Braving *the* New World
Readings in Contemporary Politics

Thomas M.J. Bateman
Augustana University College

Manuel Mertin
Mount Royal College

David M. Thomas
Malaspina University College

Nelson
Thomson Learning™

Australia • Canada • Denmark • Japan • Mexico • New Zealand • Philippines
Puerto Rico • Singapore • South Africa • Spain • United Kingdom • United States

1120 Birchmount Road
Scarborough, Ontario M1K 5G4
www.nelson.com
www.thomson.com

Canadian Cataloguing in Publication Data

Main entry under title:

Braving the new world : readings in contemporary politics

2nd ed.
Includes bibliographical references.
ISBN 0-17-616745-5

1. Political science. 2. World politics – 1945–   . I. Bateman, Thomas Michael Joseph,
1962–   . II. Mertin, Manuel. III. Thomas, David M. (David Martin), 1943–   .

JA83.B72 1999   320.9'045   C99-932649-X

Acquisitions Editor   Nicole Gnutzman
Marketing Manager   Kevin Smulan
Project Editor   Jenny Anttila
Production Editor   Tracy Bordian
Copy Editor   Marcia Miron
Proofreader   Erika Krolman
Art Director   Angela Cluer
Cover and Interior Design   Ken Phipps
Production Coordinator   Hedy Later
Senior Composition Analyst   Zenaida Diores
Printer   Webcom

Printed and bound in Canada
    3   4   03 02 01

Contents

Unit One
The New World

Unit Two
The State in the New World

Unit Three
Political Ideas and Ideologies

Unit Four

Citzenship and
Democracy

Preface

This book is intended for use in introductory political science courses at the college and university level. As a new student, you may intend to major in political science, or you may be taking an introductory political science course as an interesting elective or because your academic program requires it. You will have been exposed to a great deal of electronic media coverage of world events but may be intimidated by abstract treatments of political themes. To our "typical readers," an introductory course in political science, with its schematic texts, complex readings, and references to arcane historical events, will often appear difficult.

Such misgivings are an unfortunate reaction to a course in a discipline with certain advantages over other academic pursuits. Not the least of these advantages is an abundance of current, relevant, and interesting examples and case studies to animate the concepts and generalizations at the core of the discipline. On the other hand, political events constantly challenge, and sometimes render outdated, received understandings of politics and political life and defy our most careful predictions and generalizations. The study of politics and government is, therefore, a double-edged pedagogical sword: interesting, illuminating, and current case studies are set against the complexity and unpredictability of these events and the difficulties in analyzing them.

Textbooks used in introductory political science courses must necessarily be rigorous in their coverage of the conceptual basis of the study of politics, and they tend to present this conceptual basis as fixed. Rigour and comprehensiveness, however, are sometimes gained at the expense of an understanding of the dynamism of political life, especially in the current period.

We assembled this collection of readings to complement standard textbooks in the discipline, in a sense to bring the conceptual approach to politics alive and to examine the concepts "in action." We believe this collection will illuminate fundamental concerns in the discipline, as well as stimulate readers' interest in the world around them. It is one thing to be able to define concepts such as sovereignty and liberalism. It is another to understand how these ideas are used, abused, applied, interpreted, stretched, and attacked in historical situations. Political literacy requires one to think critically about issues and concepts, not simply to memorize details and definitions. The readings in this collection challenge people to think critically about the world around them and about a number of the basic concerns preoccupying political scientists.

Aside from the essays written especially for this book, we have selected others from notable books, journals, and current affairs magazines. Some of the contributors are professional writers; most are academics. The articles themselves range from the polemical to the analytical, from the partisan defence to the critical analysis, and from the short and direct to the lengthy and complex. Some are not easy, but some subjects simply cannot, and should not, be treated superficially. We trust that a thorough reading of the essays in this collection will broaden and deepen knowledge of political issues; we also hope that readers will become familiar with some of the sources for intelligent discussions of politics.

We have inserted a number of pedagogical aids to set articles in context. Each article in the collection is preceded by an **editors' note** that sets the stage for—but does not summarize—the article to follow. These introductions set out the problems or issues and important ideas addressed in the article. Following each article is a **list of key terms and concepts** that the reader should understand after having read the article. As well, a series of **questions** tests the reader's basic understanding of the author's argument and challenges the reader to think about the argument and how it might apply to new problems and situations. Throughout each article **key quotes** are inset to emphasize important assertions. At the end of each unit are more questions challenging readers to compare and contrast the themes and arguments made in the articles they have just read.

The essays in this book are arranged in an order that facilitates the presentation and the examination of the swirl of political change defining our times. However, instructors may have their own preferences about the order in which students should examine themes and issues. Further, students may wish to pursue a theme or topic through a series of articles in the book. The **topic guide** at the beginning of the book is designed to facilitate this approach. Key themes and concepts are listed, followed by indicators of the articles in which they are considered. For example, federalism is a key theme in this book and is treated in different ways in various articles. A reader conducting research on federalism may not glean a systematic discussion of federalism from its mention in the various contributions in this book in which federalism is discussed—such a discussion will be found in lectures and textbooks—but he or she will form a solid understanding of the contexts in which federalism arises in contemporary political debates.

This new edition attempts to keep pace with developments in world politics and to respond to helpful comments from instructors, reviewers, and students regarding the first edition. The state remains a basic principle in politics and the study of politics, and in this second edition it is given concentrated attention in a unit of its own. We have also added articles on the institutional dimension of political life and have updated or replaced most others. Throughout, we have endeavoured to increase the number of Canadian authors.

In preparing this second edition of *Braving the New World,* we have benefited from the comments of students and colleagues. We owe a debt of thanks to Jenny Anttila, at Nelson, Thomson Learning, who was our primary contact in this second go-round. Thanks also are due to Nelson's reviewers: Henry J. Jacek, McMaster University; Tom W. Joseph, Lakehead University/ Confederation College; Jacqueline Krikorian, Brock University; Chris Kukucha, Douglas College; William R. McKercher, King's College, University of Western Ontario; and Richard Nutbrown, University of Waterloo. Our greatest thanks, once again, go to our spouses, Jill, Jindra, and Maureen, whose forbearance is exemplary.

Contributors

▶ Thomas M.J. Bateman is assistant professor of political studies at Augustana University College. His interests lie in constitutional law and politics, the criminal justice process, Canadian politics, and the study of political ideas.

▶ Paul Bowles is professor of economics at the University of Northern British Columbia.

▶ Wendell Berry is a Kentuckian farmer, essayist, poet, and story writer. He has also taught at many U.S. universities. His previous works include *What Are People For?* (1990) and *Sex, Economy, Freedom and Community* (1993).

▶ Jean Bethke Elshtain is Laura Spelman Rockefeller professor of social and political ethics at the University of Chicago Divinity School. She is a prolific author and popular lecturer. Among her publications are *Public Man, Private Woman: Women in Social Thought* (1981) and *Real Politics: At the Center of Everyday Life* (1997).

▶ Michael Broadway is the head of the Department of Geography at Northern Michigan University and an expert on the role of the U.S. meatpacking industry in transforming small towns. He is co-editor of the book *Any Way You Cut It: Meatprocessing and Small Town America* (1995). He serves on the editorial board of the *Canadian Journal of Urban Research*.

▶ Larry Diamond is a senior research fellow at the Hoover Institution. He is also professor of political science and sociology (by courtesy) at Stanford University and a member of the Committee on African Studies at the University. He is a specialist on democracy in Asia, Africa, and Latin America. Diamond's latest publications include (co-editor) the two-volume *Consolidating the Third Wave Democracies* (1997) and *Promoting Democracy in the 1990s: Actors and Instruments, Issues and Imperatives* (1996).

▶ David Frum is a popular journalist and commentator and is the author most recently of *Dead Right* (1994) and *What's Right: The New Conservatism and What It Means for Canada* (1996).

▶ Roger Gibbins is professor of political science at the University of Calgary and president of the Canada West Foundation. He has published extensively in the areas of Canadian constitutional politics, federalism, regionalism, political culture, and comparative politics.

▶ Thomas F. Homer-Dixon teaches political science at the University of Toronto and is director of its peace and conflict studies program. He has published extensively on the relationship between political conflict and environmental scarcity.

▶ Samuel P. Huntington is the Albert J. Weatherhead III professor at Harvard University, where he is also director of the John M. Olin Institute for Strategic Studies and chairman of the Harvard Academy for International and Area Studies. He is the author of numerous articles and books, including *The Clash of Civilizations and the Remaking of World Order* (1996).

▶ Manuel Mertin teaches political science at Mount Royal College in Calgary and is chair of the Department of Economics and Political Science. His current research interest is comparative economic policy in developed states.

▶ Gerald Owen is former editor of *The Idler* and *Books in Canada* and a contributor to *The Times Literary Supplement*. He has published essays on constitutional politics and law in Canada and on the political thought of George Grant.

▶ Thomas E. Patterson is Bradley professor of government and the press at Harvard University's Kennedy School of Government. He is the author of numerous books and articles on political communication, including *Out of Order, The Mass Media Election,* and *The Unseeing Eye*.

▶ Robert D. Putnam is Stanfield professor of international peace, and director of the Saguaro Seminar on Civic Engagement in America, John F. Kennedy School of Government, Harvard University. He is the author of the widely read article "Bowling Alone: America's Declining Social Capital," published in the *Journal of Democracy* (1995). His research interests include civic connectedness and social capital in

America, making democracy work in the United States and abroad, comparative European politics, contemporary relations among the major Western powers, and domestic roots of foreign policy.

▶ John G. Richards is associate professor of business administration at Simon Fraser University. He has published extensively in the areas of public policy, resource policy, and social policy.

▶ Steven C. Rockefeller is professor emeritus of religion at Middlebury College in Vermont and has published work on democratic thought and the integration of democratic principles with ecology and religion.

▶ Richard Rose is director of the Centre for the Study of Public Policy, University of Strathclyde, Glasgow, Scotland, and founder of the New Russia Barometer and related studies of mass response to transformation in the post-Communist societies of Central and Eastern Europe and the former Soviet Union. His latest book is *Democracy and Its Alternatives: Understanding Post-Communist Societies,* with William Mishler and Christian Haerpfer.

▶ Richard Rosecrance is professor of political science and director of the Center for International Relations at the University of California, Los Angeles.

▶ James N. Rosenau is university professor of international affairs at George Washington University. His latest book is *Along the Domestic–Foreign Frontier: Exploring Government in a Turbulent World* (1997).

▶ Jennifer Smith teaches political science at Dalhousie University. Her recent publications include articles on representative democracy and constitutional reform, democratic rights and electoral reform, and the influence of American federalism on Canadian Confederation.

▶ Susan Strange was, until her death in 1998, professor of politics and international studies at the University of Warwick, Coventry, U.K. Her books include *Rival States, Rival Firms: Competition for World Market Shares* (1991), co-written with John Stopford, and *The Retreat of the State: The Diffusion of Power in the World Economy* (1996).

▶ David M. Thomas is vice-president of instruction at Malaspina University College. He is the editor of *Canada and the United States: Differences That Count* (1993) and is the author most recently of *Whistling Past the Graveyard: Constitutional Abeyances, Quebec, and the Future of Canada* (1997).

▶ Goh Chok Tong succeeded Lee Kuan Yew as prime minister of Singapore in 1990 and still holds that office. He received his education in Singapore and the United States. He is also secretary-general of the ruling People's Action Party.

▶ Linda Trimble is associate professor of political science at the University of Alberta. Her research interests include those aspects of Canadian politics concerning gender, citizenship, and representation; women and the constitutional order; female legislative behaviour in Alberta; and the impact of restructuring (deficit reduction, deregulation, and privatization) on women. She is co-editor, with Jane Arscott, of *In the Presence of Women: Representation in Canadian Governments* (1996).

▶ Richard Vernon is professor of political science at the University of Western Ontario and has published work on liberal political thought.

▶ Barnet Wagman holds a Ph.D. in economics.

▶ Meredith Woo-Cumings is associate professor of political science at Northwestern University. Her teaching and research interests include the development and organization of the Pacific Rim economy, study of the developmental state in comparative perspective, and U.S. economic relations with East Asia. She is co-author of *Race to the Swift: State and Finance in Korean Industrialization* (1991) and co-editor of *Past as Prelude: History in the Making of a New World Order* (1993).

▶ Loleen Youngman-Berdahl, who holds a Ph.D. in political science from the University of Calgary, is director of research at the Canada West Foundation. She has co-authored, with Keith Archer and Roger Gibbins, *Explorations: A Navigator's Guide to Quantitative Research in Political Science* (1998) and, with Roger Gibbins, *Mindscapes: Political Ideologies Toward the Twenty-First Century* (1996).

Topic Guide

Introduction

In the spring of 1999, NATO forces, including Canadian personnel, launched a sustained, surgical air campaign to force the Yugoslav military from the province of Kosovo, bringing the latest in military technology to bear on a conflict whose roots, in the minds of many of the combatants, go back over six hundred years. Many of the ironies and complexities of our political age are found in this conflict. In this respect, the Kosovo conflict provides a sobering illustration of many themes contained in this volume.

The first irony is that NATO's first military exercise was conducted not in the context of the Cold War antagonism between the U.S.S.R.-led Warsaw pact and the U.S.-led Western alliance, but rather in a messier Yugoslav ethnic debacle. Yugoslavia, once in the Communist fold but nonetheless a darling of the West for its defiance of the heavy Soviet hand, stood as a multicultural success story, if only because of the domineering leadership of Marshall Tito. A scant 10 years after Tito's death, the federation blew apart, and Europe witnessed ethnic hatred and atrocities that it thought had ended with World War II. After the Bosnian conflict left Yugoslavia a rump containing Serbia and its once-autonomous provinces of Kosovo and Montenegro, activists in ethnic Albanian-dominated Kosovo began to appeal for independence from Yugoslavia, a move answered by Yugoslav President Slobodan Milosevic with brutal military reprisals.

Not wishing to be seen dragging their heels, as was the case with the Bosnian massacres in the early 1990s, and with the memories of Nazi genocide brought once again to the fore, Western leaders, including Canada's, resolved to intervene on behalf of the beleaguered Kosovars. The NATO alliance, created in the old paradigm of the Cold War but now including as members some former Communist states, was engaged for new purposes. These new purposes have to do with the security of peoples within the borders of sovereign states. NATO's Kosovo intervention represents a watershed in world politics and may provide a precedent for future interventions, with consequences no one can predict.

The second complexity is that the Kosovo conflict dramatically highlighted the complex relationship between ethnicity and the state at the dawn of the 21st century. Very few states are or ever have been ethnically and linguistically homogeneous. Yet the nation-state ideal has been the bedrock of the international order for generations and still excites nationalists who seek political security for the national community. For decades Yugoslavia seemed to defy the notion that states can house only one nation. Yet the dream came crashing down in the 1990s, as separate ethnic groups sought, with horrific consequences, their own political entities. So-called ethnic cleansing is a particularly extreme case of forced human migration. The millions of newly stateless persons mock the idea that the world is neatly carved up into accepted entities: the ideal of the nation-state is contradicted by the reality of almost every existing state, but the ideal makes those states unstable. Canadians are all too familiar with this truth, as are the Spanish, the French, the Belgians, the Irish, the South Africans, the Nigerians, the Rwandans, and so many others. The number of states in the world has ballooned since World War II—the United Nations had 35 member states in 1948 and now has almost two hundred—and the number of national minorities seeking greater political security does not appear to be decreasing.

In Kosovo was revealed a third feature of the pattern of world politics: the active presence of nonstate actors on the world stage. As the conflict unfolded, dozens of humanitarian groups, international organization agencies, and media outlets descended upon Kosovo. To these ranks must be added the thousands of corporations, nongovernmental organizations, and social movements that pursue interests spanning the globe. The international electronic media are as effective as any interest group in influencing policy and public opinion. The state is now just one actor among a range of human groupings influencing the course of world politics.

With the challenges presented to the nation-state by other international actors has come a fourth important feature illustrated by the Kosovo conflict. A historical predicate of the state system is that states act in their national interests, a view typified by the political and academic career of former U.S. secretary of state Henry Kissinger. However, many observers point to Kosovo as a prime example of the limitations of such an explanation for policy. Speaking to the two houses of the Canadian Parliament in April 1999, Czech Republic

President Václav Havel argued that the Kosovo conflict represents "the recognition that human beings are more important than the state." Speaking specifically of NATO's bombing campaign, he claimed that "this is probably the first war that has not been waged in the name of 'national interests' but rather in the name of principles and values. If one can say of any war that it is ethical, or that it is being waged for ethical reasons, then it is true of this war."[1] One can quarrel with Havel's position, but he does touch an important development in his remark in the same speech that "human rights are superior to the rights of states." The norms of state sovereignty are not the only or the highest norms. Contemporary politics grapple with a plurality of values and a plurality of actors.

At the same time, the Kosovo conflict represents a fifth complexity of our age, namely the decline of easy faith in steady human progress. A long line of Western philosophical and theological thinkers dating to the 18th century held that history inexorably marched toward greater prosperity, scientific knowledge and understanding, rationality, peace, and happiness. Prejudice, groundless hatred, and barbarism would fade. The 20th century seems to have soundly discredited this idea. We have witnessed human brutality of staggering proportions. Consider the Third Reich, the Khmer Rouge, East Timor, Tibet, Argentina, Chile, Stalin's and Mao's agricultural failures, the gulags—to name but a few examples. Grinding poverty and disease plague most of the world's population. Environmental degradation accompanies economic growth.

The Enlightenment vision was of the dawning of a universal civilization, of some sort of global citizenship. And, indeed, organizations like the United Nations and documents such as the UN Universal Declaration of Human Rights bespeak a potent universalism. The indictment of Yugoslav President Slobodan Milosevic marked the first time a sitting head of state was indicted for war crimes. At the same time, while representatives of different countries were able to agree on the contents of the Declaration, they would never have been able to agree on *why* they believed in the rights therein contained. It may be that the Declaration would never have been adopted by signatory countries if it had contained mechanisms for its enforcement on signatory government. Today, many non-Western leaders easily dismiss the Declaration as so much Western ideology parading as universal ideals. The universal aspirations embodied in documents like the Declaration are reinforced by globalizing economic and technological trends. But they rest awkwardly alongside the resurgence of particularistic ethnic identities, many of them indeed stimulated by globalizing forces.

A powerful international movement has rallied in favour of a permanent international criminal court under the auspices of the United Nations, a potent expression of universal human rights ideals. Yet, many of the most powerful countries, including the United States and China, oppose the idea, indicating that human rights universalism has not supplanted the national interest as an organizing principle of world politics.

Political changes illustrated by the Kosovo conflict have produced changes in the core concerns of political science. States are more porous than they once were. They are affected in myriad ways by forces beyond their borders. Their capacity to act domestically in accordance with their citizens' demands and interest is impaired. States will not disappear anytime soon, but rather will coexist with supranational and transnational entities.

Citizenship is now a more complicated concept, partly because of these changes to the nature of the state. Citizenship is under constant legal and political revision as states adjust to greater human mobility and more sophisticated demands. Further, political scientists have long wondered why democratic government thrives in some settings and not in others. It was naively thought by many that with the end of communism, Russia and the Eastern European countries would automatically become democratic. This happened in only a few cases—Poland, Hungary, the Baltic states, and the former Czechoslovakia—and even here not without difficulty, as indicated, for example, by the Czech Republic's troubles with persecution of its gypsy minority. What explains democratic success in some countries and failure in others? Political scientists examine the institutions of civil society—that intermediate range of human activity between the private sphere and the formal institutions of the state—for answers.

The relationship between state and society is also in flux. Although "harder" forms of socialism went into terminal decline decades ago and global trade and capital mobility pose major challenges for the state's management of its economy, it is, to say the least, premature to applaud the rise of the global free market. Observers note that though capitalism is clearly ascendant, two points must be borne in mind: first, any economic system, capitalist or otherwise, requires a supportive political-legal framework; and second, capitalism is socially embedded and, as a result, takes different forms depending on the cultural and political milieu in which it functions. There are capitalisms, not just capitalism.[2] Accordingly, there is no one relationship between state and economy.

What has become of the relationship between political community and territory? Land has for centuries been a principal object of political contest. Territory has defined the state and the bounds of community. Federal political arrangements have been an attempt to fudge the relationship between territory and political community. Now, political scientists regularly speak of nonterritorial communities—groups of people linked not by place of residence and regular face-to-face contact but by interest or identity. One contributor to this volume even writes of the "virtual state." Others wonder if genuine community and genuine democracy can exist without locality.

In short, the political world is in great flux, making the study of politics both fascinating and challenging. The units in this volume attempt to reflect some of the major changes both in the politics of the early 21st century and in the study of politics.

Unit One contains readings that identify some of the major forces in world politics. Samuel Huntington examines the universality of notions of democracy and human rights and considers whether a truly global civilization is dawning, or whether the "West" should consider itself one civilization among others. James Rosenau introduces the concept of globalization, and Thomas Homer-Dixon explores the relationship between environmental degradation and political conflict.

Unit Two contains three articles examining the fate of the state, how it is changing, whether it is being eroded by globalizing forces, and what effect trade and capital mobility have on the domestic social policy structures.

The study of politics is inescapably normative. We ask questions like, What causes war? and, What types of political institutions are most conducive to equitable distributions of wealth? But we also ask questions such as, What should be the purpose of government? What interests among citizens should the laws help satisfy? Should the constitution make provision for the preservation of cultural identity? and, Should party discipline be relaxed? These latter questions are normative in character. They invite us to reflect on what *should* happen or prevail in the political world. Normative concerns take us explicitly into the realm of political ideology. Unit Three explores several of the major contending ideological forces in contemporary politics.

People do not merely demand things from their governments, though they do a lot of this. They also support their governments, participate in their functioning, and contribute to their direction. Participation is largely what democratic citizenship is all about. Authoritarian regimes seek to depoliticize the citizenry, directing it to nonpolitical interests. But democratic regimes ostensibly encourage participation. Unit Four examines the many issues surrounding democratic participation and the rights and obligations of citizenship.

Unit Five considers the nuts and bolts of politics—the institutions that not only foster and channel popular participation in government but also define the legislative, executive, and judicial branches of government. But these nuts and bolts are not mere technical details. Basic questions of priorities and principles are at stake in the operation of political institutions and the public policies they help to shape.

Unit Six concerns a basket of issues dealing with regimes and political change. Many countries attempted a transition from communism to democracy in the 1990s, but only a few have made it. Russia is faring quite badly, for reasons Richard Rose discusses in his contribution. Many countries have to deal with the bitterness associated with the persecution and violence of an earlier era, and how they deal with it will influence those countries' futures. Other regimes fare much better by comparison, but not because they wish to emulate Western democracies. Some Asian political leaders insist that their systems would be doomed if they sought to copy the Western economic and political model. Canada's constitutional struggles proceed apace, and the latest installment in the war of words is the Supreme Court of Canada's opinion regarding the constitutionality of Quebec's unilateral secession. That opinion is excerpted in this unit.

The concluding essay brings together many of the strands and themes that are reflected throughout the book, but does so in the context of systems and situations where there have been crimes against humanity, sanctioned hatred, and systemic violence. What then can be done to recover and create a culture where some forgiveness is possible, and where democratic politics can take place? Can we confront "the sheer weight of history"? Elshtain believes that we must find ways to do so.

---

1. The speech is reprinted in Václav Havel, "Kosovo and the End of the Nation-State," *New York Review of Books* (June 10, 1999), 4–6.

2. John Gray, *False Dawn: The Delusions of Global Capitalism* (London: Granta, 1998).

Braving *the* New World
Readings in Contemporary Politics

Unit One

The New World

* * *

Most of those who grew up between the end of World War II and 1990 lived in a fairly stable world. The Cold War defined international and, to some extent, national politics. This stability was not without its horrors: the spectre of nuclear war; the chronic, simmering wars, such as the Middle East conflict, in which both East and West were involved and to which they supplied plenty of arms; and the Berlin Wall, which divided families with a shoot-to-kill border, made everyone nervous, some neurotic, and spawned strong peace and disarmament movements. But stability meant predictability, and the threat of nuclear holocaust at least contained regional conflicts and restrained the major powers' behaviour toward each other.

With the fall of communism and the end of the Soviet Union, we are now said to be in a New World Order. But the phrase escapes definition. We are in a stage of flux, of instability, and, therefore, of unpredictability.

The Cold War was fought by two types of regimes, totalitarianism and liberal democracy, and also between two economic systems, capitalism and socialist central planning. The label "communist" came to be applied to those totalitarian political regimes with centrally planned economies. Although totalitarianism has almost disappeared—even China, with its substantial private sector, no longer fully qualifies—and its weaker cousin, authoritarianism, is in retreat, democracy has not become the universal regime and, as Samuel Huntington tells us in this

unit, is unlikely to become so in the near future. Even socialism, with the almost anachronistic exception of Castro's Cuba, is on the defensive. Capitalism has been the driving force behind globalization but could never truly become global as long as communism held sway over substantial parts of the world.

Although it is generally acknowledged that socialism is ideologically rooted (despite Marx's calling it scientific), capitalism is often considered grounded in the natural order of things. Economists typically speak of the "laws" of supply and demand. But untrammelled free enterprise is an unstable mode of economic organization, full of excesses and with the potential to wreak grievous social harm. For example, destructive effects have been brought about by unregulated international currency markets, increasing disparity within states and among states, and the fostering of corporate values of ever higher profits, which results in the sale of profitable production units.

We forget that capitalism is also rooted in an ideology, which assumes predictable human behaviour and includes a set of values that places the utility-maximizing individual on a pedestal. Critics of capitalism arguing from the Left perspective are dismissed mockingly. But even capitalists who pub-

Photo courtesy of Canapress.

In the emerging global order, internal conflicts increasingly provoke intervention by groups of states through international organizations like the UN and NATO.

lish their doubts—such as financier George Soros, who authored a controversial article entitled "The Capitalist Threat,"[1] or Rainer Mohn, the builder of the Bertelsmann publishing and media empire, who argues that "the top goal of an entrepreneur isn't profit maximization, but a contribution to society"[2]—are viewed with suspicion by some and downright scorn by others.

Economic growth, without which capitalism in its present form cannot exist, has serious effects on the environment and, as Thomas Homer-Dixon makes clear, the increasing scarcity of renewable resources, largely growth induced, has a negative effect on peace and security. But Homer-Dixon and the other contributors to this unit maintain that the logic of capitalist development is not beyond alteration.

1. George Soros, "The Capitalist Threat," *The Atlantic Monthly* (February 1997).
2. Cacilie Rohwedder, "Bertelsmann Chief Likes the Slow Lane," *The Globe and Mail* (January 15, 1997), reprinted from *The Wall Street Journal.*

[Handwritten margin notes:]
globalization is Americanization
coca-globalization.
Consumerism → globalization
modernization is about
tech changes. e.g.,
agriculture ?

The West: Unique, Not Universal

Samuel P. Huntington

Editors' Note

History is not over. Globalization and the end of the Cold War will not bring about democracy everywhere. And we need to be vigilant to ensure that Western civilization is not subverted from outside or inside. This is the appraisal of Harvard political science professor Samuel P. Huntington.

In this article, which is drawn from *The Clash of Civilizations and the Remaking of World Order* (1996), Professor Huntington focuses on the policy implications of his analysis of future geopolitics first presented in his 1993 article "The Clash of Civilizations?" He rejects both the thesis of globalization—called "Coca-colonization" here, "McWorld" elsewhere[1]—and those who declare that democracy has won the contest among regimes. He does this by uncoupling modernization from westernization.[2] He predicts that the modernization of non-Western nations, particularly Islamic and Confucian states, will occur on indigenous, not Western, terms.[3] As a consequence, the West has to stand strong and united against increasingly powerful states that will be hostile to Western values of liberal democracy and international order.

The political science student should note that Huntington combines a political culture with a realist or power approach. For Huntington, culture, much more so than economics, will shape institutions, but culture spreads primarily through the traditional tools of political conquest, not through television or the Internet.

◆ ◆ ◆

In recent years Westerners have reassured themselves and irritated others by expounding the notion that the culture of the West is and ought to be the culture of the world. This conceit takes two forms. One is the Coca-colonization thesis. Its proponents claim that Western, and more specifically American, popular culture is enveloping the world: American food, clothing, pop music, movies, and consumer goods are more and more enthusiastically embraced by people on every continent. The other has to do with modernization. It claims not only that the West has led the world to modern society, but that as people in other civilizations modernize they also westernize, abandoning their traditional values, institutions, and customs and adopting those that prevail in the West. Both theses project the image of an emerging homogeneous, universally Western world—and both are to varying degrees misguided, arrogant, false, and dangerous.

Advocates of the Coca-colonization thesis identify culture with the consumption of material goods. The heart of a culture, however, involves language, religion, values, traditions, and customs. Drinking Coca-Cola does not make Russians think like Americans any more than eating sushi makes Americans think like Japanese.

---

1. Benjamin Barber, "Jihad Vs. McWorld," *The Atlantic Monthly* (March 1992), 53–63; also reprinted in the first edition of *Braving the New World*.
2. Francis Fukuyama, *The End of History and the Last Man* (New York: Avon, 1992).
3. For an example of this approach, see Chapter 23 in this volume, by Goh Chok Tong, prime minister of Singapore.

From *Foreign Affairs* (Nov./Dec. 1996). Reprinted by permission of the author.

Throughout human history, fads and material goods have spread from one society to another without significantly altering the basic culture of the recipient society. Enthusiasms for various items of Chinese, Hindu, and other cultures have periodically swept the Western world, with no discernible lasting spillover. The argument that the spread of pop culture and consumer goods around the world represents the triumph of Western civilization depreciates the strength of other cultures while trivializing Western culture by identifying it with fatty foods, faded pants, and fizzy drinks. The essence of Western culture is the Magna Carta, not the Magna Mac.

The modernization argument is intellectually more serious than the Coca-colonization thesis, but equally flawed. The tremendous expansion of scientific and engineering knowledge that occurred in the nineteenth century allowed humans to control and shape their environment in unprecedented ways. Modernization involves industrialization; urbanization; increasing levels of literacy, education, wealth, and social mobilization; and more complex and diverse occupational structures. It is a revolutionary process comparable to the shift from primitive to civilized societies that began in the valleys of the Tigris and Euphrates, the Nile, and the Indus about 5000 B.C. The attitudes, values, knowledge, and culture of people in a modern society differ greatly from those in a traditional society. As the first civilization to modernize, the West is the first to have fully acquired the culture of modernity. As other societies take on similar patterns of education, work, wealth, and class structure, the modernization argument runs, this Western culture will become the universal culture of the world.

That there are significant differences between modern and traditional cultures is beyond dispute. A world in which some societies are highly modern and others still traditional will obviously be less homogeneous than a world in which all societies are comparably modern. It does not necessarily follow, however, that societies with modern cultures should be any more similar than are societies with traditional cultures. Only a few hundred years ago all societies were traditional. Was that world any less homogeneous than a future world of universal modernity is likely to be? Probably not. "Ming China ... was assuredly closer to the France of the Valois," Fernand Braudel observes, "than the China of Mao Tsetung is to the France of the Fifth Republic."[1] Modern societies have much in common, but they do not necessarily merge into homogeneity. The argument that they do rests on the assumption that modern society must

approximate a single type, the Western type; that modern civilization is Western civilization, and Western civilization is modern civilization. This, however, is a false identification. Virtually all scholars of civilization agree that Western civilization emerged in the eighth and ninth centuries and developed its distinctive characteristics in the centuries that followed. It did not begin to modernize until the eighteenth century. The West, in short, was Western long before it was modern.

WHAT MAKES THE WEST WESTERN?

◆ ◆ ◆

What were the distinguishing characteristics of Western civilization during the hundreds of years before it modernized? The various scholars who have answered this question differ on some specifics but agree on a number of institutions, practices, and beliefs that may be legitimately identified as the core of Western civilization. They include:

The Classical legacy. As a third-generation civilization, the West inherited much from earlier civilizations, including, most notably, Classical civilization. Classical legacies in Western civilization are many, and include Greek philosophy and rationalism, Roman law, Latin, and Christianity. Islamic and Orthodox civilizations also inherited from Classical civilization, but to nowhere near the same degree as the West.

When Westerners went out to conquer the world in the sixteenth century, they did so for God as well as gold.

Western Christianity. Western Christianity, first Catholicism and then Protestantism, is the single most important historical characteristic of Western civilization. Indeed, during most of its first millennium, what is now known as Western civilization was called Western Christendom. There was a well-developed sense of community among Western Christian peoples, one that made them feel distinct from Turks, Moors, Byzantines, and others. When Westerners went out to conquer the world in the sixteenth century, they did so for God as well as gold. The Reformation and Counter Reformation and the division of Western Christendom into Protestantism and Catholicism—and the political and intellectual consequences of that rift—are also distinctive features of

Western history, totally absent from Eastern Orthodoxy and removed from the Latin American experience.

European languages. Language is second only to religion as a factor distinguishing people of one culture from those of another. The West differs from most other civilizations in its multiplicity of languages. Japanese, Hindi, Mandarin, Russian, and even Arabic are recognized as the core languages of other civilizations. The West inherited Latin, but a variety of nations emerged in the West, and with them developed national languages grouped loosely into the broad categories of Romance and Germanic. By the sixteenth century these languages had generally assumed their contemporary forms. Latin gave way to French as a common international language for the West, and in the twentieth century French succumbed to English.

Separation of spiritual and temporal authority. Throughout Western history, first the Church and then many churches existed separate from the state. God and Caesar, church and state, spiritual authority and temporal authority had been a prevailing dualism in Western culture. Only in Hindu civilization were religion and politics as clearly separated. In Islam, God is caesar; in China and Japan, caesar is God; in Orthodoxy, God is caesar's junior partner. The separation and recurrence between church and state that typify Western civilization have occurred in no other civilization. This division of authority contributed immeasurably to the development of freedom in the West.

Rule of law. The concept of the centrality of law to civilized existence was inherited from the Romans. Medieval thinkers elaborated the idea of natural law, according to which monarchs were supposed to exercise their power, and a common law tradition developed in England. During the phase of absolutism in the sixteenth and seventeenth centuries, the rule of law was observed more in the breach than in practice, but the idea of subordinating human power to some external restraint persisted: *Non sub homine sed sub Deo et lege.* The tradition of the rule of law laid the basis for constitutionalism and the protection of human rights, including property rights, against the arbitrary exercise of power. In other civilizations law has been a much less important factor in shaping thought and behavior.

Social pluralism and civil society. Western society historically has been highly pluralistic. What is distinctive about the West, as Karl Deutsch noted, "is the rise and persistence of diverse autonomous groups not based on blood relationship or marriage."[2] Beginning in the sixth and seventh centuries these groups initially included monasteries, monastic orders, and guilds, but afterwards expanded in many areas of Europe to include a variety of other associations and societies. For more than a millennium, the West has had a civil society that distinguished it from other civilizations. Associated pluralism was supplemented by class pluralism. Most Western European societies included a relatively strong and autonomous aristocracy, a substantial peasantry, and a small but significant class of merchants and traders. The strength of the feudal aristocracy was particularly important in limiting absolutism's ability to take firm root in most European nations. This European pluralism contrasts sharply with the poverty of civil society, the weakness of the aristocracy, and the strength of the centralized bureaucratic empires that existed during the same time periods in Russia, China, the Ottoman lands, and other non-Western societies.

Representative bodies. Social pluralism gave rise at an early date to estates, parliaments, and other institutions that represented the interests of the aristocracy, clergy, merchants, and other groups. These bodies provided forms of representation that in the course of modernization evolved into the institutions of modern democracy. In some instances during the era of absolutism they were abolished or their powers greatly limited. But even when that happened, they could, as in France, be resurrected as a vehicle for expanded political participation. No other civilization today has a comparable heritage of representative bodies stretching back a millennium. Movements for self-government also developed at the local level, beginning in the ninth century in the cities of Italy and then spreading northward, wresting power from bishops and nobles and finally, in the thirteenth century, leading to such confederations of "strong and independent cities" as the Hanseatic League.[3] Representation at the national level was thus supplemented by a measure of autonomy at the local level not seen in other regions of the world.

Individualism. Many of the above features of Western civilization contributed to the emergence of a sense of individualism and a tradition of individual rights and liberties unique among civilized societies. Individualism developed in the fourteenth and fifteenth centuries, and acceptance of the right of individual choice, which Deutsch terms "the Romeo and Juliet revolution," prevailed in the West by the seventeenth century. Even claims for equal rights for all—"the poorest he in England has a life to live as much as the richest he"—were articulated if not universally accepted. Individualism remains a distinguishing feature of the West in twentieth-century civilizations. In one analysis involving similar population groups from 50 countries, the 20 countries scoring highest on the individualism index included 19 of the 20 Western countries in the sample. Another cross-cultural survey of individualism and collectivism similarly highlighted the dominance of individualism in the West compared with the prevalence of collectivism elsewhere, concluding that "the values that are most important in the West are least important worldwide."⁴ Again and again both Westerners and non-Westerners point to individualism as the central distinguishing mark of the West.

Individualism remains a distinguishing feature of the West in twentieth-century civilizations.

The above list is not an exhaustive enumeration of the distinctive characteristics of Western civilization. Nor is it meant to imply that those characteristics were always and everywhere present in Western society. They obviously were not: the many despots in Western history regularly ignored the rule of law and suspended representative bodies. Nor is it meant to suggest that none of these characteristics have appeared in other civilizations. They obviously have: the Koran and the sharia constitute basic law for Islamic societies; Japan and India had class systems paralleling that of the West (and perhaps as a result are the only two major non-Western societies to sustain democratic governments for any length of time). Individually, almost none of these factors is unique to the West. But the combination of them is, and has given the West its distinctive quality. These concepts, practices, and institutions have been far more prevalent in the West than in other civilizations. They form the essential continuing core of Western civilization. They are what is Western, but not modern, about the West.

They also generated the commitment to individual freedom that now distinguishes the West from other civilizations. Europe, as Arthur M. Schlesinger, Jr., has said, is "the source—the *unique* source" of the "ideas of individual liberty, political democracy, the rule of law, human rights, and cultural freedom ... These are *European* ideas, not Asian, nor African, nor Middle Eastern ideas, except by adoption...."⁵ These concepts and characteristics are also in large part the factors that enabled the West to take the lead in modernizing itself and the world. They make Western civilization unique, and Western civilization is precious not because it is universal but because it is unique.

CAN THE REST COPY THE WEST?

♦ ♦ ♦

To modernize, must non-Western societies abandon their own cultures and adopt the core elements of Western culture? From time to time leaders of such societies have thought it necessary. Peter the Great and Mustafa Kemal Ataturk were determined to modernize their countries and convinced that doing so meant adopting Western culture, even to the point of replacing traditional headgear with its Western equivalent. In the process, they created "torn" countries, unsure of their cultural identity. Nor did Western cultural imports significantly help them in their pursuit of modernization. More often, leaders of non-Western societies have pursued modernization and rejected westernization. Their goal is summed up in the phrases *ti-yong* (Chinese learning for the fundamental principles, Western learning for practical use) and *woken, yosei* (Japanese spirit, Western technique), articulated by Chinese and Japanese reformers of a century ago, and in Saudi Arabia's Prince Bandar bin Sultan's comment in 1994 that "'foreign imports' are nice as shiny or high-tech 'things.' But intangible social and political institutions imported from elsewhere can be deadly—ask the Shah of Iran ... Islam is for us not just a religion but a way of life. We Saudis want to modernize but not necessarily westernize." Japan, Singapore, Taiwan, Saudi Arabia, and, to a lesser degree, Iran have become modern societies without becoming Western societies. China is clearly modernizing, but certainly not westernizing.

Interaction and borrowing between civilizations have always taken place, and with modern means of transportation and communication they are much more extensive. Most of the world's great civilizations, however, have existed for at least one millennium and in some cases for several. These civilizations have a demonstrated record of borrowing from other civilizations in ways that enhance their own chances of survival. China's absorption of Buddhism from India, scholars agree, failed to produce the "Indianization" of China; it instead caused the Sinification of Buddhism. The Chinese adapted Buddhism to their purposes and needs. The Chinese have to date consistently defeated intense Western efforts to Christianize them. If at some point they do import Christianity, it is more than likely that it will be absorbed and adapted in such a manner as to strengthen the continuing core of Chinese culture.

Similarly, in past centuries Muslim Arabs received, valued, and used their "Hellenic inheritance for essentially utilitarian reasons. Being mostly interested in borrowing certain external forms or technical aspects, they knew how to disregard all elements in the Greek body of thought that would conflict with 'the truth' as established in their fundamental Koranic norms and precepts." Japan followed the same pattern. In the seventh century Japan imported Chinese culture and made the "transformation on its own initiative, free from economic and military pressures," to high civilization. "During the centuries that followed, periods of relative isolation from continental influences during which previous borrowings were sorted out and the useful ones assimilated would alternate with periods of renewed contact and cultural borrowing." In similar fashion, Japan and other non-Western societies today are absorbing selected elements of Western culture and using them to strengthen their own cultural identity. It would, as Braudel argues, almost "be childish" to think that the "triumph of civilization in the singular" would lead to the end of the plurality of cultures embodied for centuries in the world's great civilizations.[6]

CULTURAL BACKLASH

◆ ◆ ◆

Modernization and economic development neither require nor produce cultural westernization. To the contrary, they promote a resurgence of, and renewed commitment to, indigenous cultures. At the individual level, the movement of people into unfamiliar cities, social settings, and occupations breaks their traditional local bonds, generates feelings of alienation and anomie, and creates crises of identity to which religion frequently provides an answer. At the societal level, modernization enhances the economic wealth and military power of the country as a whole and encourages people to have confidence in their heritage and to become culturally assertive. As a result, many non-Western societies have seen a return to indigenous cultures. It often takes a religious form, and the global revival of religion is a direct consequence of modernization. In non-Western societies this revival almost necessarily assumes an anti-Western cast, in some cases rejecting Western culture because it is Christian and subversive, in others because it is secular and degenerate. The return to the indigenous is most marked in Muslim and Asian societies. The Islamic Resurgence has manifested itself in every Muslim country; in almost all it has become a major social, cultural, and intellectual movement, and in most it has had a deep impact on politics. In 1996 virtually every Muslim country except Iran was more Islamic and more Islamist in its

outlook, practices, and institutions than it was 15 years earlier. In the countries where Islamist political forces do not shape the government, they invariably dominate and often monopolize the opposition to the government. Throughout the Muslim world people are reacting against the "Westoxification" of their societies.

Modernization and economic development neither require nor produce cultural westernization.

East Asian societies have gone through a parallel rediscovery of indigenous values and have increasingly drawn unflattering comparisons between their culture and Western culture. For several centuries they, along with other non-Western peoples, envied the economic prosperity, technological sophistication, military power, and political cohesion of Western societies. They sought the secret of this success in Western practices and customs, and when they identified what they thought might be the key they attempted to apply it in their own societies. Now, however, a fundamental change has occurred. Today East Asians attribute their dramatic economic development not to their import of Western culture but to their adherence to their own culture. They have succeeded, they argue, not because they became like the West, but because they have remained different from the West. In somewhat similar fashion, when non-Western societies felt weak in relation to the West, many of their leaders invoked Western values of self-determination, liberalism, democracy, and freedom to justify their opposition to Western global domination. Now that they are no longer weak but instead increasingly powerful, they denounce as "human rights imperialism" the same values they previously invoked to promote their interests. As Western power recedes, so too does the appeal of Western values and culture, and the West faces the need to accommodate itself to its declining ability to impose its values on non-Western societies. In fundamental ways, much of the world is becoming more modern and less Western.

One manifestation of this trend is what Ronald Dore has termed the "second-generation indigenization phenomenon." Both in former Western colonies and in continuously independent, non-Western countries, "the first 'modernizer' or 'post-independence' generation has often received its training in foreign (Western) universities in a Western cosmopolitan language. Partly because they first go abroad as impressionable teenagers, their absorption of Western values and lifestyles may well be profound." Most members of the much larger second generation, in contrast, receive their education at home in universities the first generation established, where the local language, rather than its colonial replacement, is used for instruction. These universities "provide a much more diluted contact with metropolitan world culture" and "knowledge is indigenized by means of translations—usually of limited range and of poor quality." Graduates of these universities resent the dominance of the earlier Western-trained generation and thus often "succumb to the appeals of nativist opposition movements."[7] As Western influence recedes, young and aspiring leaders cannot look to the West to provide them with power and wealth. They have to find the means of success within their own society, and hence accommodate the values and culture of that society.

Indigenization is furthered by the democracy paradox: when non-Western societies adopt Western-style elections, democracy encourages and often brings to power nativist and anti-Western political movements. In the 1960s and 1970s westernized and pro-Western governments in developing countries were threatened by coups and revolutions; in the 1980s and 1990s they have been increasingly in danger of being ousted in elections. Democracy tends to make a society more parochial, not more cosmopolitan. Politicians in non-Western societies do not win elections by demonstrating how Western they are. Electoral competition stimulates them to fashion what they believe will be the most popular appeals, and those are usually ethnic, nationalist, and religious in character. The result is popular mobilization against Western-oriented elites and the West in general. This process, which began in Sri Lanka in the 1950s, has spread from country to country in Asia, Africa, and the Middle East, and is manifest in the victories of religiously oriented parties in India, Turkey, Bosnia, and Israel in elections in 1995 and 1996. Democratization is thus at odds with westernization.

The powerful currents of indigenization at work in the world make a mockery of Western expectations that Western culture will become the world's culture. The two central elements of any culture are language and religion. English, it has been asserted, is becoming the world's language. It clearly has become the lingua franca for communication in multinational business, diplomacy, international institutions, tourism, and aviation. This use of English for intercultural communication, however, presupposes the existence of different cultures; like translation and interpretation, it is a way of coping with those differences, not eliminating them. In fact, the proportion of the world's population speaking English is small and declining. According to the most reliable data, compiled by Sidney S. Culbert, a professor at the University of Washington, in 1958 roughly 9.8 percent of human beings spoke English as a first or second language; in 1992, 7.6 percent did. A language foreign to 92 percent of the world's population is not the world's language. Similarly, in 1958, 24 percent of humans spoke one of the five major Western languages; in 1992, less than 21 percent did. The situation is similar for religion. Western Christians now make up perhaps 30 percent of the world's population, but the proportion is declining steadily, and at some point in the next decade or so the number of Muslims will exceed the number of Christians. With respect to the two central elements of culture, language and religion, the West is in retreat. As Michael Howard has observed, the "common Western assumption that cultural diversity is a historical curiosity being rapidly eroded by the growth of a common, Western-oriented, Anglophone world culture, shaping our basic values ... is simply not true."[8]

What is universalism to the West is imperialism to the rest.

As indigenization spreads and the appeal of Western culture fades, the central problem in relations between the West and the rest is the gap between the West's, particularly America's, efforts to promote Western culture as the universal culture and its declining ability to do so. The collapse of communism exacerbated this disparity by reinforcing the view in the West that its ideology of democratic liberalism had triumphed globally and was thus universally valid. The West—and especially the United States, which has always been a missionary nation—believes that the non-Western peoples should commit themselves to the Western values of democracy, free markets, limited government, separation of church and state, human rights, individualism, and the rule of law, and should embody these values in their institutions. Minorities in other civilizations embrace and promote these values, but the dominant attitudes toward them in non-Western cultures range from skepticism to intense opposition. What is universalism to the West is imperialism to the rest.

Non-Westerners do not hesitate to point to the gaps between Western principle and Western practice. Hypocrisy and double standards are the price of universalist pretensions. Democracy is promoted, but not if it brings Islamic fundamentalists to power; nonproliferation is preached for Iran and Iraq, but not for Israel; free trade is the elixir of economic growth, but not for agriculture; human rights are an issue with China, but not with Saudi Arabia; aggression against oil-owning Kuwaitis is repulsed with massive force, but not so aggression against oil-less Bosnians.

The belief that non-Western peoples should adopt Western values, institutions, and culture is, if taken seriously, immoral in its implications. The almost universal reach of European power in the late nineteenth century and the global dominance of the United States in the latter half of the twentieth century spread many aspects of Western civilization across the world. But European globalism is no more, and American hegemony is receding, if only because it is no longer needed to protect the United States against a Cold War Soviet threat. Culture follows power. If non-Western societies are once again shaped by Western culture, it will happen only as a result of the expansion and deployment of Western power. Imperialism is the necessary, logical consequence of universalism, yet few proponents of universalism support the militarization and brutal coercion that would be necessary to achieve their goal. Furthermore, as a maturing civilization, the West no longer has the economic or demographic dynamism required to impose its will on other societies. Any effort to do so runs contrary to Western values of self-determination and democracy. This March, Prime Minister Mahathir of Malaysia told the assembled heads of European governments: "European values are European values; Asian values are universal values." As Asian and Muslim civilizations begin to assert the universal relevance of their cultures, Westerners will come to appreciate the connection between universalism and imperialism and to see the virtues of a pluralistic world.

SHORING UP THE WEST

◆ ◆ ◆

The time has come for the West to abandon the illusion of universality and to promote the strength, coherence, and vitality of its civilization in a world of civilizations. The interests of the West are not served by promiscuous intervention into the disputes of other peoples. In the era that is dawning, primary responsibility for containing and resolving regional conflicts must rest with the leading states of the civilizations dominant in those regions. "All politics is local politics," Thomas P. "Tip" O'Neill, the former Speaker of the House, observed, and the

corollary to that truth is "All power is local power." Neither the United Nations nor the United States can impose on local conflicts long-lasting solutions that deviate from the realities of local power. As anyone knowledgeable about crime knows, local law and order are best insured by a cop walking the beat, not by the potential appearance over the horizon of a squad of motorized police. In a multipolar, multicivilizational world, the West's responsibility is to secure its own interests, not to promote those of other peoples nor to attempt to settle conflicts between other peoples when those conflicts are of little or no consequence to the West.

The future of the West depends in large part on the unity of the West. Scholars of civilizations see them evolving through times of trouble and a period of warring states, eventually leading to a universal state for the civilization that may be either a source of renewal or a prelude to decay and disintegration. Western civilization has moved beyond its warring states phase and is heading toward its universal state phase. That phase is still incomplete, with the nation-states of the West cohering into two semi-universal states in Europe and North America. These two entities and their constituent units are, however, bound together by an extraordinarily complex network of formal and informal institutional ties. The universal states of previous civilizations were empires. Since democracy is the political form of Western civilization, the emerging universal state of Western civilization is not an empire but rather a compound of federations, confederations, and international regimes.

The problem for the West, in this situation, is to maintain its dynamism and to promote its coherence. Western unity depends more on events in the United States than on those in Europe. At present the United States is pulled in three directions. It is pulled south by the continuing immigration of Latin Americans and the growing size and power of its Hispanic population; by the incorporation of Mexico into the North American Free Trade Agreement and the possibility of extending NAFTA to other western hemisphere countries; and by the political, economic, and cultural changes in Latin America that make it more like the United States. At the same time, the United States is pulled westward by the increasing wealth and influence of East Asian societies; by the ongoing efforts to develop a Pacific community, epitomized in the Asia-Pacific Economic Cooperation (APEC) forum; and by migration from Asian societies. If democracy, free markets, the rule of law, civil society, individualism, and Protestantism take firm root in Latin America, that continent, whose culture has always been closely related to that of the West, will merge with the West and become the third pillar of Western civilization. No such convergence is possible with Asian societies. Asia is instead likely to pose continuing economic and political challenges to the United States specifically and the West more generally. The third pull, toward Europe, is the most important. Shared values, institutions, history, and culture dictate the continuing close association of the United States and Europe. Both necessary and desirable is the further development of institutional ties across the Atlantic, including negotiation of a European-American free trade agreement and creation of a North Atlantic economic organization as a counterpart to NATO.

The major current differences between Europe and America arise not from direct conflicts of interest with each other, but from their policies toward third parties. Among other questions, these include the provision of support to a Muslim-dominated Bosnia, the priority of Israeli security needs in Middle Eastern policy, U.S. efforts to penalize foreign companies that do business with Iran and Cuba, the maintenance of full economic sanctions against Iraq, and the part human rights and weapons proliferation concerns should play in dealing with China. Non-Western powers, especially China, have actively attempted to exploit these differences and play one Western country off against another. The differences themselves arise largely from different geopolitical perspectives and domestic political and economic interests. Maintaining the unity of the West, however, is essential to slowing the decline of Western influence in world affairs. Western peoples have far more in common with each other than they have with Asian, Middle Eastern, or African peoples. The leaders of Western countries have institutionalized patterns of trust and cooperation among themselves that, with rare exceptions, they do not have with the leaders of other societies. United, the West will remain a formidable presence on the international scene; divided, it will be prey to the efforts of non-Western states to exploit its internal differences by offering short-term gains to some Western countries at the price of long-term losses for all Western countries. The peoples of the West, in Benjamin Franklin's phrase, must hang together, or most assuredly they will hang separately.

Promoting the coherence of the West means both preserving Western culture within the West and defining the limits of the West. The former requires, among other things, controlling immigration from non-Western societies, as every major European country has done and as the United States is beginning to do, and ensuring the assimilation into Western culture of the immigrants who are admitted. It also means recognizing that in the post-Cold War world, NATO is the security organization of Western civilization and that its primary purpose is to defend and preserve that civilization. Hence states that are Western in their history, religion, and culture should, if they desire, be able to join NATO. Practically speaking, NATO membership would be open to the Visegrad states, the Baltic states, Slovenia, and Croatia, but not countries that have historically been primarily Muslim or Orthodox. While recent debate has focused entirely on the expansion rather than the contraction of NATO, it is also necessary to recognize that as NATO's mission changes, Turkish and Greek ties to NATO will weaken and their membership could either come to an end or become meaningless. Withdrawal from NATO is the declared goal of the Welfare Party in Turkey, and Greece is becoming as much an ally of Russia as it is a member of NATO.

The peoples of the West ... must hang together, or most assuredly they will hang separately.

The West went through a European phase of development and expansion that lasted several centuries and an American phase that has dominated this century. If North America and Europe renew their moral life, build on their cultural commonality, and develop closer forms of economic and political integration to supplement their security collaboration in NATO, they could generate a third Euroamerican phase of Western affluence and political influence. Meaningful political integration would in some measure counter the relative decline in the West's share of the world's people, economic product, and military capabilities and revive the West's power in the eyes of the leaders of other civilizations. The principal responsibility of Western leaders is not to attempt to reshape other civilizations in the image of the West—which is increasingly beyond their ability—but to preserve and renew the unique qualities of Western civilization. That responsibility falls overwhelmingly on the most powerful Western country, the United States of America. Neither globalism nor isolationism, neither multilateralism nor unilateralism will best serve American interests. Its interests will be most effectively advanced if the United States eschews those extremes and instead adopts an Atlanticist policy of close cooperation with its European partners, one that will protect and promote the interests, values, and culture of the precious and unique civilization they share.

Notes

1. Fernand Braudel, *On History,* Chicago: University of Chicago Press, 1980, p. 213.
2. Karl Deutsch, "On Nationalism, World Regions, and the Nature of the West," in Per Torvik, ed., *Mobilization, Center-Periphery Structures and Nation-Building,* Bergen: Universitetsforlaget, 1981, p. 77.
3. Stein Rokkan, "Dimensions of State Formation and Nation-Building," in Charles Tilly, ed., *The Formation of Nation-States in Western Europe,* Princeton: Princeton University Press, 1975, p. 576.
4. Geert Hofstede, "National Cultures in Four Dimensions," *International Studies of Management and Organization,* 1983, Vol. 13, p. 53; Harry C. Triandis, "Cross-Cultural Studies of Individualism and Collectivism," *Nebraska Symposium on Motivation 1989,* Lincoln: University of Nebraska Press, 1990, pp. 44–133, quoted in Daniel Coleman, "The Group and the Self: New Focus on a Cultural Rift," *The New York Times,* December 25, 1990, p. 41.
5. Arthur M. Schlesinger, Jr., *The Disunity of America,* New York: W.W. Norton, 1992, p. 127.
6. Adda B. Bozeman, "Civilizations under Stress," *Virginia Quarterly Review,* Winter 1975, p. 7; William E. Naff, "Reflections on the Question of 'East and West' from the Point of View of Japan," *Comparative Civilizations Review,* Fall 1985–Spring 1986, p. 222; Braudel, *On History,* pp. 212–213.
7. Ronald Dore, "Unity and Diversity in Contemporary World Culture," in Hedley Bull and Adam Watson, eds., *Expansion of International Society,* Oxford: Oxford University Press, 1984, pp. 420–421.
8. Michael Howard, *America and the World* (Annual Lewin Lecture), St. Louis: Washington University, 1984, p. 6.

Terms & Concepts

civil society
Coca-colonization
imperialism
rule of law

second-generation indigenization
separation of church and state
social pluralism
universalism

Western civilization
Westoxification

Questions

1. Huntington predicts antidemocratic outcomes from democratic decision making in non-Western societies. Is this a paradox?

2. Is there any evidence that modernization does, eventually, lead to democracy as understood in the Western world?

3. Huntington argues that immigrants from non-Western societies have to be quickly assimilated in Western countries to preserve Western culture. Do you agree that immigrants have to be made to assimilate, or that assimilation is desirable?

4. Does "globalization" affect political culture? What are the limits of this effect?

5. Why is Huntington less alarmed about Latin America than he is about Asia?

The Complexities and Contradictions of Globalization

James N. Rosenau

Editors' Note

Is *globalization* merely a buzzword, a lazy way of putting a name to the changes that affect the ability of states to run their affairs and that lead to economic and cultural integration around the globe? James Rosenau thinks not: he argues that we need such a term in order to describe and capture what is happening as the human condition, in his words, "undergoes profound transformations in all of its aspects." Nonetheless, he urges us to be careful when using the term, and he makes the particularly important point that globalization is a *process* of transformation and change. It is not an end in itself, nor does it presume a set of shared values, even though it embodies the spread of similar forms of behaviour, processes, and systems.

Along with globalization comes its supposed opposite, localism. In a widely read and much-quoted book, Benjamin Barber has referred to this tension as a clash between the forces of McWorld—a world defined by technology, culture, commerce, communications, capital, and consumerism—and the world of Jihad.[1] Jihad is the realm of fanaticism, parochial hatreds, tribalism, and ultranationalism. The forces of McWorld and Jihad sometimes exert themselves within the same society, often creating instability or worse—for example, cosmopolitan Sarajevo has been torn apart by ethnic hatreds and pure savagery.

Rosenau's views on global versus local conflicts are illuminating because he does not see these tensions as inherently contradictory. Although he does not claim that globalization's triumph is assured or free of unhealthy consequences, he remains optimistic that contradictions will work themselves out. He coins the term *fragmegration* to argue that we will indeed be able to combine our loyalty to the state (assuming we have one we wish to be loyal to) with multiple memberships in other communities that increasingly matter to us.

◆ ◆ ◆

The mall at Singapore's airport has a food court with 15 food outlets, all but one of which offering menus that cater to local tastes; the lone standout, McDonald's, is also the only one crowded with customers. In New York City, experts in *feng shui*, an ancient Chinese craft aimed at harmonizing the placement of man-made structures in nature, are sought after by real estate developers in order to attract a growing influx of Asian buyers who would not be interested in purchasing buildings unless their structures were properly harmonized.

Most people confronted with these examples would probably not be surprised by them. They might even view them as commonplace features of day-to-day life late in the twentieth century, instances in which local practices have spread to new and distant sites. In the first case the spread is from West to East and in the second it is from East to West, but both share a process in which

---

1. Benjamin Barber, *Jihad Vs. McWorld: How Globalism and Tribalism Are Reshaping the World* (New York: Ballantine, 1995).

practices spread and become established in profoundly different cultures. And what immediately comes to mind when contemplating this process? The answer can be summed up in one word: globalization, a label that is presently in vogue to account for peoples, activities, norms, ideas, goods, services, and currencies that are decreasingly confined to a particular geographic space and its local and established practices.

Indeed, some might contend that "globalization" is the latest buzzword to which observers resort when things seem different and they cannot otherwise readily account for them. That is why, it is reasoned, a great variety of activities are labeled as globalization, with the result that no widely accepted formulation of the concept has evolved. Different observers use it to describe different phenomena, and often there is little overlap among the various usages. Even worse, the elusiveness of the concept of globalization is seen as underlying the use of a variety of other, similar terms—world society, interdependence, centralizing tendencies, world system, globalism, universalism, internationalization, globality—that come into play when efforts are made to grasp why public affairs today seem significantly different from those of the past.

Such reasoning is misleading. The proliferation of diverse and loose definitions of globalization as well as the readiness to use a variety of seemingly comparable labels are not so much a reflection of evasive confusion as they are an early stage in a profound ontological shift, a restless search for new ways of understanding unfamiliar phenomena. The lack of precise formulations may suggest the presence of buzzwords for the inexplicable, but a more convincing interpretation is that such words are voiced in so many different contexts because of a shared sense that the human condition is presently undergoing profound transformations in all of its aspects.

WHAT IS GLOBALIZATION?

◆ ◆ ◆

Let us first make clear where globalization fits among the many buzzwords that indicate something new in world affairs that is moving important activities and concerns beyond the national seats of power that long served as the foundations of economic, political, and social life. While all the buzzwords seem to cluster around the same dimension of the present human condition, useful distinctions can be drawn among them. Most notably, if it is presumed that the prime character-istic of this dimension is change—a transformation of practices and norms—then the term "globalization" seems appropriate to denote the "something" that is changing humankind's preoccupation with territoriality and the traditional arrangements of the state system. It is a term that directly implies change, and thus differentiates the phenomenon as a process rather than as a prevailing condition or a desirable end state.

Conceived as an underlying process, in other words, globalization is not the same as globalism, which points to aspirations for the state of affairs where values are shared by or pertinent to all the world's more than 5 billion people, their environment, and their role as citizens, consumers, or producers with an interest in collective action to solve common problems. And it can also be distinguished from universalism, which refers to those values that embrace all of humanity (such as the values that science or religion draws on), at any time or place. Nor is it coterminous with complex interdependence, which signifies structures that link people and communities in various parts of the world.

Although related to these other concepts, the idea of globalization developed here is narrower in scope. It refers neither to values nor to structures, but to sequences that unfold either in the mind or in behavior, to processes that evolve as people and organizations go about their daily tasks and seek to realize their particular goals. What distinguishes globalizing processes is that they are not hindered or prevented by territorial or jurisdictional barriers. As indicated by the two examples presented at the outset, such processes can readily spread in many directions across national boundaries, and are capable of reaching into any community anywhere in the world. They consist of all those forces that impel individuals, groups, and institutions to engage in similar forms of behavior or to participate in more encompassing and coherent processes, organizations, or systems.

Contrariwise, localization derives from all those pressures that lead individuals, groups, and institutions to narrow their horizons, participate in dissimilar forms of behavior, and withdraw to less encompassing processes, organizations, or systems. In other words, any technological, psychological, social, economic, or political developments that foster the expansion of interests and practices beyond established boundaries are both sources and expressions of the processes of globalization, just as any developments in these realms that limit or reduce interests are both sources and expressions of localizing processes.

Note that the processes of globalization are conceived as only capable of being worldwide in scale. In fact, the activities of no group, government, society, or company have ever been planetary in magnitude, and few cascading sequences actually encircle and encompass the entire globe. Televised events such as civil wars and famines in Africa or protests against governments in Eastern Europe may sustain a spread that is worldwide in scope, but such a scope is not viewed as a prerequisite of globalizing dynamics. As long as it has the potential of an unlimited spread that can readily transgress national jurisdictions, any interaction sequence is considered to reflect the operation of globalization.

Obviously, the differences between globalizing and localizing forces give rise to contrary conceptions of territoriality. Globalization is rendering boundaries and identity with the land less salient while localization, being driven by pressures to narrow and withdraw, is highlighting borders and intensifying the deep attachments to land that can dominate emotion and reasoning.

Some globalization dynamics are bound, at least in the long run, to prevail.

In short, globalization is boundary-broadening and localization is boundary-heightening. The former allows people, goods, information, norms, practices, and institutions to move about oblivious to or despite boundaries. The boundary-heightening processes of localization are designed to inhibit or prevent the movement of people, goods, information, norms, practices, and institutions. Efforts along this line, however, can be only partially successful. Community and state boundaries can be heightened to a considerable extent, but they cannot be rendered impervious. Authoritarian governments try to make them so, but their policies are bound to be undermined in a shrinking world with increasingly interdependent economies and communications technologies that are not easily monitored. Thus it is hardly surprising that some of the world's most durable tensions flow from the fact that no geographic borders can be made so airtight to prevent the infiltration of ideas and goods. Stated more emphatically, some globalization dynamics are bound, at least in the long run, to prevail.

The boundary-expanding dynamics of globalization have become highly salient precisely because recent decades have witnessed a mushrooming of the facilities, interests, and markets through which a potential for worldwide spread can be realized. Likewise, the boundary-contracting dynamics of localization have also become increasingly significant, not least because some people and cultures feel threatened by the incursions of globalization. Their jobs, their icons, their belief systems, and their communities seem at risk as the boundaries that have sealed them off from the outside world in the past no longer assure protection. And there is, of course, a basis of truth in these fears. Globalization does intrude; its processes do shift jobs elsewhere; its norms do undermine traditional mores. Responses to these threats can vary considerably. At one extreme are adaptations that accept the boundary-broadening processes and make the best of them by integrating them into local customs and practices. At the other extreme are responses intended to ward off the globalizing processes by resort to ideological purities, closed borders, and economic isolation.

THE DYNAMICS OF FRAGMEGRATION

◆ ◆ ◆

The core of world affairs today thus consists of tensions between the dynamics of globalization and localization. Moreover, the two sets of dynamics are causally linked, almost as if every increment of globalization gives rise to an increment of localization, and vice versa. To account for these tensions I have long used the term "fragmegration," an awkward and perhaps even grating label that has the virtue of capturing the pervasive interactions between the fragmenting forces of localization and the integrative forces of globalization.[1] One can readily observe the unfolding of fragmegrative dynamics in the struggle of the European Union to cope with proposals for monetary unification or in the electoral campaigns and successes of Jean-Marie Le Pen in France, Patrick Buchanan in the United States, and Pauline Hanson in Australia—to mention only three examples.

It is important to keep in mind that fragmegration is not a single dynamic. Both globalization and localization are clusters of forces that, as they interact in different ways and through different channels, contribute to more encompassing processes in the case of globalization and to less encompassing processes in the case of localization. These various dynamics, moreover, operate in all realms of human activity, from the cultural and social to the economic and political.

In the political realm, globalizing dynamics underlie any developments that facilitate the expansion of authority, policies, and interests beyond existing socially constructed territorial boundaries, whereas the politics of localization involves any trends in which the scope of authority and policies undergoes contraction and reverts to concerns, issues, groups, and institutions that are less extensive than the prevailing socially constructed territorial boundaries. In the economic realm, globalization encompasses the expansion of production, trade, and investments beyond their prior locales, while localizing dynamics are at work when the activities of producers and consumers are constricted to narrower boundaries. In the social and cultural realms, globalization operates to extend ideas, norms, and practices beyond the settings in which they originated, while localization highlights or compresses the original settings and thereby inhibits the inroad of new ideas, norms, and practices.

It must be stressed that the dynamics unfolding in all these realms are long-term processes. They involve fundamental human needs and thus span all of human history. Globalizing dynamics derive from people's need to enlarge the scope of their self-created orders so as to increase the goods, services, and ideas available for their well-being. The agricultural revolution, followed by the industrial and postindustrial transformations, are among the major sources that have sustained globalization. Yet even as these forces have been operating, so have contrary tendencies toward contraction been continuously at work. Localizing dynamics derive from people's need for the psychic comforts of close-at-hand, reliable support—for the family and neighborhood, for local cultural practices, for a sense of "us" that is distinguished from "them." Put differently, globalizing dynamics have long fostered large-scale order, whereas localizing dynamics have long created pressure for small-scale order. Fragmegration, in short, has always been an integral part of the human condition.

GLOBALIZATION'S EVENTUAL PREDOMINANCE

◆ ◆ ◆

Notwithstanding the complexities inherent in the emergent structures of world affairs, observers have not hesitated to anticipate what lies beyond fragmegration as global history unfolds. All agree that while the contest between globalizing and localizing dynamics is bound to be marked by fluctuating surges in both directions, the underlying tendency is for the former to prevail over the latter. Eventually, that is, the dynamics of globalization are expected to serve as the bases around which the course of events is organized.

Consensus along these lines breaks down, however, over whether the predominance of globalization is likely to have desirable or noxious consequences. Those who welcome globalizing processes stress the power of economic variables. In this view the globalization of national economies through the diffusion of technology and consumer products, the rapid transfer of financial resources, and the efforts of transnational companies to extend their market shares is seen as so forceful and durable as to withstand and eventually surmount any and all pressures toward fragmentation. This line acknowledges that the diffusion that sustains the processes of globalization is a centuries-old dynamic, but the difference is that the present era has achieved a level of economic development in which it is possible for innovations occurring in any sector of any country's economy to be instantaneously transferred to and adapted in any other country or sector. As a consequence,

> when this process of diffusion collides with cultural or political protectionism, it is culture and protectionism that wind up in the shop for repairs. Innovation accelerates. Productivity increases. Standards of living improve. There are setbacks, of course. The newspaper headlines are full of them. But we believe that the time required to override these setbacks has shortened dramatically in the developed world. Indeed, recent experience suggests that, in most cases, economic factors prevail in less than a generation....
>
> Thus understood, globalization—the spread of economic innovations around the world and the political and cultural adjustments that accompany this diffusion—cannot be stopped.... As history teaches, the political organizations and ideologies that yield superior economic performance survive, flourish, and replace those that are less productive.[2]

While it is surely the case that robust economic incentives sustain and quicken the processes of globalization, this line of theorizing nevertheless suffers from not allowing for its own negation. The theory offers no alternative interpretations as to how the interaction of economic, political, and social dynamics will play out. One cannot demonstrate the falsity—if falsity it is—of the theory because any contrary evidence is seen merely as "setbacks," as expectable but temporary deviations from the predicted course. The day may come, of course, when events so perfectly conform to the predicted patterns of globalization that one is inclined to conclude that the theory has been affirmed. But in the absence of alternative scenarios, the theory offers little guidance as to how to interpret intervening events, especially those that highlight the tendencies toward fragmentation. Viewed in this way, it is less a theory and more an article of faith to which one can cling.

Other observers are much less sanguine about the future development of fragmegration. They highlight a litany of noxious consequences that they see as following from the eventual predominance of globalization: "its economism; its economic reductionism; its technological determinism; its political cynicism, defeatism, and immobilism; its de-socialization of the subject and resocialization of risk; its teleological subtext of inexorable global 'logic' driven exclusively by capital accumulation and the market; and its ritual exclusion of factors, causes, or goals other than capital accumulation and the market from the priority of values to be pursued by social action."[3]

Still another approach, allowing for either desirable or noxious outcomes, has been developed by Michael Zurn. He identifies a mismatch between the rapid extension of boundary-crossing activities and the scope of effective governance. Consequently, states are undergoing what is labeled "uneven denationalization," a primary process in which "the rise of international governance is still remarkable, but not accompanied by mechanisms for ... democratic control; people, in addition, become alienated from the remote political process.... The democratic state in the Western world is confronted with a situation in which it is undermined by the process of globalization and overarched by the rise of international institutions."[4]

While readily acknowledging the difficulties of anticipating where the process of uneven denationalization is driving the world, Zurn is able to derive two scenarios that may unfold: "Whereas the pessimistic scenario points to instances of fragmentation and emphasizes the disruption caused by the transition, the optimistic scenario predicts, at least in the long run, the triumph of centralization." The latter scenario rests on the presumption that the increased interdependence of societies will propel them to develop ever more effective democratic controls over the very complex arrangements on which international institutions must be founded.

UNEVEN FRAGMEGRATION

◆ ◆ ◆

My own approach to theorizing about the fragmegrative process builds on these other perspectives and a key pre-

sumption of my own—that there is no inherent contradiction between localizing and globalizing tendencies— to develop an overall hypothesis that anticipates fragmegrative outcomes and that allows for its own negation: *the more pervasive globalizing tendencies become, the less resistant localizing reactions will be to further globalization.* In other words, globalization and localization will coexist, but the former will continue to set the context for the latter. Since the degree of coexistence will vary from situation to situation (depending on the salience of the global economy and the extent to which ethnic and other noneconomic factors actively contribute to localization), I refer, borrowing from Zurn, to the processes depicted by the hypothesis as *uneven fragmegration.* The hypothesis allows for continuing pockets of antagonism between globalizing and localizing tendencies even as increasingly (but unevenly) the two accommodate each other. It does not deny the pessimistic scenario wherein fragmentation disrupts globalizing tendencies; rather it treats fragmentation as more and more confined to particular situations that may eventually be led by the opportunities and requirements of greater interdependence to conform to globalization.

There is no inherent contradiction between localizing and globalizing tendencies.

For globalizing and localizing tendencies to accommodate each other, individuals have to come to appreciate that they can achieve psychic comfort in collectivities through multiple memberships and multiple loyalties, that they can advance both local and global values without either detracting from the other. The hypothesis of uneven fragmegration anticipates a growing appreciation along these lines because the contrary premise, that psychic comfort can only be realized by having a highest loyalty, is becoming increasingly antiquated. To be sure, people have long been accustomed to presuming that, in order to derive the psychic comfort they need through collective identities, they had to have a hierarchy of loyalties and that, consequently, they had to have a highest loyalty that could only be attached to a single collectivity. Such reasoning, however, is a legacy of the state system, of centuries of crises that made people feel they had to place nation-state loyalties above all others. It is a logic that long served to reinforce the predominance of the state as the "natural" unit of political organization and that probably reached new heights during the intense years of the cold war.

But if it is the case, as the foregoing analysis stresses, that conceptions of territoriality are in flux and that the failure of states to solve pressing problems has led to a decline in their capabilities and a loss of legitimacy, it follows that the notion that people must have a "highest loyalty" will also decline and give way to the development of multiple loyalties and an understanding that local, national, and transnational affiliations need not be mutually exclusive. For the reality is that human affairs are organized at all these levels for good reasons; people have needs that can only be filled by close-at-hand organizations and other needs that are best served by distant entities at the national or transnational level.

In addition, not only is an appreciation of the reality that allows for multiple loyalties and memberships likely to grow as the effectiveness of states and the salience of national loyalties diminish, but it also seems likely to widen as the benefits of the global economy expand and people become increasingly aware of the extent to which their well-being is dependent on events and trends elsewhere in the world. At the same time, the distant economic processes serving their needs are impersonal and hardly capable of advancing the need to share with others in a collective affiliation. This need was long served by the nation-state, but with fragmegrative dynamics having undermined the national level as a source of psychic comfort and with transnational entities seeming too distant to provide the psychic benefits of affiliation, the satisfactions to be gained through more close-at-hand affiliations are likely to seem ever more attractive.

THE STAKES

◆ ◆ ◆

It seems clear that fragmegration has become an enduring feature of global life; it is also evident that globalization is not merely a buzzword, that it encompasses pervasive complexities and contradictions that have the potential both to enlarge and to degrade our humanity. In order to ensure that the enlargement is more prevalent than the degradation, it is important that people and their institutions become accustomed to the multiple dimensions and nuances as our world undergoes profound and enduring transformations. To deny the complexities and contradictions in order to cling to a singular conception of what globalization involves is to risk the many dangers that accompany oversimplification.

Notes

1. For an extensive discussion of the dynamics of fragmegration, see James N. Rosenau, *Along the Domestic-Foreign Frontier: Exploring Governance in a Turbulent World* (Cambridge: Cambridge University Press, 1997), ch. 6.
2. William W. Lewis and Marvin Harris, "Why Globalization Must Prevail," *The McKinsey Quarterly*, no. 2 (1992), p. 115.
3. Barry K. Gills, "Editorial: 'Globalization' and the 'Politics of Resistance,'" *New Political Economy*, vol. 2 (March 1997), p. 12.
4. Michael Zurn, "What Has Changed in Europe? The Challenge of Globalization and Individualization," paper presented at a meeting on What Has Changed? Competing Perspectives on World Order (Copenhagen, May 14–16, 1993), p. 40.

Terms & Concepts

boundary-broadening

boundary-heightening

cultural protectionism

de-socialization and resocialization

economic reductionism

fragmegration

globalism

globalizing dynamics

norms

ontological shift

psychic comfort

technological determinism

teleological subtext

traditional mores

uneven fragmentation

universalism

world society/system

Questions

1. How does Rosenau see the forces of fragmegration working themselves out?

2. Are states disaggregating into their separate, functionally distinct parts and creating new networks of collaboration and cooperation? Provide examples.

3. How do new technologies—fax, Internet, e-mail, satellites, etc.—undermine the state, assist globalization, and change people's perceptions of community?

4. Does Rosenau have an overly optimistic view of both globalization and fragmegration, one that, despite his protestations, does tend to assume a predicted and predictable course of events?

Environmental Scarcity, Mass Violence, and the Limits to Ingenuity

Thomas F. Homer-Dixon

Editors' Note

Social scientists and public-policy makers are concerned about the varieties and intensities of political conflict, but it is just as important to understand its causes and effects. In public policy, as in medicine, treating the symptom of a malady should not be mistaken for treating its causes. Thomas Homer-Dixon makes this basic concern central to his analysis of environmental scarcity and brings together two phenomena often considered in isolation. In this article, he argues that renewable resource scarcity in varying degrees causes political conflict. Environmental health and the stewardship of natural resources are becoming security issues, just as military buildups are a security issue.

This is a novel way of looking at environmental scarcity. Most people consider the problem in nonpolitical terms. The pollution of underground water supplies, for example, is considered bad because it can adversely affect human health. Homer-Dixon sees the lines of causality in more complex terms. Aquifer contamination means less potable water, putting stress on irrigation supplies and causing farmers to become impoverished, lose their farms, and move into overcrowded cities. The farmers clamour for government action and contest the privileges of the wealthy, yet the state may be unable or unwilling to meet their demands.

States may come into conflict with each other over freshwater supplies. The depletion of a renewable resource can have rippling political consequences, which are made all the more grave as governments and citizens alike work to maximize economic growth and thus place greater stress on natural resources.

Is there hope for the world as environmental scarcity proceeds apace? Homer-Dixon's outlook is neither particularly hopeful, nor is it bleak. He still places great stock in human ingenuity.

◆ ◆ ◆

Scarcities of critical environmental resources—in particular cropland, freshwater, and forests—are contributing to mass violence in several areas of the world. While these "environmental scarcities" do not cause wars between countries, they do sometimes sharply aggravate stresses within countries, helping stimulate ethnic clashes, urban unrest, and insurgencies. This violence affects Western national interests by destabilizing trade and economic relations, provoking migrations, and generating complex humanitarian disasters that divert militaries and absorb huge amounts of aid.

Policymakers and citizens in the West ignore these pressures at their peril. In Chiapas, Mexico, Zapatista insurgents recently rose up against land scarcity and insecure land tenure produced by longstanding inequalities in land distribution, by rapid population growth among groups with the least land, and by changes in laws governing land access. The insurgency rocked Mexico to the core, helped trigger the peso crisis, and reminded the world that Mexico remains—despite the North American Free Trade Agreement (NAFTA) and the pretenses of the country's elites—a poor and profoundly unstable developing country.

In Pakistan, shortages and the maldistribution of good land, water, and forests have encouraged the migration of huge numbers of rural poor into major cities such as Karachi and Hyderabad. The conjunction of this in-migration with high fertility rates is causing urban populations to grow at a staggering 4 to 5 percent a year, producing fierce competition and often violence among ethnic groups over land, basic services, and political and economic power. This turmoil exacts a huge cost on the national economy. It may also encourage the Pakistani regime to buttress its internal legitimacy by adopting a more belligerent foreign policy on issues such as Kashmir and nuclear proliferation.

In South Africa, severe land, water, and fuelwood scarcity in the former black homelands has helped drive millions of poor blacks into teeming squatter settlements in the major cities. The settlements are often constructed on the worst urban land, in depressions prone to flooding, on hillsides vulnerable to slides, or near heavily polluting industries. Scarcities of land, water, and fuelwood in these settlements provoke interethnic rivalry and violent feuds between settlement warlords and their followers. This strife jeopardizes the country's transition to democratic stability and prosperity.[1]

THREE FORMS OF SCARCITY

◆ ◆ ◆

It is easy for the 1 billion or so people living in rich countries to forget that the well-being of about half the world's population of 5.8 billion remains directly tied to local natural resources. Nearly 3 billion people rely on agriculture for their main income; perhaps 1 billion of these are subsistence farmers who survive by eating what they grow. More than 40 percent of the world's people—some 2.2 billion—use fuelwood, charcoal, straw, or cow dung as their main source of energy; 50 to 60 percent rely on these biomass fuels for at least some of their energy needs. Over 1.2 billion people lack access to clean drinking water.

The cropland, forests, and water supplies that underpin the livelihoods and well-being of these billions are renewable. Unlike nonrenewable resources such as oil and iron ore, renewables are replenished over time by natural processes. If used prudently, they should sustain an adequate standard of living indefinitely. Unfortunately, in the majority of regions where people are highly dependent on renewable resources, these

resources are being depleted or degraded faster than they are being renewed. From Gaza and the Philippines to Honduras, the evidence is stark: aquifers are being overdrawn and salinized, coastal fisheries are disappearing, and steep uplands have been stripped of their forests, leaving their thin soils to erode into the sea.

Renewables are replenished over time by natural processes. If used prudently, they should sustain an adequate standard of living indefinitely.

These environmental scarcities usually have complex causes. Resource depletion and degradation are a function of the physical vulnerability of the resource, the size of the resource-consuming population, and the technologies and practices this population uses. The size of the population and its technologies and practices are in turn a result of a wide array of other variables, from the status of women to the availability of human and financial capital.

Moreover, resource depletion and degradation, taken together, are only one of three sources of environmental scarcity. Depletion and degradation produce a decrease in total resource *supply*—that is, a decrease in the size of the total resource "pie." But population growth and changes in consumption behavior can also cause greater scarcity by boosting the *demand* for a resource. Thus, if a rapidly growing population depends on a fixed amount of cropland, the amount of cropland per person—the size of each person's slice of the resource pie—falls inexorably. In many countries resource availability is being squeezed by both supply and demand pressures.

In many countries resource availability is being squeezed by both supply and demand pressures.

The third cause of scarcity is a severe imbalance in the *distribution* of wealth and power, which results in some groups in a society receiving disproportionately large slices of the resource pie while others get slices that are too small to sustain their livelihoods. This unequal distribution, which we call structural scarcity, has been a key factor in every case our research team examined. Often the imbalance is deeply rooted in the institutions and class and ethnic relations inherited from the colonial period. Often it is sustained and reinforced by international economic relations that trap developing countries into dependence on a few raw material exports. It can also be reinforced by heavy external debts that encourage countries to use their most productive environmental resources—such as their best croplands and forests—to generate hard currency rather than to support the most impoverished segments of their populations.

HOW SCARCITIES INTERACT

◆ ◆ ◆

In the past, scholars and policymakers have usually addressed these three sources of scarcity independently. But supply, demand, and structural scarcities interact and reinforce each other in extraordinarily pernicious ways.

One type of interaction is resource capture. This occurs when powerful groups within a society recognize that a key resource is becoming more scarce (due to both supply and demand pressures) and use their power to shift resource access in their favor. This shift imposes severe structural scarcities on weaker groups. In Chiapas, worsening land scarcity (caused in part by rapid population growth) encouraged powerful landowners and ranchers to exploit weaknesses in the state's land laws in order to seize land from campesinos and indigenous farmers. Gradually these peasants were forced deeper into the state's lowland rain forest, further away from the state's economic heartland and further into poverty.

In the Jordan River basin, Israel's critical dependence on groundwater flowing out of the West Bank—a dependence made acute by a rising Israeli population and salinizing aquifers along the Mediterranean coast—encouraged Israel to restrict groundwater withdrawals on the West Bank during the occupation. These restrictions were far more severe for Palestinians than for Israeli settlers. They contributed to the rapid decline in Palestinian agriculture in the region, to the increasing dependence of young Palestinians on day labor within Israel and, ultimately, to rising frustrations in the Palestinian community.

Another kind of interaction, ecological marginalization, occurs when a structural imbalance in resource distribution joins with rapid population growth to drive resource-poor people into ecologically marginal areas, such as upland hillsides, areas at risk of desertification, and tropical rain forests. Higher population densities in these vulnerable areas—along with a lack of the capital and knowledge needed to protect local resources—causes resource depletion, poverty, and eventually further migration, often to cities.

Ecological marginalization affects hundreds of millions of people around the world, across an extraordinary range of geographies and economic and political systems. We see the same process in the Himalayas, the Sahel, Central America, Brazil, India's Rajasthan, and Indonesia. For example, in the Philippines an extreme imbalance in cropland distribution between landowners and peasants has interacted with high population growth rates to force large numbers of landless poor into interior upland regions of the archipelago. There, the migrants use slash and burn agriculture to clear land for crops. As millions more arrive from the lowlands, new land becomes hard to find, and as population densities on the steep slopes increase, erosion, landslides, and flash floods become critical. During the 1970s and 1980s, the resulting poverty helped drive many peasants into the arms of the communist New People's Army insurgency that had a stranglehold on upland regions. Poverty drove countless others into wretched squatter settlements in cities like Manila.

Ecological marginalization affects hundreds of millions of people around the world ...

Of course, many factors unique to the Filipino situation have combined with environmental and demographic stress to produce these outcomes. Environmental scarcity is never a determining or sole cause of large migrations, poverty, or violence; it always joins with other economic, political, and cultural factors to produce its effects. In the Filipino case the lack of clear property rights in upland areas encouraged migration into these regions and discouraged migrants from conserving the land once they arrived. And President Ferdinand Marcos's corrupt and authoritarian leadership reduced regime legitimacy and closed off options for democratic action by aggrieved groups.

Analysts often overlook the importance of such contextual factors and, as a result, jump from evidence of simple correlation to unwarranted conclusions about causation. Thus some commentators have asserted that rapid population growth, severe land scarcity, and the resulting food shortfalls caused the Rwandan genocide. In an editorial in August 1994, *The Washington Post* argued that while the Rwandan civil war was "military, political, and personal in its execution," a key underlying cause was "a merciless struggle for land in a peasant society whose birthrates have put an unsustainable pressure on it." Yet, while environmental scarcities in Rwanda were serious, close analysis shows that the genocide arose mainly from a conventional struggle among elites for control of the Rwandan state. Land scarcity played at most a peripheral role by reducing regime legitimacy in the countryside and restricting alternatives for elite enrichment outside the state.

Despite these caveats, in many cases environmental scarcity powerfully contributes to mass violence. Moreover, it is not possible entirely to subordinate its role to a society's particular institutions and policies. Some skeptics claim that a society can fix its environmental problems by fixing its institutional and policy mistakes; thus, they assert, environmental scarcity's contribution to conflict does not merit independent attention. But our research shows that such arguments are incomplete at best.

First, environmental scarcity is not only a consequence of institutions and policy: it also can reciprocally influence them in harmful ways. For example, during the 1970s and 1980s the prospect of chronic food shortages and a serious drought encouraged governments along the Senegal River to build a series of irrigation and flood-control dams. Because of critical land scarcities elsewhere in the region, land values in the basin shot up. The Mauritanian government, controlled by Moors of Arab origin, then took control of this resource by changing the laws governing land ownership and abrogating the traditional rights of black Mauritanians to farm, herd, and fish along the river.

Second, environmental scarcity should not be subordinated to institutions and policies because it is partly a function of the physical context in which a society is embedded. The original depth of soils in the Filipino uplands and the physical characteristics that make Israel's aquifers vulnerable to salt intrusion are not functions of human social institutions or behavior. And third, once environmental scarcity becomes irreversible (as when a region's vital topsoil washes into the sea), then the scarcity is, by definition, an external influence on society. Even if enlightened reform of institutions and policies removes the original political and economic causes of the scarcity, it will be a continuing burden on society.

RESOURCE SCARCITY AS A CAUSE OF INTERSTATE WAR

◆ ◆ ◆

Scarcity-induced resource capture by Moors in Mauritania helped ignite violence over water and cropland in the Senegal River basin, producing tens of thousands of refugees. Expanding populations, land degradation, and drought spurred the rise of the Shining Path guerrillas in the southern highlands of Peru. In Haiti, forest and soil loss worsens a chronic economic crisis that generates strife and periodic waves of boat people. And land shortages in Bangladesh, exacerbated by fast population growth, have prompted millions of people to migrate to India—an influx that has, in turn, caused ethnic strife in the Indian states of Assam and Tripura.

Severe environmental scarcity can ... undermine a state's moral authority and capacity to govern.

Close examination of such cases shows that severe environmental scarcity can reduce local food production, aggravate the poverty of marginal groups, spur large migrations, enrich elites who speculate on resources, and undermine a state's moral authority and capacity to govern. These long-term stresses can slowly tear apart a poor society's social fabric, causing chronic popular unrest and violence by boosting grievances and changing the balance of power between contending social groups and the state.

The violence that results is usually chronic and diffuse, and almost always subnational, not international. There is virtually no evidence that environmental scarcity causes major interstate war. Yet among international relations scholars, it has been conventional wisdom for some time that critical scarcities of national resources can produce international conflict. During the 1970s, for example, Nazli Chourci and Robert North argued that countries facing high resource demands and limited resource availability within their territories would seek the needed resources through trade or conquest beyond their boundaries.[2] Although this "lateral pressure" theory helped explain some past wars, such as World War I, our more recent research highlights a number of the theory's errors. Most important, the theory makes no distinction between renewable and nonrenewable resources.

There is no doubt that some major wars in this century have been motivated in part by one country's desire to seize another's nonrenewable resources, such as fossil fuels or iron ore. For example, before and during World War II, Japan sought to secure coal, oil, and minerals in China and Southeast Asia. But the story is different for renewables like cropland, forests, fish, and freshwater. It is hard to find clear examples from this century of major war motivated mainly by scarcities of renewables.

There are two possible explanations. First, modern states cannot easily convert cropland and forests seized from a neighbor into increased state power, whereas they can quickly use nonrenewables like iron and oil to build and fuel the military machines of national aggression. Second, countries with economies highly dependent on renewables tend to be poor, and poor countries cannot easily buy large and sophisticated conventional armies to attack their neighbors. For both these reasons, the incentives and the means to launch resource wars are likely to be lower for renewables than for nonrenewables.

The "wars of the next century will be over water," not oil.

The exception, some might argue, is water, especially river water: adequate water supplies are needed for all aspects of national activity, including the production and use of military power, and rich countries are as dependent on water as poor countries (often they are more dependent). Moreover, about 40 percent of the world's population lives in the 214 river basins shared by more than one country. Thus at a meeting in Stockholm in August 1995, Ismail Serageldin, the World Bank's vice president for environmentally sustainable development, declared that the "wars of the next century will be over water," not oil.

The World Bank is right to focus on the water crisis. Water scarcity and pollution are already hindering economic growth in many poor countries. With global water use doubling every 20 years, these scarcities—and the subnational social stresses they cause—are going to get much worse. But Serageldin is wrong to declare that we are about to witness a surge of "water wars."

Wars between upstream and downstream neighbors over river water are likely only in a narrow set of circumstances: the downstream country must be highly dependent on the water for its national well-being; the upstream country must be able to restrict the river's flow; there must be a history of antagonism between the two countries; and, most important, the downstream country must be much stronger militarily than the upstream country.

There are very few river basins around the world where all these conditions hold. The most obvious example is the Nile. Egypt is wholly dependent on the river's water, has historically turbulent relations with its upstream neighbors, Sudan and Ethiopia, and is vastly more powerful than either. And Egypt has several times threatened to go to war to guarantee an adequate supply of Nile waters.

But more common is the situation along the Ganges, where India has constructed a huge dam—the Farakka Barrage—with harsh consequences on downstream cropland, fisheries, and villages in Bangladesh. Bangladesh is so weak that the most it can do is plead with India to release more water. There is little chance of a water war here between upstream and downstream countries (although the barrage's effects have contributed to the migrations out of Bangladesh into India). The same holds true for other river basins where alarmists speak of impending wars, including the Mekong, Indus, Paraná, and Euphrates.

PIVOTAL STATES

◆ ◆ ◆

The chronic and diffuse subnational strife that environmental scarcity helps generate is exactly the kind of conflict that bedevils conventional military institutions. Around the world we see conventional armies pinned down and often utterly impotent in the face of interethnic violence or attacks by ragtag bands of lightly armed guerrillas and insurgents. As yet, environmental scarcity is not a major factor behind most of these conflicts. But we can expect it to become a far more powerful influence in coming decades because of larger populations and higher resource consumption rates.

The world's population is growing by 1.6 percent a year; on average, real economic product per capita is also rising by 1.5 percent a year. These increases combine to boost the earth's total economic product by about 3 percent annually. With a doubling time of approximately 23 years, the current global product of $25 trillion should exceed $50 trillion in today's dollars by 2020.

A large component of this increase will be achieved through greater consumption of the planet's natural resources. Already, as a group of geographers has noted, "transformed, managed, and utilized ecosystems constitute about half of the ice-free earth; human-mobilized material and energy flows rival those of nature."[3] Such changes are certain to grow because of the rapidly increasing scale and intensity of our economic activity.

At the level of individual countries, these changes often produce a truly daunting combination of pressures. Some of the worst-affected countries are "pivotal states"—to use the term recently coined in *Foreign Affairs* by historian Paul Kennedy. These countries—including South Africa, Mexico, India, Pakistan, and China—are key to international stability in their regions.

India deserves particularly close attention. Since independence, it has often seemed on the brink of disintegration. But it has endured, despite enormous difficulties, and by many measures India has made real progress in bettering its citizens' lives. Yet, although recent economic liberalization has produced a surge of growth and a booming middle class, India's prospects are uncertain at best.

Population growth stubbornly remains around 2 percent a year; the country's population of 955 million (of which about 700 million live in the countryside) grows by 17 million people annually, which means it doubles every 38 years. Demographers estimate that India's population will reach 1.4 billion by 2025. Yet severe water scarcities and cropland fragmentation, erosion, and salinization are already widespread. Fuelwood shortages, deforestation, and desertification also affect sweeping areas of countryside.

Rural resource scarcities and population growth have combined with an inadequate supply of rural jobs and economic liberalization in cities to widen wealth differentials between the countryside and urban areas. These differentials propel huge waves of rural-urban migration. The growth rates of many of India's cities are nearly twice that of the country's population, which means that cities like New Delhi, Mumbai, and Bangalore double in size every 20 years. Their infrastructures are overtaxed: New Delhi has among the worst urban air pollution levels in the world, power and water are regularly unavailable, garbage is left in the streets, and the sewage system can handle only a fraction of the city's wastewater.

India's rapidly growing population impedes further loosening of the state's grip on the economy: as the country's workforce expands by 6.5 million a year, and as resentment among the poor rises against those castes and classes that have benefited most from liberalization, left-wing politicians are able to exert strong pressure to maintain subsidies for fertilizers, irrigation, and inefficient industries and to keep statutory restrictions against corporate layoffs. Rapid population growth also leads to fierce competition for limited status and job opportunities in government and education. Attempts to hold a certain percentage of such positions for lower castes cause bitter intercaste conflict. The right-wing Bharatiya Janata Party capitalizes on upper- and middle-caste resentment of encroachment on their privileges, mobilizing this resentment against minorities like Muslims.

These pressures are largely beyond the control of India's increasingly corrupt and debilitated political institutions. At the district and state levels, politicians routinely hire local gang leaders or thugs to act as political enforcers. At the national level, kickbacks and bribes have become common in an economic system still constrained by bureaucracy and quotas. The central government and many state governments are widely seen as unable to manage India's rapidly changing needs, and as a result have lost much of their legitimacy. Furthermore, the 1996 national elections dealt a dramatic blow to the Congress Party, which has traditionally acted to aggregate the interests of multiple sectors of Indian society. The parties that gained at Congress's expense represent a profusion of narrow caste, class, religious, and regional interests.

The fast expansion of urban areas in poor countries like India may have the dual effect of increasing both the grievances and the opportunities of groups challenging the state: people concentrated in slums can communicate more easily than those in scattered rural villages, which might reinforce incipient economic frustrations and, by reducing problems of coordination, also increase their power in relation to the police and other authorities. While there is surprisingly little historical correlation between rapid urbanization and civil strife, India shows that the record may be changing: the widespread urban violence in early 1993 was concentrated in the poorest slums. Moreover, although Western commentators usually described the rioting as strictly communal, between Hindus and Muslims, Hindus directed many of their attacks against recent Hindu migrants from rural areas. B.K. Chandrashekar, a sociology professor at the Indian Institute of Management, has noted that "the communal violence was quite clearly a class phenomenon. Indian cities became the main battlegrounds because of massive migrations of the rural poor in the past decades."

Indian social institutions and democracy are now under extraordinary strain. The strain arises from a rapid yet incomplete economic transition, from widening gaps between the wealthy and the poor, from chronically weak political institutions, and—not least—from continued high levels of population growth and resource depletion. Should India suffer major internal violence as a result—or, in the worst case, should it fragment into contending regions—the economic, migratory, and security consequences for the rest of the world would be staggering.

BANKING ON INGENUITY

◆ ◆ ◆

Some reading this account of India will say "nonsense!" As long as market reforms and adequate economic growth continue, India should be able to solve its problems of poverty, population growth, and environmental stress.

The most rigorous representatives of this optimistic position are neoclassical economists. They generally claim that few if any societies face strict limits to population or consumption. Properly functioning economic institutions, especially markets, can provide incentives to encourage conservation, resource substitution, the development of new sources of scarce resources, and technological innovation. Increased global trade allows resource-rich areas to specialize in the production of goods (like grain) that are derived from renewables. These optimists are commonly opposed by neo-Malthusians—often biologists and ecologists—who claim that finite natural resources place strict limits on the growth of human population and consumption both globally and regionally; if these limits are exceeded, poverty and social breakdown result.

Neoclassical economists are right to stress the extraordinary ability of human beings to surmount scarcity and improve their lot.

The debate between these two camps is now thoroughly sterile. Each grasps a portion of the truth, but neither tells the whole story. Neoclassical economists are right to stress the extraordinary ability of human beings to surmount scarcity and improve their lot. The dominant trend over the past two centuries, they point out, has not been rising resource scarcity but increasingly aggregate wealth. In other words, most important resources have become less scarce, at least in economic terms.

The optimists provide a key insight: that we should focus on the supply of human ingenuity in response to increasing resource scarcity rather than on strict resource limits. Many societies adapt well to scarcity, without undue hardship to their populations, and often end up better off than they were before. These societies supply enough ingenuity in the form of new technologies and new and reformed social institutions—like efficient markets, clear property rights, and rural development banks—to alleviate the effects of scarcity.

What determines a society's ability to supply this ingenuity? The answer is complex: different countries, depending on their social, economic, political, and cultural characteristics, will respond to scarcity in different ways and with varying amounts and kinds of ingenuity.

Optimists often make the mistake of assuming that an adequate supply of the right kinds of ingenuity is always assured. However, in the next decades population growth, rising average resource consumption, and persistent inequalities in resource access guarantee that scarcities of renewables will affect many regions in the developing world with a severity, speed, and scale unprecedented in history. Resource substitution and conservation tasks will be more urgent, complex, and unpredictable, increasing the need for many kinds of ingenuity. In other words, these societies will have to be smarter—socially and technically—to maintain or increase their well-being in the face of rising scarcities.

Simultaneously, the supply of ingenuity will be constrained by a number of factors, including the brain drain from many poor societies, their limited access to capital, and their chronically incompetent bureaucracies, corrupt judicial systems, and weak states. Moreover, markets in developing countries often do not work well: property rights are unclear; prices for water, forests, and other common resources do not adjust accurately to reflect rising scarcity; and thus incentives for entrepreneurs to respond to scarcity are inadequate.

Most important, the supply of ingenuity can be restricted by stresses generated by the very resource crises the ingenuity is needed to solve. In Haiti, for example, severe resource shortages—especially of forests and soil—have inflamed struggles among social groups, struggles that, in turn, obstruct technical and institutional reform. Scarcities exacerbate poverty in rural Haitian communities and produce significant profit opportunities for powerful elites. Both deepen divisions and distrust between rich and poor and impede beneficial change. Thus, for example, the Haitian army has blocked reforestation projects by destroying tree seedlings; the army and the notorious Tonton Macoutes fear such projects will bring disgruntled rural people together and threaten their highly profitable control of forest resource extraction.

Similar processes are at work in many places. In the Indian state of Bihar, which has some of the highest population growth rates and rural densities in the country, land scarcity has deepened divisions between land-holding and peasant castes, promoting intransigence on both sides that has brought land reform to a halt. In South Africa, scarcity-driven migrations into urban areas and the resulting conflicts over urban environmental resources (such as land and water) encourage communities to segment along lines of ethnicity or residential status. This segmentation shreds networks of trust and debilitates local institutions. Powerful warlords, linked to the Inkatha Freedom Party or the African National Congress, have taken advantage of these dislocations to manipulate group divisions within communities, often producing violence and further institutional breakdown.

Societies like these may face a widening "ingenuity gap" as their requirement for ingenuity to deal with scarcity rises while their supply of ingenuity stagnates or drops. A persistent and serious ingenuity gap boosts dissatisfaction and undermines regime legitimacy and coercive power, increasing the likelihood of widespread and chronic civil violence. Violence further erodes the society's capacity to supply ingenuity, especially by causing human and financial capital to flee. Countries with a critical ingenuity gap therefore risk entering a downward and self-reinforcing spiral of crisis and decay.

A focus on ingenuity supply helps us rethink the neo-Malthusian concept of strict physical limits to

Some societies are locked into a "race" between a rising requirement for ingenuity and their capacity to supply it.

growth. The limits a society faces are a product of both its physical context and the ingenuity it can bring to bear on that context. If a hypothetical society were able to supply infinite amounts of ingenuity, then that society's maximum sustainable population size and rate of resource consumption would be determined by biological and physical laws, such as the second law of thermodynamics. Since infinite ingenuity is never available, the resource limits societies face in the real world are more restrictive than this theoretical maximum. And since the supply of ingenuity depends on many social and economic factors and can therefore vary widely, we cannot determine a society's limits solely by examining its physical context, as neo-Malthusians do. Rather than speaking of limits, it is better to say that some societies are locked into a "race" between a rising requirement for ingenuity and their capacity to supply it.

In coming decades, some societies will win this race and some will lose. We can expect an increasing bifurcation of the world into those societies that can adjust to population growth and scarcity—thus avoiding turmoil—and those that cannot. If several pivotal states fall on the wrong side of this divide, humanity's overall prospects will change dramatically for the worse.

Notes

1. Over the last six years a diverse group of 100 experts from 15 countries has closely studied cases such as these. Organized by the Peace and Conflict Studies program at the University of Toronto and the American Academy of Arts and Sciences in Cambridge, Massachusetts, its research and that of other groups provides a clear picture of how and where environmental scarcity produces social breakdown and violence. This article surveys these findings.

2. *Nations in Conflict* (San Francisco: Freeman, 1975).

3. B.L. Turner et al., eds., *The Earth as Transformed by Human Action: Global and Regional Changes in the Biosphere over the Past 300 Years* (Cambridge: Cambridge University Press, 1990), p. 13.

Terms & Concepts

ecological marginalization
environmental scarcity
demand scarcity
human ingenuity

ingenuity gap
ingenuity supply
neoclassical economists
neo-Malthusians

pivotal states
resource capture
structural scarcity
supply scarcity

Questions

1. What is environmental scarcity and what are its causes?

2. Why has renewable resource scarcity not been considered a cause of major interstate war?

3. In what ways is India one of the key countries to watch?

4. How does environmental scarcity affect the state's capacity to govern?

5. What is the ingenuity gap? How can it be closed?

Unit One   Discussion Questions

1. The editors claim that the political world is undergoing a major transition. What forces drive this change, and do we have any control over these forces?

2. Do the analyses in this section imply that we face new challenges, or have we coped with similar problems before?

3. Can we ignore the effects of the changes discussed in this section, or will it be impossible to isolate ourselves morally, physically, spiritually, and materially from changes of this magnitude?

Annotated Bibliography

Barber, Benjamin. *Jihad Vs. McWorld: How Globalism and Tribalism Are Reshaping the World.* New York: Ballantine, 1995. In an expansion of his popular 1992 article, Barber sees the trajectory of world politics as being dominated by opposing forces of universalism and particularism.

Elkins, David J. *Beyond Sovereignty: Territory and Political Economy in the Twenty-First Century.* Toronto: University of Toronto Press, 1995. A provocative look at the future of the nation-state and other conventional forms of political organization.

Heilbroner, Robert. *Visions of the Future: The Distant Past, Yesterday, Today, Tomorrow.* Oxford: Oxford University Press; New York: New York Public Library, 1994. Heilbroner's latest collection of essays reflects a considerable amount of pessimism about our ability to save our environment and continue our systems of "ceaseless accumulation."

Hobsbawm, Eric. *The Age of Extremes: A History of the World, 1914–1991.* New York: Pantheon Books, 1994. Hobsbawm is an eminent British historian. This ambitious, sweeping work focuses on the economic and social forces that have shaped the 20th century, particularly capitalism and socialism. He does not find much to look forward to!

Huntington, Samuel P. *The Clash of Civilizations and the Remaking of World Order.* New York: Touchstone, 1996. The author examines the forces of modernization and alignment of civilizations and their implications for world politics.

Ignatieff, Michael. *The Warrior's Honour: Ethnic War and the Modern Conscience.* Toronto: Viking, 1998. A thought-provoking collection of essays reflecting on moral intervention in conditions of modern brutality.

Kaplan, Robert D. *The Ends of the Earth: A Journey to the Frontiers of Anarchy.* New York: Vintage, 1996. A thoughtful, sobering political travelogue probing familiar and remote regions of Africa and Asia.

Magnusson, Warren. "De-Centring the State." In *Canadian Politics,* 2nd ed., edited by James P. Bickerton and Alain-G. Gagnon. Peterborough, Ont.: Broadview, 1994. An examination of environmentalism, new politics, and sovereignty at the end of the 20th century.

O'Brien, Conor Cruise. *On the Eve of the Millennium.* Concord, Ont.: Anansi, 1994. A reflection on the status and future of Enlightenment values at the end of the second millennium.

Todorova, Mariia Nikolaeva. *Imagining the Balkans.* New York: Oxford University Press, 1997. This critical look at the history of Balkans provides an important perspective on recent conflicts.

Unit Two

The State in the New World

◆ ◆ ◆

The term *state* conjures up, for most of us, strong images and emotions. We often write as if states were individuals with personalities: "France was in her hour of greatest need." We have created myths about the ways states developed, fashioning master narratives to account for the kinds of states that have been created. Our symbols are still extraordinarily powerful: currencies, flags, teams, armies, cultures, character traits. ... The list is long.

Yet even in the case of that archetypal example of state growth—the United Kingdom—what we think we see (a unitary state governed by a single sovereign crown-in-parliament) has always been more complex in reality. The United Kingdom can be seen as a union-state with very odd subunits that is now attempting to recognize historic distinctions in a more formal way. Thus, when historians and social scientists look backward at "the state," they, and we, now do so through the lens of what we might call deconstructive discourse.

This is a discourse and an analytical framework that questions the confident, often imperial, Eurocentric, statist, and overtly nationalistic assumptions of yesteryear. We had a sort of "rise and fall" model of states and empires, which dominated our thinking. The concept at the centre of it all—the state—was often treated as a given; it was something we thought we understood and could take for granted. We believed we knew what states were and how, once created, they could play their roles upon the world stage. This approach, apart from being overly simplistic, is

reductionist and all encompassing (something either is or isn't a state). It is also frequently overtly teleological, which is to say that states had missions and roles to fulfill, they represented progress and destiny, they were analyzed in masculine terms, and they were led by great men.

All this has changed, so that now, as we look ahead to the future of the state, we attempt to move away from our older, simpler, and more confident assertions. Now we are not nearly as certain that we know what's going on out there or where it's all leading. We are unsure about how to define the thing we are studying. We can't decide where sovereignty begins and ends, and how nongovernmental organizations (nonstate actors) are affecting the way states operate. We attempt to analyze the global forces that are at work, many of which are discussed in the essays in this book, including multinational business, resource usage, immigration, stock markets, international crime, and communication technologies. Regional organizations and institutions occupy a large portion of the "territory" formerly inhabited by states alone.

After three and a half centuries, perhaps we are indeed at a point where, as Jessica Mathews notes, it takes "a mental leap to think of

Local identity and globalization co-exist: these young women abide by traditional Islamic dress codes while sporting backpacks emblazoned with the images of pop stars.

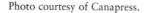
Photo courtesy of Canapress.

world politics in terms other than occasionally co-operating but generally competing states, each defined by its territory and representing all the people therein."[1] But at the same time that old forms of state analysis seem no longer convincing, it is apparent that the state is very much alive and kicking. We cannot simply argue that its time has past and that we are entering a world where states will disappear. What we have to do, as David Cannadine has argued recently in his study *The Rise and Fall of Class in Britain,* is face the task of "defining our subject afresh and envisioning it anew."[2] The articles in this and the preceding section were chosen with this end in view.

---

1. Jessica Mathews, "Power Shift," *Foreign Affairs* (January–February 1997), 61.
2. David Cannadine, *The Rise and Fall of Class in Britain* (New York: Columbia University Press, 1999), 17.

The Erosion of the State

Susan Strange

Editors' Note

For the past two centuries nation-states have grown ever more powerful, and the appeal of "statehood"—whatever this really means—is still enormous. As this book goes to press there are almost 50 members of what is called the Unrepresented Nations and People's Organization (UNPO). Each member wants to become a recognized political unit, with full statehood as the ultimate goal. Yet the nation-state may have already passed its zenith, and if Susan Strange is correct, it is already in serious decline in terms of its ability to control events and to provide services and protection to its population. Her conclusion, strongly stated, is that the power of even advanced industrial/technological/welfare states has been weakened at the expense of their most vulnerable citizens and of the environment. Societies are now "at the mercy of big business."

Many would argue that societies are also still at the mercy of big governments and big bureaucracies, some of them now supranational and even less accountable (the European Union's annual budget is now about $100 billion annually). Paradoxically, however, what may be happening is that as distinctions between national politics and supranational politics (and bodies) become ever more blurred, national governments themselves may take a more active role in policy planning and implementation, leaving the new bureaucrats to become a more traditional civil service.

Strange's vision of the contemporary state may be in some senses an updated late-20th-century version of the jingle that was associated with the large-scale enclosure of common land in Britain:

The fault is great in man or woman
Who steals a goose from off a common;
But what can plead that man's excuse
Who steals the common from the goose?

Should we resuscitate the state to protect the common, and how do we do so without recreating the old problems, which include protectionism, imperialism, and nativism, or a sense of belonging and place that gets out of control? And how do we argue that we should shore-up existing states and redress democratic deficits, if we are not prepared to advocate the creation of many more state-like entities, with all that this entails? Paradoxes abound, and principles clash.

◆ ◆ ◆

I hear two choruses of voices raised against the whole notion of globalization. I have some sympathy with one and none at all with the other. Explaining this requires me to say—briefly—what I understand the term to mean and forms the first part of this essay. It also helps to make clear what I understand to be the root causes behind the process of globalization. This is the essay's second part. And, for the last part I explain what I understand to be the main consequences of globaliza-tion for the state in the context of consequences for other political institutions and social and economic groups.

THE NAYSAYERS

◆ ◆ ◆

The chorus of voices with whom I have no sympathy—or very little—is that which denies the reality of globalization and claims that nothing has really changed. According to this chorus it is all "globaloney," a great myth, an illusion, and therefore not to be taken seriously. Globalization according to them is an illusion because the state still exists, because enterprises still belong to one particular state in the sense that their headquarters are located in the territory of the state from which they sprang, because their directors are almost exclusively of one national origin, and because their corporate culture is markedly different from that of other national firms.

They are wrong, however; the fact that states still exist does not prove that globalization is not a part of the reality in which we all live. Nor does the fact that firms are referred to as "American," "British," or "Japanese" mean that the nature and behavior of firms like that of states has not been changed by globalization. Although it is hard to measure the process of globalization, it is no myth. It exists, and it changes things on several levels. As an international political economist, I perceive these changes first of all in what the French historian Fernand Braudel called "material life"—the production structure that determines what material goods and services are produced by human societies for their survival and comfort. Instead of goods and services being predominantly produced by and for people living in the territory of a state, they are now increasingly produced by people in several states, for a world market instead of for a local market.

Second, globalization involves changes in the financial structure—the system by which credit is created to finance production and trade in goods and services. Where once the creation and use of credit mostly took place within the societies of territorial states, it now takes place across territorial frontiers, in global markets electronically linked into a single system. True, within that system there are local banks and markets creating credit for local use. But these are no longer autonomous; they are part of the larger system, more vulnerable to its ups and downs than it is to their ups and downs.

Finally, globalization takes place on a third level, the level of perceptions, beliefs, ideas, and tastes. Here, while cultural differences persist, the sensitivities and susceptibilities of individual human beings are increasingly being modified by the processes of global homogenization. While made easier and faster by the so-called information revolution and the falling costs of international communication, these are only channels, the means by which the processes of globalization take place. Although this third level of globalization is the hardest to quantify or monitor, it may in the long run be the most significant of all the changes brought by globalization.

Yet this level is the one most often overlooked by those economists and others who join in the chorus denying the reality of globalization. While some merely question whether the extent of change attributable to globalization is being exaggerated, others call the whole concept of globalization into question, denying that there has been any real change.[1]

Many of these voices belong to my former colleagues in that branch of social science called international relations. It is a branch that did not exist before the First World War, and in America, not until after the Second World War. The terrible destruction and waste in both conflicts prompted intellectuals to ask the question, "Why do states wage war on each other?" The problematic of international relations, therefore, was the causes of interstate conflict and war, and whether, and how war could be prevented and peace preserved. Always, the state was the primary focus of attention and was often habitually treated also as a unitary actor. Because discussion of globalization introduces other actors—markets and firms, and other forces of change, like technology, the media, and communications—such discussion implies the growing obsolescence of the study of international relations. On top of these longer-term secular changes, moreover, came the end of the cold war, removing one of the main dangers inherent in the international political system.

Like a stag at bay, the professor of international relations is apt to turn and hurl defiance at those who would bring him down. For myself, as an international political economist, I believe study of the world we live in should adapt to change, not resist it. I have little sympathy with those who deny the reality of globalization and cling to an obsolescing paradigm and a problematic superseded by others. As I have argued elsewhere, the danger of major wars between states has paled beside the danger of long-lasting economic depression resulting from flaws in the financial system and of irreversible environmental damage resulting from worldwide industrialization.[2]

THREE DILEMMAS AND AN EXPLANATION

◆ ◆ ◆

With the other chorus that acknowledges the reality but urges resistance to it, I have more sympathy. Change always creates losers as well as winners. It is never pain-less for everyone. There are costs, and it can be (and is) argued that the costs are not worth the benefits and that the pace of change is so fast that the risks are greater than the opportunities. If globalization cannot be reversed or even resisted, it should at least be slowed down. For reasons that will be clearer when I come to the consequences of globalization, I think this may be a tenable view. It seems to be especially prevalent in Europe. A recent book, *The Global Trap,* by Harald Schumann and Hans-Peter Martin of *Der Spiegel,* proved an unexpected bestseller in Germany in 1996.[3] Germans generally prefer the deutsche mark to the euro, the national past to the globalized future.

If globalization cannot be reversed or even resisted, it should at least be slowed down.

Three dilemmas for the world political economy result from the effects of globalization on the state. One is economic. A market economy, whether global or national, needs a lender of last resort, an authority—call it hegemonic, though the term misleads—able to disci-pline but also to give confidence to banks and financial markets, and able to apply Keynesian logic in times of slow growth and recession. The dilemma is that neither former hegemons nor international organizations can be relied on for either task.

Another dilemma is environmental. The motivations of corporate players in the world market economy lead most of them to destroy and pollute the planet while the necessary countervailing power of states is handicapped by principles of international law, sovereignty, and the like.

The third dilemma is political. The long struggle for liberty and accountability gradually made at least some states accountable to the people, but globalization, by shifting power from states to firms, has allowed interna-tional bureaucracies to undermine that accountability. None of the new nonstate authorities are accountable; few are even transparent. There is a democratic deficit, not only in Europe, but in America, Japan—the entire globalized economy.

As to the underlying causes of globalization—and the consequential retreat of the state from its predomi-nant position of authority in the economy and society—I would point first to the accelerating rate of technological change, and second to the accelerated mobility of capital, as the two indispensable factors affecting production in a modern economy.[4] Both are too often overlooked and neglected by social scientists. An appreciation of their importance surely requires a historical perspective. Their origins go back at least 200 years to the late eighteenth century—or in the case of technological change, as far back as Galileo and da Vinci. Both men believed that science held the answers to the great puzzles of life on the planet and had the poten-tial to change the human condition for the better. That belief (reinforced by the competition of states for techni-cal advantage in waging war) has sustained the pursuit of scientific discovery and technological innovation from the Industrial Revolution onward. Yet the application of the discoveries and the innovations beyond the place where they were made would have been impossible if capital had not been mobile enough to move from where credit was created to where it could be profitably invested. The international mobility of capital, in short, which began to be seen in small ways by the late eigh-teenth century, has been the sine qua non of twentieth-century globalization.

What must be additionally explained is why both technological change and capital mobility began to accelerate around the middle of this century. The two are interrelated but the cause of one was mainly economic, the other mainly political. Technological change has typ-ically involved the substitution of capital for labor. That was the essence of Fordism: by installing a capital-inten-sive assembly line and the management to go with it at Willow Run, Henry Ford could employ cheap unskilled labor instead of skilled expensive labor. Afterward, even cheaper robots replaced the workers, once again involv-ing higher capital costs as the price of lower running costs. In Marxist terms, technological change altered the organic composition of capital, thus increasing the demand for capital and lowering the demand for labor.

By mid-century, this substitution was fueling the expansion of international trade since newcomers like the Japanese could lower marginal costs by producing for export as well as the home market. In sector after sector, from steel to beer, production for the world mar-ket became imperative. Every technological innovation called for more capital investment. And as the pace of technological innovation accelerated under the pressure of competition between firms for market shares, it became less and less possible to survive on the basis of profits in a home market. Firms, in short, did not choose to produce for foreign markets; they were forced to do so or go under. The price of entry, in many cases but especially in developing countries with potentially large markets, was often relocation of manufacturing capacity inside the trade barriers against competitive imports.[5]

THE NEW DIPLOMACY

◆ ◆ ◆

None of this would have been possible without the greater mobility of capital. For this, the Europeans and especially the British were responsible during the long nineteenth century to 1914, and the Americans thereafter. Mobility slowed almost to a standstill after the crash of 1929, but even then United States firms continued to invest in international production in Europe and Latin America. After 1945, successive American governments pushed for the reduction of exchange controls over capital movements. This, more than the reduction of tariffs and other barriers to trade, created the necessary and sufficient conditions for the internationalization of production. Firms found it increasingly easy to borrow in one country or currency—not necessarily their own—and invest it in another. It could be done through banks or through stock markets, and the whole business was greatly aided by the creation of the unregulated, untaxed Eurocurrency markets.

First in the new postwar wave of foreign investment were the American multinationals. They soon overtook the British, Swiss, and Dutch as the major holders of the stock of foreign direct investment. The big enterprises were soon followed by much smaller firms. The American multinationals were soon joined by the Japanese, Koreans, Taiwanese, and others. Their spread into other markets was made easier by the concurrent change in the attitudes of host countries. Where these had initially been hostile to foreign firms, by the 1980s most had realized that the foreign firms held three keys to earning the foreign exchange so necessary for industrialization. These three keys were command of technology; ready access to mobile capital; and (often the most important) the brand name and distribution network that gave ready access to the rich markets of America and Europe.

The significance of this "new diplomacy" (as John Stopford and I called it) has been largely lost on conventional writers on international relations. For it means that states are joined by firms as the authorities exercising power over the course of national and global economic development. The governments of states may still be the gatekeepers to the territory over which other states recognize their authority. But if no foreign firms want to go through their gate, their countries have a slim chance of keeping up with the competition from other, more welcoming governments for world market shares. Even if firms do seek entry, governments have to negotiate with them over terms. The balance of power between host and foreign firm then becomes an important field of study in comparative political economy, with much depending on the size of the host market and the firm's standing in the kind of business it is in.

Another aspect of the new diplomacy is also of growing importance in world politics and world economics. Corporate takeovers and strategic alliances between firms increasingly determine future trends in economic growth, employment, and trade. Recall the fuss in Europe over Boeing's takeover of McDonnell-Douglas. It created an aircraft manufacturer likely to dominate the world market, a competitor for Europe's Airbus even more formidable than before. Recall the alarm felt in Hong Kong last August when Li Ka-shing bought 3 percent of shares in Jardine Mathieson, raising doubts over how long Beijing would allow non-Chinese interests to survive the new regime. Such questions—both political and economic in their implications—call for more serious study of firm-firm relations than exists at the moment. It is a new field where experts in international business and management have to work with those in international relations, and to listen carefully, too, to business historians.

Although neglected, the growing importance of state-firm and of firm-firm diplomacy is only one aspect of the rising power of firms and other non-state actors and the corresponding decline in the authority of the state in the world economy and society. But before attempting to demonstrate this decline in a more systematic manner, it should be pointed out that "decline" may have been preceded by "rise," and that it may be dangerous to extrapolate decline into the future. This is to say that the predominance of the nation-state as the foremost authority over society and economy may turn out to have been exceptional, not normal. In a longer historical perspective, multiple sources of authority were perhaps the norm, and the concentration of power in the hands of state governments in this century and the last may have been a deviation. Second, those of us who perceive decline in state authority in the last decade or two are not necessarily predicting that the decline will continue indefinitely into the future. We simply do not know.

ERODING THE STATE'S AUTHORITY

◆ ◆ ◆

There are three main areas in which state authority has declined. Other aspects of decline are almost all subsidiary to these three. The first is defense: the security of society from violence. The second is finance: the preservation of money as a reliable means of exchange, unit of account, and store of value (this is especially necessary to a market, as opposed to a state-planned economy). And the third is the provision of welfare: the assurance that some of the benefits of greater wealth go to the poor, the weak, the sick, and the old. This too is particularly necessary in a capitalist market economy, where the system tends to make the rich conspicuously richer and the gap wider between them and the disadvantaged. It can be quickly and easily shown that the power of most states in all three—and therefore the justification for their claims on society—has seriously declined. And it has done so as a result of the forces of globalization already described.

Defense against foreign invasion is no longer necessary if—as is now mostly the case—neighbors show no sign of wanting to invade for the sake of command over territory. There are now only three exceptional cases where neighbors may be so tempted. One is for command over oil or gas fields. Another is for control over water supplies. The third is irredentism, where societies or their governments feel a moral or emotional compulsion to incorporate territory inhabited by ethnic or religious groups into the state to safeguard their interests and security (there are more cases today where this might have happened but has not, than there are where it has).

For the most part, the obsolescence of major interstate war is implicit in state policies, for the very good reason that people recognize that success in gaining world market shares has replaced territorial acquisition as the means to survival. Armies and navies continue to exist—not least because of competition for world market shares in the arms trade—but more because they are needed to preserve civil order rather than to repel invaders. Where there is no risk of civil disorder, they are merely an ornamental anachronism. Where there is such a risk parts of society will regard national armed forces as a threat to their security, not as an impartial guardian of the peace. The decline of support for conscription in many countries is one indicator of this change.

The second justification for state authority—that it maintains the value of the currency—is also fast disappearing. With probably the sole exception of the United States (and possibly the Swiss Confederation), states are no longer able to resist the foreign exchange markets. It is not that speculators have run amok, but that the mobility of capital mentioned earlier means that flows of money in and out of currencies, not trade balances, trigger market responses, which in turn move exchange rates. And only a powerful coalition of major central banks led by the United States (as in the Mexican peso crisis in 1994) can stop a collapsing currency.

With one of the three legs of monetary stability so weak, what of the other two, interest rates and inflation rates? Governments can determine the first, but only within limits set by the markets. Too high an interest rate may keep money flowing in but—as in Germany recently, or Britain under Gordon Brown as finance minister—this will impose excruciating costs on small business and will push the exchange rate too high to make exports competitive.

As for inflation rates, governments pretend to control the money supply, and thus the value of money, mainly by varying interest rates. But technology is about to frustrate their efforts. Credit card spending is rising quickly in the United States and now in Britain. It is purchasing power over which the state has no control. Digital money and digital shopping on the Internet will be even less under state control and potentially even more disruptive. Much depends on the banks as major players in the money markets. Yet the central banks' Bank for International Settlements in Basel confessed just this past year that its concordats on bank regulation cannot be relied on to preserve the global financial system against the dangers besetting it. Rules of thumb on reserve requirements that used to limit growth in the money supply, and therefore the value of money, no longer work. Commercial banks therefore must be trusted (and helped) to regulate themselves. But trusting the bankers to discipline themselves is like asking poachers to see that there is no poaching. So far, so good....

The state as social safety net, redistributing resources and entitlements to make good the shortcomings of the market, has been a recent but important justification for its authority and one most powerfully appreciated by the Europeans. The superiority of "Rhenish capitalism" in the vocabulary of Michel Albert (over Anglo-Saxon capitalism) was precisely that it ensured a measure of social justice denied by the market.[6]

This justification is still made, but it lacks credibility. Globalization has opened tax-evading doors for multinationals and many individuals. As more tax havens open up and more use is made of them, states'

Society is at the mercy of big business.

---

revenues suffer; everywhere, welfare services are cut back (the age at which state pensions are paid will soon be raised in Italy, France, and probably Germany). In desperation, states raise money by selling off state-owned enterprises. The public sector that once—even in the United States in World War II—was an important lever of state power over the economy cannot survive the pressures of global competition. Even the power of the state to use trade protection as an economic weapon against foreign competition and a supplementary safety net for those (such as farmers, fishermen, miners, or steelworkers) in declining occupations is fast disappearing. The global consensus declares protectionism wrong, liberalization right. National experience is that it often protects the inefficient and uncompetitive and is therefore counterproductive.

The "globaloney" school is not only wrong, but by trying to persuade people that nothing has changed, is also encouraging an ostrich-like response to recent changes in the world economy. If, as I have argued, the states' power to provide economic and financial stability, to protect the vulnerable in society, and to preserve the environment has been weakened, society is at the mercy of big business. That is not a prospect I suspect most Europeans and many Americans really want for their children and their grandchildren in the years to come.

Notes

1. See, for example, Paul Hirst and Grahame Thompson, *Globalization in Question: The International Economy and the Possibilities of Governance* (Cambridge Policy Press, 1996).
2. See Susan Strange, States and Markets, 2d ed. (London: Pinter, 1994), pp. 60–63, and ibid., *The Retreat of the State: The Diffusion of Power in the World Economy* (Cambridge: Cambridge University Press, 1996), pp. 66–87.
3. Harald Schumann and Hans-Peter Martin, *The Global Trap* (London: Zed Books, 1997).
4. This argument is developed at greater length in *The Retreat of the State*, op. cit.
5. See John Stopford and Susan Strange, *Rival States: Rival Firms' Competition for World Market Shares* (Cambridge: Cambridge University Press., 1991), pp. 1–64.
6. See Michel Albert, *Capitalism against Capitalism* (London: Whurr, 1993).

Terms & Concepts

changes in material life
democratic deficit
digital money
exchange controls
Fordism
gatekeeper states

global homogenization
irredentism
Keynesian logic
lender of last resort
mobility of capital
new diplomacy

nonstate authorities
Rhenish capitalism
transparency
worldwide industrialization

Questions

1. What does "globalization" mean to Strange, and does her view of it differ from Rosenau's (Chapter 2)?
2. Strange argues that armies (and armed forces) are becoming "ornamental anachronisms." In the light of NATO's actions in Kosovo and other recent events, is this judgment premature? Or does this prove the general rule that defence against invasion is no longer necessary?
3. What, according to Strange, should the state's role be, and in what ways can a strong public sector survive the pressures of global competition and capital mobility?
4. The process of globalization "changes things on different levels." What things? And what changes?

⑤

The Rise of the Virtual State

Richard Rosecrance

Editors' Note

States in the future will be downsized and will fall into two classes: "head" states and "body" states. This is the astonishing prediction of Richard Rosecrance. For clearly, there is no unanimity among social scientists about the future of either the state or the international state system.

Using a political economy approach in his analysis, Rosecrance argues that land was the crucial resource of state power when primary production was most important. When secondary production and manufacturing eclipsed agriculture and resource exploitation, a large urban workforce and trade links became crucial. With the move to tertiary (service) industry, people in fixed locations have become dispensable, as capital and information can move at the push of a key-stroke, and the labour force can be moved or cheaper labour can be found elsewhere. What remains is either a headquarters state, where research takes place, products are designed and financed, and marketing strategies are planned, or a production state, where the production of goods is contracted for final use in both types of states but where no decisions about the products are made.

Interestingly, Rosecrance sees opportunities for all types of states. Skilled labour can remove Third World countries from reliance on decreasingly important primary production. Expensive education and connectivity, such as through E-commerce, can provide the skills that the head state needs. For this interdependent economy international peace is a must, and the governments of states that place economy above culture (cf. Huntington, Chapter 1) will try to ensure that stability is preserved. However, the outlook for democracy is cloudy. How do people control their destiny when so much of it lies beyond their state borders?

You might be glad (or perhaps alarmed) to know that this American thinks Canada is already well on the way to virtual statehood, having moved from being a country of "hewers of wood and drawers of water" to a "contracting-out" state.

◆ ◆ ◆

TERRITORY BECOMES PASSÉ

◆ ◆ ◆

Amid the supposed clamor of contending cultures and civilizations, a new reality is emerging. The nation-state is becoming a tighter, more vigorous unit capable of sustaining the pressures of worldwide competition. Developed states are putting aside military, political, and territorial ambitions as they struggle not for cultural dominance but for a greater share of world output. Countries are not uniting as civilizations and girding for conflict with one another. Instead, they are downsizing—in function if not in geographic form. Today and for the foreseeable future, the only international civilization worthy of the name is the governing economic culture of the world market. Despite the view of some contemporary observers, the forces of globalization have successfully resisted partition into cultural camps.

Yet the world's attention continues to be mistakenly focused on military and political struggles for territory. In beleaguered Bosnia, Serbian leaders sought to create an independent province with an allegiance to

Reprinted by permission of *Foreign Affairs*, Vol. 75 No. 4, 1996. Copyright 1996 by the Council on Foreign Relations, Inc.

Belgrade. A few years ago Iraqi leader Saddam Hussein aimed to corner the world oil market through military aggression against Kuwait and, in all probability, Saudi Arabia; oil, a product of land, represented the supreme embodiment of his ambitions. In Kashmir, India and Pakistan are vying for territorial dominance over a population that neither may be fully able to control. Similar rivalries beset Rwanda and Burundi and the factions in Liberia.

These examples, however, look to the past. Less developed countries, still producing goods that are derived from land, continue to covet territory. In economies where capital, labor, and information are mobile and have risen to predominance, no land fetish remains. Developed countries would rather plumb the world market than acquire territory. The virtual state—a state that has downsized its territorially based production capability—is the logical consequence of this emancipation from the land.

In recent years the rise of the economic analogue of the virtual state—the virtual corporation—has been widely discussed. Firms have discovered the advantages of locating their production facilities wherever it is most profitable. Increasingly, this is not in the same location as corporate headquarters. Parts of a corporation are dispersed globally according to their specialties. But the more important development is the political one, the rise of the virtual state, the political counterpart of the virtual corporation.

The ascent of the trading state preceded that of the virtual state. After World War II, led by Japan and Germany, the most advanced nations shifted their efforts from controlling territory to augmenting their share of world trade. In that period, goods were more mobile than capital or labor, and selling abroad became the name of the game. As capital has become increasingly mobile, advanced nations have come to recognize that exporting is no longer the only means to economic growth; one can instead produce goods overseas for the foreign market.

As more production by domestic industries takes place abroad and land becomes less valuable than technology, knowledge, and direct investment, the function of the state is being further redefined. The state no longer commands resources as it did in mercantilist yesteryear; it negotiates with foreign and domestic capital and labor to lure them into its own economic sphere and stimulate its growth. A nation's economic strategy is now at least as important as its military strategy; its ambassadors have become foreign trade and investment representa-tives. Major foreign trade and investment deals command executive attention as political and military issues did two decades ago. The frantic two weeks in December 1994 when the White House outmaneuvered the French to secure for Raytheon Company a deal worth over $1 billion for the management of rainforests and air traffic in Brazil exemplifies the new international crisis.

Timeworn methods of augmenting national power and wealth are no longer effective. Like the headquarters of a virtual corporation, the virtual state determines overall strategy and invests in its people rather than amassing expensive production capacity. It contracts out other functions to states that specialize in or need them. Imperial Great Britain may have been the model for the nineteenth century, but Hong Kong will be the model for the 21st.

The virtual state is a country whose economy is reliant on mobile factors of production.

The virtual state is a country whose economy is reliant on mobile factors of production. Of course it houses virtual corporations and presides over foreign direct investment by its enterprises. But more than this, it encourages, stimulates, and to a degree even coordi-nates such activities. In formulating economic strategy, the virtual state recognizes that its own production does not have to take place at home; equally, it may play host to the capital and labor of other nations. Unlike imperial Germany, czarist Russia, and the United States of the Gilded Age—which aimed at nine-teenth-century omnicompetence—it does not seek to combine or excel in all economic functions, from min-ing and agriculture to production and distribution. The virtual state specializes in modern technical and research services and derives its income not just from high-value manufacturing, but from product design, marketing, and financing. The rationale for its econ-omy is efficiency attained through productive downsiz-ing. Size no longer determines economic potential. Virtual nations hold the competitive key to greater wealth in the 21st century. They will likely supersede the continent-sized and self-sufficient units that prevailed in the past. Productive specialization will dominate internationally just as the reduced instruction set, or "RISC," computer chip has outmoded its more versatile but slower predecessors.

THE TRADING STATE

◆ ◆ ◆

In the past, states were obsessed with land. The international system with its intermittent wars was founded on the assumption that land was the major factor in both production and power. States could improve their position by building empires or invading other nations to seize territory. To acquire land was a boon: a conquered province contained peasants and grain supplies, and its inhabitants rendered tribute to the new sovereign. Before the age of nationalism, a captured principality willingly obeyed its new ruler. Hence the Hapsburg monarchy, Spain, France, and Russia could become major powers through territorial expansion in Europe between the sixteenth and nineteenth centuries.

With the Industrial Revolution, however, capital and labor assumed new importance. Unlike land, they were mobile ingredients of productive strength. Great Britain innovated in discovering sophisticated uses for the new factors. Natural resources—especially coal, iron, and, later, oil—were still economically vital. Agricultural and mineral resources were critical to the development of the United States and other fledgling industrial nations like Australia, Canada, South Africa, and New Zealand in the nineteenth century. Not until late in the twentieth century did mobile factors of production become paramount.

By that time, land had declined in relative value and become harder for nations to hold. Colonial revolutions in the Third World since World War II have shown that nationalist mobilization of the population in developing societies impedes an imperialist or invader trying to extract resources. A nation may expend the effort to occupy new territory without gaining proportionate economic benefits.

In time, nationalist resistance and the shift in the basis of production should have an impact on the frequency of war. Land, which is fixed, can be physically captured, but labor, capital, and information are mobile and cannot be definitively seized; after an attack, these resources can slip away like quicksilver. Saddam Hussein ransacked the computers in downtown Kuwait City in August 1990 only to find that the cash in bank accounts had already been electronically transferred. Even though it had abandoned its territory, the Kuwaiti government could continue to spend billions of dollars to resist Hussein's conquest.

Today, for the wealthiest industrial countries such as Germany, the United States, and Japan, investment in land no longer pays the same dividends. Since mid-century, commodity prices have fallen nearly 40 percent relative to prices of manufactured goods.[1] The returns from the manufacturing trade greatly exceed those from agricultural exports. As a result, the terms of trade for many developing nations have been deteriorating, and in recent years the rise of prices of international services has outpaced that for manufactured products. Land prices have been steeply discounted.

Amid this decline, the 1970s and 1980s brought a new political prototype: the trading state. Rather than territorial expansion, the trading state held trade to be its fundamental purpose. This shift in national strategy was driven by the declining value of fixed productive assets. Smaller states—those for which, initially at any rate, a military-territorial strategy was not feasible—also adopted trade-oriented strategies. Along with small European and East Asian states, Japan and West Germany moved strongly in a trading direction after World War II.

Countries tend to imitate those that are most powerful. Many states followed in the wake of Great Britain in the nineteenth century; in recent decades, numerous states seeking to improve their lot in the world have emulated Japan. Under Mikhail Gorbachev in the 1980s, even the Soviet Union sought to move away from its emphasis on military spending and territorial expansion.

The most efficient corporations are those that can maintain or increase output with a steady or declining amount of labor.

In recent years, however, a further stimulus has hastened this change. Faced with enhanced international competition in the late 1980s and early 1990s, corporations have opted for pervasive downsizing. They have trimmed the ratio of production workers to output, saving on costs. In some cases productivity increases resulted from pruning of the work force; in others output increased. These improvements have been highly effective; according to economist Stephen Roach in a 1994 paper published by the investment banking firm Morgan Stanley, they have nearly closed the widely noted productivity gap between services and manufacturing. The gap that remains is most likely due to measurement problems. The most efficient corporations are those that can maintain or increase output with a steady or declining amount of labor. Such corporations grew on a worldwide basis.

Meanwhile, corporations in Silicon Valley recognized that cost-cutting, productivity, and competitiveness could be enhanced still further by using the production lines of another company. The typical American plant at the time, such as Ford Motor Company's Willow Run factory in Michigan, was fully integrated, with headquarters, design offices, production workers, and factories located on substantial tracts of land. This comprehensive structure was expensive to maintain and operate, hence a firm that could employ someone else's production line could cut costs dramatically. Land and machines did not have to be bought, labor did not have to be hired, medical benefits did not have to be provided. These advantages could result from what are called economies of scope, with a firm turning out different products on the same production line or quality circle. Or they might be the result of small, specialized firms' ability to perform exacting operations, such as the surface mounting of miniaturized components directly on circuit boards without the need for soldering or conventional wiring. In either case, the original equipment manufacturer would contract out its production to other firms. SCI Systems, Solectron, Merix, Flextronics, Smartflex, and Sanmina turn out products for Digital Equipment, Hewlett-Packard, and IBM. In addition, AT&T, Apple, IBM, Motorola, MCI, and Corning meet part of their production needs through other suppliers. TelePad, a company that makes pen-based computers, was launched with no manufacturing capability at all. Compaq's latest midrange computer is to be produced on another company's production line.

Thus was born the virtual corporation, an entity with research, development, design, marketing, financing, legal, and other headquarters functions, but few or no manufacturing facilities: a company with a head but no body. It represents the ultimate achievement of corporate downsizing, and the model is spreading rapidly from firm to firm. It is not surprising that the virtual corporation should catch on. "Concept" or "head" corporations can design new products for a range of different production facilities. Strategic alliances between firms, which increase specialization, are also very profitable. According to the October 2, 1995, *Financial Times,* firms that actively pursue strategic alliances are 50 percent more profitable than those that do not.

TOWARD THE VIRTUAL STATE
◆ ◆ ◆

In a setting where the economic functions of the trading state have displaced the territorial functions of the expansionist nation, the newly pruned corporation has led to the emerging phenomenon of the virtual state. Downsizing has become an index of corporate efficiency and productivity gains. Now the national economy is also being downsized. Among the most efficient economies are those that possess limited production capacity. The archetype is Hong Kong, whose production facilities are now largely situated in southern China. This arrangement may change after 1997 with Hong Kong's reversion to the mainland, but it may not. It is just as probable that Hong Kong will continue to govern parts of the mainland economically as it is that Beijing will dictate to Hong Kong politically. The one country–two systems formula will likely prevail. In this context, it is important to remember that Britain governed Hong Kong politically and legally for 150 years, but it did not dictate its economics. Nor did this arrangement prevent Hong Kong Chinese from extending economic and quasi-political controls to areas outside their country.

The model of the virtual state suggests that political as well as economic strategy push toward a downsizing and relocation of production capabilities. The trend can be observed in Singapore as well. The successors of Lee Kuan Yew keep the country on a tight political rein but still depend economically on the inflow of foreign factors of production. Singapore's investment in China, Malaysia, and elsewhere is within others' jurisdictions. The virtual state is in this sense a negotiating entity. It depends as much or more on economic access abroad as it does on economic control at home. Despite its past reliance on domestic production, Korea no longer manufactures everything at home, and Japanese production (given the high yen) is now increasingly lodged abroad. In Europe, Switzerland is the leading virtual nation; as much as 98 percent of Nestlé's production capacity, for instance, is located abroad. Holland now produces most of its goods outside its borders. England is also moving in tandem with the worldwide trend; according to the Belgian economic historian Paul Bairoch in 1994, Britain's foreign direct investment abroad was almost as large as America's. A remarkable 20 percent of the production of U.S. corporations now takes place outside the United States.

A reflection of how far these tendencies have gone is the growing portion of GDP consisting of high-value-added services, such as concept, design, consulting, and financial services. Services already constitute 70 percent of American GDP. Of the total, 63 percent are in the high-value category. Of course manufacturing matters, but it matters much less than it once did. As a proportion of foreign direct investment, service exports have grown strikingly in most highly industrialized economies. According to a 1994 World Bank report, *Liberalizing International Transactions in Services,* "The reorientation of [foreign direct investment] towards the services sector has occurred in almost all developed market economies, the principal exporters of services capital: in the most important among them, the share of the services sector is around 40 percent of the stock of outward FDI, and that share is rising."

Manufacturing, for these nations, will continue to decline in importance. If services productivity increases as much as it has in recent years, it will greatly strengthen U.S. competitiveness abroad. But it can no longer be assumed that services face no international competition. Efficient high-value services will be as important to a nation as the manufacturing of automobiles and electrical equipment once were.[2] Since 1959, services prices have increased more than three times as rapidly as industrial prices. This means that many nations will be able to prosper without major manufacturing capabilities.

Australia is an interesting example. Still reliant on the production of sheep and raw materials (both related to land), Australia has little or no industrial sector. Its largest export to the United States is meat for hamburgers. On the other hand, its service industries of media, finance, and telecommunications—represented most notably by the media magnate Rupert Murdoch—are the envy of the world. Canada represents a similar amalgam of raw materials and powerful service industries in newspapers, broadcast media, and telecommunications.

As a result of these trends, the world may increasingly become divided into "head" and "body" nations, or nations representing some combination of those two functions. While Australia and Canada stress the headquarters or head functions, China will be the 21st-century model of a body nation. Although China does not innately or immediately know what to produce for the world market, it has found success in joint ventures with foreign corporations. China will be an attractive place to produce manufactured goods, but only because sophisticated enterprises from other countries design, market, and finance the products China makes. At present China cannot chart its own industrial future.

While Australia and Canada stress the headquarters or head functions, China will be the 21st-century model of a body nation.

Neither can Russia. Focusing on the products of land, the Russians are still prisoners of territorial fetishism. Their commercial laws do not yet permit the delicate and sophisticated arrangements that ensure that "body" manufacturers deliver quality goods for their foreign "head." Russia's transportation network is also primitive. These, however, are temporary obstacles. In time Russia, with China and India, will serve as an important locus of the world's production plant.

THE VESTIGES OF SERFDOM

◆ ◆ ◆

The world is embarked on a progressive emancipation from land as a determinant of production and power. For the Third World, the past unchangeable strictures of comparative advantage can be overcome through the acquisition of a highly trained labor force. Africa and Latin America may not have to rely on the exporting of raw materials or agricultural products; through education, they can capitalize on an educated labor force, as India has in Bangalore and Ireland in Dublin. Investing in human capital can substitute for trying to foresee the vagaries of the commodities markets and avoid the constant threat of overproduction. Meanwhile, land continues to decline in value. Recent studies of 180 countries show that as population density rises, per capita GDP falls. In a new study, economist Deepak Lal notes that investment as well as growth is inversely related to land holdings.[3]

These findings are a dramatic reversal of past theories of power in international politics. In the 1930s the standard international relations textbook would have ranked the great powers in terms of key natural resources: oil, iron ore, coal, bauxite, copper, tungsten, and manganese. Analysts presumed that the state with the largest stock of raw materials and goods derived from land would prevail. CIA estimates during the Cold War were based on such conclusions. It turns out, however, that the most prosperous countries often have a negligible endowment of national resources. For instance, Japan has shut down its coal industry and has no iron ore, bauxite, or oil. Except for most of its rice, it imports much of its food. Japan is richly endowed with human capital, however, and that makes all the difference.

The implications for the United States are equally striking. As capital, labor, and knowledge become more important than land in charting economic success, America can influence and possibly even reshape its pattern of comparative advantage. The "new trade theory," articulated clearly by the economist Paul Krugman, focuses on path dependence, the so-called QWERTY effect of past choices. The QWERTY keyboard was not the arrangement of letter-coded keys that produced the fastest typing, except perhaps for left-handers. But, as the VHS videotape format became the standard for video recording even though other formats were technically better, the QWERTY keyboard became the standard for the typewriter (and computer) industry, and everyone else had to adapt to it. Nations that invested from the start in production facilities for the 16-kilobyte computer memory chip also had great advantages down the line in 4- and 16-megabyte chips. Intervention at an early point in the chain of development can influence results later on, which suggests that the United States and other nations can and should deliberately alter their pattern of comparative advantage and choose their economic activity.

American college and graduate education, for example, has supported the decisive U.S. role in the international services industry in research and development, consulting, design, packaging, financing, and the marketing of new products. Mergers and acquisitions are American subspecialties that draw on the skills of financial analysts and attorneys. The American failure, rather, has been in the first 12 years of education. Unlike that of Germany and Japan (or even Taiwan, Korea, and Singapore), American elementary and secondary education falls well below the world standard.

Economics teaches that products should be valued according to their economic importance. For a long period, education was undervalued, socially and economically speaking, despite productivity studies by Edward Denison and others that showed its long-term importance to U.S. growth and innovation. Recent studies have underscored this importance. According to the World Bank, 64 percent of the world's wealth consists of human capital. But the social and economic valuation of kindergarten through 12th-grade education has still not appreciably increased. Educators, psychologists, and school boards debate how education should be structured, but Americans do not invest more money in it.

In international economic competition, human capital has turned out to be at least as important as other varieties of capital.

Corporations have sought to upgrade the standards of teaching and learning in their regions, but localities and states have lagged behind, as has the federal government. Elementary and high school teachers should be rewarded as patient creators of high-value capital in the United States and elsewhere. In Switzerland, elementary school teachers are paid around $70,000 per year, about the salary of a starting lawyer at a New York firm. In international economic competition, human capital has turned out to be at least as important as other varieties of capital. In spite of their reduced functions, states liberated from the confines of their geography have been able, with appropriate education, to transform their industrial and economic futures.

THE REDUCED DANGER OF CONFLICT

◆ ◆ ◆

As nations turn to the cultivation of human capital, what will a world of virtual states be like? Production for one company or country can now take place in many parts of the world. In the process of downsizing, corporations and nation-states will have to get used to reliance on others. Virtual corporations need other corporations' production facilities. Virtual nations need other states' production capabilities. As a result, economic relations between states will come to resemble nerves connecting heads in one place to bodies somewhere else. Naturally, producer nations will be working quickly to become the brains behind emerging industries elsewhere. But in time, few nations will have within their borders all the components of a technically advanced economic existence.

To sever the connections between states would undermine the organic unit. States joined in this way are therefore less likely to engage in conflict. In the past, international norms underlying the balance of power, the Concert of Europe, or even rule by the British Raj helped specify appropriate courses of action for parties in dispute. The international economy also rested partially on normative agreement. Free trade, open domestic economies, and, more recently, freedom of movement for capital were normative notions. In addition to specifying conditions for borrowing, the International Monetary Fund is a norm-setting agency that inculcates market economics in nations not fully ready to accept their international obligations.

Like national commercial strategies, these norms have been largely abstracted from the practices of successful nations. In the nineteenth century many countries emulated Great Britain and its precepts. In the British pantheon of virtues, free trade was a norm that could be extended to other nations without self-defeat. Success for one nation did not undermine the prospects for others. But the acquisition of empire did cause congestion for other nations on the paths to industrialization and growth. Once imperial Britain had taken the lion's share, there was little left for others. The inability of all nations to live up to the norms Britain established fomented conflict between them.

In a similar vein, Japan's current trading strategy could be emulated by many other countries. Its pacific principles and dependence on world markets and raw materials supplies have engendered greater economic cooperation among other countries. At the same time, Japan's insistence on maintaining a quasi-closed domestic economy and a foreign trade surplus cannot be successfully imitated by everyone; if some achieve the desired result, others necessarily will not. In this respect, Japan's recent practices and norms stand athwart progress and emulation by other nations.

President Clinton rightly argues that the newly capitalist developmental states, such as Korea and Taiwan, have simply modeled themselves on restrictionist Japan. If this precedent were extended to China, the results would endanger the long-term stability of the world economic and financial system. Accordingly, new norms calling for greater openness in trade, finance, and the movement of factors of production will be necessary to stabilize the international system. Appropriate norms reinforce economic incentives to reduce conflict between differentiated international units.

DEFUSING THE POPULATION BOMB

◆ ◆ ◆

So long as the international system of nation-states lasts, there will be conflict among its members. States see events from different perspectives, and competition and struggle between them are endemic. The question is how far conflicts will proceed. Within a domestic system, conflicts between individuals need not escalate to the use of physical force. Law and settlement procedures usually reduce outbreaks of hostility. In international relations, however, no sovereign, regnant authority can discipline feuding states. International law sets a standard, but it is not always obeyed. The great powers constitute the executive committee of nation-states and can intervene from time to time to set things right. But, as Bosnia shows, they often do not, and they virtually never intervene in the absence of shared norms and ideologies.

In these circumstances, the economic substructure of international relations becomes exceedingly important. That structure can either impel or retard conflicts between nation-states. When land is the major factor of production, the temptation to strike another nation is great. When the key elements of production are less tangible, the situation changes. The taking of real estate does not result in the acquisition of knowledge, and aggressors cannot seize the needed capital. Workers may flee from an invader. Wars of aggression and wars of punishment are losing their impact and justification.

Eventually, however, contend critics such as Paul Ehrlich, author of *The Population Bomb*, land will become important once again. Oil supplies will be depleted; the quantity of fertile land will decline; water will run dry. Population will rise relative to the supply of natural resources and food. This process, it is claimed, could return the world to the eighteenth and nineteenth centuries, with clashes over territory once again the engine of conflict. The natural resources on which the world currently relies may one day run out, but, as before, there will be substitutes. One sometimes forgets that in the 1840s whale oil, which was the most common fuel for lighting, became unavailable. The harnessing of global energy and the production of food does not depend on particular bits of fluid, soil, or rock. The question, rather, is how to release the energy contained in abundant matter.

But suppose the productive value of land does rise. Whether that rise would auger a return to territorial competition would depend on whether the value of land rises relative to financial capital, human capital, and information. Given the rapid technological development of recent years, the primacy of the latter seems more likely. Few perturbing trends have altered the historical tendency toward the growing intangibility of value in social and economic terms. In the 21st century it seems scarcely possible that this process would suddenly reverse itself, and land would yield a better return than knowledge.

Diminishing their command of real estate and productive assets, nations are downsizing, in functional if not in geographic terms. Small nations have attained peak efficiency and competitiveness, and even large nations have begun to think small. If durable access to assets elsewhere can be assured, the need to physically possess them diminishes. Norms are potent reinforcements of such arrangements. Free movement of capital and goods, substantial international and domestic investment, and high levels of technical education have been the recipe for success in the industrial world of the late twentieth century. Those who depended on others did better than those who depended only on themselves. Can the result be different in the future? Virtual states, corporate alliances, and essential trading relationships augur peaceful times. They may not solve domestic problems, but the economic bonds that link virtual and other nations will help ease security concerns.

THE CIVIC CRISIS

◆ ◆ ◆

Though peaceful in its international implications, the rise of the virtual state portends a crisis for democratic politics. Western democracies have traditionally believed that political reform, extension of suffrage, and economic restructuring could solve their problems. In the 21st century none of these measures can fully succeed. Domestic political change does not suffice because it has insufficient jurisdiction to deal with global problems. The people in a particular state cannot determine international outcomes by holding an election. Economic restructuring in one state does not necessarily affect others. And the political state is growing smaller, not larger.

The rise of the virtual state portends a crisis for democratic politics.

If ethnic movements are victorious in Canada, Mexico, and elsewhere, they will divide the state into smaller entities. Even the powers of existing states are becoming circumscribed. In the United States, if Congress has its way, the federal government will lose authority. In response to such changes, the market fills the vacuum, gaining power.

As states downsize, malaise among working people is bound to spread. Employment may fluctuate and generally decline. President Clinton observed last year that the American public has fallen into a funk. The economy may temporarily be prosperous, but there is no guarantee that favorable conditions will last. The flow of international factors of production—technology, capital, and labor—will swamp the stock of economic power at home. The state will become just one of many players in the international marketplace and will have to negotiate directly with foreign factors of production to solve domestic economic problems. Countries must induce foreign capital to enter their domain. To keep such investment, national economic authorities will need to maintain low inflation, rising productivity, a strong currency, and a flexible and trained labor force. These demands will sometimes conflict with domestic interests that want more government spending, larger budget deficits, and more benefits. That conflict will result in continued domestic insecurity over jobs, welfare, and medical care. Unlike the remedies applied in the insulated and partly closed economies of the past, purely domestic policies can no longer solve these problems.

THE NECESSITY OF INTERNATIONALIZATION

◆ ◆ ◆

The state can compensate for its deficient jurisdiction by seeking to influence economic factors abroad. The domestic state therefore must not only become a negotiating state but must also be internationalized. This is a lesson already learned in Europe, and well on the way to codification in East Asia. Among the world's major economies and polities, only the United States remains, despite its potent economic sector, essentially introverted politically and culturally. Compared with their counterparts in other nations, citizens born in the United States know fewer foreign languages, understand less about foreign cultures, and live abroad reluctantly, if at all. In recent years, many English industrial workers who could not find jobs migrated to Germany, learning the language to work there. They had few American imitators.

The virtual state is an agile entity operating in twin jurisdictions: abroad and at home. It is as prepared to mine gains overseas as in the domestic economy. But in large countries, internationalization operates differentially. Political and economic decision-makers have begun to recast their horizons, but middle managers and workers lag behind. They expect too much and give and learn too little. That is why the dawn of the virtual state must also be the sunrise of international education and training. The virtual state cannot satisfy all its citizens. The possibility of commanding economic power in the sense of effective state control has greatly declined. Displaced workers and businesspeople must be willing to look abroad for opportunities. In the United States, they can do this only if American education prepares the way.

Notes

1. See, for example, Enzo R. Grilli and Maw Cheng Yang, "Primary Commodity Prices, Manufactured Goods Prices, and the Terms of Trade of Developing Countries: What the Long Run Shows," *The World Bank Economic Review,* 1988, Vol. 2, No. 1, pp. 1–47.

2. See José Ripoll, "The Future of Trade in International Services," *Center for International Relations Working Paper,* UCLA, January 1996.

3. Daniel Garstka, "Land and Economic Prowess" (unpublished mimeograph), UCLA, 1995; Deepak Lal, "Factor Endowments, Culture and Politics: On Economic Performance in the Long Run" (unpublished mimeograph), UCLA, 1996.

Terms & Concepts

body nations

comparative advantage

downsized states

factors of production

head nations

path dependence

QWERTY effect

virtual corporation

virtual state

Questions

1. What effect will the downsized state have on manufacturing workers in virtual states?

2. What are the challenges to democracy in the world Rosecrance predicts? Is democracy safer in "head" states or in "body" states?

3. Do you agree with the author that Canada is already well on the way to becoming a virtual state? What evidence can you identify?

4. What is the danger of the Japanese example?

5. Do any changes have to be made to the international system before this new division of states can work smoothly?

Globalization and the Welfare State: Four Hypotheses and Some Empirical Evidence

Paul Bowles and Barnet Wagman

Editors' Note

This article attempts to test some of the major theories about the effects of globalization on domestic social policy. Bowles and Wagman bring globalization down to earth, and in so doing investigate a number of competing hypotheses. Such hypotheses are not merely academic speculations, disconnected from the world of ordinary political and social choice, for our beliefs about globalization can and do drive public policy decisions and set public agendas. Is there a "race to the bottom"? Are the forces of globalization incompatible with the welfare state and its assumed inefficiencies, rigidities, and tax structures? Has the composition of welfare spending changed, moving from health and social security to education and training? Do open economies—which attract capital—also require a strong public sector and higher levels of government intervention to reduce risks? Has there been a race not to the top but to the middle, and are there significant differences between state systems that are corporatist and those that take a more laissez-faire approach? How such questions are posed and answered has significant consequences for citizens (who, in any event, take their beliefs about the welfare state and government and globalization into the polling booths with them).

A crucial consequence of the Bowles and Wagman approach is that our picture of globalization becomes more nuanced and more complex—yet clearer. In some cases, their findings are counterintuitive: noncorporatist states, for example, find it more difficult to restrict welfare spending than do corporatist states. Although this article demands of the reader a working knowledge of key economic terms and concepts (often not a requirement in a political studies text), it is well worth making the effort to understand them. The authors' conclusion is heartening, for the data lead them to believe that "multiple responses to globalization are possible" and that these responses will matter a great deal to citizens.

◆ ◆ ◆

INTRODUCTION

◆ ◆ ◆

The "new globalism" of the late 1980s and 1990s has widely been viewed as having profound implications for national economic policy autonomy and domestic policy choices. Policy discussions in many countries have become increasingly internationalized in the sense that the impacts of foreign actors and forces—foreign investors, international financial markets and the global economy—are invoked as justification for particular policy positions.

In this paper, we examine the implications of this "new globalism" for one of the most important areas of national economic policy, the welfare state. While much has been written on "globalization" and on the "crisis of the welfare state," the relationship between these two contemporary phenomena has not been well articulated. Part of the reason for this is undoubtedly because the term "globalization" is itself nebulous. In this paper, we

From *Eastern Economic Journal*, XXIII, 3, summer 1997. Reprinted with permission.

restrict ourselves to analyzing only those facets of glob-alization which have direct bearing on the welfare state. This means primarily considering the globalization of short-term capital, of long-term capital, and of trade.

Even this leaves with us significant room for debate. Here, we provide a guide to this debate by analyzing four competing hypotheses on the relation-ship between globalization and levels of spending on the welfare state. For the purposes of this paper, we define welfare state spending as government spending on education, health, and social security and welfare. The hypotheses that we analyze we call: the "down-ward harmonization hypothesis"; the "upward con-vergence hypothesis"; the "convergence clubs hypothesis"; and the "globalization irrelevance hypothesis."

In the next section, we provide a detailed discussion of each of these four hypotheses. We then provide some preliminary evidence on these hypotheses by examining levels of welfare state spending. We restrict our attention (in both of these sections) to OECD countries since the impact of globalization on the welfare state may differ by level of economic and institutional development.[1] Given the limitations of available data, we restrict our empirical investigation to a subset of OECD countries for which reliable time-series data can be constructed. We find some evidence for convergence of welfare spending, not universally, but among countries with sim-ilar political institutions.[2]

GLOBALIZATION AND THE WELFARE STATE: FOUR HYPOTHESES

◆ ◆ ◆

The process of globalization is a complex one and there are considerable differences of opinion about its extent and its impact. Researchers differ about the causes of globalization, its importance, and the mechanisms through which it affects other variables. As a guide through this tangled web of competing views, we divide the literature into four main groups, each defined by a prediction about the observed pattern of welfare state spending. It should immediately be noted, however, that although we divide the literature into these four cate-gories, there are differences within these groups and, as will become evident, our categorization on the basis of predicted outcomes still permits different explanations within each category as to why these outcomes might be observed.

We start by considering one of the most popular hypotheses, namely, that globalization has led to a reduction in the ability of nation states to conduct inde-pendent economic policy and that this has inevitably put downward pressures on welfare state expenditure levels.

Globalization has led to a reduction in the ability of nation states to conduct independent economic policy.

The Downward Harmonization Hypothesis

The downward harmonization hypothesis (also some-times referred to as the "race to the bottom" hypothesis) is perhaps best summarized by the following quotation from Dharam Ghai, Director of UNRISD:

Global economic integration, within a free market context, now poses new challenges for the welfare state. The virtually instantaneous mobility of capital in unregulated markets seriously affects the capacity of governments to regulate national economies; competition for capital and markets increases pres-sure to adopt a low wage strategy, including a reduc-tion in the cost of social benefits and weakening labour standards; and the twin goals of maintaining acceptable levels of employment and defending the principles of equity and solidarity seem increasingly incompatible. (1994, i)

The argument identifies increasing capital mobility and competition, both to attract capital and to maintain export markets, as key elements of globalization which are undermining national economic policy autonomy and adversely affecting the welfare state.

Evidence of increased capital mobility and increased internationalization of capital markets during the 1980s has been documented by Cosh et al. They argue that "the financial markets of the advanced industrial coun-tries have undergone far-reaching changes since the mid-1970s. These changes essentially stem from the following interrelated factors: the progressive deregula-tion of financial markets both internally and externally in the leading countries; the internationalization of these markets; the introduction of an array of new financial investments; and the emergence and the increasing role of new players, particularly institutional investors, in the markets" (1992, 19). Cosh et al., following Levich (1987) and Feldman (1986), argue that capital markets have become more integrated during this period.

Table 6.1   The Role of FDI in World Economic Activity 1960–91

Item	1960	1975	1980	1985	1991
World FDI Stock as a Share of World Output	4.4	4.5	4.8	6.4	8.5
World FDI Inflows as a Share of World Output	0.3	0.3	0.5	0.5	0.7
World FDI Inflows as a Share of World Gross Fixed Capital Formation	1.1	1.4	2.0	1.8	3.5

Source: Crotty et al. (1995, 52).

The reasons for this internalization of capital markets are identified closely with the policies followed by the major industrial nations in Cosh et al.'s analysis, a point also made forcefully by Helleiner (1994). This is not, however, the only reason; others place more emphasis on the reductions in transactions costs and the information revolution as central explanations of the trend to capital market internationalization.

The argument refers not only to short-term financial assets (such as bonds and equities) but also extends to foreign exchange markets. Data on the volume of foreign exchange transactions would also support the general argument that international financial transactions have increased substantially during the past 20 years.[3] The French macroeconomic policy reversal in 1983 served as an early example of the rising power of international financial markets, but the currency crises which the British, Italian, and Swedish governments encountered in 1992 as a result of their participation in the European exchange rate mechanism fully illustrated the impotence of national governments in the face of currency flight. The Mexican peso crisis of 1995 offered further evidence of this.

The importance of long-term capital (i.e., foreign direct investment) flows has also risen sharply in the 1980s and 1990s as indicated in Table 6.1. As well as increased (especially short-term) capital mobility, globalization also has a trade dimension. Certainly, national economies have become more open as the ratio of trade to GNP has generally risen in OECD countries over the past few decades, although it is important to note that, in contrast to the increases in capital flows which occurred primarily in the 1980s, increasing trade volumes were primarily a phenomenon of the 1970s.[4]

This summary of the trends in selected dimensions of globalization gives some indication of the sorts of changes underway in the international economy to which supporters of the downward harmonization hypothesis might appeal. These changes, it is argued, represent a "new globalism" qualitatively different from previous periods.[5]

The implication of this process of globalization, as suggested by Ghai above, is that there is downward pressure on the levels of spending on the welfare state. Such an outcome might be expected especially since, as Helleiner has argued, the original architects of the Bretton Woods agreement, John Maynard Keynes and Harry Dexter White, originally regarded capital controls as necessary to preserve the "political autonomy of the welfare state" (1994, 165). Agreement with this outcome is not, however, limited to those with Keynesian sympathies. In fact, it is possible to find arguments from across a wide ideological spectrum that globalization is constraining national policy choices and that this has important implications for the welfare state; what differs is an assessment of the desirability of these implications.

As indicated above, the effects of globalization on the welfare state may come through two channels, namely, the greater mobility of capital and the greater openness of international trade. We discuss each channel in turn. As a point of entry into this discussion consider the view of two influential European economists, Drèze and Malinvaud, who argue that the welfare state may have adverse economic consequences because:

(i) measures of income protection or social insurance introduce undesired rigidities in the functioning of labor markets;

(ii) welfare programmes increase the size of government at a risk of inefficiency; their funding enhances the amount of revenue to be raised, and so the magnitude of tax distortions;

(iii) ... welfare programmes may lead to cumulative deficits and mounting public debts. (1994, 95)

Part of the argument made by Drèze and Malinvaud refers to the alleged microeconomic efficiency and incentive problems with the welfare state, but their arguments are also relevant to the globalization debate. With respect to their first point, concerning the functioning of labour markets, it has been argued that the welfare state, by increasing rigidities in labour markets, has slowed down the adjustment of the economy to the changes required by globalization and a more extensive international division of labour. Furthermore, such "adjustment gradualism" has been harmful as it has led to higher adjustment costs and induced hysteresis in labour markets.

For an example of this type of reasoning consider the arguments made by Canadian economists Courchene and Lipsey. Brown summarizes their position thus:

> In their view, the social contract must change to complement the nature of the economy on which it rests. In other words, the welfare state should complement the underlying structure of the economy, and should not—and probably cannot—be used in the long run merely to offset fundamental changes happening there ... [they] believe that the old social contract has been rendered obsolete by global events beyond the control of any national government. Canada's current dilemmas result partly from the social contract's sluggishness in adapting to the new globalized economy. (1994, 116–17)

The welfare state therefore needs to be reconstituted on a more "flexible," less universal, and less expensive basis.

With regard to the second and third points made by Drèze and Malinvaud, namely those concerning the level of taxes needed to support the welfare state and the potential for deficits arising from commitments to meet welfare spending, these too have clear relevance for the role that globalization might play in constraining national policy choices.

With respect to taxation, Drèze and Malinvaud argue that taxes are distortionary and that they should therefore be kept to "reasonable" levels, which implies similarly "reasonable" levels of government spending on the welfare state. This argument also has resonance with the globalization literature in that low taxes are required not only to minimize "distortions" but also to prevent capital, in this case foreign direct investment, from relocating (or to remain attractive to new investment) in a world of few restrictions on capital mobility.

As an example of this type of argument consider, for example, Connolly and Kroger. They argue that:

> The liberalization of capital markets adds ... a further dimension [to policy making]. As investment decisions depend upon expectations (i.e., what really matters is the expected rate of real return), it is important to establish a high degree of micro-economic credibility. A lack of supply-side credibility would result in micro-economic risk premium, which would require a real rate of return which is superior to that of other countries. The credibility of any micro-economic regime depends upon various factors among which the operation of the labour market, the taxation system and infrastructure conditions are the most important. In addition, public interference in the market process could become an important obstacle to attracting private capital. (1993, 45)

The "taxation system," presumably meaning low taxes on capital, is identified therefore as one factor determining the location of increasingly mobile capital. This obviously has direct implications for the level of government expenditure. Indirectly, some of the other factors identified as important by Connolly and Kroger also have implications for the welfare state. For example, they suggest that labour market operations and perceptions of "public interference in the market process" are all important for corporate investment decisions; it is unlikely that an extensive welfare state will be viewed as contributing to "microeconomic credibility." We would thus expect welfare state spending to fall to competitors' levels, converging at the level of the lowest spender.

With respect to budget deficits, it has been argued that governments' ability to finance such deficits on more integrated international capital markets has been increasingly constrained. In this scenario, international capital markets are seen as making judgments as to the fiscal responsibility of governments, and credit ratings depend upon such judgments. For some, such a development is not unwelcome since global financial markets are now seen as providing the disciplining device that national governments failed to develop. Thus, we might expect that as the power of global financial markets increases, the ability of states to borrow to finance their spending would come under increasing scrutiny and the necessity of reducing the size of the welfare state to the level of more frugal and "financially responsible" countries would become more evident.

All of these arguments point to downward pressure on welfare state spending. This prediction is also supported by "political resource" models of the determinants of relative welfare state spending, which suggest that welfare state spending depends on the strength of interest groups which support the welfare state.[6] It can be argued that all countries are experiencing downward pressures on their levels of welfare state spending because capital, as a class, has become more powerful with the process of globalization and that it is not in capital's interests to have an extensive and expensive welfare state. Thus, globalization has been accompanied by a fundamental shift of political power towards capital and away from other groups who might support an extensive welfare state; the result is that the welfare state, whose existence and level depends upon the political resources it can rely upon to support it, is under attack.

These arguments, stemming from Drèze and Malinvaud's analysis, have primarily been concerned with greater capital mobility but there is a second channel of the possible influence of globalization on the welfare state through the globalization of trade. At first, this may seem implausible since the welfare state provides primarily non-tradeable goods and any trade effects should be felt primarily by the tradeable goods sector. However, Alesina and Perotti (1994) develop a model in which the income transfers necessary to finance the welfare state reduce the competitiveness of the tradeable goods sector.[7] As a result, pressures to reduce the size of the welfare state arise in order to maintain the competitiveness of the tradeable goods sector.

In addition to the general hypothesis that we would expect globalization to lead to downward pressure on average levels of welfare state expenditure, we might also expect to observe changes in the composition of welfare state spending. In particular, it has been argued that the welfare state has been transformed by the pressures of globalization into the "competitor state." The process of globalization, it is argued, has dramatically changed the relation of states to the international economy; whereas states could previously be seen as "gatekeepers" insulating domestic economies from the ravages of the international economy, their policy autonomy has now been reduced to the point where they have in fact become agents transmitting the requirements of the globalizing economy to the domestic economy.[8] We would expect to see, therefore, not only a reduction in the size of the welfare state but also to see education expenditures and labour market retraining programmes

It has been argued that the welfare state has been transformed by the pressures of globalization.

expand relative to health and social security and welfare spending over time as states seek not only to reduce the level of welfare state spending, but to redirect it to those activities which are believed to enhance competitiveness in the global economy.

The Upward Convergence Hypothesis

While the arguments above view the "new globalism" as a predominantly post mid-1980s phenomenon, others view the integration of the international economy as being a phenomenon characteristic of the past century, particularly the post-1945 period. During this period, according to some, there has been an international diffusion of technology so that levels of total factor productivity, and therefore per capita income, have converged over time (Abramowitz, 1986; Baumol, 1986). The benefits of an open trading system have accrued, therefore, to follower countries that have been able to take advantage of the possibilities of technological catch-up.[9]

Thus, many neoclassical economists have been concerned about exploring the extent to which national economies have converged to higher per capita income levels in the post–World War II period.[10] The implications of this convergence, if it occurs, for the welfare state are not explicitly made. However, it is argued that consumer preferences tend to become more homogenous as income levels converge and hence we might expect similar patterns of welfare state spending to emerge. As Abramowitz notes, "as followers' levels of per capita income converge on the leader's, so do their structures of consumption and prices" (1986, 389). Furthermore, the income elasticities of demand for public spending in general, and health and education spending in particular, are relatively high and hence we would expect rising expenditures on these items.[11]

This latter prediction can also be found in structuralist theories, popular with welfare state theorists in the 1960s and 1970s, which viewed the rise of the welfare state as a "modern" phenomenon accompanying industrialization and rising levels of per capita GNP. As Esping-Andersen argues:

One variant begins with a theory of industrial society, and argues that industrialization makes social policy both necessary and possible—necessary because pre-industrial modes of social reproduction, such as the family, the church, *noblesse oblige*, and guild solidarity are destroyed by the forces attached to modernization, such as social mobility, urbanization, individualism, and market dependence. The crux of the matter is that the market is no adequate substitute because it caters only to those who are able to perform in it. Hence, the "welfare function" is appropriated by the nation-state. (1990, 13)

The view that the welfare state grows up with industrial society also finds support in the structuralist Marxist literature. Here it is argued that capitalist industrial society requires both a well-educated and relatively healthy workforce and a legitimacy which can only be achieved by social spending. The result is that the state acts to provide these needs of the capitalist system as a whole through welfare spending (O'Connor, 1973).

Seen in this light, globalization can be seen as a new stage during which we might expect to see increased levels of welfare state spending. This arises because, given the arguments above that the welfare state arose in large part out of a desire to provide income security for individuals in the face of structural changes in the economy, then globalization might be expected to increase the need for the welfare state. A more extensive welfare state would be required to meet the increasing social strains caused by an increased international division of labour or, in the structuralist Marxist analysis, to provide continued legitimacy for capitalist accumulation on a global scale.

A recent argument which bears resemblance to some of these points has been made by Rodrik (1996). Rodrik finds that there is a strong positive statistical relationship between size of government and degree of trade openness in a sample of over 100 countries. He further concludes that "the estimated coefficient on initial government spending is strongly negative, implying a (conditional) convergence effect on government spending.... Not only is openness an important determinant of government consumption levels across countries, openness in the early 1960s turns out to be a significant predictor of the *expansion* of government consumption in the subsequent three decades" (1996, 8).[12] Rodrik suggests that the explanation for this statistical finding can be found in the role that government spending plays in reducing the role of external risk to which economies are exposed; since more open economies have higher degrees of such risk they compensate by having larger public sectors. Or, to use Rodrik's words, "societies seem to demand (and

receive) a larger government sector as the price for accepting larger doses of external risk" (1996, 1) with the result that "globalization may well require, big, not small, government" (1996, 26). Rodrik's results indicate that the relationship between trade openness and higher government spending holds for both education and health expenditures although there is some ambiguity about the spending on social security and welfare.[13] Certainly, we would expect the argument to hold for social security and welfare spending in OECD countries.

The theories outlined above, although derived from a variety of theoretical frameworks, all share a common prediction about the relationship between globalization and welfare state spending levels, namely, that the relationship is expected to be positive and that this relationship would also hold for the three categories of welfare state spending considered here: education, health, and social security and welfare. All theories point to a rising average level of welfare state expenditure and some suggest, more strongly, a convergence towards the higher level.

The Convergence Clubs Hypothesis

The two hypotheses considered above both predict that the responses to globalization will be similar for all OECD countries. However, given the significant institutional differences between these countries it may be argued that we would expect a variety of responses. Consider the following argument by Esping-Andersen:

> We should ... not exaggerate the degree to which global forces overdetermine the fate of national welfare states. One of the most powerful conclusions in comparative research is that political and institutional mechanisms of interest representation and political consensus building matter tremendously in terms of managing welfare, employment and growth objectives.... Countries ... vary in their capacity to manage conflicting interests. (1994, 4)

In analyzing these institutional differences between OECD countries one oft-made distinction is between those countries whose economies utilize corporatist institutions to manage conflicting interests and those which take a more laissez-faire approach. This division has been argued to be especially important in determining policy responses and policy outcomes to the world economic slowdown after the oil price shocks of the 1970s. Specifically, it has been argued that in countries with high degrees of corporatism the social bargain has enabled economies to adjust more rapidly and efficiently to changes in external conditions.[14] The centralized bargaining structures of corporatist states, with their inclusion of business, labour, and government in national economic policy-making, has enabled them to more efficiently strike social bargains which involve greater degrees of real wage flexibility in return for higher employment levels and a higher social wage (i.e., more extensive welfare state). The globalization of the mid-1980s and 1990s could plausibly be argued to be a similarly important change in external conditions which requires coordinated policy responses. If it is true that globalization puts downward pressure on welfare states then we might expect that corporatist countries would be better able to adapt their policy choices in response. Reducing welfare state expenditures is a politically divisive process and corporatist countries might have the institutional structures more capable of managing such a process. However, corporatist countries' structures depend to a considerable degree on the provision of welfare state benefits as part of the social bargain underpinning their structures. We would therefore expect reductions in welfare state spending to have a definite lower bound and we would not expect the size of the welfare state to shrink to that of non-corporatist countries.[15] In the latter countries, we might again expect downward pressure on the welfare state although perhaps with some variation in achieving this objective given the political obstacles to welfare state reductions and the absence of well-developed institutional mechanisms to overcome them. We might expect to find, therefore, that responses to globalization vary with the degree of corporatism, with both high and low corporatist countries facing downward pressure on welfare state spending but with the highly corporatist set of countries still having higher levels of welfare state spending and being capable of pursuing more coordinated responses than the low corporatist countries.

It is possible that the relevant categorization of countries is by their regional affiliation.

It is possible that the relevant categorization of countries is not by the degree to which their institutions may be regarded as corporatist but by their regional affiliation. Characterizing the current phase of the world economy as one dominated by globalization is not without its critics and one alternative would be to view regionalization as a more dominant force. Hirst and Thompson, for example, argue that "perhaps the most significant post-1970s development, and the most enduring, is the formation of supra-national trading and economic blocs" (1992, 369).[16] If this is the case, then we might plausibly expect to see "convergence clubs" emerging on the basis of regional affiliation. In particular, we might expect to see welfare state spending converging among members of regional trade blocs.

The concern over the possibility of downward harmonization has led to attempts to provide safeguards in regional trading agreements as the environmental and labour side agreements negotiated in NAFTA and the Social Chapter of the EU 1992 project illustrate. In general though, there is a large difference between the policies of the two most powerful economies in the regional blocs of NAFTA and of the EU. Specifically, Germany has a much more extensive welfare state model than the U.S. The outcome of European integration may be more favourable to the welfare state than that of NAFTA as a result, although the difficulties of positive integration (as opposed to the negative integration represented by the removal of regulations) remain real in the European case.[17] Nevertheless, we would expect pressures for upward harmonization to be highest in Europe and the pressures for downward harmonization to be greatest in NAFTA. The two regions may therefore exhibit quite different convergence patterns with two distinct convergence clubs emerging.

The Globalization Irrelevance Hypothesis

The arguments made above all rely on the assumption that globalization (or regionalization) is taking place to a significant degree and that this has implications for the autonomy of national economic policy making. However, other theorists dispute the importance of globalization and it is certainly valid to question the reliability of the theoretical links between globalization, even if it is occurring, and the welfare state.

Consider first the arguments about the existence of globalization. With respect to the global integration through increased trade argument, although economies are more open as a result of tariff reductions there has been a simultaneous rise in nontariff barriers; the degree of increased trade openness is therefore open to doubt and trade figures alone undoubtedly overstate the case. Furthermore, although production is said to be becoming more global in the sense that increasingly greater amounts of production are occurring in host countries, Lipsey et al. find this increase to be modest and conclude that:

Given all the attention that "globalization" has received from scholars, international organizations, and the press, [our data] are a reminder of how large a proportion of economic activity is confined to single geographical locations and home country ownership. Internationalization of production is clearly growing in importance, but the vast majority of production is still carried out by national producers within their own borders.[18] (1995, 60–61)

Perhaps the case for globalization is strongest when considering the growth of short-term financial markets. Even here, however, the argument is not unambiguous and Zevin (1992), for example, argues that international capital mobility in the 1980s is similar to that found in the 1880s. In his view, it is not the 1980s which are new but the immediate post–World War II period which is exceptional in the degree to which international capital mobility was restricted.

The increased mobility of long-term capital, another alleged dimension of globalization, is also open to dispute. Despite its growth during the post–World War II period, there is still evidence that there are considerable barriers to the movement of long-term capital. As Epstein (1994) argues, it does not appear that we have moved to a Walrasian world where we have a pool of world savings with countries freely borrowing from it. Epstein further shows that for U.S. multinationals in the period 1951–86, there was no tendency for profit rates to equalize across countries or for the variance of profit rates to fall over time, suggesting that significant barriers to the mobility of long-term capital remain.

Whilst these arguments question the degree to which globalization has taken place, others question the hypothesized links between globalization and the welfare state. For example, the argument advanced by Drèze and Malinvaud that welfare states may lead to "cumulative deficits and mounting public debts" is straightforward but controversial. It is controversial in that it implies an analysis of state spending behaviour which may not be accurate and on the specific grounds that although spending on the welfare state may be a large budget item, it is not the only item and deficits could equally be reduced or eliminated by reducing spending in other areas. Furthermore, the integration of global capital markets may enable governments to borrow *more* not less by increasing their access to global capital supplies.

The argument that increased capital mobility will constrain the ability of governments to raise taxes to finance the welfare state and constrain the type of inter-

ventions that it can make remains a hypothesis. It may turn out to be false because a large body of literature of firm location decisions find little evidence that tax rates are a major factor and, as suggested earlier, it appears that there are still significant barriers to long-term capital mobility.[19] Furthermore, evidence from two highly integrated areas shows that even the restrictions placed on countries who have joined the European exchange rate mechanism have not led to significant levels of labour market convergence (Anderton and Barrell, 1995) and that the U.S. states still exhibit substantial differences in social welfare provision despite over a century of free capital movements.

If one accepts these arguments then, we should not expect globalization to have had any significant impact on welfare state spending levels. If we do find any trends, or more strongly convergence, in welfare state spending levels then we should look elsewhere for their explanations. This suggests that countries continue to have policy choices, albeit constrained by their own history and institutional structures, but that such choices are made for non-globalization related reasons, of which the most important might be government ideology. In this case, whilst right-wing governments may invoke the forces of globalization to assert that there are no alternatives to their reductions in welfare state spending (or spending growth), they are no more than that: assertions designed to demobilize the opposition rather than statements of fact. Thus, we might expect countries to differ in their patterns of welfare state expenditure but these differences would be explained by political affiliation of the ruling party and there is no necessary reason to believe that a convergence of expenditures would be observed.

Before considering the data, we conclude this section by providing a summary of the four hypotheses. Figure 6.1 illustrates differences between the hypotheses in terms of how important they judge globalization to be, what they consider the implications of globalization to be for average welfare state spending over time, and whether they predict, more strongly, a convergence of welfare state spending.

TRENDS IN WELFARE STATE SPENDING

◆ ◆ ◆

The four globalization hypotheses summarized in Figure 6.1—"Downward Harmonization," "Upward Convergence," "Convergence Clubs," and "Globalization

Figure 6.1   Summary
Globalization and the Welfare State: Four Hypotheses

Hypothesis	Globalization Important?	Mean Welfare State Spending	Convergence of Welfare State Spending
I. Downward Harmonization	Yes	Lower	Yes
II. Upward Convergence	Yes	Higher	Yes
III. Convergence Clubs			
a. Corporatist	Yes	Lower: Non-corporatist Lower (?): Corporatist	No: Non-corporatist Yes: Corporatist
b. Regional	Regionalization more important	Lower: North America Higher (?): Europe	Yes: North America Yes: Europe
IV. Globalization Irrelevance	No	Lower (?): Right-wing Gov'ts Left-wing Gov'ts	? ?

Note: (?) indicates an uncertain effect

Irrelevance"—have differing implications for trends in welfare state spending. In this section, we examine those trends as a means of evaluating these competing views.

We use national expenditures on education, health, and social security and welfare (as percentages of GDP) as measures of welfare state size. The main difficulty in doing so is the paucity of comparable cross-country data for the relevant period, from the early 1970s to the present. Using two data sources, the OECD study *Social Expenditures 1960-1990* (OECD 1985)[20] and the *Government Financial Statistics Yearbook* (IMF, 1995), we were able to assemble statistics on education and social security and welfare spending for ten OECD countries, and on government health expenditures for eight countries.[21] These statistics contain spending by all levels of government. The use of such aggregate data as a measure of welfare state size is not beyond criticism, but as Freeman notes, "indicators of the extent of the welfare state like the share of public expenditures or of taxes in GDP are imperfect, but probably give a reasonable picture of differences in the magnitude of social policy activity across countries and over time" (1995, 247).

In addition to examining average levels of welfare state spending, we also wish to test for convergence. However, testing for convergence is problematic because of "the absence of an agreed upon definition of conver-

gence" (Hall et al., 1992, 99). Given this, we report two simple statistics as indicators of changes in the variation of social spending as a percentage of GDP—the standard deviation and the coefficient variation of spending by countries in the sample. If both decline over time, we will conclude that convergence has occurred.

Important components of welfare state spending are likely to be counter-cyclical. Obviously, welfare and unemployment payments will increase during recessions, but other welfare state expenditures may vary cyclically as well. For example, expenditures on post-secondary education may increase during economic downturns as individuals choose schooling instead of competing in a tight labour market. Consequently, cross-sectional comparisons of welfare state spending in any one year may be inappropriate, if countries are at different points in their business cycles.[22]

To mitigate this potential source of bias, we will limit our analysis to welfare state spending in business cycle peak years. For each country in the sample, we identified peak years of the business cycle by linearly detrending real GDP. We then used the business cycle peaks closest to 1970, 1980, and 1990, within the period 1970–1992. Our cross-country analysis is carried out in terms of three periods for which these business cycle peak years are proxies: the early 1970s, the late

Table 6.2   Total Welfare State Spending as % of GDP

	Period 1: Early 1970s	Period 2: Late 1970s to Early 1980s	Period 3: Late 1980s
Australia	13.1%	18.2%	15.3%
Austria	22.3%	27.1%	28.8%
Canada	19.7%	20.3%	23.4%
Denmark	27.4%	33.3%	32.8%
Germany	26.3%	30.5%	28.3%
Norway	27.1%	27.2%	28.1%
United Kingdom	19.4%	21.3%	20.8%
United States	16.9%	18.6%	16.9%
Mean	21.5%	24.6%	24.3%
Standard deviation	0.049	0.054	0.058
Coefficient of variation	0.226	0.219	0.240

Note: Welfare state spending is defined as expenditures on education, health, and social security and welfare, by all levels of government.

Sources: See Table A1.

1970s to early 1980s, and the late 1980s. (See Table A1 for the years used for each country.) Of course, since the severity of business cycle volatility is not uniform across countries, this procedure may not fully correct for cyclical variations in welfare state spending. Nevertheless, we believe this to be a reasonable first approximation.

Table 6.2 shows total welfare state spending for our sample of eight countries. Spending increased between the first two periods and then remained stable—i.e., while welfare state size increased in the 1970s, the 1980s are not characterized by the sharp decline in welfare state size that some hypotheses might suggest. The absence of welfare state growth in the 1980s (after the ubiquitous growth of welfare state spending in the 1970s) could, however, be taken as indicative of a response to pressures from globalization.[23] We do not observe convergence based on either test statistic, which is evidence against both the "Downward Harmonization" and the "Upward Convergence" hypotheses.

If globalization fosters the development of "competitor states," then change may occur in the composition rather than in the overall level of welfare state spending. A strong version of the competitor states hypothesis would predict an upward convergence in spending on education and/or downward convergence in spending on health and social security and welfare.[24] However, disaggregating the data by type of spending

did not reveal this pattern.[25] Average national spending on education declined in the 1980s, with no indication of convergence. Social security and welfare spending increased in the 1970s and remained roughly level in the 1980s; we observe a *divergence* of spending levels among our sample countries during this period. In the 1970s, government spending on health increased and converged; the upward trend in spending continued in the 1980s, but convergence did not. Available data allows us to include Japan and Sweden in the sample for spending on education and on social security and welfare but their inclusion does not change the patterns discussed above.

The apparent divergence of spending on social security and welfare in the 1980s suggests the possibility of convergence clubs. To explore this possibility, we have divided our sample of countries into corporatist and non-corporatist states, based on the corporatism index developed by Crouch (1983).[26]

As one might expect, corporatist and non-corporatist have substantially different average levels of total welfare state spending in all periods (Table 6.3). In corporatist countries, the absence of welfare state spending growth during the 1980s is consistent with the view that downward pressures resulting from globalization were evident. However, average welfare state spending levels were maintained during the 1980s and convergence is seen during this period, suggesting that corporatist states

Table 6.3   Total Welfare State Spending as % of GDP, Corporatist vs. Non-Corporatist States

		Period 1: Early 1970s	Period 2: Late 1970s to Early 1980s	Period 3: Late 1980s
Corporatist	Austria	22.3%	27.1%	28.8%
	Denmark	27.4%	33.3%	32.8%
	Germany	26.3%	30.5%	28.3%
	Norway	27.1%	27.2%	28.1%
	Mean	25.8%	29.5%	29.5%
	Standard deviation	0.020	0.025	0.019
	Coefficient of variation	0.079	0.086	0.065
Non-corporatist	Australia	13.1%	18.2%	15.3%
	Canada	19.7%	20.3%	23.4%
	United Kingdom	19.4%	21.3%	20.8%
	United States	16.9%	18.6%	16.9%
	Mean	17.3%	19.6%	19.1%
	Standard deviation	0.027	0.013	0.032
	Coefficient of variation	0.154	0.065	0.167

Note: Corporatist states are those with Crouch index > 2.

Welfare state spending is defined as expenditures on education, health, and social security and welfare by all levels of government.

Sources: See Table A1.

had institutional structures which elicited a common response to those pressures.

The story is somewhat different for the set of non-corporatist states. Their mean levels of total spending fell slightly in the 1980s and their individual spending levels diverged (after converging in the 1970s). This was particularly true for spending on social security and welfare (Table 6.4). The fact that two of the non-corporatist states, Japan and Canada, experienced substantial increases in this category of spending suggests that either they were not experiencing global pressure to reduce social spending or that in the absence of corporatist institutions, restricting welfare state spending may prove difficult.

Although we have controlled for business cycle variations by drawing data from business cycle peak years, it could be argued that secular differences in macroeconomic conditions can influence trends in welfare state spending. It is possible that the convergence of social spending among corporatist states reflects similar long-run economic conditions, particularly since these coun-

tries are all European.[27] As a rough check on this possibility, we considered national unemployment rates in business cycle peak years.[28] We observe a secular increase in average unemployment rates for both corporatist *and* non-corporatist states. This suggests that the apparently systematic difference in social spending patterns between corporatist and non-corporatist states does not reflect differing economic conditions, but rather differing responses to the pressures of globalization.

CONCLUSIONS

◆ ◆ ◆

In the first part of this paper, we identified four hypotheses concerning the relationship between globalization and the welfare state. This relationship is an important one because globalization is the subject of great controversy, and has become an important factor in the ongoing and often acrimonious debate over the reform of the welfare state. The statistics on welfare state spending

Table 6.4   Spending on Social Security and Welfare as % of GDP, Corporatist vs. Non-Corporatist States

		Period 1: Early 1970s	Period 2: Late 1970s to Early 1980s	Period 3: Late 1980s
Corporatist	Austria	15.6%	18.8%	19.1%
	Denmark	14.9%	20.0%	21.0%
	Germany	16.2%	19.2%	17.7%
	Norway	13.6%	14.4%	15.0%
	Sweden	10.4%	16.6%	18.83%
	Mean	14.1%	17.8%	18.3%
	Standard deviation	0.020	0.020	0.020
	Coefficient of variation	0.145	0.113	0.107
Non-corporatist	Australia	5.0%	7.9%	6.2%
	Canada	8.8%	9.1%	12.0%
	United Kingdom	9.3%	11.5%	10.5%
	United States	8.4%	9.5%	7.3%
	Japan	3.6%	6.8%	8.0%
	Mean	7.0%	9.0%	8.8%
	Standard deviation	0.023	0.016	0.021
	Coefficient of variation	0.328	0.174	0.243

Note: Corporatist states are those with Crouch index > 2.

Sources: See Table A1.

described in the previous section of this paper lead us to several conclusions:

- The mean levels of welfare state spending decreased slightly in the 1980s, in contrast to the 1970s, when all countries in our sample experienced increased spending as a percentage of GDP. This is consistent with the hypothesis that the process of globalization in the 1980s resulted in downward pressure on welfare state spending.

- There is evidence of neither a downward convergence nor of an upward harmonization of welfare state spending in the full sample of countries.

- We do, however, observe a convergence of welfare state spending in the 1980s among the corporatist states in our sample. The same is *not* true of spending by non-corporatist states; welfare state spending by non-corporatist states diverged in the 1980s.

- Average spending on education and on social security and welfare both declined in the 1980s, while spending on health increased. This is inconsistent with the strong version of the competitor states hypothesis which predicts an *increase* in spending on education and a decrease in other forms of welfare state spending.

Our results suggest that globalization may indeed have posed a challenge to the welfare state in the 1980s. However, the responses to that challenge were not uniform across the set of countries in our sample. The fact that corporatist states did show a similarity in their response is an indicator of the importance of institutional structures in determining how countries respond to economic conditions that are beyond their direct control.

It should again be noted that our results should be viewed as suggestive rather than definitive. The number of countries in our sample was relatively small and our analysis of welfare state spending trends has been concerned with finding consistency with the four hypotheses outlined in the first part of this paper, rather than with tests of

Should nations passively accept, and comply with, such pressures?

causality. Nevertheless, on the basis of our findings, it has been possible to draw some tentative conclusions.

If, in fact, countries are obliged to respond to global pressures, then a central policy question is: should nations passively accept, and comply with, such pressures, or should they seek ways to limit the destructive tendencies which globalization may hold for the welfare state? The experience of the 1980s suggests that multiple responses to globalization are possible; the fate of the welfare state appears to depend on institutional structures and policy decisions, rather than on an inevitable capitulation to global forces.

Table A1   Business Cycle Peak Years, Data Sources, and Crouch Index

| | Business Cycle Peak Years | | | |
	Period 1: Early 1970s	Period 2: Late 1970s to Early 1980s	Period 3: Late 1980s	Crouch index of corporatism
Australia	1973	1978	1989	0.0
Austria	1974	1980	1991	4.0
Canada	1974	1979	1988	0.0
Denmark	1973	1979	1986	3.0
Germany	1973	1979	1991	4.0
Japan	1973	1979	1991	1.5
Norway	1976	1980	1986	4.0
Sweden	1970	1979	1989	4.0
United Kingdom	1973	1979	1989	0.0
United States	1973	1978	1989	0.0

Sources: For periods 1 and 2, OECD (1985). For period 3, IMF (1995). For Crouch index, Crouch (1983).

References

Abramowitz, M. "Catching Up, Forging Ahead, and Falling Behind." *Journal of Economic History,* June 1986, 385–406.

Alesina, A., and Perotti, R. "The Welfare State and Competitiveness." *NBER Working Paper No. 4810,* 1994.

Amenta, E. "The State of the Art in Welfare State Research on Social Spending Efforts in Capitalist Democracies since 1960." *American Journal of Sociology,* November 1993, 750–63.

Anderton, R., and Barrell, R. "The ERM and Structural Change in European Labour Markets: A Study of 10 Countries." *Weltwirtschaftliches Archiv,* January 1995, 47–66.

Baumol, W. "Productivity Growth, Convergence, and Welfare: What the Long-Run Data Show." *American Economic Review,* December 1986, 1072–1085.

Brown, D. "Economic Change and New Social Policies," in *The Case for Change: Reinventing the Welfare State,* edited by W. Watson, J. Richards, and D.C. Brown. D. Howe Institute, 1994.

Bruno, M., and Sachs, J. *The Economics of Worldwide Stagflation,* Cambridge, MA: Harvard University Press, 1985.

Connolly, B., and Kroger, J. "Economic Convergence in the Integrating Community Economy and the Role of Economic Policies." *Recherches Economiques de Louvain,* March 1993, 37–68.

Cosh, A., Hughes, A., and Singh, A. "Openness, Financial Innovation, Changing Patterns of Ownership, and the Structure of Financial Markets," in *Financial Openness and National Autonomy: Constraints and Opportunities*, edited by T. Banuri and J. Schor. Oxford: Clarendon Press, 1992.

Cox, R. "Global Restructuring: Making Sense of the Changing International Political Economy," in *Political Economy and the Changing Global Order*, edited by R. Stubbs and G. Underhill. Toronto: McLelland and Stewart, 1994, 45–59.

Crotty, J., Epstein, G., and Kelly, P. "Multinational Corporations and Technological Change: Global Stagnation, Inequality and Unemployment." *Mimeo*, 1995.

Crouch, C. "The Conditions for Trade Union Restraint." *Mimeo*, 1983.

Drèze, J., and Malinvaud, E. "Growth and Employment: The Scope for a European Initiative." *European Economy*, January 1994, 77–106.

Durlauf, S. "On the Convergence and Divergence of Growth Rates: An Introduction." *Economic Journal*, July 1996, 1016–1018.

Epstein, G. "International Profit Rate Equalization and Investment," in *Macroeconomics After the Conservative Era: Studies in Investment, Saving and Finance*, edited by G. Epstein and H. Gintis. Cambridge University Press, 1994.

Esping-Andersen, G. *The Three Worlds of Welfare Capitalism*. London: Polity Press, 1990.

———. "After the Golden Age: The Future of the Welfare State in the New Global Order." *Occasional Paper No. 7, World Summit for Social Development*. Geneva: UNRISD, 1994.

Feldman, R. *Japanese Financial Markets*. Cambridge, MA, 1986.

Frankel, J. "How Well Do Foreign Exchange Markets Function: Might a Tobin Tax Help?" *NBER Working Paper No. 5422*, 1996.

Freeman, R. "W(h)ither the Welfare State in an Epoch of Rising Inequality?" in *Labour Market Polarization and Social Policy Reform*, edited by K. Banting and C. Beach. School of Policy Studies, Queen's University, Ontario, 1995, 243–56.

Friedman, J., Gerlowski, D., and Silberman, J. "What Attracts Foreign Multinational Corporations? Evidence from Branch Plant Location in the United States." *Journal of Regional Science*, November 1992, 403–418.

Ghai, D. Preface to "After the Golden Age: The Future of the Welfare State in the New Global Order," by G. Esping-Andersen. *Occasional Paper No. 7, World Summit for Social Development*, Geneva: UNRISD, 1994.

Green, F., Henley, A., and Tsakalotos, E. "Income Inequality in Corporatist and Liberal Economies: A Comparison of Trends Within OECD Countries." *International Review of Applied Economics*, September 1994, 303–331.

Hall, S.G., Robertson, D., and Wickens, M. "Measuring Convergence of the EC Economies." *Manchester School*, LX Supplement, 1992, 99–111.

Helleiner, E. "From Bretton Woods to Global Finance: A World Turned Upside Down," in *Political Economy and the Changing Global Order*, edited by R. Stubbs and G. Underhill. Toronto: McLelland and Stewart, 1994, 163–175.

Hirst, P., and Thompson, G. "The Problem of 'Globalization': International Economic Relations, National Economic Management and the Formation of Trading Blocs." *Economy and Society*, November 1992, 357–396.

International Monetary Fund. *Government Financial Statistics Yearbook*, Washington, D.C.: IMF, 1995.

Levich, R. "Financial Innovations in International Financial Markets." *NBER Working Paper No. 2277*, 1987.

Lipsey, R., Blomstrom, M., and Ramstetter, E. "Internationalised Production in World Output." *NBER Working Paper No. 5385*, 1995.

McCallum, J. "Unemployment in OECD Countries in the 1980s." *Economic Journal*, December 1986, 942–966.

O'Connor, J. *The Fiscal Crisis of the State*, New York: St. Martin's Press, 1973.

OECD. *Social Expenditures, 1960–1990*. Paris: OECD, 1985.

Oman, C. "The Policy Challenges of Globalization and Regionalisation." *Policy Brief No. 11*, Paris: OECD Development Centre, 1996.

Rhodes, M. "The Future of the 'Social Dimension': Labour Market Regulation in Post-1992 Europe." *Journal of Common Market Studies*, March 1992, 23–51.

Rodrik, D. "Why Do More Open Economies Have Bigger Governments?" *NBER Working Paper No. 5537*, 1996.

Zevin, R. "Are World Financial Markets More Open? If so, Why and With What Effects?" in *Financial Openness and National Autonomy: Opportunities and Constraints*, edited by T. Banuri and J Schor. Oxford: Clarendon Press, 1992, 43–84.

Notes

1. In particular, the effects of increasing international economic integration on the countries in Eastern Europe, Latin America, and East Asia may be quite different given their diverse institutional histories and levels of development. An analysis of the effects of globalization on these countries lies beyond the scope of this paper. See Esping-Andersen (1994) for discussion.

2. However, we caution that in the light of the above mentioned data limitations, our results should be regarded as preliminary rather than definitive.

3. For example, Frankel (1996, 5–6) shows that foreign exchange trading increased rapidly during the 1980s and 1990s and, by April 1995, amounted to approximately U.S. $1,200 billion per day, some 40–50 times larger than world trade flows per day.

4. For example, exports plus imports as a percentage of GDP rose from 30.0 to 43.0 percent between 1970 and 1980 for the G-7 countries. The figure then fell slightly to 41.5 percent in 1990. See World Bank, *World Tables 1992*.

5. It has been argued that the last decades of the nineteenth century can be seen as the period of "internationalization" when the world economy expanded on the basis of greater links between national economies, the 1960s and 1970s as a period of "multinationalization" when the world economy became more integrated as the activities of multinational corporations increased, but that the 1990s are characterized by a period of "globalization" where production, trade, and finance become truly global. See Oman (1996) for more details on the differences between the three periods.

6. For a review of this literature see, for example, Amenta (1993).

7. Alesina and Perotti argue that redistributive taxation will cause wage-earners to bargain for higher wages, thereby increasing costs and prices and reducing the competitiveness of the economy. The ability of wage-earners to attain such higher wages depends upon union strength, although Alesina and Perotti argue that the effects of union strength on wage outcomes will be non-linear.

8. For more on this hypothesis see Cox (1994).

9. Abramowitz (1986) argues that countries' ability to catch up depends on their social capabilities.

10. The "convergence hypothesis" has proved to be an extremely controversial one even within mainstream economics. The initial studies of Abramowitz and Baumol cited here were criticized for a number of reasons including the fact that they used data only from industrialized countries. Theoretical work from the endogenous growth literature and empirical work using larger data sets have subsequently been used to challenge the convergence hypothesis although the latter still has its share of supporters. For review see, for example, the exchanges introduced by Durlauf (1996).

11. A rising share of government consumption in GDP as per capita income increases, reflecting an income elastic demand for government services, is sometimes referred to as "Wagner's law."

12. Conditional convergence in this context means that countries' levels of government spending converge if we allow for differences in specified demographic and structural conditions. (For the conditions included see Rodrik [1996, 6]).

13. Specifically, higher social security and welfare spending is associated with higher degrees of openness in Rodrik's results for 1990–92 data but not for the 1985–89 data. Rodrik suggests that the inclusion of developing countries in his sample may explain this result since social security and welfare systems are difficult to devise in these economies and they may therefore "rely on a broader set of instrumentalities to achieve risk reduction" (1996, 14).

14. See, for example, Bruno and Sachs (1985) and McCallum (1986).

15. See Green et al. (1994) for further discussion of the relationship between corporatism and the welfare state.

16. Hirst and Thompson (1992, 393) take the view that "globalization has not taken place and is unlikely to do so" although others argue, less strongly, that regionalization is the more important of the two forces.

17. For a discussion, see for example, Rhodes (1992).

18. Using home-country data for FDI, Lipsey et al. (1995, 45) find that "the share of internationalized, or affiliate production has risen from about 4 per cent to between 6 and 7 per cent of world output since 1970." Using host country data, two calculations were made. Both resulted in a lower figure for internationalized production although in one case the increase was rapid in the late 1980s (in the other case there was no discernible trend).

19. For evidence on firm location decisions see, for example, Friedman et al. (1992).

20. This report contains data through 1981.

21. The countries for which we have full data are Australia, Austria, Canada, Denmark, Germany, Norway, United Kingdom, and United States. In addition we have spending figures on education and social security and welfare for Japan and Sweden. Missing data for at least some years precludes the inclusion of more OECD countries.

22. As Esping-Andersen notes, "In Britain, total social expenditure has grown during the Thatcher period, yet this is almost exclusively a function of very high unemployment. Low expenditure on some programs may signify a welfare state more seriously committed to full employment" (1990, 20).

23. This interpretation assumes that globalization is a 1980s phenomenon.

24. We call this a strong version of the hypothesis since it requires changes in the composition of welfare state spending unadjusted for demographic change. In fact, all of the countries in our sample experienced a rise in the ratio of the population over the age of 64 to that under the age of 25. This may be expected to affect education and health expenditures. The small number of data points precluded our adjusting welfare

state spending in these categories for demographic changes which might have also permitted testing a weaker version of the "competitor states" hypothesis.

25. A full set of tables providing details of all of the results discussed in this paper is available from the authors upon request.

26. The Crouch corporatism index ranges from 0.0 to 4.0, with countries scoring one point for each of the following criteria met: work councils, centralized union movement, low shop floor autonomy, and coordination among employers. We designate as corporatist countries with a Crouch score greater than 2. See Table A1 for country scores. Of course, this a static notion of corporatism and ignores the important changes in corporatist institutions which have taken place in the past 25 years. The index which we have adopted is used simply because it permits empirical testing.

27. Disaggregating by regional affiliation yields no discernible trends, although our ability to test for regional convergence blocks was severely limited by the countries in our sample.

28. We are grateful to Dr. Javid Taheri for providing us with internationally comparable unemployment rates.

Terms & Concepts

adjustment gradualism
conditional convergence
convergence clubs
corporatist institutions/countries
GDP
globalization irrelevance
hysteresis

income elasticities
micro-economic credibility
micro-economic risk premium
political resource models
progressive deregulation
real rate of return
social contract

tax distortions
tradeable goods sector
trade openness coefficient
upward convergence
Wagner's law
Walrarian world

Questions

1. Compare and contrast Bowles and Wagman's evidence with Susan Strange's conclusions (Chapter 4). Do their findings tend to support her views?

2. Which of the four competing hypotheses seem to have been dominant in Canadian political life, and with what consequences?

3. What are the key differences between corporatist and noncorporatist states? Does this distinction hold for Canada, which has a significantly higher level of total welfare spending than the United States and other noncorporatist states?

4. Summarize the major reasons why the authors are drawn to the view that multiple responses to globalism are possible and desirable.

Unit Two   Discussion Questions

1. Why is there such divergence of opinion regarding what is happening to "the state" as we thought we knew it? Why can't experts agree? Give examples.

2. What responses to the "forces of globalization" seem possible and desirable?

3. To what extent do the analyses in this section imply that states face new challenges? Do we tend to exaggerate both our inability to cope and the magnitude of what is happening?

Annotated Bibliography

Daedalus 124, 2 (1995). A special issue of a prestigious journal, containing articles on the changing role of states in the contemporary world.

Resnick, Philip. *The Masks of Proteus: Canadian Reflections on the State*. Montreal: McGill-Queen's University Press, 1990. A philosophical account of the role of the state in Canadian politics.

Waters, Malcom. *Globalization*. London: Routledge, 1995. A comprehensive introduction to the subject.

Watson, William. *Globalization and the Meaning of Canadian Life*. Toronto: University of Toronto Press, 1998. Watson argues that globalization is wrongly thought to constrain states. Canada has been subjected to globalizing forces for four hundred years and, he argues, has considerable room to manoeuvre.

Weiss, Linda. *The Myth of the Powerless State*. Ithaca, N.Y.: Cornell University Press, 1998. A sustained critique of the view that globalization has disabled the modern state.

Unit Three

Political Ideas and Ideologies

◆ ◆ ◆

Much ink has been spilt to define the concept of ideology. While there is no need to rehearse the long and tortured history of the idea, it is helpful to set out a few of its major themes. The Marxian account suggests that ideology is a complex of ideas and principles explaining and justifying an economic and political system whose oppressive, exploitive character would otherwise ruin it. Ideologies, therefore, prop up an illegitimate system and dupe their victims into thinking that their fate is necessary or somehow worth enduring. More recent versions of this notion suggest that ideology is tantamount to all those opinions and suppositions we consider to be common sense and not worth thinking about, questioning, or contesting. Ideology, in this view, governs ideas of the age and converts uncertain, contestable, and changeable states of affairs into conditions that are taken for granted.

Another view of ideologies associates them with the grand, revolutionary systems of thought that have directed their champions to transform society and human nature according to the dictates of some revolutionary blueprint. This view is often held by those who criticize the radical pretensions of leftists and fascists. In other words, those who see the status quo as inevitable, good, or both slap the label "ideological" on those who see the status quo as corrupt, evil, and open to concerted improvement. One observer defines ideology this way: "What persuades men and women to mistake each other from time to time for gods or vermin is ideol-

ogy."[1] Ideologies allow two people to look at the same thing and see two different objects. For example, consider two friends who are walking along a downtown street and who pass a prostitute. One remarks that the prostitute is an unfortunate victim of an oppressive cultural and political order in which women are reduced to sexual objects for men's enjoyment, as commodities in the market for women's bodies. "If women had real political influence and if dominant patriarchal assumptions could be rooted out of society," she might say, "women would not feel the need to prostitute themselves." The other replies that in a liberal society people are in control of their lives and can decide what to do with themselves and their bodies. "Your moral judgments regarding their choices are quite irrelevant," he retorts. "You may disapprove of the prostitute's choices, but you should still respect them. What we should do is legalize prostitution, regulate it for the safety and health of prostitutes, and tax it for the benefit of society." A passerby of more conservative bent overhears the conversation. She declaims both of these interpretations, suggesting that prostitution, whether legalized or criminalized, is a sign of the decay of moral order in any self-governing society. Of necessity, she avers, law enforces moral norms: "Decency is the province of the law."

Communist ideology, once a towering presence, is now toppled. For some, it is the object of scorn; for others, indifference. Political ideologies can move societies as well as challenge those who do.

Photo courtesy of Canapress.

Ideology helps to explain these different perceptions of the otherwise uncontroversial fact of prostitution. Ideologies provide us with answers to some important questions: Who are we? What is human nature? What is wrong with us? Why are we not happy, content, perfect, or self-directing? What are the causes of the evil surrounding us? How can we make things better? Political ideologies emphasize, in particular, the answer to this last question. Ideologies direct people to political action and give them a general guide to what must be done. It is one thing to have some general ideas about human nature, women's oppression, or the subversion of the "common sense of the common people," as populists like to say. It is quite another to have a developed theory of political change based on an analysis of society and the causes of its various ills. Political ideologies provide the theoretical fuel for concerted political action.

In one way or another, each article in this unit gives its own answer to these questions. The authors discuss what they consider the correct ordering of political society and the obstacles that stand in the way of that correct ordering. They also give a sense,

explicitly or not, of what they consider human nature to be and what dimensions of the human condition are most politically consequential.

There is no standard list of political ideologies. Students years ago were given a thin gruel of conservatism, liberalism, socialism, and maybe nationalism and fascism. At the dawn of the 21st century, the ideological landscape is harder to negotiate, or perhaps we are more sensitive to nuances that were always there. Feminism in its many varieties exerts a major influence on political discourse, as do liberal political and economic ideas. Multiculturalism receives much attention. Different shades of conservative ideas compete for space on the right, while nationalist thinking, thought to be in decline owing to economic globalization, has proved reports of its demise to be premature.

This unit invites you to consider the following questions: Where do political ideologies come from? What causes ideologies to move in and out of fashion? Do political ideas and ideologies exert independent influence on political life and public policy? and, What influence do ideologies exert on one another?

---

1. Terry Eagleton, *Ideology: An Introduction* (London: Verso, 1991), xiii.

Comment

Steven C. Rockefeller

Editors' Note

What makes you "you"? How are you different from others? How did you acquire your distinct identity? Did you "make yourself," or did others aid in your development? Is a community of others crucial to your identity? How is that community defined? How important is it that other people affirm and respect your identity? Are you harmed when others despise, ridicule, and disparage it? Do all people form their identities in the same way? And should all identities be equally recognized and affirmed in a liberal society?

An influential school of thought holds that if the purpose of society is individual self-development, society must make room for the many ways in which people develop and live out their identities. Philosophers such as Charles Taylor support multicultural societies—not merely in the sense that the empirical diversity in ways of life and patterns of identity formation should be tolerated, but in the deeper sense that political structures should protect distinctive identities and the means by which they sustain themselves over time. This liberal multiculturalism is born of the recognition that whereas dominant cultures are secure by virtue of their very dominance, minority cultures do not have the social and political influence to withstand pressures of conformity. And since one cannot say that one culture is better than any other, all cultures initially deserve equal concern and respect, at least until we are sure that some aspect of them is intolerable. At issue for societies like Canada's is the appropriate definition of equality, as either individualistic, "colour-blind" equality, wherein all people are treated the same according to a uniform standard, or as "the legal recognition of difference," which posits an equality of cultures and an equality of means by which individuals acquire and protect their identities. The following reading is a critical commentary on the theory of liberal multiculturalism set out by Charles Taylor.

❖ ❖ ❖

The liberal democratic tradition has been formed by an ideal of universal freedom, equality, and fulfillment, which even in the best situations has been only partially realized and which may not yet be fully imagined. The spiritual meaning of American history and the history of other democratic nations is chiefly the story of the quest for this ideal. The heart of the liberal tradition is a creative process, a social and individual method of transformation, designed to enable men and women to pursue the embodiment of this ideal. Charles Taylor has made clear the way multiculturalism and the politics of difference and equal recognition are currently influencing this process of transformation. He has explained in a most instructive fashion the historical origins in modern thought of ideas that are playing a central role in the current debate over these matters.

At a minimum, the politics and ethics of equal dignity need to be deepened and expanded so that respect for the individual is understood to involve not only respect for the universal human potential in every person but also respect for the intrinsic value of the different cultural forms in and through which individuals actualize their humanity and express their unique personalities. The following reflections endeavor to put this idea in perspective by considering the politics of equal recognition in relation to the values of liberal democracy, the environmental movement, and the religious dimension of experience. These perspectives can help us to appreciate the positive contributions of the politics of recognition and to clarify the dangers in the extreme forms of it that threaten to subvert the ideals of universal freedom and inclusive community.

I

◆ ◆ ◆

First of all, it is important to clarify a basic issue when discussing recognition of diversity in a democratic social and political context. From the democratic point of view, a person's ethnic identity is not his or her primary identity, and important as respect for diversity is in multicultural democratic societies, ethnic identity is not the foundation of recognition of equal value and the related idea of equal rights. All human beings as the bearers of a universal human nature—as persons—are of equal value from the democratic perspective, and all people as persons deserve equal respect and equal opportunity for self-realization. In other words, from the liberal democratic point of view a person has a right to claim equal recognition first and foremost on the basis of his or her universal human identity and potential, not primarily on the basis of an ethnic identity. Our universal identity as human beings is our primary identity and is more fundamental than any particular identity, whether it be a matter of citizenship, gender, race, or ethnic origin.

From the liberal democratic point of view a person has a right to claim equal recognition first and foremost on the basis of his or her universal human identity and potential, not primarily on the basis of an ethnic identity.

It may be that in some situations the rights of individuals can best be defended by addressing the rights of an entire group defined, for example, by gender or race, but this does not alter the situation regarding a person's primary identity. To elevate ethnic identity, which is secondary, to a position equal in significance to, or above,

a person's universal identity is to weaken the foundations of liberalism and to open the door to intolerance.

What is universally shared in human nature expresses itself in a great diversity of cultural forms. From the democratic perspective, particular cultures are critically evaluated in the light of the way they give distinct concrete expression to universal capacities and values. The objective of a liberal democratic culture is to respect—not to repress—ethnic identities and to encourage different cultural traditions to develop fully their potential for expression of the democratic ideals of freedom and equality, leading in most cases to major cultural transformations. How diverse cultures accomplish this task will vary, giving a rich variety worldwide to the forms of democratic life. Cultures can undergo significant intellectual, social, moral, and religious changes while maintaining continuity with their past.

I am uneasy about the danger of an erosion over time of fundamental human rights growing out of a separatist mentality that elevates ethnic identity over universal human identity.

These reflections raise some questions about Taylor's endorsement of a model of liberalism that allows the goals of a particular cultural group, such as the French Canadians in Quebec, to be actively supported by government in the name of cultural survival. It is one thing to support on the basis of the right to self-determination the political autonomy of a historically distinct and autonomous group such as a Stone Age tribal people in New Guinea or Tibetan Buddhist culture in Canada. The situation gets more complicated when one is considering creation of an autonomous state within a democratic nation as in the case of the Quebeckers or establishment of a separate public school system with its own curriculum for a particular group in the United States. Regarding Taylor's Quebec brand of liberalism, I am uneasy about the danger of an erosion over time of fundamental human rights growing out of a separatist mentality that elevates ethnic identity over universal human identity. American democracy has developed as an endeavor to transcend the separatism and ethnic rivalries that have had such a destructive effect on life in the "old world," the Yugoslavian civil war being only the most recent example.

II

◆ ◆ ◆

Clarification of the nature and meaning of liberal democracy provides a way to explore further the moral and political issues raised by the politics of recognition. Some contemporary liberals have argued for a view of the liberal state as neutral between conceptions of the good life. Procedural liberalism in this view involves a moral commitment to processes that ensure the fair and equal treatment of all but not a moral commitment to specific ends of life, that is, an idea of the good life. For example, procedural liberalism respects the separation of church and state. It is also argued that procedural liberalism creates a kind of universal culture in which all groups can flourish and live together. However, many multiculturalists today challenge the idea that liberalism can be neutral with regard to conceptions of the good life, arguing that it reflects a regional Anglo-American culture and has a homogenizing effect. They reject the view that liberalism is or can be a universal culture.

There is some truth in both of these interpretations of liberalism. A liberal political culture is neutral in the sense that it promotes tolerance and protects freedom of conscience, religion, speech, and assembly in a way that no other culture does. Liberalism at its best also represents a universal human aspiration for individual freedom and self-expression as no other culture does. However, this is only part of the story. As Taylor recognizes, liberalism is "a fighting creed" and "can't and shouldn't claim complete cultural neutrality." What is this "fighting creed"? What is the meaning of liberal democracy? Taylor has not articulated it as fully as John Dewey.

A variety of Americans, for different reasons, endorse the idea of a purely procedural form of political liberalism in the belief that it is morally neutral regarding conceptions of the good life. However, they miss the full moral meaning of liberal democracy, which contains within it a substantive idea of the good life. Liberalism, as Dewey argued, is the expression of a distinct moral faith and way of life.[1]

For liberals like Dewey, the good life is a process, a way of living, of interacting with the world, and of solving problems, that leads to ongoing individual growth and social transformation. One realizes the end of life, the good life, each and every day by living with a liberal spirit, showing equal respect to all citizens, preserving an open mind, practicing tolerance, cultivating a sympathetic interest in the needs and struggles of others, imag-ining new possibilities, protecting basic human rights and freedoms, solving problems with the method of intelligence in a nonviolent atmosphere pervaded by a spirit of cooperation. These are primary among the liberal democratic virtues.

Liberal democracy, from this Deweyan viewpoint, is not first and foremost a political mechanism; it is a way of individual life. Liberal democratic politics are strong and healthy only when a whole society is pervaded by the spirit of democracy—in the family, in the school, in business and industry, and in religious institutions as well as in political institutions. The moral meaning of democracy is found in reconstructing all institutions so that they become instruments of human growth and liberation. This is why issues of child abuse and sexual harassment, as well as discrimination on the basis of gender, race, or sexual orientation, are liberal democratic issues.

Liberal democratic politics are strong and healthy only when a whole society is pervaded by the spirit of democracy.

Liberal democracy is a social strategy for enabling individuals to live the good life. It is unalterably opposed to ignorance. It trusts that knowledge and understanding have the power to set people free. Its lifeblood is free communication building on freedom of inquiry, speech, and assembly. The liberating power of democracy is also closely tied to what one might call the democratic method of truth, which relies on experience and experimental intelligence. The idea of moral absolutes and a fixed hierarchy of values is rejected. No idea of the good is above criticism, but this does not lead to a directionless relativism. Through experience with the aid of experimental intelligence, one can find ample grounds for making objective value judgments in any particular situation.

Liberal democracy is a social strategy for enabling individuals to live the good life.

When a liberal society faces the question of granting special privileges, immunities, and political autonomy to one cultural group such as the French Canadians in Quebec, it cannot compromise on fundamental human rights, as Professor Taylor acknowledges. Furthermore, those who understand liberal democracy as itself a way of life grounded in a distinct moral faith cannot in good conscience agree to allow schools or government to suppress the democratic way of growth and transformation. The democratic way conflicts with any rigid idea of, or absolute right to, cultural survival. The democratic way means respect for and openness to all cultures, but it also challenges all cultures to abandon those intellectual and moral values that are inconsistent with the ideals of freedom, equality, and the ongoing cooperative experimental search for truth and well-being. It is a creative method of transformation. This is its deeper spiritual and revolutionary significance.

Taylor indicates appreciation of this significance when he describes the value of a cross-cultural dialogue that transforms human understanding, leading to a "fusion of horizons." However, it is unlikely that a society will be open to such a transformation if it is preoccupied with the protection of one particular culture to the extent of allowing the government to maintain that culture at the expense of individual freedom. There is an uneasy tension here between Taylor's defense of the political principle of cultural survival and his espousal of open-minded cross-cultural exchange. As liberal democracies wrestle today with the problems identified by the politics of difference and make adjustments in response to powerful separatist and nationalistic forces, it is essential that they not lose sight of this issue.

III

◆ ◆ ◆

Taylor considers at some length the question of how and on what basis different cultural groups are to be recognized and respected. In this regard, it is instructive to note the emergence of a politics of recognition with the environmental movement as well as with the politics of difference and multiculturalism. The environmentalists demand a respect for animals, trees, rivers, and ecosystems. They, like the multiculturalists, are concerned with a new appreciation of diversity and with the moral and legal standing of the rights of oppressed groups. Furthermore, just as multiculturalists might criticize the positing of the achievements of one group, such as white European and American males, as the norm of fully developed humanity, so some environmentalists criticize an anthropocentric outlook that posits human beings as the final end of the creation process and as inherently superior to all other beings. In both cases there is an attack on hierarchical modes of thought that tend to diminish or deny the value of other beings.

It is instructive to note the emergence of a politics of recognition with the environmental movement as well as with the politics of difference and multiculturalism.

In an attempt to address this issue, many environmentalists abandon an anthropocentric orientation that views non-human life forms as possessing instrumental value only and as existing solely as a means to human ends. They embrace a biocentric perspective that affirms the inherent value of all life forms. For example, the United Nations World Charter for Nature, which was approved by the General Assembly in 1982, includes the principle that "every form of life is unique, warranting respect regardless of its worth to man," and it goes on to assert that human beings have a moral obligation to respect all life forms.

This line of thinking can be applied to the question of the value of diverse human cultures. (In line with Taylor's definition, the concern here is with "cultures that have animated whole societies over some considerable stretch of time.") It may be argued that human cultures are themselves like life forms. They are the products of natural evolutionary processes of organic growth. Each, in its own distinct fashion, reveals the way the creative energy of the universe, working through human nature in interaction with a distinct environment, has come to a unique focus. Each has its own place in the larger scheme of things, and each possesses intrinsic value quite apart from whatever value its traditions may have for other cultures. This fact is not altered by the consideration that, like living beings, cultures may develop into disintegrated and diseased forms.

Just as some deep ecologists embrace a biocentric egalitarianism, so some multiculturalists demand that all cultures receive recognition of equal value.

Just as some deep ecologists embrace a biocentric egalitarianism, so some multiculturalists demand that all cultures receive recognition of equal value. Drawing on the insights of modern social psychology, Taylor has presented a persuasive argument for a new moral attitude that involves approaching all cultures with at least a presumption of equal value. One is reminded of the ancient rabbinic saying that a "wise person learns from everyone." Taylor's proposal seems entirely consistent with the liberal democratic spirit. However, the idea of a presumption of equal value involves the view that upon close scrutiny some cultures may not be found to be of equal value. Taylor's resistance to an outright judgment of equal value reflects a critical perspective that is concerned with the progressive evolution of civilization and the need to make distinctions about the relative merits of various achievements of different cultures. However, the ecological standpoint offers another perspective in light of which all cultures possess intrinsic value and in this sense are of equal value. Both perspectives have their place and are not mutually exclusive.

Translated into programs of responsible action, a presumption, or recognition, of equal value means, for example, rewriting basic textbooks for our schools, as has been done in California and is being done in New York. However, I share the concerns expressed by Arthur Schlesinger, Jr., that such undertakings not create increased social fragmentation.[2] We need a new, deeper appreciation of the ethnic histories of the American people, not a reduction of American history to ethnic histories.

IV

♦ ♦ ♦

Taylor states that there may be a religious ground for a presumption of the equal worth of different cultures, and it is illuminating to consider the question of recognition of equal value from a religious perspective. The arguments in defense of the idea of equal dignity in Western democracies continue to reflect the influence of the ancient biblical and classical Greek notions that there is something sacred about human personality. Likewise, in the defense of the idea of the intrinsic value of all life forms, which is put forth by environmentalists, one frequently encounters thinking that has roots in religious experience and beliefs. All life is sacred, is the claim. All of the various forms of life are ends in themselves, and none should be viewed as a means only. In the language of Martin Buber, all life forms should be respected as a "thou" and not just as an "it." As Albert

Schweitzer put it, one should respect the life in all beings as sacred and practice reverence for all life. Some ecological thinkers like Aldo Leopold have tried to give the idea of the moral rights of nature a scientific and secular defense, but the idea of the sacred is usually implicit or not far in the background.

If, as has been suggested, all cultures as well as all life forms are of intrinsic value and also sacred, then from a religious perspective all are in this sense equal in value. The fourteenth-century Christian mystic Meister Eckhart asserted: "God loves all creatures equally and fills them with his being. And we should lovingly meet all creatures in the same way."[3] In the spirit of Johann Gottfried Herder's outlook, which is cited by Taylor, Aleksandr Solzhenitsyn writes: "Every people, even the very smallest, represents a unique facet of God's design." Solzhenitsyn goes on to cite Vladimir Solovyov's reconstruction of the second great commandment: "You must love all other people as you love your own."[4]

If one employs this kind of religious argument in defense of the idea of equal value, one should recognize its full implications. It is opposed to anthropocentrism as well as to all egoisms of class, race, or culture. It calls for an attitude of humility. It encourages a respect for, and pride in, one's own particular identity only insofar as such respect and pride grow out of a recognition of the value of the uniqueness in the identity of all other peoples and life forms. Furthermore, if what is sacred in humanity is life, which is not something exclusively human, then humanity's primary identity is not just with the human species but with the entire biosphere that envelops planet Earth. Questions concerning equal dignity, respect for ethnic diversity, and cultural survival should be explored, therefore, in a context that includes consideration of respect for nature.

Finally, we can gain further insight into the meaning of the demand for equal recognition by considering the psychological dimension of the issue. Some multiculturalists may demand recognition of equal value chiefly in order to gain leverage in pressing the political agenda of a particular minority group. However, there is more to multiculturalism than this. The call for recognition of the equal value of different cultures is the expression of a basic and profound universal human need for unconditional acceptance. A feeling of such acceptance, including affirmation of one's ethnic particularity as well as one's universally shared potential, is an essential part of a strong sense of identity. As Taylor points out, the formation of a person's identity is closely connected to positive social recognition—acceptance and respect—

from parents, friends, loved ones, and also from the larger society. A highly developed sense of identity involves still more. Human beings need not only a sense of belonging in relation to human society. Especially when confronted with death, we also need an enduring sense of belonging to—of being a valued part of—the larger whole which is the universe. The politics of recognition may, therefore, also be an expression of a complex human need for acceptance and belonging, which on the deepest level is a religious need. To offer only a presumption of equal value does not fully address this deeper human need. Moreover, from a cosmic perspective, all peoples together with their diverse cultures may well possess inherent value and belong in some ultimate sense. This may be the element of truth in the idea of equal value from a religious perspective.

The politics of recognition may ... also be an expression of a complex human need for acceptance and belonging, which on the deepest level is a religious need.

It is not possible for secular politics to address fully the religious needs of individuals or groups for a sense of unconditional acceptance. However, any liberal democratic politics committed to the ideals of freedom and equality cannot escape the demand that it create inclusive and sustaining social environments that respect all peoples in their cultural diversity, giving them a feeling of belonging to the larger community. Furthermore, insofar as a liberal democracy encourages people to identify not only with their ethnic group or nation but also with humanity and other life forms more generally, it also nurtures a spiritual orientation conducive to realization of a sense of harmony with the cosmos.

If an affirmation of equal value is made on ecological or religious grounds, this does not diminish the importance of in-depth critical appraisal of the achievements and practices of different cultures. Comparative study and critical analysis are essential to the development of cross-cultural understanding and progressive social reconstruction. In a liberal democracy such work can and should be carried on, however, within a framework of mutual respect founded on recognition of the intrinsic worth of all cultures.

Notes

1. See, for example, John Dewey, "Creative Democracy—The Task Before Us," in *Later Works of John Dewey, 1925–1935,* ed. Jo Ann Boydston (Carbondale: Southern Illinois University Press, 1988), 14: 224–30.
2. Arthur Schlesinger, Jr., "A Dissenting Opinion," *Report of the Social Studies Syllabus Review Committee,* State Education Department, State University of New York, Albany, N.Y., 13 June 1991, p. 89.
3. See Matthew Fox, *Breakthrough: Meister Eckhart's Creation Spirituality in New Translation,* (Garden City, N.Y.: Doubleday, 1980), p. 92.
4. Aleksandr Solzhenitsyn, *Rebuilding Russia: Reflections and Tentative Proposals,* trans. Alexis Klimoff (New York: Farrar, Strauss & Giroux, 1991), p. 21.

Terms & Concepts

diversity
fundamental human rights
multiculturalism

primary identity
procedural liberalism
secondary identity

universal identity
unconditional acceptance

Questions

1. What is the difference between primary and secondary identity?

2. Can liberalism be culturally neutral? Should it be?

3. To what extent can secular politics satisfy the human need for belonging and acceptance?

4. In what ways are cultures like living beings, according to Rockefeller?

5. Charles Taylor supports laws mandating the use of French in select areas of life to make the Quebec francophone majority secure not only in that province, but also as a minority culture in North America. Does Rockefeller agree?

Conservatism: A Case of Life After Death

Gerald Owen

Editors' Note

A superficial glance at the Canadian political landscape suggests that conservatism has been made irrelevant by centrist, grasping Liberals on the one hand and populist, right-wing Reformers on the other. Progressive Conservative leader Joe Clark struggles to find his constituency. But this essay by Gerald Owen invites a closer look and suggests that conservative ideas are sewn into the very fabric of the modern Canadian social safety net.

Conservatism, in one famous rendering by Michael Oakeshott, is less a political ideology than a sensibility or a political disposition. Conservative-minded people are not enamoured of change; they value what is known over what an indeterminate future may promise. Accordingly, they are suspicious of revolution, whether sponsored by well-intentioned political radicals or by the transformative forces of the free market. Conservatives are not taken in by simplisitic appeals to equality.

As Owen writes, the question is "whether modern conservatism is anything at all." Is conservatism just a grumpy, reactionary force? Has the modern world, with its emphasis on technology, growth, and convenience, passed conservatism by? Owen leaves it to the reader to judge. But he does offer an uncommon conservative rationale for the welfare state, which will surprise many and perhaps stir some interest among readers who for some time have seen conservatism as a political ideology on life support.

◆ ◆ ◆

There is a widespread belief that there are still such people as "conservatives." A sophisticated twist on this belief is that there are people called "neo-conservatives," who have deviated from traditional conservatism. This deviance allegedly consists of the neo-conservatives' advocacy of free, or unregulated, markets—a liberal idea. Well, *neo-* (as in *neoclassical* or *neo-Nazi*) means "new" or "revived." *Conservative* suggests some sort of allegiance to traditions. But plainly, *neo-conservative* isn't used to mean "revived traditionalist." So could it mean "new, nontraditional traditionalist"? That would be like saying "young old people." This contradiction seems to show that neo-conservatives just aren't conservatives. At any rate, almost everybody in the Western world is a liberal of one kind or another. But different parts of the original liberal agenda have become partly detached from each other. The so-called neo-conservatives are the advocates of the economic aspects of what was once a united liberal agenda.

Even if the name fits badly, when people talk about neo-conservatives, at least we understand whom they mean. It is more difficult to point out any traditional conservatives. Still, a widespread belief in their existence is not necessarily a superstition, as with the belief in Sasquatches or the Loch Ness monster, but simply a case of weak or tenuous evidence, as with the alleged presence of cougars in Central Canada.

Though I won't venture to claim any sightings of individual conservatives, I maintain here that there is such a thing as conservatism in our time. Oddly enough, I will build my argument on a statement by someone who said (with some regret) that conservatism has become impossible. In many ways, my classification of conservatism is opposite to the prevailing one—specifi-

---

Article prepared for this publication. © Nelson, Thomson Learning 2000.

cally, I assert that *the welfare state is and always has been a conservative institution.*

The welfare state is and always has been a conservative institution.

But first, let's look at what was conservatism was when it certainly did exist, and then I will present a brief catalogue of various themes that are called conservative.

The pedigree of conservatives plainly goes back to one response to the French Revolution: to the capital-R Reaction. Conservatives were the "throne-and-altar" party—the upholders of an old and hereditary monarchy (with real power) and the established church, that is, the religion of the state and, in fact or theory, of the people.

The word *conservative* first appears in French (in a political sense) at the time of Thermidor, when the Revolutionary government began to exercise some caution, pulling back from the Terror. But it is in Britain that the concept really caught on, as a replacement for *Tory,* the name of the-throne-and-altar party that goes back to the 17th century. This change signified some sort of adaptation to modern times, and in particular to the Reform Bill of 1832, which allowed the middle class to vote, though the word *conservative* had been launched politically in a magazine article two years earlier. Arguably, it was a euphemism: the Irish leader Daniel O'Connell called it in 1832 "the fashionable term, the new-fangled phrase now used in polite society to designate the Tory ascendancy." The young Benjamin Disraeli, who would become English prime minister in 1868, objected that conservatism had no content; as a dissident Tory, he argued that aristocratic government had been abolished by the Reform Bill, without being replaced by democracy or any other principle. In his novel *Coningsby,* he has two Tory organizers talking:

> "Hush!" said Mr. Tadpole. "The time has gone by for Tory governments; what the country requires is a sound Conservative government."
>
> "A sound Conservative government," said Taper musingly. "I understand: Tory men and Whig measures."

In other words, conservatism, even then, meant liberalism administered by a formerly nonliberal men's club. This is not just the view of two fictional characters. In one speech of the 1840s, Disraeli said that the Tory/Conservative leaders had "caught the Whigs bathing and run away with their clothes," that is, with their policies, specifically free trade; in another speech he said that Conservative government meant "organized hypocrisy."

This is startling enough from someone who later became a very successful Conservative leader. I raise it here to show that the question of whether conservatism is anything at all has been around for at least 150 years—almost as long as the term itself.

Here, then, is a quick catalogue of various themes that have often been often put forward as conservative and can hardly be called varieties of liberalism:

1. The preservation of remnants of throne-and-altar Toryism (a position best represented by T.S. Eliot)
2. A temperament of caution, or a belief in the virtue of moderation
3. Tradition in the sense of evolution and development, in contrast to clear ideals and "rights talk" (Edmund Burke, a Whig who passionately opposed the French Revolution, is the originator of this theme)
4. Plutocracy: the dominance of big business as a new version of aristocracy (i.e., Wall Street or Bay Street having the greatest power in a nominal or partial democracy)
5. Strenuous adherence to the reforms of a generation before (a shrewd criticism made by a liberal, G.K. Chesterton, whom most people now classify as a conservative)
6. Natural law: a belief that there is a permanent human nature and that duties and rights should be in accord with each other and with that human nature—in short, rights have no priority over duties
7. Nationality or nationalism and other kinds of "communitarianism," including preservation of strong municipal governments
8. Enjoyment or gusto: an ecstatic spirit that knows it needs to be reined in by authority
9. Skepticism, as opposed to earnestness and faith in inevitable progress: this quality appears in the philosopher David Hume, in Benjamin Disraeli, and in John A. Macdonald
10. Shared values or common culture of some kind, as a substitute for the established churches of the past
11. The mixed regime: an ancient theme that praises limited government and a complex constitution to prevent the tyranny of any one class or individual, including a tyranny of the majority
12. An "organic" as opposed to a "mechanical" structure of society and government

On this last theme, I will pause. The liberal view of society is of similar individual "atoms" that are free of large complex structures except for the state itself and that are pushed and pulled by impersonal economic forces. The young Disraeli advanced an "organic" view that classes should be represented in the political order by a new version of the medieval principle of "the state of estates," *estates* meaning "statuses," or walks of life. Thus, British Parliament reflected the order of communities: the clergy, the great landowners (lords temporal), the lesser landowners (knights of the shire), and the merchants and craftsmen of the towns (the commons, burgesses of boroughs, and the bourgeoisie). In *Coningsby*, Disraeli proposed that there should be a House of the Peasants, as well as of a House of Lords and House of Commons; a couple of Scandinavian countries have actually had such things. If he had persisted with this thinking, he would logically have proposed a House of the Factory Workers, too.

This organic view of the political order strikes us now as quaint or as a bit crazy. In this century, two fascist tyrants, Mussolini and Salazar, toyed with it under the name of *corporatism.* (This word refers to organized classes or estates as corporations, not to limited-liability business corporations.) Still, the idea is not altogether farfetched; in Canada some Red Tories (Conservatives who promote liberal social policies) favour a degree of corporatism. In practice, all corporatism amounts to is the attempt to get government, business, and labour together at conferences to arrive at a three-way consensus. Bob Rae attempted this in Ontario, as did Lucien Bouchard in a conference on how to cut the deficit in Quebec. Such forums were more in evidence when inflation was high, and some people sought consensus on levels of wages, prices, and profits.

The main objections to the corporatist arrangement are (1) that it is an undemocratic and unparliamentary coalition of Big Government, Big Business, and Big Labour, in other words, of three elites ganging up on the little people (and on political party machines), and (2) that it assumes that all or most wages, prices, and profits should move at uniform rates, rather than varying flexibly among firms, industries, and products according to various demands and various supplies.

What, if anything, could these themes of conservatism in my catalogue mean in practice? If we turn to the Canadian Tories who set themselves apart from what they and others call neo-conservatism, it is not easy to see what, in principle and practice, really distinguishes them from the Liberal Party or from moderate New

Democrats. Look, for example, at the following books of Hugh Segal, recently the second-place federal Conservative leadership candidate and a ubiquitous commentator: *No Surrender: Reflections of a Happy Warrior in the Tory Crusade* and *Beyond Greed.* Segal calls himself a traditional conservative, as opposed to a neo-conservative. One of his leading themes is civility, a quality that he argues is somehow more conservative than liberal or socialist. However, the term is vague, and the Liberals do not advocate rudeness or incivility. If traditional conservatives believe, as they say they do, in private property and limited government but also accept certain elements of socialism, it strongly suggests that they are centrists, just like the 20th-century Liberals, rather than some stranger, more interesting mixture of the Left and the Right. Look also at *Six Journeys* and *Radical Tories,* two books by the late journalist and horse breeder Charles Taylor (a Torontonian not to be confused with the Montreal philosopher of the same name), especially the last chapter of *Radical Tories,* in which Taylor meets Robert Stanfield and David Crombie.

Red Tory was a term coined in an attempt to classify a hard-to-classify Canadian philosopher, George Grant, who said that conservatism is now impossible. Since his writings are short and readily available, I will not restate or rehash his views here. Instead, I will elaborate on one practical remark in his *Lament for a Nation.* I will first outline one socioeconomic matter that confirms the impossibility of traditional conservatism in our time, then I will move to another matter that show the feasibility and even the present-day reality of some sort of social-democratic conservatism.

Once upon a time, people believed in the "just price." In fact, people still believe that there are fair and unfair prices, but we are hard put to explain what we mean. The just price was not a pure market price at the equilibrium point where supply and demand curves meet, and it was certainly not a price fixed by a government plan, as in the command economy of the late Soviet Union.

Just price theory in the Middle Ages took into account supply and demand, but it also assumed that there was a sin called greed, which was unjust. How does one measure just price? Partly by custom—a fair wage or fair price was one by which a person could maintain his or her accustomed standard of living, according, that is, to his or her status or condition in life. Built into the theory of just price, then, are stable social relationships and class divisions. We can imagine such a system bringing about an equal standard of living, but even this would be based on a more or less static economy—on not getting ahead. For the past few centuries, we have heavily committed ourselves to instability and to the reasonable hope that most people will get ahead.

In this modern regime, lenders create money, giving credit to entrepreneurs. When entrepreneurs make new things or do things in a new way, they have a temporary monopoly and make an exceptional profit, which would once have been considered an excess profit. Others then catch up by imitating the new thing, the price of which sinks down. The issuance of new credit is viable in the long run only because new things are brought into being to match the new money. But this whole pattern has inflationary and deflationary phases, ups and downs.

Spooky as it seems to many, most money is created by credit, and the whole system has been underpinned by loans to government. This is the most solid credit because the government has the ability to compel people to pay taxes, so it can pay back its lenders. Even when the government has a budget surplus, it never quite pays off all its debt. The main banks lend to other people with the backup of what the government owes them. And the government is supposed to have a reliable schedule for repaying its debts. This system goes back to the Dutch in the 17th century, not simply to J.M. Keynes or Franklin Roosevelt in the 20th.

In short, our whole economy is built upon change and hope and the expectation of gain, qualities that conflict with the ideas of traditional conservatism. It means a cycle of booms and busts, in which some suffer. But to put a stop to it all would be catastrophic.

The sight of a superhighway expressed much the same thing for George Grant. "I never forget returning home [in 1960] to Toronto after many years in Halifax," he said in an interview. "Driving in from the airport, I remember being gripped in the sheer presence of the booming, pulsating place which had arisen since 1945. What did it mean? Where was it going? What had made it? How could there be any stop to its dynamism without disaster, and, yet, without a stop, how could there not be disaster?"

I can't answer those questions, but I want to develop another passage of his here. In *Lament for a Nation*, Grant says that "the failure of socialism to recognize itself as an essentially conservative force has nowhere been so patently obvious as in the confusions of the Canadian socialist movement." What does he mean? This:

There is confusion in the minds of those who believe in socialism and the emancipation of the passions. It

is surely difficult to deny that greed in some form is a desire that belongs to man *qua* man, and is not simply produced by the society of scarcity. If this is so, to emancipate the passions is to emancipate greed. Yet what is socialism, if it is not the use of the government to restrain greed in the name of social good? In actual practice, socialism has always had to advocate inhibition in this respect. In doing so, was it not appealing to the conservative idea of social order against the liberal idea of freedom?

Grant almost makes it sound as though this confusion were just a blunder that could be corrected. What I was getting at a little earlier in writing about the just price is that there is now no criterion for recognizing greed, the sin of avarice, in a dynamic society that invites everyone to get ahead.

There are some elements of "the conservative idea of social order" that we do associate with socialist politicians. In Canada, we are often told that we should thank—or blame—the NDP and its predecessor the CCF for Canada's social programs. Liberals and Conservatives, this partly true story goes, have borrowed or stolen the Left's platform. But this is misleading. The founders of the welfare state were, as Ian Hacking, a deservedly famous Canadian philosopher and historian of science, puts it, "not socialists but preservers of traditional order in new economic conditions."

Otto von Bismarck, the most important founder of social programs, was on the Right. As premier of Prussia in the 1860s, he attempted to bring in government-subsidized insurance for workers. In the 1880s, as Chancellor of Germany, he successfully introduced social insurance for health care, industrial accidents ("workers' compensation"), old age, and disability. No doubt, these policies were partly designed as a way of opposing the Social Democratic Party. (The Social Democrats decided to go along with Bismarck's legislation, while making numerous amendments or introducing rival bills of their own; for example, they said that all contributions should come from employers.) But whatever we may conclude about his motives, Bismarck was not stealing or borrowing a policy from the Social Democrats. Socialism meant, and still means, public ownership of the major means of production and equal distribution of wealth, not schemes like the Canada and Quebec Pension Plans, to which workers, employers, and the government all have to contribute.

Again, such plans were not part of the Labour Party program when Liberals—notably Lloyd George and

Winston Churchill—implemented them in Britain (for the first time in the English-speaking world), a few years before World War I. When social insurance or social security was new, workers themselves (not to mention socialist leaders) had mixed feelings at best about deductions from their pay—about being forced to save. But in time they and the socialist politicians found that these programs are an acquired taste.

Well, you may object, right-wingers may have started these programs, but so what? Let's go back and see what Ian Hacking could mean by describing social insurance as a way of preserving the traditional social order.

Bismarck and others were trying to imitate some elements of the old agricultural society in a world of factories and offices, of big cities.

To put it differently, Bismarck and others were trying to imitate some elements of the old agricultural society in a world of factories and offices, of big cities. Medieval peasants suffered many things, and if we measure their income, they do appear to have been worse off than the factory workers of even the worst days of unregulated industrialization in 19th-century England, not to mention all the depressions and recessions that have followed. But preindustrial peasants could only fall so far. They lived on arable land, and to various extents they had an entitlement to it. Unemployment and retirement were hardly known, so unemployment insurance and old age pensions were not an issue. People had children partly as a kind of pension plan. Most people lived in villages that were essentially extended families, among people who knew them and would hardly let them starve. The landowners had, in theory, an obligation to their tenants, and some of them acted on the theory. People did not think about economic cycles; there were famines, but the peasants at least went hungry together.

To find a contrast to preindustrial life, we don't have to conjure up sordid Dickensian scenes. Today, the vast majority of modern employees have many consumer assets but no productive land and no productive equipment of their own. Many of us live far from our extended families, who are indeed now "extended." We can fall alone and become nameless.

To legally force people to save and to legally force employers to help them save is an attempt to imitate the old order, to provide stability and security through income-earning assets, and, more broadly, to establish a regime of mutual obligation. The welfare state is not primarily about those who cannot provide for themselves; almost every society has provided for the destitute. It is more about protecting or creating a lower middle class and a "respectable" working class.

Arguably, conservatives—assuming for a moment that they exist—are best at managing the welfare state. They invented it, and they do not want to bend it out of shape to make it look more socialist. Unlike liberals and socialists, conservatives are not addicted to stimulating the economy because they are not so keen on change; in their hearts, they do not love economic growth, though they know that we are now committed to it. For generations now, socialists have been strong advocates of the welfare state; in recent decades, most of them have also adopted a distorted version of Keynesian economics, which means that many of them have become advocates of permanent budget deficits. In contrast, conservative prudence can pay for and maintain social programs.

Remember that according to this classification, the Reagan Administration, which ran huge deficits, was liberal. But believing themselves to be conservative, the Reaganites had an uneasy conscience about deficit finance. They told themselves that they had to spend a lot on arms to exhaust Soviet Russia, and that the only way to make the Democratic Congress cut spending was to cut tax revenues and run up interest payments to induce an eventual crisis. More broadly, the spirit of Reaganism was sunny and hopeful, often inclined to wishful thinking—not considered conservative vices.

Remember also that the great socialist parties of the West are older than Keynesianism; the German Social Democrats, in particular, are in touch with an old Bismarckian consensus. And in some countries, voters are more willing to pay for their social security in taxes. A combination of a social policy tradition with self-discipline can make for conservatism in the name of social democracy.

The first two Labour governments in Britain were all too attached to pre-Keynesian economic orthodoxy, in other words to an older liberalism; though the Labour Party was still socialist then, they could not overcome their attachment to the gold standard and balanced-budgeting. Similarly (but more happily) when the Co-operative Commonwealth Federation (CCF) government came to power in Saskatchewan in 1944, Tommy

Douglas postponed bringing in medicare until he could get the public finances in order; the Liberals had left them in a mess. As it turned out, Saskatchewan did not enact medicare until 1961, after Douglas had left for federal politics. But in 1944, popularized Keynesianism was not yet the new orthodoxy, and it may be that the Saskatchewan NDP to this day owes its considerable sanity to older traditions. In the 1980s and early 1990s, one would sometimes hear New Democrats shyly invoke the precedent of Tommy Douglas to suggest that deficits could indeed be troublesome, not just bogeys held up by bondholders or matters of accounting interpretation.

This is a detour from my main argument, in which I have let myself get drawn into using conventional party labels. But it is worth wondering if socialists may have been more conservative when they were staunch socialists with a coherent, comprehensive account of what they actually hoped to accomplish.

I am not trying to present social insurance or social security as a kind of a utopia. The clearest, sharpest criticism of such institutions (as far as I know) is provided in an odd book from 1912, *The Servile State* by Hilaire Belloc. Though remembered now mostly for his *Cautionary Tales for Children*, Belloc was a dissident Liberal MP who favoured redistribution of property. He argued that social insurance was a step backward from a hard-won legal equality of status, toward a new institutionalization of class division.

Conservatives are not much troubled by resemblances to patriarchal authority, by a fair amount of bureaucracy, or by policies that acknowledge inequality of wealth.

Certainly, payroll deductions for CPP, QPP, and unemployment insurance are in some sense a tax that the rich do not have to pay; this is comparable to the tax-free status of French nobles before the Revolution. Income from stocks and bonds and other property is exempt. Salaries, above a certain point, are also exempt. So CEOs, sports heroes, and heirs and heiresses are all largely free of payroll deductions.

To use a phrase common in discussions of health care, social insurance is always two-tier. Put another way, it is paternalistic. But conservatives—in the sense I am using the term—are not much troubled by resemblances to patriarchal authority, by a fair amount of bureaucracy, or by policies that acknowledge inequality of wealth.

In continental Western Europe, the legacy of Bismarck has been generously built upon. Higher payroll costs mean that the cost of employing someone there has risen; therefore, it is likely not coincidental that unemployment is higher than in North America (and often more persistent for individuals). So pure free-marketeers can make the case that social insurance increases poverty, and they make the same kind of objection to the minimum wage (a well-ensconced remnant of the just price). The principle of social insurance is that the state, employers, and employees all have a duty to provide for the misfortunes and old age of employees; one price for this principle is that some people may not get employed at all and consequently are not "socially insured."

It is worth pointing out what social insurance is *not*. This essential part of the welfare state does not exclude what we call welfare, but it is not the same thing. It is also not a guaranteed annual income; that would be a kind of right to live, and social insurance is based on duties, rather than rights. It is not financed through the general tax system, unlike our current medicare scheme, to which we no longer make any specific contributions.

A contributory scheme is not some sort of giant RRSP, and it is still less a self-directed one; RRSPs are a tax shelter designed as an *incentive* to save, rather than as a legal *obligation* to do so. Some people propose replacing the CPP with RRSPs because the return on investment is likely to be better. The conservative reply would be that some people will invest badly and will be reduced to poverty and welfare. In practice, social insurance is rarely insurance; it is not calculated on probabilities of losses. In other words, the CPP is a "pay as you go" plan, and it is not actuarially sound. The Canadian Liberal government in the 1960s was hopeful that economic cycles could be smoothed out, and they apparently did not foresee that efficient birth control would actually reduce the birth rate. The upshot is that requiring one generation to pay for another is very expensive. The CPP/QPP's bite out of paycheques is becoming large, perhaps unbearably so. And to start it all over again on an actuarial basis would be difficult. At present, people want these contributory schemes to survive, but many fear they will not.

In 1976, Ronald Reagan tried to become the Republican candidate for president of the United States, and failed. One major reason was that he lost the Florida primary, in a state with many elderly people. We generally expect the elderly to be conservative, and Mr. Reagan was by all normal accounts the conservative candidate. But modern elderly people are usually retired, and retired people like their public pensions. Reagan had proposed to reduce or possibly do away with the social security system, brought in by President Franklin Delano Roosevelt in the 1930s.

In 1980, Mr. Reagan became president after a campaign in which he was emphatic that he would not disturb social security, and he expressed admiration for FDR. I mention this to illustrate how the purer advocates of self-regulating markets would prefer to let people save for themselves—or not, if they choose. These classical liberals whom we call conservatives accept institutions like the CPP and QPP as a necessary or prudent concession. But conservatives—if they exist—would favour obligatory saving as something desirable and practicable. To socialists, social insurance and the whole welfare state are at best a transition.

This brings us back to the present range of political parties. What could a reclassification of the spectrum tell us about our own situation and the current state of conservative parties in Canada? About the United Alternative? Since this essay has set out to clarify a distinction (between conservative and neo-conservative), it tends naturally against "uniting the Right," rather than toward searching for a new, unifying basis. The Reform Party is true to its name: as in England and Canada in the 19th century, Reformers are liberals, with an underlying nonconformist or sectarian Protestantism. (Fundamentalism is hardly more than name-calling.) Preston Manning's party arose in large part from a reaction against the Meech Lake Accord, in defence of the Canadian Charter of Rights and Freedoms. Being liberals, Reformers accept the priority of rights over obligations. (Others no doubt interpret the Charter differently, but genuine conservatives would oppose the Charter itself. The disagreements among Reformers, Liberals, and politically correct postmodern radicals are quarrels within the liberal family. This is by no means to say that they are foolish or unimportant.) Being liberals, Reformers are individualists, suspicious of nationality and community, and clearly opposed to complicated nationality, including nations within nations, distinct societies, and Aboriginal self-government. Preston Manning apparently believes that the people of Quebec must either want to stay in Canada or just leave.

Reformers want to apply abstract principles to politics: a comparatively pure free market, a pure democracy that expresses the will of the people, and equality of the provinces as represented in the Senate. Tories accept the reality of nations and mixed, ambivalent allegiances, and they do not believe that "ordinary people" are more virtuous than politicians. They adhere to parliamentary representation and to constitutional tradition generally, not to delegate democracy and frequent referendums.

Tories accept the reality of nations and mixed, ambivalent allegiances, and they do not believe that "ordinary people" are more virtuous than politicians.

In some ways, the Reform Party is more like the NDP than like the Tories or the Liberals. The saying goes that you go to Tory conventions to get drunk, to Liberal conventions to get laid, and to NDP conventions to get a thick file of policy papers. Reform clearly belongs to the third category; they take policy resolutions very seriously. On the one hand, their party is doctrinaire, attached to clear (not to say simplistic) principles and policies. On the other hand, it aspires to be so democratic as not to be constrained by dogma: it is designed as a consciousness-raising forum of ordinary people, not quite as a political party. Thomas Flanagan in *Waiting for the Wave,* testifies to Manning's desire to emulate the Civic Forum founded by Václav Havel and others, not as a party but as an society to discuss and prepare politics after communism. If one reads C.B. Macpherson's *Democracy in Alberta,* one sees that this is no quirk of Manning's, but rather a long tradition in Alberta, dating back to the Non-Partisan League started in 1916. The league tended toward one-party government: if the party is an expression of all the people, why present a choice of parties to the people? A non-partisan party is a contradiction in terms.

Some long-time and grassroots Reformers resent Rick Anderson, an Ottawa lobbyist and former Liberal turned Reform strategist, and blame him for various compromises. But he was attracted to Reform because of his adherence to party democracy, a cause he had been interested in for years—that is, to democracy within a political party, and to the use of internal party activities as a form of participatory democracy. Even Anderson's father-in-law, Blair Williams, a former National Director of the Liberal Party, on the far Left of that party, has expressed some admiration for Reform on these grounds.

Like the NDP, Reform praises itself for being a new party and offers a New Canada. This is plainly a progressive party, not a party of tradition like the Conservatives or indeed the Liberals.

Reform is plainly a progressive party, not a party of tradition like the Conservatives or indeed the Liberals.

At the recent United Alternative conference, Quebec nationalists such as Jean Allaire were greeted warmly, in spite of Reform's history of opposition to Quebec nationalism. This is because the cause of smaller government is associated with decentralization or devolution. But such an alliance is less hopeful than the Meech Lake Accord was in its day. Canadian national feeling does not favour a weakened federal government. The Tory party, by contrast, has sometimes been able to appeal to both Canadian and Québécois national feeling. However, it is unclear whether it will easily recover to do so again.

What about Reform and the welfare state? The 1993 Reform program called for social programs to be delivered through the income tax system—a plan that is partly designed to get rid of a lot of social workers and civil servants, but perhaps more importantly is technocratic, in keeping with Manning's career as a management consultant. Though Reform has never specifically called for winding up the Canada Pension Plan, the party shows no particular attachment to contributory schemes.

As for the federal Progressive Conservative Party, it needs to justify its existence by rebuilding a broad coalition and by showing that it has something to offer that is distinct from the other parties. These tasks will not be easy. One of the less obvious possibilities is that the Liberals will become a centrist conservative party, absorbing moderate Tories and opening up an opportunity for the NDP on the Liberals' left flank.

Earlier, I rashly spoke of a social-democratic conservatism that would be a mixture of genuine Left and Right, not just a fence-sitting centrism. But if any party were to adopt principles and practice of the kind sketched here, it would probably be a centrist party such as the Liberals or the Conservatives, not a strange-bedfellow alliance of extremes.

Some readers will accuse me of thinking that contributory schemes are a panacea, the be-all and end-all. So I repeat that they are presented here as an example of the possibility that conservatism has some specific practical meaning in our times.

A stronger criticism of this essay would be that I have swerved from saying that almost nobody is a conservative to saying that almost everybody is. There is, after all, widespread support for the Canada Pension Plan. Even in the allegedly neo-conservative United States, there is widespread support for social security. Well, maybe almost everybody *is* implicitly conservative—and explicitly liberal, in which case this essay amounts to an attempt to articulate some principles, probably centrist ones.

I complained earlier about the vagueness of certain strains of conservatism. Here, as I close, I will partly recant: a temperament, a spirit, even a principle can be vague or diffuse, but by being diffuse it can pervade many persons and things and run deep, too deep to be quite grasped. Still, specific institutions can be grasped and do matter.

Though perhaps there is widespread conservatism, the present range of parties does not express it well. But it cannot just be an accident (to slightly misquote George Grant) that socialists fail to see that they are really conservatives.

Though perhaps there is widespread conservatism, the present range of parties does not express it well.

Many now say, with much truth, that the Left–Right distinction is out of date or inadequate, that it does not correspond to various important disagreements. Yet when it comes to elections—and to the looser tribal formations in public opinion—we still group ourselves into Left and Right. Why?

There are stronger forces than thoughts of the kind that led to the foundation of the welfare state. On the one hand, there are compelling, impassioning principles that move us to strive for the greatest possible equality or freedom, or both; on the other hand, there are economic needs and interests that push and pull everybody, businesses and public sector employees alike. Classes still exist. But, from time to time, there are and will be opportunities for principled and practical statecraft.

Terms & Concepts

just price theory
mechanical structure of government
organic structure of government

patriarchal authority
Red Tories
social insurance

throne-and-altar Toryism

Questions

1. How does conservatism differ from neo-conservatism and the politics of the Reform Party?

2. How does Owen place social democratic policies on a conservative foundation?

3. Conservatives see at least some parts of the welfare state as the preservation of order in new industrial social conditions. Does this confirm or challenge Trimble's analysis of feminism and the welfare state in Chapter 10?

4. Conservatives favour an organic over a mechanical conception of society. What does this mean?

5. What advice, if any, does this article contain for Joe Clark in his plans to rebuild the Progressive Conservative Party of Canada?

9

Introduction to *What's Right: The New Conservatism and What It Means for Canada*

David Frum

Editors' Note

Liberal political thinkers consider the facilitation of individual liberty and self-fulfillment one of the highest goals of a political order. Historically, this belief has led them to support private property rights, economic freedom, and a relatively free market. Under these conditions, people are able to make unfettered decisions about their own interests, and the resultant allocation of economic resources tends to advance the larger principles of efficiency and social utility. Liberals assumed that individual citizens would exercise personal restraint and community obligations to maintain the conditions for market life. If government is to be restricted to law enforcement, defence, and the minimal provision of public goods, citizens need to assume responsibility for social order and the care of the young and helpless. Furthermore, citizens need to be self-disciplined to delay the gratification of immediate desires in order to participate effectively in the capitalist order.

It is becoming increasingly evident, according to some observers, that "market liberalism is in its workings ineluctably subversive of tradition and community."[1] The social and moral underpinnings of a market order, in this view, are eroded by constant advertising that appeals to the satisfaction of momentary desires and, in general, by the veneration of individualism. As a result, market liberalism undermines the conditions for its own functioning.

The welfare state arose in part to ameliorate some of the corrosive side effects of liberal market behaviours, as the essay by Gerald Owen, Chapter 8 in this volume, suggests. But this solution seems to have its own limitations. Critics charge that by insuring people against the vagaries of life, such as unemployment and sickness, the welfare state actually removes people's incentive to find and keep jobs and stay healthy. Accordingly, the welfare state creates more demand for its services and becomes unsus-

tainable. An influential school of thought, then, contends that liberal markets and the welfare state both fail to sustain the prerequisites of a liberal economic order.

Neo-conservatism arose in response to these new conditions, as well as to the threats communism allegedly posed to liberal societies in the 1960s. But as this essay indicates, neo-conservatives put the blame for society's moral decay not on the market, but on the interventionist, paternal state, whose public policies create dependency and moral permissiveness. A new political formula is needed, Frum argues, one that combines market principles with older bourgeois virtues such as thrift, restraint, self-reliance, community-mindedness, fidelity, and moderation. In Frum's view, these virtues, which have been systematically undermined by the state, will assume their rightful place when we see the nanny-welfare state for what it is.

---

1. John Gray, *Enlightenment's Wake: Politics and Culture at the Close of the Modern Age* (London: Routledge, 1995), 97.

If I had to pick the moment I began calling myself a conservative, it would be the summer of 1975. I was fourteen going on fifteen, and I was working—improbable as this is going to sound—as a volunteer for an NDP candidate for the provincial legislature. Not that I considered myself a New Democrat—or anything else. My political views at the beginning of that summer were still hazy, to put it charitably. But the candidate was a friend of my parents', and I had wanted to watch a political campaign close up. Somehow my parents persuaded the candidate to let me hang around his office, fetch sandwiches, type letters, and generally subtract from the efficiency of the struggle for socialism in west Toronto.

The campaign's headquarters was a 45-minute bus and subway ride from my parents' house. I devoted the resulting reading time to a book that my mother had given me: the first volume of Aleksandr Solzhenitsyn's *Gulag Archipelago*. The horror of Soviet communism burst upon me like a bomb. A kind of evangelical fervor gripped me: everybody had to know about this! (Remember, I was fourteen.) I couldn't accost my parents—they'd already read the book. I couldn't accost my school friends—it was summer holiday. So I went to work on my campaign colleagues.

Theoretically, of course, there's no reason why one couldn't be a fully paid-up member of the NDP and also a vehement anticommunist. But as I quickly discovered, very few of my fellow-volunteers were much influenced by this interesting ideological possibility. I soon became an office nuisance. Quarrels erupted whenever I hoved into view. Eventually the office manager sat me down for a quiet little chat. I didn't finish out the campaign.

One of the other volunteers in the office liked to sing to himself the old trade-union anthem, "Which Side Are You On?" By the end of that summer, I knew.

Back then, of course, it was rather an eccentric thing for a teenager to be "right wing" (as my co-workers on the 1975 campaign termed it). In the Toronto where I grew up, everyone who mattered agreed that there was something inherently un-Canadian about conservatism. Canada, it was once painstakingly explained to me, was not a *nation-state*, like Ireland or France. It was a *state-nation*, like the Austro-Hungarian Empire, assembled in defiance of logic by a strong central government. The stronger that government, the stronger the country. Weaken the government, and Canada would fly apart like the Habsburg domains in 1918. As for those of us who wanted to restrain the expansion of government, we were not merely cold and heartless, etc., etc.; we stood accused of subversion.

> *All hailed Big Government and moral permissiveness—in a word, liberalism—as the political fundaments that defined Canada.*

In those days—really, until very recently—Canada possessed an official ideology in more or less the same way that Britain possesses an established church. Not everybody adhered to it, but it set the tone of polite society. The textbooks studied in school, the programs broadcast on television, the news published in the papers, the speeches bellowed at election time, all hailed Big Government and moral permissiveness—in a word, liberalism—as the political fundaments that defined Canada. Doubters who wondered whether it really made sense to build railways to nowhere, to regulate the songs radio stations could play, to outlaw private medicine, to invite fishermen and loggers to spend three-quarters of the year on unemployment insurance, were dismissed as reactionary skinflints, unwilling to pay the necessary "price of being Canadian."

Suddenly that all seems a very long time ago. The doubters have been winning the day for nearly a decade, spectacularly so over the past two or three years. Increasingly, Canadians—and young Canadians in particular—have been wondering, "To be a patriot, do I really have to be such a sucker?" … No, of course you don't.

> *If it takes medicare, the CBC, and cheap tuition to distinguish us from the Americans or the Mexicans, how in the world are we to explain the generations of self-confident Canadians who lived without any of these things?*

Social programs are all very well, in moderation. But they hardly constitute a national identity. Medicare did not climb the cliffs to the Plains of Abraham in General Wolfe's knapsack. We copied it from Britain three years after we imported the Twist. The Dominion of Canada antedates the oldest of its social programs by nearly three-quarters of a century. If it takes medicare, the CBC, and cheap tuition to distinguish us from the Americans or the Mexicans, how in the world are we to explain the generations of self-confident Canadians who lived without any of these things?

In truth, it is not the ethic of personal responsibility and limited government that we call conservatism that betrays Canada's national character. On the contrary, it is the statism and moral weakness of the past thirty years that have traduced the real nature of our country. A country whose people settled some of the world's bleakest terrain without even the gift of a free bag of seed—did these people need welfarism to provide them with their nationhood? A country that left 100,000 of its sons dead on the world's battlefields between 1914 and 1953—was this nation well served by the palaver that authentic Canadians are a uniquely peaceable lot?

Has any group of self-proclaimed patriots ever felt so little interest in the actual traditions of their country as did the liberal nationalists of the 1960s and 1970s? Is it not bizarre to convene symposia on the national identity while systematically wiping away all traces of the past from the nation's currency, its post office boxes, even its flagpoles? Our liberal nationalists celebrated a Canada that never existed. The Canada that sang "The Maple Leaf Forever," that hanged Louis Riel, that listened to black-clad priests denounce the theory of evolution, that erected statues to Queen Victoria, that volunteered for the trenches, that shunned the New Deal reforms of Franklin Delano Roosevelt, that made a hero of Soviet defector Igor Gouzenko—*that* Canada, historical Canada, was erased from our textbooks, its monuments destroyed, its achievements disparaged. Instead of taking pride in the construction of a vast, rich, and free nation, we were instead—as Margaret Atwood argued in a hugely influential 1972 book—humbly to think of ourselves as "survivors."

Is it not bizarre to convene symposia on the national identity while systematically wiping away all traces of the past from the nation's currency, its post office boxes, even its flagpoles?

This disparity, between what we are and what we were told we are, has led to something close to national schizophrenia. Canada is a big, rich, North American nation, where people live in suburbs, drive to work, shop in malls, invest their money in mutual funds, listen to country music, and resent paying taxes. But watch a Canadian movie, read a Canadian novel, flip through most Canadian magazines, or turn on the news, and you'll see a different country: a poor, struggling hinter-

land of the American empire, where people live in outports, work for the government if they work at all, collect groceries from food banks, listen to folk singers, and enjoy paying taxes.

Actual Canada began to make itself heard in 1988, when it swatted down the self-proclaimed nationalists to vote for free trade with the United States.
NAFTA

What the political convulsions of the 1990s tell us, however, is that our schizophrenia may at last have found a cure. Like a nervous middle-aged man in a James Thurber story, official Canada has rounded a corner, only to bump into the actual Canada heading in the opposite direction. Actual Canada began to make itself heard in 1988, when it swatted down the self-proclaimed nationalists to vote for free trade with the United States. It was heard from again in 1992, when it defeated the Charlottetown accord—an agreement that would have perversely inscribed a further dose of socialism into a constitution that already regarded welfare, but not private property, as a fundamental right. And again in 1993, when outraged Westerners crumpled up the Progressive Conservative Party and replaced it with the steelier Reform Party. And once more when voters in Alberta, Ontario, and New Brunswick voted overwhelmingly for provincial governments that explicitly promised dramatic cuts in spending. Perhaps the best way to understand the politics of our country today is to think of them not as some radical transformation of Canada, but as a simple rediscovery of a country that was there all along.

Detractors of this old-new Canada—defenders of the liberal Canada that now feels so beleaguered—complain that the coming era of smaller government threatens to sever the bonds of community so that a few greedy individuals can indulge their lust for gain. If true, that charge would sting. But is it true?

In a disused corner of my local library, a puppet stage gathers dust. "Do you ever perform shows for the children?" we once asked the librarian. "Not any more," she answered bitterly—"it's the cutbacks." The city, you see, used to send round a professional puppeteer once a month. Now it doesn't.

So if, by the weakening of "community," you mean the loss of puppet shows performed by government employees, then yes, I suppose, the shrinkage of government stands guilty as charged.

where's? Social Capital. Civic engagement

civic

But I'd like to know something else. When *we* were children, the puppet shows at the local libraries were performed by library volunteers—people from the neighbourhood who loved reading and loved children. What happened to them? How is it that so elementary an act of community spirit as an afternoon's amusement at the local library can collapse once the political authorities cease to pay for it? Alexis de Tocqueville suggested the answer in *Democracy in America*: "There are countries … where the native considers himself as a kind of settler, indifferent to the fate of the spot he inhabits. The greatest changes are effected there without his concurrence, and (unless chance may have apprised him of the event) without his knowledge; nay, more, the condition of his village, the police of his street, the repairs of the church or the parsonage, do not concern him; for he looks upon all these things as unconnected with himself and as the property of a powerful stranger whom he calls the government."

decline in Social Capital

As government grows, the ambit for real community shrinks. Conservatives want to roll back the state not because they envision human beings as selfish individualists who must be left alone to make as much money as they can, but because they see the functions of real communities being usurped by overweening governments—a usurpation that ends with the citizens ultimately unable to do anything for themselves without the aid of the central authorities. To an endless refrain of "We need more funding!" the job of putting on puppet shows at the library passes from my neighbours and myself to some municipal or provincial employee and his supervisors. And—who knows?—from there someday to Public Service Alliance of Canada workers at the federal Ministry of Mimes, Clowns and Puppets.

As government grows, the ambit for real community shrinks.

Nor is that the worst of it. Our very understanding of the meaning of community has been degraded. Canadians take shockingly little interest in their immediate environs. Municipal politics is barely reported, and voter turnout in local elections seldom rises much above twenty-five percent. The parent-teacher associations so prevalent in the United States ignite very little enthusiasm here, largely because our schools receive their money from bureaucrats who can ignore parental preferences with impunity. The civic pride that inspired pri-

decline in votes

vate citizens in the United States and Britain to donate their money and artworks to found great museums, libraries, and universities never seemed to flourish here. Never mind the Metropolitan Museum or Oxford; Canada has nothing to compare with Chicago's Art Institute or Atlanta's Emory University. We have learned to transfer the community's responsibilities to the government, and we have ceased to understand the difference between the two. We are *not*, in fact, a highly community-spirited people; we are merely a highly taxed people.

It is the expansion of government that has accelerated the decay of our old "obligation culture."

Having arrogated to itself the functions of real communities, modern Canadian government has proceeded to attack the very preconditions of communities' existence: the moral norms that they enforce on their members. An old adage tells us that Spain suffered arbitrary government for so many centuries because the Spanish failed to understand that "freedom" entailed something more than a certificate declaring that *this* Spaniard was free to do anything he wished to. Self-governing communities demand a very high degree of personal restraint from their members. Many people fear that this spirit of self-restraint is weakening in Canada. If so, it's not because of free markets: markets encourage self-restraint, a virtue essential to economic success. Nor is it because there's too little government spending. We imposed many more restraints upon ourselves in 1965, before the great expansion of government, than we do today. It is the expansion of government that has accelerated the decay of our old "obligation culture," as David Gelertner calls it in his wonderful book *1939: The Lost World of the Fair*, to an "entitlement culture"; from an era when people said "I must" to one in which they say "I want."

One small but telling example. Toronto formerly forbade women to remove their tops in public. Not an unreasonable rule, one would think. But a passel of feminist activists launched a court challenge against the ordinance, and an obliging court struck it down as a violation of the Charter guarantee of sexual equality. A legal revolution? Not exactly. Toronto's women have not yet made much use of their new freedom; the parks do not swarm with topless sunbathers.

But the significance of the court decision extends far beyond the single law at issue. One of the thousands of little rules and conventions—the vast majority of them unlegislated—that maintain Toronto as a pleasant place to live was set aside at the whim of a single judge. Think of that the next time someone agues that "capitalism" dissolves community. Most of the time, the acid eating away at the restraints and rules of civilization is modern liberal government—in the form of judges and human rights commissioners operating in the service of grievance-bearers with ever-expanding lists of claims on the rest of society.

Yes, corporations can undermine community standards too. I dislike it as much as the next parent when Calvin Klein puts up a quasi-pornographic billboard on my street corner. Writers like Daniel Bell and the late Christopher Lasch tell us something of the truth when they warn that a marketplace undisciplined by morality can inflict real harm. Advertisers may attempt to exploit pervasive feelings of entitlement.

But it is our public policies that *foment* those feelings. In our heroic—but alas, inevitably futile—determination to use the state to wipe away every human tear, we have inculcated in ourselves a spooky certainty that failure everywhere and always reflects on society. Are you poor? Ignorant? Unhappy? The fault is not yours, but everyone else's—and you have a right to demand that some large new social program come into existence to redress the fault at once.

We have inculcated in ourselves a spooky certainty that failure everywhere and always reflects on society. Are you poor? Ignorant? Unhappy? The fault is not yours, but everybody else's.

Flip open the report of Ontario's *1994 Royal Commission on Learning* for a spectacular example:

There must not be the slightest doubt that this Commission shares the concern, the desperation even, of the black community, about the under-achievement of black students as a group. We can hardly stress too strongly our conviction that the school system must better accommodate the needs of black children and young black men and women. Schools must become more inclusive, staff must become more representative of our society as a whole, courses must reflect the perspectives and contributions of minority groups.

But even that is not enough….

Black students are performing poorly, the commissioners report, *and therefore society is failing*! The possibility that the blame for poor performance lies with the students or their parents is simply inadmissible. That would be "blaming the victim." The possibility that we shouldn't be tracking the performance of racial groups—that we should applaud individual success without measuring the skin colour of the successful—is inadmissible too. That would be averting our eyes from a "crying social need."

I don't doubt that the educrats responsible for producing the Royal Commission report regard the critics who oppose their project for reengineering the schools in the name of racial equality as opponents of "community." But isn't community spirit attacked far more viciously and directly by promoting racial aggrievement? Isn't community responsibility for schooling certain to be the first casualty of orders from Central Education HQ?

Newcomers to a country tend to respect the rules of their new home. They intend to be good citizens. They hope to prosper here, and they begin full of confidence that they can. But once here, respected authority figures tell them to blame all the inevitable difficulties and disappointments of life in a strange country on the bigotry and unfairness of the old inhabitants, and to look to—and vote for!—an ever-expanding state as their only protection against the enemies that supposedly lurk all around them.

The accusation that limitations upon government threaten to sap the strength of our communities is diametrically opposed to the truth. Under our present circumstances, reductions in the arrogance and ambition of government are the very first steps that must be taken by those who hope to strengthen and revitalize communities. The late C.B. Macpherson, a Marxist political theorist at the University of Toronto, coined the intentionally unattractive phrase "possessive individualism" to describe the democratic capitalist societies he disliked. But contemporary Canadian conservatism is only incidentally concerned with acquisition, and defends individualism only within limits. At its core, conservatism is a doctrine dedicated to the vindication of a good society—and to the preservation of that society from the ideologies and interest groups bent on destroying it.

Terms & Concepts

actual Canada	liberalism	self-restraint
Big Government	modern liberal government	statism
community	moral permissiveness	
conservatism	official Canada	

Questions

1. Frum argues that government is opposed to community. How so?

2. Are people fundamentally risk takers or risk avoiders?

3. In what ways can government be seen to encourage moral permissiveness? On what bases can this view be criticized?

4. How does Frum's conservatism compare with Owen's?

5. Frum draws a distinction between official Canada and actual Canada. Explain.

10

The Politics of Feminism: An Introduction

Linda Trimble

Editors' Note

In the following article written for this volume, Linda Trimble argues that feminist advances in recent decades have stimulated a misinformed backlash against both feminism and those who identify themselves as feminists. She responds to this backlash, evaluates feminist achievements in politics and political theory, and suggests what challenges for women still lie ahead.

Feminists contend that contemporary gender inequality is rooted in patriarchy, which has been entrenched for millennia. It has shaped human values, beliefs, culture, religion, institutions, and, in the last couple of centuries, even science, to perpetuate male domination. The earliest philosophers ranked men above women, arguing that

women's inferiority was grounded in nature. Organized religion has also, for the most part, relegated women to inferior status. Indeed, the study of history often involves exploring major civilizations through the actions of their almost invariably male rulers, with the help of records kept by male scribes according to what they saw as important, and then interpreted by mostly male historians.[1] Feminists reject the view that the preeminence of men must be part of the natural order and provide evidence to the contrary.[2]

The problem in understanding feminist critiques is one common to all ideologies: the need to separate premises based on assumptions (e.g., women are more nurtur-

ing than men) from those based on facts (e.g., women bear children) and then to evaluate the conventions derived from both. This task is made difficult by the pervasiveness of the conventions. They are around us everywhere, from the wedding veil to the chador.

Some progress has been made, but tasks still to be accomplished by feminists and their supporters are complicated by the shifting ground of the future. As states shrink (see Richard Rosecrance's article, Chapter 5) and globalization shifts many areas of former state responsibility to the international level, the battles already won by feminists may have to be fought again in this new and unfamiliar forum.

◆ ◆ ◆

INTRODUCTION

◆ ◆ ◆

On the first meeting of my women and politics class, I ask my students whether or not they identify themselves

as feminists. Generally, about half the class is comfortable with the term because they see feminism as a positive, proactive, and vital social movement. But the others are reluctant to adopt the label because, in popular discourse, feminists are portrayed as man-hating, anti-fam-

---

1. Germaine Greer makes a compelling case of the historical suppression of female artists *in The Obstacle Race: The Fortunes of Women Painters and Their Work* (New York: Farrar Strauss Giroux, 1979).
2. For example, see Rianne Eisler, *The Chalice and The Blade: Our History, Our Future* (San Francisco: Harper and Row, 1988).

ily, unfeminine, and usually lesbian radicals.[1] Some scholars, politicians, and journalists describe feminism as a socially and politically destructive instrument of indoctrination which blames all of women's troubles on men. Male students are unsure whether men are "allowed" to be feminists. Students sense that these characterizations of feminism are homophobic, unfounded, and misleading, but they don't want to call themselves feminists and thus be (mistakenly) seen as anti-male. Many of the students in the class adopt an "I'm not a feminist, but ..." stance; they avoid the label while identifying with goals of the women's movement, such as equal rights, recognition of women's unpaid work, and an end to discrimination based on sex, ethnicity, ability, and sexual orientation.

Male students are unsure whether men are "allowed" to be feminists.

My students are reflecting the backlash against feminism in contemporary Canadian society, a backlash so extensive that, in 1989, a prominent political journalist declared feminism "the new F-word."[2] As we enter the new millennium, women's groups are deemed special-interest groups that supposedly want their marginal interests imposed on ordinary Canadians. Feminism-bashing is increasingly popular, even among those who call themselves feminists. Donna Laframboise, a columnist with a women's studies degree, claims that the women's movement is increasingly plagued by anti-male hostility, extremism, and intolerance of viewpoints other than its own.[3] It is hardly surprising to find that male and female students alike are confused and ambivalent about feminism.

This chapter tries to clear up some of the confusion. I begin with an overview of feminism, which is no easy task since feminist thought and practice are complex and diverse. The first section of the chapter defines feminism and the basic concepts important to understanding different feminist theories. Anti-feminist ideas, such as the myth of feminist orthodoxy and the notion that feminists have won the so-called battle of the sexes, are described in the second section. The third part of the chapter provides a brief overview of the ways in which feminism has influenced Canadian political life and public policy, and it highlights the work that remains to be done. I conclude with some thoughts about the future of feminism in an era of globalization, the shrinking state, and new information technologies.

WHAT IS FEMINISM?

◆ ◆ ◆

Feminism is, at one and the same time, a constantly evolving and internally complex ideology (or system of ideas), an epistemological framework (that is, a way of understanding how human beings know, who the knowers are, and what constitutes genuine knowledge), and a social movement (a constellation of diverse citizen groups pressing for social, cultural, economic, and political change).[4] The ideology, the epistemology, and the sociopolitical action arising from the feminist movement reinforce, challenge, and change one another because of the necessary interaction between ideas and their practice in everyday life (praxis). In short, feminism provides ways of looking at and understanding human societies, these ideas fuel a transformative social movement with significant political consequences, and the movement in turn generates challenges and alternatives to feminist theories. Defining what feminism is, however, does not help us understand what it involves. What ideas underpin feminist thought and action, and why are they important agents of political change?

At heart, feminism is concerned with gender, patriarchy, and oppression. Gender is the social construction of sex characteristics such that being male or female helps determine a person's social, economic, cultural, and political status. Gender is what society does or does not make of sex distinctions. In other words, biology determines whether a person is labelled male or female, but much of what it means to be male or female is socially determined. Societies design gender codes—different roles, characteristics, resources, norms, and expectations—for men and women because of their sex. For instance, that women menstruate until menopause is a function of their sex; that societies have treated menstruation as a taboo, even to the extent of segregating menstruating women, is a function of gender codes. Gender codes form part of our taken-for-granted world. We expect girls and women to look and act "feminine," and any deviation from social norms of femininity, like Hollywood actor Julia Roberts's decision to attend the premier of her latest movie sporting unshaven armpits, provokes comment and even condemnation.[5] Gender codes are not unidimensional and unshifting; indeed, they change over time and are informed by the social construction of ethnicity, sexual orientation, social class, and physical or mental ability. That Canadian society prescribes different roles, rules, possibilities, and expectations for upper-class heterosexual white women than it does for women who do not fit this mould is illustrated by the experience of Judith Zelman, a disabled woman who mobilizes in a wheelchair. Zelman was disturbed by the consternation expressed by co-workers and friends when she announced her pregnancy. As she wrote, in a *Globe and Mail* column,

> Why do people have such a hard time dealing with disability and pregnancy together? Is it because the disabled as a group are seen as asexual or childlike and are thus not supposed to reproduce? Is it because people are afraid we are irresponsible and unable to care for our children properly?... Whatever the reason, I am writing this to ask that the next time you see a visibly pregnant woman with a disability, treat her just as you would an able-bodied pregnant woman.[6]

---

*Gender codes form part of our
taken-for-granted world.*

Gender codes, like the continued expectation that women will perform the majority of domestic and nurturing tasks, are constructed both discursively (through discourse—language, mass media, propaganda, and other communications) and materially (through material and physical realities such as threats of physical harm, individual and state coercion, economic necessity, or lack of mobility). Contemporary North American mass media construct an idealistic image of the "supermom," as epitomized by a 1998 Coca-Cola movie theatre advertisement featuring a curvaceous, caped superhero for whom saving the world was secondary to rushing home with bottles of Coke for her daughter and son. While discourses of popular culture reify the (white, privileged, attractive) mother, material realities literally cast many women into the role of supermoms struggling to manage a double shift of full-time work in the paid labour force plus full-time unpaid work in the home. Many more women cannot find paid work, are underemployed, or live below the poverty line.

As these examples of gender coding indicate, the social construction of gender is far from neutral. In fact,

an examination of gender norms, roles, and rules within any society reveals patriarchy, or male privilege and female subordination. Patriarchal ideas and practices have changed over time, and patriarchy is expressed differently in different cultures, but at a minimum the concept means rule by men in both the private realm of home and family and the public sphere of the economy, formal politics, organized religion, and other non-domestic pursuits. Patriarchy is male dominance of sexual, social, cultural, economic, and political relations; in patriarchal societies, men have more power than women and greater access to what is valued by the social group.[7] In patriarchal societies, male dominance is institutionalized (that is, a feature of key social, political, economic, and cultural institutions) and normalized (assumed to be natural and functional). For example, the fact that Canadian legislators are predominantly male was considered unworthy of comment until recently. Since male politicians are considered the norm, elected women in Canada are subjected to media scrutiny that highlights their femininity (that is, their *difference* from their male colleagues) by focusing on their personal relationships, domestic skills, wardrobe, hair, makeup, and weight.[8]

Male dominance of economic and political power relations is accompanied, in patriarchal societies, by control of knowledge. The production of knowledge includes the framing of what can possibly be true, who can know it, and how truth is to be represented. As feminist philosopher Simone de Beauvoir put it, "Representation of the world, like the world itself, is the work of men; they describe it from their own point of view, which they confuse with absolute truth."[9] The exclusion of women from the public sphere and their confinement to the household was based in part on knowledge claims, namely the assumption of male superiority and female inferiority. Until this century, political, scientific, and intellectual elites accepted as a universal truth that women were the weaker sex, by nature designed principally to perform domestic and nurturing tasks. This patriarchal epistemological framework characterized women as incapable of being objective "knowers," thereby denying women a role in knowledge production. Contemporary mainstream epistemology claims to be gender neutral and universally applicable, when in fact it is masculinist (constructed from the standpoint of typically white men). For instance, until recently a great deal of medical research used only adult males in trials of prescription medicines; the results were assumed to apply equally to women. Feminist theorists show how masculinist epistemology upholds patriarchal ideas, institutions, and practices.

The oppression of women is central to the maintenance of patriarchal power relations. Feminist philosopher Marilyn Frye defines oppression as "a system of interrelated barriers and forces which reduce, immobilize and mould people who belong to a certain group, and effect their subordination to another group."[10] The idea that women as a group are oppressed by men as a group, however, is an oversimplified characterization of feminist thought. For one thing, feminist scholars and practitioners are increasingly sensitive to the fact that women's oppression often transcends the category "women" to include subordination based on ethnicity, sexual orientation, disability, class, and other social groupings. In other words, many women confront multiple forms of oppression. Many Aboriginal women, for example, experience the devastating impact of gender, cultural, and class discrimination:

> They are often single mothers without the benefit of culturally appropriate child care programs. They and their children are often the subject of sexual abuse and "unconscionable levels of domestic violence." They have a disproportionately high rate of incarceration in correctional institutions, and they still have no matrimonial property rights on reserves if their marriages break down.[11]

A second difficulty is that recognizing these various and overlapping sources of oppression leads to the conclusion that, in some circumstances, certain *women* may be in a position to subordinate men or other women. Economically privileged women may use their wealth to exploit the labour of lower-class men and women, for instance, by employing migrant workers, contracting the services of working-class women as surrogate mothers, or hiring ethnic minority women as live-in domestic servants.

The third problem is that the word *oppression* implies a constant and unremitting state of passive victimhood. Many feminists wish to celebrate women's tenacity, courage, victories, and even power without denying the reality of women's continued oppression.[12] Still, the recognition of "power feminism,"[13] as journalist Naomi Wolf calls it, and the many advancements in women's rights lead observers to say that women are no longer oppressed (we will explore this argument later in the chapter). Feminists recognize that surmounting oppression is more than an issue of rights. In sum, feminist theorists and practitioners have concluded that

relations of domination and subordination are complex, variable, and constantly shifting. Because there is no one true way of understanding the creation of gender codes through patriarchy and oppression, feminist thought is, of necessity, diverse.

No feminist orthodoxy exists, despite the frequent assertions of critics of feminism. While, in general, a feminist perspective offers "explanations for the pervasiveness of relationships of domination and subordination between men and women, for different perceptions of the relevance of class, racial, and ethnic differences among women, and for a range of understandings about the changes required to redress exploitative and oppressive relationships,"[14] variants of feminist thought offer different, and sometimes competing, explanations for these phenomena. There are many ideas about the origins of inequality, how oppression can be eliminated, and what kinds of social arrangements should replace patriarchal societies.[15] Contemporary scholarship describes a panoply of feminisms, including liberal, socialist, radical, Marxist, maternal, left-wing, psychoanalytic, Black, anti-racist, lesbian, separatist, cultural, French/postmodern, equal rights, poststructuralist, ecological, and now cyberfeminist. For the sake of clarity, I will briefly outline the most commonly cited or applied feminist theories, then provide an example of how theory informs practical politics.

Most contemporary examinations of feminism include liberal, radical, socialist, and postmodern variants of feminist thought.[16] To summarize these strands briefly, they must be stripped of their complexity, so what follows is an extremely oversimplified account of these feminist theories. Liberal feminism is perhaps the most familiar approach because most people identify feminism with claims for equal rights. Liberal feminists consider women's oppression to originate from unequal treatment, namely denial of access to equal opportunity in education, politics, and employment—in sum, an absence of basic equality rights associated with citizenship. It was not until this century that women were granted the right to vote, stand for political office, sign contracts, stay in certain paid jobs after marriage, join the medical and legal professions, obtain loans from financial institutions in their own names, and so on. Denied the opportunity to become free, self-actualizing individuals, women form dependency relationships with men. For liberal feminists, the solution lies in achieving equal civil and political rights, judicial fairness, and free choices for women. This means rooting out bias and discrimination in the workplace. Also, gender socialization must be changed in order for girls to recognize the available range of educational and labour-force opportunities and to realize their full potential as autonomous human beings.

Radical feminists see liberal feminism as an inadequate challenge to patriarchal power relations because it seeks reform, not transformation. Radical feminists challenge all aspects of patriarchal societies, not just their public institutions, and focus in particular on the sex/gender system, that is, the ways in which biological imperatives like women's reproductive roles, combined with gender codes and compulsory heterosexuality, have been used to uphold women's subordination to men. Veiling, foot binding, arranged marriage, genital mutilation, witch burning, wife killing, chastity belts, sexual assault, wife battering, and sexual harassment are all examples of male control of women's bodies and sexuality. Explanations and solutions vary according to the radical feminist theorist. Some early writers advocated androgyny (each individual equally valuing their feminine and masculine characteristics), while others suggested opting out of heterosexual relationships through celibacy, lesbianism, or separatism (living apart from men). More contemporary radical feminist writers, however, accept bisexual, same-sex, and heterosexual relationships on the grounds that a woman's sexuality is hers to determine.

Liberal feminists reveal legal, social, and political practices that prevent women from making free choices and competing on an equal footing with men, while radical feminists focus on the ways in which biological determinism (the belief that "a woman's nature and all of her possibilities are determined by her biology"[17]) and sexual control construct male dominance and female subordination. Socialist feminists point out yet another source of oppression, the capitalist mode of economic production, and build on the insights of radical feminist thinkers by showing how patriarchy and capitalism act, often with the assistance of the state, as intersecting and mutually reinforcing systems. Socialist feminists bring material realities into the picture, arguing that a woman's status is shaped by her role in economic production and in biological (and social) reproduction. The sexual division of labour in the family assigns to women domestic and nurturing responsibilities, thereby reinforcing the sexual division of labour in the workplace, funnelling the majority of women into part-time or casual, low-paying "pink collar" jobs. Moreover, capitalist economies are fuelled by the unpaid labour of women in the household as well as the underpaid labour

of women who make up a readily exploitable and disposable reserve army of labour upon which capitalism can draw in times of need. Governments enact laws and policies that uphold patriarchy and capitalism, such as banning birth control, supporting the monogamous heterosexual marriage, and reinforcing women's economic dependency on men or the state. For instance, "spouse in the house" rules for social welfare cut single mothers off social assistance when they have sexual relationships with men, on the assumption that any man enjoying sexual intimacy with a woman should support her economically. Socialist feminists believe that patriarchy cannot be dismantled as long as state-supported capitalism goes unchallenged.

Women's diversity makes it impossible to conceive of a unified women's identity or political project.

Postmodern variants of feminism question the existence of meta-narratives, or universal truths, on the grounds that since the symbolic order is socially constructed, there can be no single version of any event or communication. Accordingly, reality is not set, but rather is continually being structured, deconstructed, and reconstituted by discourses (ideas, words, texts, images). Postmodern feminists contest any integration of feminist thought or practice into a unified whole. For that matter, postmodern feminist writers challenge the concept of "woman" because women's diversity makes it impossible to conceive of a unified women's identity or political project. Seeing language as the main instrument of patriarchy, postmodern feminists employ counter-discourses to disrupt and even displace the masculinist symbolic order. This is difficult because of male domination of language and knowledge; therefore, postmodern feminists must somehow challenge the symbolic order when the only instruments available are those that are products of this order. One method adopted by some postmodern feminists is to disrupt the male view of reality by offering an alternative female/feminine view. In other words, women can "write themselves out of the world men have constructed for them by putting into words the unthinkable/unthought," including subversive and transformative ideas.[18]

While it is difficult to get a fix on much postmodern thought, as it is often deliberately obscure and even self-contradictory, postmodern feminism has been important to the evolution of feminist thinking and practice because of its emphasis on women's diversity. Early feminism was often inattentive to multiple sources of oppression and tended to speak from a white, middle-class, able-bodied, heterosexist standpoint. Many women pointed out that this standpoint (the falsely constructed universal woman) did not encompass their experiences or social positions. Postmodern fracturing of the category "woman" has reinforced the need for recognizing and celebrating women's differences from one another, especially when coalition building and solidarity falter.

How do these different theoretical positions translate into political practice? Sometimes different variants of feminism lead to different positions on policy issues, while in other instances feminists take a similar stance, but for different reasons. Prostitution provides a good example of the former response. Socialist and radical feminists tend to regard prostitution as a practice that degrades, abuses, and exploits women. For the radical feminist, prostitution epitomizes the victimization and objectification of women, with the male customer or pimp in the role of the oppressor, and the female sex-trade worker in the character of the vulnerable, dependent victim. A radical feminist tends to see prostitution as the exploitation of women's bodies. State regulation of the buying and selling of sexual services is supported by some radical feminists on the grounds that women need protection from sexual subordination and from the violence that takes place within the sex trade. For instance, a radical feminist might applaud the B.C. government's decision to provide Vancouver-area prostitutes, who are under threat from a possible serial killer, with cell phones set up to make 911 calls.

Similarly, socialist feminists would see prostitution as gender-based exploitation characteristic of patriarchal societies but would also examine it as an example of capitalist exploitation of labour. A woman's sexuality is commodified by prostitution. On the one hand, by selling their sexual services, prostitutes defiantly assign economic value to physical labour that is otherwise unpaid, thereby challenging the sex/gender order. On the other hand, sex-trade workers normally don't control their livelihood because their work is regulated by pimps or escort agencies. And, socialist feminists would maintain, it is typically economic inequality based on gender, class, ethnicity, and so on, that leads women into the sex trade. State action, including criminalization of prostitution, only masks the true problem, namely the inequalities of wealth propagated by capitalism. There is no easy solu-

tion in a capitalist society. Socialist feminists might support the creation of collectives or cooperatives; while still commodified, their labour would be controlled by the sex-trade workers themselves.

A liberal might argue that women freely choose to work in the sex trade. A liberal *feminist* would point out the paucity of employment options, especially for women without much formal education, and say that it is not an autonomous choice. Women are constrained in the workplace by unequal pay, by lack of access to permanent, full-time, well-paying jobs, and by sexual harassment and inadequate child care. Moreover, without a postsecondary education, most women have little to choose from besides low-wage jobs, so prostitution is often a rational option that ensures economic survival. The long-term solution lies in greater access to education and job training, as well as reform of the workplace. A liberal feminist is likely to support government regulation of child prostitution, arguing that children have not yet reached the age of consent or autonomy and should receive the protection of the state. Most liberal feminists would be opposed to criminal sanctions against sex-trade workers themselves because prostitutes deserve economic independence and the right to make decisions about their own bodies.

A postmodern feminist may challenge any totalizing characterization of the prostitute. Women who do this work for pay have different family histories, stories, ethnicities, class positions, and life goals. They cannot be homogenized, and their interests cannot be reduced to a single policy solution. As well, the project of the postmodern feminist is to show how the discursive construction of prostitutes and prostitution via words and images is as important as the physical and material realities associated with the act of prostitution itself. How is the sex-trade worker characterized through different texts, such as news reports, movies, and books? Is she seen voyeuristically through a male gaze, or is she allowed to speak for herself? Is she stereotyped as the drug-addicted, pimp-dependent victim (the imagery conveyed in many news reports), or is she portrayed as the woman with a heart of gold who is temporarily down on her luck and merely needs rescuing by "the right man" (see the Hollywood movies *Pretty Woman* and *Milk Money*)? Postmodern feminists would certainly recommend the creation of new images of the sex-trade worker through texts imagined and communicated by the prostitute herself.

A vast array of methodologies, questions, ideas, and normative foundations fuels scholarly studies based on feminism. Likewise, feminism as a social movement is characterized by a wide variety of groups, goals, projects, and ways of organizing.[19] Feminism in theory and practice features competing ideas, internal debates, and frequent reformulation of core assumptions and perspectives. This diversity is a source of both weakness and strength. Because feminism defies easy description or characterization, its critics can stereotype feminist theory or practice by highlighting the most radical or provocative ideas (this problem is illustrated in the next section, on anti-feminism). Conversely, by pointing out apparent contradictions in feminist thought, critics can say feminism is too inconsistent to generate coherent ideas or to facilitate concrete political action. Diversity in thought and practice can also be a source of strength. Feminism's flexibility means that when new ideas appear or old ideas are challenged, theories and projects may be demobilized but are not destroyed. Because a multiplicity of voices and ideas exist within feminist praxis, feminism is permeable and adaptable. Feminism is constantly reinventing itself.

Feminism is of necessity woman-centred, so can men be feminists? A feminist historian such as Gerda Lerner would answer no, because she defines feminist consciousness as the awareness *of women* that because they belong to a subordinate and oppressed group they must *join with other women* to remedy discrimination and to create a society in which women as well as men will enjoy autonomy and self-determination.[20] But can't men share the awareness that women tend to be subordinated whereas men are privileged by patriarchal societies? Can't men join with women to remedy injustice and dismantle restrictive gender codes? In my view, of course they can. There are plenty of Canadian examples of the fact that men can, and do, employ feminist theory and methodology and participate in feminist movements for social change. Men were active participants in the Canadian suffrage movement, which sought the vote for women. Toronto academic and activist Michael Kauffman created the White Ribbon Campaign, a group of men working to end male violence toward women. However, a great deal of the most important work of critiquing the status quo and working for social change must be done by women themselves. Men can help, especially by changing attitudes, but women themselves must come to know that they have been subordinated and seek their own emancipation.

ANTI-FEMINISM

◆ ◆ ◆

Anti-feminists contest the very core of feminist thought by asserting that gender is biologically determined, not socially constructed. As the following quotation illustrates, anti-feminists see patriarchal gender codes as natural outcomes of sex differences:

> Moms are moms and dads are dads. So far no pill or twisted thinking can change the fact that women produce babies and, as nature intended, feed them from their breasts. Let us honour the father as the breadwinner, the hero who brings home the bacon. This is his position in the animal kingdom. Let the mother be the nurturer, the caregiver, the producer of the next generation, the homemaker.[21]

Anti-feminists regard the hetero-patriarchal family as the cornerstone of our society. For instance, vocal anti-feminist author William Gairdner says society as we know it will crumble if the traditional family is disrupted, and he calls radical feminists "the new barbarians of modern society" because they challenge the strict assignment of nurturing roles to women.[22]

Anti-feminists contest the very core of feminist thought by asserting that gender is biologically determined, not socially constructed.

Few Canadians believe biology is destiny, and the vast majority support equal rights for women, including reproductive choice, equality in the workplace, and equal benefit of the law.[23] Still, anti-feminism enjoys a certain currency because its proponents successfully employ two myths about feminism. The first is the myth of feminist orthodoxy—the idea that there exists a unified and homogeneous feminist position that is rigidly anti-male and anti-family. The second myth holds that feminism has triumphed and gender equality is now a reality. Journalist Danielle Crittenden claims feminism has been so "wildly effective" that it has "infiltrated the establishment" and has been absorbed by "the main institutions of society."[24] She asserts that the women's movement is no longer relevant because it has achieved all of its goals. In Crittenden's words, "the war's over."

These two myths are often linked in a circular pattern of reasoning that goes something like this. The feminist movement has emerged victorious, but feminist activists do not want to relinquish their power and notoriety, so they continue to insist that women are oppressed. Since the idea of women's oppression by men is no longer tenable, feminists promote extremist, intolerant, anti-male ideas and support these ideas with dodgy statistics and even outright lies. Journalist Donna Laframboise argues this case, insisting that, since the "big battles have been won," a few radical feminist "nut cases" have taken over the women's movement.[25] These "extreme elements," she says, promote the notion that "the entire male population is a menace," rail against heterosexual marriage, and attack the family. Their credibility is now in question, asserts Laframboise, because these feminists use "sloppy arithmetic and skewed data" to mislead the public about issues like male violence against women. Similarly, *Edmonton Journal* columnist Lorne Gunter says feminists have perpetrated the lie that men are largely responsible for domestic violence, denying or covering up the "fact" that "women are as likely, perhaps even a little more so, to abuse their partners severely."[26] Feminists do this, claims Gunter, so they can preserve their "grip over politics, the media and, particularly, the courts."

Feminism challenges the patriarchal family, not the family per se; it is woman-centred, not anti-male; and while it includes radical and transformative ideas, these ideas do not dominate feminist thought and practice, nor do they preclude competing ideas. We have seen that feminism is far from a unified system of thought. For example, popular wisdom (and anti-feminist rhetoric) has it that feminism single-mindedly lobbies for women's rights in the paid workforce and ignores the plight of homemakers. Yet in 1997 Canada's largest umbrella feminist organization, the National Action Committee on the Status of Women (NAC), organized a conference to seek greater support and recognition for women's unpaid work in the home and to articulate the policy needs of stay-at-home mothers.[27] But what about the argument that the women's movement has achieved most, if not all, of its goals, rendering feminism irrelevant and unnecessary? And are feminists suppressing the "truth" about their success in order to maintain their grip on political power? Feminism has helped reshape Canadian politics and society, but, as the Statistics Canada data cited in the next section show, substantive equality is far from the reality for most women.

FEMINISM AND POLITICAL ACTION IN CANADA

◆ ◆ ◆

Feminism, as expressed through the women's movement, has had a measurable effect on Canadian society. The women's movement "has touched the lives of many Canadian women, radically transforming the nature of their everyday experiences."[28] My mother, who came with her family to Canada from Czechoslovakia in 1937, had her name changed by immigration authorities and school teachers,[29] ran away from home at age 16 to escape her parent's insistence that she marry a middle-aged farmer, and was pressured by social norms to quit her job after marrying my father, even though they needed both incomes. My life choices have been much freer, thanks to the persistence of the women's movement. I was able to make choices about reproduction, marriage, child care, and work that were simply not available to women of my mother's generation. For instance, the sale, distribution, and use of birth control was prohibited and defined as a criminal act until 1969. Abortion was also banned by the Criminal Code until 1969, then allowed only under strict conditions. Maternity leave and child-care centres were virtually unknown, women could be fired from their jobs if they became pregnant, and women abandoned by their husbands were often left destitute.[30] Until the 1940s, and even later, laws and policies promoted the traditional family, assuming that women would marry, become financially dependent on their husbands, and bear and raise children.

At the time of Confederation, women were denied many basic citizenship rights because individual rights for women were seen as incompatible with the proper functioning of the patriarchal family. "Woman's first and only place is in the home," asserted political, clerical, and medical elites in turn-of-the-century Canada.[31] The early women's movement worked hard for many decades to claim civil and political rights for women, such as the right to vote, own and control wages and property, enter the professions, stay in the workplace after marriage, and claim Canadian citizenship status. These rights were not extended to all women at the same time, however; for instance, the right to vote in federal elections was granted to white women in 1918, Asian and Indo-Canadians in 1947 and 1948, status Indians in 1960, and persons with mental disabilities in 1991. Some women still find rights elusive, even though equality rights have been entrenched in the constitution via section 15 of the Canadian Charter of Rights and Freedoms. Rights in law don't necessarily translate into access to and enjoyment of formal entitlements. Immigration laws and regulations still work to keep women out of Canada on the basis of their race, class, and gender.[32] Sexual orientation was not explicitly listed as one of the prohibited grounds of discrimination in section 15 of the Charter, so gays and lesbians have turned to legislatures and the courts in an effort to claim rights that heterosexuals take for granted, including protection from discrimination by employers and landlords, the right to claim spousal benefits, and the right to adopt children.

A major goal of the women's movement has been to engender rights, that is, to interpret basic citizenship rights in ways that recognize women's experiences and needs. These projects have required transforming the definition of what is political, as captured by the feminist slogan "the personal is political." For example, the right to bodily autonomy has only recently been conceptualized to include women's sexual autonomy within marriage. Until 1983 men could not be charged with raping their wives because it was assumed that a woman was in a constant state of sexual consent to her husband. In other words, as his sexual property she had no right to say no. Similarly, the right to security of person, necessarily accompanied by the state's obligation to provide protection from bodily harm, was not extended to battered women before the mid-1980s. Women's groups have tried to politicize a wide range of issues, including child care, the sexual division of labour in the home and workplace, unequal pay, reproduction, sex-role stereotyping in education, and continued discrimination based on sex, ethnicity, sexual orientation, and ability. The Canadian women's movement has pursued a variety of goals, including but certainly not limited to legal rights. Some groups do not focus on the state and its legislative function at all, choosing instead to devote their efforts to helping groups of women by providing services such as job counselling, rape crisis intervention, shelters for those forced to flee domestic violence, and language training.

The creation of the Canadian welfare state, which took place roughly between the 1930s and 1970s, provided some measure of social citizenship for women. Social citizenship, the right to basic economic welfare and security, is often referred to as the *social safety net*. The term *welfare state* means an approach to governance which includes a certain type of fiscal policy and government provision of universal social programs, such as public education, health care, income security, and wage replacement programs. Through the activities of the welfare state, some women received help with some domestic responsibilities, such as caring for people with special needs. As well, women have filled public sector jobs, working as nurses, teachers, social workers, and clerical staff. Yet the welfare state has always been premised on the existence of stable, self-sufficient nuclear families with men as breadwinners and women in the role of domestic labourer. As a result, welfare state policies have done little to change the fact that many women must choose between economic dependency on men (marriage) or reliance on the state (social assistance). Woman-centred demands for programs including but not limited to national child care, recognition of midwifery, shelters for battered women, and culturally sensitive social welfare services have largely been ignored.

The welfare state, which never fully incorporated women's realities and needs, is now being dismantled by Canadian governments that are battling staggering debt loads. Federal funding to the provinces has been reduced, resulting in spending cuts to education, health, and social programs, as well as restructuring measures such as privatization, deregulation, and decentralization. These shifts in fiscal and social policy are driven by changes to the ideological order. Neoliberalism is a globalization-era ideology whose proponents want the freest possible market for transnational capital, would gladly have government services replaced with private arrangements, insist on individual self-reliance, and envision a minimalist role for government. For most women, who rely more heavily than do most men on the employment and services provided by the welfare state, who do not compete on a level playing field, and who are far from being economically self-reliant in many cases, the shrinking welfare state is cause for alarm.[33] Equally disturbing is the dogmatic neoliberal condemnation of women's demands as "special interests" that are characterized as being somehow antagonistic to the common good. For example, the Alberta government recently announced that it will stop funding job-placement services specifically directed at women and other groups. According to the minister responsible for the program, the jobless should be helped as individuals, not as members of particular groups.[34] Women who formerly could receive counselling for their experience of spousal abuse in preparation for seeking employment now must make do with generic job training, which may not address their particular social and psychological needs.

If we accept the anti-feminist claim that most patriarchal practices have been erased and women are now equal, the neoliberal edict of individual self-sufficiency is of little concern. If feminism has triumphed, women should be able to survive in an increasingly competitive marketplace. This view hinges on the assumption that women now have as much power as men and share equal access to the resources and goods valued by our society. Do Canadian women now enjoy economic autonomy, political equality, and personal liberty? On the whole, the answer is still no. Women's economic independence remains elusive, as the majority of women are underemployed and underpaid. The majority of part-time, casual, and minimum-wage employees are women. Women earn, on average, 70 percent of what men earn when working full time because women continue to work in the lowest-paying jobs.[35] Immigrant women, ethnic minority women, Aboriginal women, and women with disabilities are significantly more likely to be unemployed than other workers, male or female.[36] Women run greater risks than men of living in poverty, especially single mothers, elderly women, and women with disabilities.[37] The majority of women who do not have a man to support them are poor.

Women's economic independence remains elusive, as the majority of women are underemployed and underpaid.

Women's share of political power is also far from equal. As of July 1, 1999, women compose about 18 percent of the legislators at the provincial and territorial level and 20 percent at the federal level. Particular populations of women—ethnic minority, lesbian, Aboriginal, disabled—remain even more profoundly underrepresented in elected political institutions. In 1998, only 14 percent of provincially appointed judges and 20 percent of federally appointed members of the judiciary were women. Government agencies designed to represent women's policy interests, such as the Canadian Advisory Council on the Status of Women and the Alberta Advisory Council on Women's issues, have been dismantled. At present, the political currency of the women's movement is at an all-time low because "it is being recast as just another special interest group whose claims for state intervention are both self-interested and oppositional to the collective interest."[38]

Women continue to shoulder most of the responsibility for child-rearing and domestic duties, layering paid work on top of their household and community obligations. According to Statistics Canada, women perform two-thirds of the total unpaid work.[39] These duties limit women's workplace choices and personal autonomy. Moreover, women have less physical security and freedom of movement than do men because of high levels of violence against women. Statistics Canada found that about half of all adult women surveyed in 1993 had experienced at least one incident of physical or sexual violence since the age of 16, and 20 percent of these incidents resulted in physical injury.[40] Fear of sexual violence keeps women from moving freely in public spaces; according to Statistics Canada, 60 percent of women fear walking alone in their area after dark, and 76 percent worry about waiting for or using public transit alone after sunset.

Attitudes about a woman's place have indeed changed, but patriarchal notions persist and are still voiced by political and judicial elites. Consider Alberta Court of Appeal Justice John McClung's suggestion that a sexual assault victim invited the attack because she didn't "present herself to [the accused] in a bonnet and crinolines," or Quebec Justice Jean Bienvenue's claim that women are "naturally" inclined to greater depravity than are men, or Alberta MLA Julius Yankowsky's characterization of mothers receiving support payments from ex-husbands as "vindictive leech moms." As the information provided by Statistics Canada shows, feminists do not need to tell lies or fudge data when arguing that although progress for some Canadian women has been considerable, there is much ground yet to gain.

CONCLUSION
♦ ♦ ♦

The political realm is changing rapidly. The state is shrinking, national boundaries are being eroded by the forces of globalization, knowledge-based economies are redefining work, and some citizens are joining the wired world of the information superhighway. What does all of this mean for feminism? Those who take a unidimensional view of feminism might say its proponents are so mired in old paradigms that the movement is doomed to extinction, but evidence suggests otherwise. Feminism continues to evolve. The movement has gone global, and international organizing allows feminist activists from all areas of the world to share theories and experiences.

Women's groups from around the world are analyzing the impact of globalization on women, examining everything from the control of plant genetics by transnational agribusiness to the international sex trade in girls and women. Women's groups are inventing new ways to manoeuvre in a world that features minimalist states and permeable national boundaries.

The reaction of feminist thinkers and women's groups to new information technologies illustrates the continued evolutionary potential of feminism. Some feminist theorists and activists are joining the wired world at the same time as they are challenging its underlying power dynamics. They are analyzing the relationship between global capitalism and digital technology, measuring the impact of technological restructuring on women's work, and deconstructing digital culture. Women's groups increasingly use the Internet to create virtual communities, communicate, and organize. A new breed of activists called cyberfeminists believe that the Internet presents women with unlimited possibilities for engineering social change. Cyberfeminist online groups like geekgirl, Cybergrrl, and Riotgrrl[41] are but one illustration of the continued vitality and adaptability of feminism in an age of technological, political, and ideological transformation. Yet the ideas of the pioneers retain their importance. Feminists continue to analyze the social construction of gender codes, the nature of oppression in its various forms, and the persistence of patriarchal power relations. Postmodern and other contemporary variants of feminism have supplemented, and not supplanted, liberal, socialist, and radical feminist approaches.

Because feminism challenges the status quo and envisions significant social, economic, and political transformations, it provokes responses from those who resist change. Feminist action is met with anti-feminist reaction. Despite rumours of its demise and anti-feminist insistence on its irrelevance, feminism is alive and well because it lies at the heart of women's continued struggles for justice, equality, and independence. As the economic and political context for these struggles changes, so does feminist thought and activism. Internal debates and external challenges alike will help feminism hold its course as an important social, cultural, and political project in the new millennium.

Notes

1. William Gairdner espouses this view in *The War Against the Family* (Toronto: Stoddart, 1992), 116.

2. Charlotte Gray, "The New F-word," *Saturday Night* (April 1989), 17–20.

3. Donna Laframboise, "You've Come a Long Way, Baby ... and for What?" *Globe and Mail* (July 26, 1997), D1, D3.

4. Karen Offen, "Defining Feminism: A Comparative Historical Approach," *Signs* 14, 1 (1988), 119–57.

5. "Big Hairy Deal for Julia," *Edmonton Journal* (May 1, 1999), C1.

6. Judith Zelman, "Pregnant with Disability: Expecting but Unexpected," *Globe and Mail* (October 8, 1997), A28.

7. Lorraine Code, "Feminist Theory," in Sandra Burt et al., *Changing Patterns: Women in Canada*, 2nd ed. (Toronto: McClelland & Stewart, 1993), 19.

8. Gertrude Robinson and Armande Saint-Jean, "Women Politicians and Their Media Coverage: A Generational Analysis," in Kathy Megyery, ed., *Women in Canadian Politics: Toward Equity in Representation* (Toronto: Dundurn Press, 1991), 127–69.

9. Quoted in Lorraine Code, *What Can She Know? Feminist Theory and Construction of Knowledge* (Ithaca and London: Cornell University Press, 1991), ix.

10 Marilyn Frye, *The Politics of Reality: Essays in Feminist Theory* (Freedom, Calif.: The Crossing Press, 1983), 33.

11. Sally Weaver, "First Nations Women and Government Policy, 1970–92: Discrimination and Conflict," in Burt et al., *Changing Patterns*, 2nd ed., 128.

12. See Jean Bethke Elshtain, "The Power and Powerlessness of Women," in Gisela Bock and Susan James, eds., *Beyond Equality and Difference: Citizenship, Feminist Politics and Female Subjectivity* (London: Routledge, 1992), 110–25.

13. Naomi Wolf, *Fire with Fire* (Toronto: Random House, 1993), 135–42.

14. Roberta Hamilton, *Gendering the Vertical Mosaic: Feminist Perspectives on Canadian Society* (Toronto: Copp Clark, 1996), 4.

15. Jill Vickers, *Reinventing Political Science: A Feminist Approach* (Halifax: Fernwood, 1997), 196.

16. Rosemarie Tong, *Feminist Thought: A Comprehensive Introduction* (Boulder & San Francisco: Westview Press, 1980).

17. Code, "Feminist Theory," 22–23.

18. Tong, *Feminist Thought*, 224–25.

19. See, for instance, Nancy Adamson, Linda Briskin, and Margaret McPhail, *Feminist Organizing for Change: The*

Contemporary Women's Movement in Canada (Toronto: Oxford University Press, 1988).

20. George Lerner, *The Creation of Feminist Consciousness: From the Middle Ages to Eighteen-Seventy* (New York: Oxford University Press, 1993), 14.

21. Letter to the editor of the *Toronto Star*, quoted in Pat Armstrong and Hugh Armstrong, *The Double Ghetto*, 3rd ed. (Toronto: McClelland & Stewart, 1994), 144.

22. Gairdner, *The War Against the Family*, 302.

23. Adamson et al., *Feminist Organizing for Change*, 4.

24. Danielle Crittenden, "Let's Junk the Feminist Slogans: The War's Over," *Chatelaine* (August 1990), 38.

25. Laframboise, "You've Come a Long Way, Baby."

26. Lorne Gunter, "Women Must Share Spousal Abuse Blame," *Edmonton Journal* (September 28, 1997), G8.

27. Paula Brook, "Every Mother Is a Working Mother," *Globe and Mail* (October 25, 1997), D1, D3.

28. Burt et al., "Introduction," in *Changing Patterns*, 2nd ed., 9.

29. My mother's given name is Katrinka. Immigration authorities put "Katarina" on her immigration papers. Her elementary school teacher, under pressure from other parents who said my mother's name sounded "too foreign," insisted on calling her Kathleen.

30. See Sandra Burt, "The Changing Patterns of Public Policy," in Burt et al., *Changing Patterns*, 2nd ed., 213–15.

31. Alison Prentice et al., *Canadian Women: A History* (Toronto: Harcourt Brace, 1988), 143.

32. Yasmeen Abu-Laban, "Keeping 'Em Out: Gender, Race and Class Biases in Canadian Immigration Policy," in Joan Anderson et al., eds., *Painting the Maple: Essays on Race, Gender and the Construction of Canada* (Vancouver: UBC Press, 1999), 69–82.

33. See Janine Brodie, *Politics on the Margins: Restructuring and the Canadian Women's Movement* (Halifax: Fernwood, 1995), and Gurston Dacks, Joyce Green, and Linda Trimble, "Road Kill: Women in Alberta's Drive Toward Deficit Elimination," in Trevor Harrison and Gordon Laxer, eds., *The Trojan Horse: Alberta and the Future of Canada* (Montreal: Black Rose, 1995), 271–80.

34. Allyson Jeffs, "Job-Placement Programs for Women at Risk," *Edmonton Journal* (April 19, 1999), B1.

35. Jane Gadd, "Canadians Got Poorer in 90s," *Globe and Mail* (May 13, 1998), A1, A4, A5.

36. Brian Laghi, "Minorities Don't Share in Canada's Boom," *Globe and Mail* (May 13, 1998), A4.

37. Statistics Canada, *Women in Canada* (Ottawa: Supply and Services Canada, 1995). Much of this data is available on the Internet; see the Statistics Canada Web site at http://www.statcan.ca

38. Janine Brodie, "Restructuring and the Politics of Marginalization," in Manon Tremblay and Caroline Andrew, eds., *Women and Political Representation in Canada* (Ottawa: University of Ottawa Press, 1998), 34.

39. Margaret Philp, "Unpaid Work Worth at Least $234-Billion," *Globe and Mail* (December 21, 1995), A5. Statistics Canada found that husbands do no more work around the house than do unmarried men.

40. Statistics Canada, "The Violence Against Women Survey," *The Daily* (November 18, 1993). The survey of 12,300 women over the age of 18 defined assault as those behaviours considered offences under the Criminal Code.

41. Melanie Stewart Millar, *Cracking the Gender Code* (Toronto: Second Storey Press, 1998), 60.

Terms & Concepts

backlash
biological determinism
feminisms: liberal, radical, socialist, and postmodern

gender and sex
gender codes
male as norm and female as deviant
patriarchy

private realm and public sphere
socialization

Questions

1. Simone de Beauvoir wrote that "one is not born, but rather becomes a woman." What did she mean?

2. Have the battles of feminism been largely won? What is left to be done?

3. Is there a common core of beliefs among the varieties of feminism?

4. Can you identify remnants of institutionalized gender discrimination in Canada?

5. Does feminism challenge the family as a social organization?

An Act Respecting the Future of Quebec (Bill 1) Introduced in the National Assembly of Quebec on September 7, 1995

Editors' Note

At the time, it was high drama. Millions of Canadians watched in amazement as the results of the Quebec referendum on October 30, 1995, came in. For most of that memorable evening, the contest was too close to call, and when it was all over the "No" forces had barely eked out a victory. In retrospect, it seems even more amazing. Almost 94 percent turnout, a 49.4 to 50.6 percent split, and yet not a single major disturbance afterward (unless you count Jacques Parizeau's "money and ethnics" speech). Some electoral irregularities occurred, but they were few by most standards. Recriminations abounded, but life just went on. It was yet another triumph for federalism and the Canadian way.

But was it really? Were we simply lucky to have escaped the passing of Bill 1, *An Act Respecting the Future of Quebec*? Whether we were or not, the usual debates concerning centralization versus decentralization of federal powers have taken over, punctuated occasionally by well-aimed salvos fired at the Quebec government and the Parti Québécois by Stephane Dion and enlivened also by a potentially crucial Supreme Court decision (excerpted in Chapter 25 of this volume).

So why should we now read Bill 1? Won't a devolutionary agenda satisfy Quebec, and aren't Quebeckers anyway rather like the Scots who want, still, to be both British and Scottish (and whose agendas and policy preferences are somewhat indistinct from those of their English neighbours)? Canadian federalism is often, after all, about not having to make tough either/or choices.

Quebeckers may now realize, far more than before, that the terms proposed in Bill 1 beg a number of absolutely key questions and therefore lead to the hard choices that would inevitably have to be made with full nationhood and sovereignty.

As you read Bill 1, note what it assumes, what it omits, and what it portends if Quebec nationalism is able to more strongly reassert itself. And it surely could, for even though Quebec's present powers may look wonderful to someone who wants to be recognized as, say, a Ruthenian, the appeal of sovereignty is hard to match. A seat at the table, a vote at the UN, national teams—sovereignty can still trump other cards if federalists are not careful and creative.

◆ ◆ ◆

The Parliament of Quebec Enacts as Follows

Self-Determination

1. The National Assembly is authorized, within the scope of the Act, to proclaim the sovereignty of Quebec.

The proclamation must be preceded by a formal offer of economic and political partnership with Canada.

From Bill 1, *An Act Respecting the Future of Quebec*, National Assembly of Quebec, 1995.

Sovereignty

2. On the date fixed in the proclamation of the National Assembly, the Declaration of sovereignty appearing in the Preamble shall take effect and Quebec shall become a sovereign country; it shall acquire the exclusive power to pass all its laws, levy all its taxes and conclude all its treaties.

Quebec shall become a sovereign country.

Partnership Treaty

3. The Government is bound to propose to the Government of Canada the conclusion of a treaty of economic and political partnership on the basis of the tripartite agreement of June 12, 1995 reproduced in the schedule.

   The treaty must be approved by the National Assembly before being ratified.

4. A committee charged with the orientation and supervision of the negotiations relating to the partnership treaty, composed of independent personalities appointed by the Government in accordance with the tripartite agreement, shall be established.

5. The Government shall favor the establishment in the Outaouais region of the seat of the institutions created under the partnership treaty.

New Constitution

6. A draft of a new constitution shall be drawn up by a constituent commission established in accordance with the prescriptions of the National Assembly. The commission, consisting of an equal number of men and women, shall be composed of a majority of non-parliamentarians, and shall include Quebecers of various origins and from various backgrounds.

   The proceedings of the commission must be organized so as to ensure the fullest possible participation of citizens in all regions of Quebec, notably through the creation of regional sub-commissions, if necessary.

   The commission shall table the draft constitution before the National Assembly, which shall approve the final text. The draft constitution shall be submitted to a referendum and shall, once approved, become the fundamental law of Quebec.

7. The new constitution shall state that Quebec is a French-speaking country and shall impose upon the Government the obligation of protecting Quebec culture and ensuring its development.

8. The new constitution shall affirm the rule of law, and shall include a charter of human rights and freedoms. It shall also affirm that citizens have responsibilities towards their fellow citizens.

   The new constitution shall guarantee the English-speaking community that its identity and institutions will be preserved. It shall also recognize the right of the aboriginal nations to self-government on lands over which they have full ownership and their right to participate in the development of Quebec; in addition, the existing constitutional rights of the aboriginal nations shall be recognized in the constitution. Such guarantee and such recognition shall be exercised in a manner consistent with the territorial integrity of Quebec.

The new constitution shall guarantee the English-speaking community that its identity and institutions will be preserved. It shall also recognize the right of the aboriginal nations to self-government.

Representatives of the English-speaking community and of each of the aboriginal nations must be invited by the constituent commission to take part in the proceedings devoted to defining their rights. Such rights shall not be modified otherwise than in accordance with a specific procedure.

9. The new constitution shall affirm the principle of decentralization. Specific powers and corresponding fiscal and financial resources shall be attributed by law to local and regional authorities.

Territory

10. Quebec shall retain its boundaries as they exist within the Canadian federation on the date on which Quebec becomes a sovereign country. It shall exercise its jurisdiction over the land, air and water forming its territory and over the areas adjacent to its coast, in accordance with the rules of international law.

Quebec shall retain its boundaries as they exist within the Canadian federation.

Citizenship

11. Every person who, on the date on which Quebec becomes a sovereign country, holds Canadian citizenship and is domiciled in Quebec acquires Quebec citizenship.

    Every person born in Quebec who, on the date on which Quebec becomes a sovereign country, is domiciled outside Quebec and who claims Quebec citizenship also acquires Quebec citizenship.

    In the two years following the date on which Quebec becomes a sovereign country, any person holding Canadian citizenship who settles in Quebec or who has established a substantial connection with Quebec without being domiciled in Quebec may claim Quebec citizenship.

12. Quebec citizenship may be obtained, once Quebec has become a sovereign country, in the cases and on the conditions determined by law. The law must provide, in particular, that Quebec citizenship shall be granted to every person born in Quebec, or born outside Quebec to a father or mother holding Quebec citizenship.

13. Quebec citizenship may be held concurrently with Canadian citizenship or that of any other country.

Currency

14. The currency having legal tender in Quebec shall remain the Canadian dollar.

Treaties and International Organizations and Alliances

15. In accordance with the rules of international law, Quebec shall assume the obligations and enjoy the rights set forth in the relevant treaties and international conventions and agreements to which Canada or Quebec is a party on the date on which Quebec becomes a sovereign country, in particular in the North American Free Trade Agreement.

16. The Government is authorized to apply for the admission of Quebec to the United Nations Organization and its specialized agencies. It shall take the necessary steps to ensure the participation of Quebec in the World Trade Organization, the Organization of American States, the Organization for Economic Co-operation and Development, the Organization for Security and Co-operation in Europe, the Francophonie, the Commonwealth and other international organizations and conferences.

17. The Government shall take the necessary steps to ensure the continuing participation of Quebec in the defence alliances of which Canada is a member. Such participation must, however, be compatible with Quebec's desire to give priority to the maintenance of world peace under the leadership of the United Nations Organization.

Continuity of Laws, Pensions, Benefits, Licences and Permits, Contracts and Courts of Justice

18. The Acts of the Parliament of Canada and the regulations thereunder that apply in Quebec on the date on which Quebec becomes a sovereign country shall be deemed to be the laws and regulations of Quebec. Such legislative and regulatory provisions shall be maintained in force until they are amended, replaced or repealed.

19. The Government shall ensure the continuity of the unemployment insurance and child tax benefit programs and the payment of the other benefits paid by the Government of Canada to individuals domiciled in Quebec on the date on which Quebec becomes a sovereign country. Pensions and supplements payable to the elderly and to veterans shall continue to be paid by the Government of Quebec according to the same terms and conditions.

20. Permits, licences and other authorizations issued before October 30, 1995 under an Act of the Parliament of Canada that are in force in Quebec on the date on which Quebec becomes a sovereign country shall be maintained. Those issued or renewed on or after October 30, 1995 shall also be maintained unless they are denounced by the Government within one month following the date on which Quebec becomes a sovereign country.

    Permits, licences and other authorizations that are so maintained will be renewable according to law.

21. Agreements and contracts entered into before October 30, 1995 by the Government of Canada or its agencies or organizations that are in force in Quebec on the date on which Quebec becomes a sovereign country shall be maintained, with the Government of Quebec substituted, where required, for the Canadian party. Those entered into on or after October 30, 1995 shall also be maintained, with the Government of Quebec substituted, where required,

for the Canadian party, unless they are denounced by the Government within one month following the date on which Quebec becomes a sovereign country.

22. The courts of justice shall continue to exist after the date on which Quebec becomes a sovereign country. Cases pending may be continued until judgment. However, the law may provide that cases pending before the Federal Court or before the Supreme Court shall be transferred to the Quebec jurisdiction it determines.

The Court of Appeal shall become the court of highest jurisdiction until a Supreme Court is established under the new constitution, unless otherwise provided for by law.

Judges appointed by the Government of Canada before October 30, 1995 who are in office on the date on which Quebec becomes a sovereign country shall be confirmed in their functions and shall retain their jurisdiction. The judges of the Federal Court and of the Supreme Court of Canada who were members of the Quebec Bar shall become, if they so wish, judges of the Superior Court and the Court of Appeal respectively.

Federal Public Servants and Employees

23. The Government may, in accordance with the conditions prescribed by law, appoint the necessary personnel and take appropriate steps to facilitate the application of the Canadian laws that continue to apply in Quebec pursuant to section 18. The sums required for the application of such laws shall be taken out of the consolidated revenue fund.

The government shall ensure that the public servants and other employees of the Government of Canada and of its agencies and organizations, appointed before October 30, 1995 and domiciled in Quebec on the date on which Quebec becomes a sovereign country, shall become, if they so wish, public servants or employees of the Government of Quebec. The government may, for that purpose, conclude agreements with any association of employees or any other person in order to facilitate such transfers. The Government may also set up a program of voluntary retirement; it shall honor any retirement or voluntary departure arrangement made with a transferred person.

Interim Constitution

24. The Parliament of Quebec may adopt the text of an interim constitution which will be in force from the date on which Quebec becomes a sovereign country until the coming into force of the new constitution of Quebec. The interim constitution must ensure the continuity of the democratic institutions of Quebec and of the constitutional rights existing on the date on which Quebec becomes a sovereign country, in particular those relating to human rights and freedoms, the English-speaking community, access to English-language schools, and the aboriginal nations.

The interim constitution must ensure the continuity of the democratic institutions of Quebec.

Until the coming into force of the interim constitution, the law, rules and conventions governing the internal constitution of Quebec shall remain in force.

Other Agreements

25. In addition to the partnership treaty, the Government is authorized to conclude with the Government of Canada any other agreement to facilitate the application of this Act, in particular with respect to the equitable apportionment of the assets and liabilities of the Government of Canada.

The proclamation of sovereignty may be made as soon as the partnership treaty has been approved.

Coming into Force

26. The negotiations relating to the conclusion of the partnership treaty must not extend beyond October 30, 1996 unless the National Assembly decides otherwise.

The proclamation of sovereignty may be made as soon as the partnership treaty has been approved by the National Assembly or as soon as the latter, after requesting the opinion of the orientation and supervision committee, has concluded that the negotiations have proved fruitless.

27. This Act comes into force on the day on which it is assented to.

Terms & Concepts

citizenship

constituent commission

continuity

Court of Appeal

interim constitution

partnership treaty

political partnership

proclamation of sovereignty

sovereignty

Questions

1. In what respects would Quebec *not* be sovereign under the terms outlined in Bill 1?

2. How does Bill 1 deal with the rights of citizenship, both Canadian and Québécois?

3. Is Bill 1 a reasonable basis for a future agreement if Quebec decides to separate?

4. What assumptions are made about Aboriginal rights and about Quebec's territorial integrity?

5. Would Quebec continue to be a member of NAFTA, under international law, as stated?

A Primer on Market and
Political Failures

John Richards

Editors' Note

What follows is an excerpt from John Richards's *Retooling the Welfare State*. At a time when every political party seems to be moving to the centre, looking for a "third way," and attempting to be economically and fiscally conservative without surrendering the welfare state (this would be true even of the Reform Party), it is important for us to reconsider some of the conventional wisdom about markets and social policy.

Richards does precisely this; his views will be anathema to those who refuse to think anew about what we should do to shake up the status quo to achieve greater efficiencies and better results. There are still those on the Right who believe that big government must be attacked vigorously if anything major is to happen to expenditures and practices. To be fair, right-wingers have considerable ammunition, and Richards makes good use of it (one of his early chapters is entitled "The Irresponsibility of Canada's Traditional Left" and details how we must avoid its "traditional syndromes").

At the same time, Richards does defend the state's public, collective role, and in the chapter excerpted here, he provides three criteria for doing so. His examples clearly illustrate what one might call the "real world" of market forces and market failures. If we do not use his kind of assessment criteria, we will continue to formulate public policy based not on what actually happens, but on what we believe will or should happen. According to Richards, if we refuse to face the facts, the future of the welfare state will be more problematic than if we are willing to suspend our historic judgments (be they left or right wing). Richards argues that we must consider not simply some compromise or supposed "middle way" that really amounts to pleasing the median voter, but rather we must create effective new policies that further our social goals when we "trade for the public good."

◆ ◆ ◆

For readers who are not economists, this chapter introduces the theory of market and government failure as it applies to social policy. It is divided into three sections. The first deals with reasons why markets can generate inefficient outcomes. To the extent social policy redresses genuine market failures, the rationale for social policy is relatively noncontroversial. The second discusses more controversial rationales for social policy—namely, the realization of certain shared values. Among the values that civilized communities pursue is realization of an acceptable distribution of income and of what are called merit goods. The third section, on government failure, introduces generic problems that arise when governments intervene. The concepts of government failure are, in a sense, the obverse of market failure: they are the reasons not to intervene in markets.

MARKET FAILURES
◆ ◆ ◆

... Wherever the structure of private markets is such that individuals acting in their own rational self-interest produce an inefficient outcome, a *market failure* is said to arise. If present, such failures often provide "virtuous" rationales for government social policy.

From *Retooling the Welfare State* (C.D. Howe Institute, 1998) by John Richards. Reprinted with permission.

The three market failures most relevant to any discussion of social policy involve public goods, externalities, and asymmetrical information.

Public Goods

The first market failure concerns *public goods and services*: items that have the characteristic of being *nonrivalrous* in consumption (my use of the good in no way hampers your use of it) and *nonexcludable* (it is expensive or technically impossible to exclude potential users once the good is in place). Textbook examples are uncongested roads, parks, and lighthouses. Privately owned lighthouses have existed. Their owners collected a fee from boats docking in an adjacent port, so, in effect, provision of the dock and the lighthouse became a joint service; no boat could be excluded from using the lighthouse, but it could be prevented from tying up at the wharf if it failed to pay. Lighthouses remain a dubious prospect as a source for private profit because there is usually no practical means to deny the service to a passing ship that refuses to pay. Here is a classic example of a universal problem associated with public goods. Once they are supplied, nonexcludability means that people will free ride.

Lighthouses are also perfectly nonrivalrous. Unlike parks or roads, which can become congested and hence cease to be nonrivalrous, use of the lighthouse's service by one ship in no way detracts from use by the next ship and in no way imposes any incremental cost on running the lighthouse.

The reason for labeling this category of market failure as public goods is that private markets usually do not supply them. To the extent that society wants public goods, public agencies must organize the supply—either via a state-owned enterprise (that is, direct supply) or via regulations that enable a private firm to operate profitably.[1] Urban sanitation is close to being a pure public good. Once the water and sewage system is in place, the cost of additional water use is negligible—provided it does not bump up against a capacity constraint or exacerbate environmental pollution. (Regulating increased use of the system is obviously hard to do, as water authorities discover whenever a drought occurs and gardeners seek to preserve their roses.)

Although public goods may entail no costs from incremental beneficiaries, building and running lighthouses and urban sanitary water systems do have costs. These can be usefully categorized as

- *Administrative costs.* Governments must incur costs to raise taxes and limit evasion by taxpayers. Taxpayers must incur compliance costs to gather the relevant information and calculate their tax liability.

- *Private sector opportunity costs.* These are the costs of forgone opportunities in the private market as governments raise revenues to pay for public goods. As tax rates increase, taxpayers face larger incentives to undertake tax-avoidance behavior, behavior that is inefficient relative to that which would be undertaken in a tax-free economy. In a recent study, Kesselman (1995) cites estimates that show that, on average, raising $1.00 of tax revenue in Canada engenders a *gross* cost to the private economy of $1.33. The net cost depends on the value of what the government does with the revenue. If it supplies a service of value equal to what taxpayers would have purchased with $1.00 in the market, the *net* cost is not $1.33 but $0.33. Thus, to be efficient, the value of the program to which the government devotes the $1.00 must be at least a third greater than the value of the market goods or services that taxpayers have had to forgo.[2]

Higher tax rates increase the economic costs.

- *Political costs.* Rising tax rates increase citizens' incentives to engage in political activities to avoid paying tax. Frequently, this activity takes the form of special interest groups' lobbying for particular exemptions. At any given level of social spending, exemptions for one interest group raise the average and marginal tax rates to be imposed on everyone else. In turn, higher tax rates increase the economic costs discussed above. Political activity may also induce outright corruption, which, in turn, may contaminate the entire public service. High tariffs provide a classic example. In addition to causing direct economic inefficiencies (arising from distorted domestic prices), tariffs generate multiple unintended costs. They divert resources to smuggling; they lead to endemic corruption of public officials engaged in management of ports, borders, and customs, which further increases transaction costs for importing firms; and they divert entrepreneurial energy into the exercise of political influence and away from economically productive activities.

Externalities

Externalities arise when exchanges between two agents inevitably have an impact on nonconsenting third parties. The third-party effect may be negative.... Or it may be positive. When parents inoculate their child against polio, that particular child is not the only one who benefits. Since she now cannot communicate the infectious disease, the inoculation benefits all other children with whom she comes in contact.

A simple but dramatic example of an externality arising from education is the effect on the life expectancy of a woman's future children, who are clearly nonconsenting third parties. Educated mothers earn more and can better afford to feed their children; they make better use of health services and pay more attention to sanitation. On the basis of a sample from Africa, Asia, and Latin America, the World Bank (1995a, 30–31) reports that, on average, four to six years of education reduces the death rate of young children (under age two) by more than a quarter from that for children whose mothers have no formal education (see Figure 12.1).

Asymmetrical Information

Information asymmetry arises when one party to an exchange has information of value to the other party

Figure 12.1   Chances of Children's Dying before Age Two, by Mother's Education

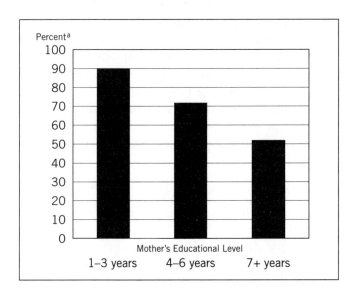

ᵃThe comparison is the chance of death before age two for children of mothers with various amounts of education vis-à-vis the chance for children of mothers with no schooling (represented by 100 percent on the vertical axis). Data are from a sample of 25 countries in Africa, Asia, and Latin America.

Source: World Bank 1995, which cites Hobcraft 1993.

that he could transmit at a cost below its value to the recipient. Two ideas are crucial here: that parties to an exchange do not have an equivalent basis of knowledge, and that the relevant knowledge could be transferred at a cost below its value to the recipient. (In contrast, in a doctor-patient exchange, the physician and the patient usually have vastly unequal knowledge about medicine, but the physician could not transform the patient into a physician at any reasonable cost; hence information asymmetry does not necessarily arise.)

The classic case of information asymmetry occurs in the market for second-hand cars. The salesperson knows that she is flogging a lemon and chooses not to inform the unsuspecting customer. The customer knows that lemons abound in the market but not whether this particular car is a lemon. Such markets are hard to analyze, and government intervention can potentially render them more efficient.

The first two market failures I discussed—those involving public goods or externalities—provide a rationale for government to regulate certain kinds of behavior, and below I provide a rationale for government to intervene over the distribution of income. None of these arguments, however, provides justification for government *supply* of any goods or services. The presence of information asymmetry may do so.[3]

In the case of education, for example, externality (and myopia) arguments warrant making universal education mandatory (to an appropriate level that rises with the importance of technology-based employment in the economy). Such arguments do not, however, warrant government-run schools. Why not legislate that parents buy the requisite education for their children from private schools? And if redistributive arguments warrant that the state pay for education among the poor, why not provide parents with education vouchers of sufficient value to cover the fees of an average private school? Provided competition prevailed among schools, fees would reflect costs but would vary according to quality. Parents who wanted a superior school for their children could top up the value of the voucher from their own income. Those who did not much value school learning could opt for a cheap school and divert some of the voucher to another use.

So why should governments run education systems? Much of the rationale for government involvement in the supply of social services depends on two aspects of information asymmetry: experience goods and adverse selection.

Experience Goods   The value of some goods and services is exceedingly difficult for the consumer to judge at the time of purchase. In the case of *experience goods,* their value becomes apparent only after lengthy experience. The quality of elementary and secondary education provided by particular schools has this property. One partial solution is for government to control the inputs to education, supplying it via public agencies—that is, running a public school system.

Perhaps state intervention could be restricted to a regulatory and redistributive role and still realize an acceptable level of universal education. But were that option feasible, surely some country would by now have put such a policy in place. None has. Over the past two centuries, all states that have achieved a measure of industrial success—from Britain, as pioneer, to present-day Thailand—have intervened in the provision of primary and secondary education in ways far more complex than simply legislating compulsory schooling and providing an income transfer to parents.

My purpose here is not to defend the status quo in education policy. In Canada over the past half-century, provincial ministries of education and teachers' unions have promoted too many education fads and have too often resisted measuring learning outcomes. Canadians need to debate education policy, to be less parochial, and to take seriously policies pursued elsewhere in the world. But to express dissatisfaction with the status quo does not deny the central argument: education displays information asymmetry.[4] It is hard for parents to assess school quality. A system of competitive private schools would result in some very good schools, but the variance would be unacceptably high. In such a system, many bad schools would also thrive, and many children would fall between cracks.

Adverse Selection   *Adverse selection* arises whenever one party to a contingent contract can conceal relevant information from the other. In education, adverse selection arises if schools systemically restrict entry to good students and reject the poor. School administrators often have more knowledge about the potential performance of students than do parents. In a system of private schools, schools may use their superior basis of knowledge to cream off high-potential students and avoid those whose past academic record or social characteristics suggest a high probability of poor performance. Students with below-average potential, rejected by most schools, wind up warehoused in inferior schools. A universal publicly run school system can avoid this problem.

Insurance markets offer some of the most important examples of adverse selection. By pooling together many independent risky events, insurance improves efficiency by allowing those who want to avoid risk to do so. Consider hail insurance for farmers. Hail damage to crops is an unpredictable event, and insurance spreads the cost uniformly over those farmers insured. The uncertainty attached to an insurance company's portfolio of hail policies (in terms of the expected loss per policy, averaged over all policies) is far lower than the uncertainty surrounding the expected loss for any individual uninsured farmer.

In this relatively simple form of insurance, adverse selection is unimportant; both farmer and insurer can readily ascertain the relevant weather data, so both have similar *ex ante* information on the prospects of a claim. Competitive market forces induce insurance companies to segregate policies and vary premiums based on identifiable risk factors, such as differing probabilities of hail in different regions. Farmers who buy insurance reduce their average incomes by the amount of profit and overhead of the insurance companies, but they consider themselves better off because they prefer slightly lower average incomes associated with much less risk.

In contrast, consider health insurance. As with hail, an efficient insurance company uses any accessible information that indicates the probability of a claim, subdividing policyholders based on age, sex, previous medical record, lifestyle, and so on and setting the premiums for any subgroup to reflect the average costs of insuring people with that particular set of characteristics. But any such subdivision will be imperfect; the insurees usually know more about their health status than the insurer. Let one group be women over age 50 who do not smoke. For women within this group who consider themselves to be in good health, the premiums will appear high; for women who consider themselves to be in poor health, the premiums will appear low. Over time, those who seek insurance will increasingly tend to be those women with below-average health status. This is adverse selection.

To limit this perverse dynamic, insurance companies must spend large resources monitoring would-be insurees and claims, and insurees must expend resources establishing the legitimacy of their claims. For some categories of high-risk individuals, the cost of overcoming adverse selection is so high that private insurance markets simply do not exist.

COLLECTIVE GOALS

◆ ◆ ◆

More controversial rationales for social policy are based on the argument that the state should intervene to realize important shared values or collective goals (the third dimension of social policy). Implicit in the theory of market failures is that some forms of collective action unambiguously improve economic efficiency; banning leaded gasoline is a convincing example. To the extent social policy entails realization of shared values, however, the link with enhanced efficiency becomes tenuous and the rationale more controversial.

---

*Social policy inevitably entails a
certain amount of paternalism.*

Social policy inevitably entails this third dimension and hence a certain amount of paternalism. Intellectually, many people are uncomfortable with arguments that justify any state coercion on behalf of one group's values over those of some other group. But basic social policies inevitably discriminate against the minority who disagree with them. Specific social policies may entail more controversial exercises in discrimination. Central to the art of statecraft in any democracy is determining how far to go in using social policy to realize particular values.

Equalizing Income Distribution

An important collective goal that governments seek to realize is that the overall income distribution be acceptable to the majority. Market economies left to themselves tend to generate unacceptably unequal income distributions.

Inevitably, there arises the tricky question of devising a suitable mechanism to realize the redistribution. If one individual voluntarily gives $1,000 to the poor, she may consider herself better off, given her desire to exercise charity. Her act helps a few poor people and enables her free-riding neighbors to feel better about their community without actually contributing themselves—remember the medieval orphanage. But any individual act of charity has a negligible impact on overall income distribution. On the other hand, the government can require every nonpoor individual to pay $1,000 in taxes, and itself redistribute the revenue to the poor. Collective institutions, whether medieval church or modern welfare

state, are better placed than individuals to realize any significant redistribution of income.

Increasing the equality of outcomes by use of the tax-and-transfer system is akin to setting up a lighthouse inasmuch as exclusion is not possible. Once the redistribution is effected, no one is excluded from its benefit: the poor have more income and the nonpoor—at least those who favor redistribution—also realize a gain. Unlike the case of the lighthouse, however, the incremental cost is not zero. If a poor family on welfare has an additional child, the government incurs additional welfare costs to maintain the existing income distribution.

People in a democratic society disagree about how much redistribution governments should undertake. But the majority obviously want a considerable amount of it. Furthermore, the majority want rules (such as those defining the income tax system) to prevent free riding by some on the redistributive acts of others.

Supplying Merit Goods

Merit goods are those goods and services that government insists on supplying, regardless of individual preferences. Merit goods entail a particular kind of interdependent preference in which A is concerned not about the income that B has at his disposal but about his consumption of particular goods and services. Merit goods are a way of saying that social policy entails promotion of certain shared values.

An example of a merit good is primary and secondary education. In all industrial countries, government obliges parents to educate a child, whether they want to do so or not. The ultimate rationale here is that the majority think the value of an educated citizenry is so important that social policy can legitimately override the preferences of the minority of parents (and children) who object to the state's dictating what youngsters do for 200 days a year for 12 years of their lives.

Why mandate education? A first set of arguments is redistributive. The provision of universal education is a means of equalizing income distribution relative to what it would otherwise be. A second set is based on improving efficiency. Educating mothers lowers the death rate of children and hence lowers the social cost of raising the labor force for the next generation. An educated populace can more quickly implement productivity-enhancing technical changes. A more subtle argument links education to efficiency in public policy. A literate citizenry is better able than an illiterate citizenry to assess the efficiency implications of alternate political options;

literacy thereby increases the probability that efficient public policy prevails.[5] Yet another argument derives from the idea that information asymmetry would exist in a private market for loans between parents seeking to finance their children's primary and secondary education and potential lenders. In a private education market, such loans would be exceedingly difficult to negotiate. (Would the children agree to repay loans negotiated on their behalf by their parents?) Even for post-secondary education, where students borrow on their own behalf, such loans are complex. Universal state-funded primary and secondary education eliminated many financial complexities.

In addition to these redistributive and efficiency-based arguments, the majority view education as a merit good. Regardless of its contribution to equality of incomes and economic development, those of us who can read and write, who can use basic mathematics, and who understand something of science and history want others to have the benefits of this knowledge as well. Thailand's monarchy has a long tradition of wielding royal influence within government to advance universal primary education. Such policies have without doubt contributed to Thailand's exceptional economic growth in the last generation; but Thai monarchs have also defended education simply as a merit good that they want for their subjects.

Thai monarchs and Third World feminists have this much in common: both view education as a merit good. Educated women earn more than uneducated women, but that is not the feminists' central concern. Feminists argue for universal primary education because of the effect it has on the relative position of women and men. Educated girls are less subservient; they have options beyond the traditional roles of marriage, child bearing, and unpaid labor within the family. Feminists want more equality between the sexes, both in the family and in the community, regardless of what men think on the matter.

Merit goods imply the imposition of certain values via the design of social policy. Inevitably, such imposition entails frustrating those with divergent values. In many traditional societies, the majority of men are dubious about educating girls. Certainly, the majority do not favor devoting a large share of public revenues toward such programs.

Controversial merit good debates are not restricted to traditional patriarchal societies. International evidence suggests that universal state-run health insurance is more efficient than a private market alternative. But are efficiency arguments enough to force people to pay taxes for a service they do not want? Maybe, but to restrict discussion to efficiency concerns misses the heart of the matter. The majority in most industrial societies simply do not want a minority to be without free access to basic health services.

Merit good rationales for social policy are never simple and often evoke objections. When the Saskatchewan government first introduced universal medical insurance in 1962, the merit good argument was, to understate matters, controversial.... The majority of the province's doctors declared a strike and withheld services. They did not oppose government subsidy of insurance for the poor (and, at the time, any efficiency savings from overcoming adverse selection had yet to be demonstrated). The doctors' core complaint was that the government should not impose its "socialist" values on those who preferred alternate arrangements, either as health care providers or as patients. The government insisted that, in this case, imposing a widely shared value was legitimate.

In the final analysis, the legitimacy of any merit good argument rests on the legitimacy of the community value being promoted relative to the severity of any infringements being imposed on those who dissent. In political democracies, legitimacy for collective action derives from the decisions of elected legislatures, as constrained by the courts, guarantors of fundamental civil liberties. In the case of mandatory health insurance, the majority of citizens have shown in repeated elections that they find the merit good argument convincing, and, on the other side, the dissidents have been unable to convince any court that the imposition on them warrants redress.

Overcoming Myopia

Markets are wonderfully efficient institutions for allocating resources to maximize the current productivity of the economy, given its stock of capital goods (including here natural resources, physical capital, and the education and skills of the population). In almost every case across all countries, privately owned farms and private agricultural markets have proved better institutions for feeding a country's population than state-run farms and food distribution systems.

Private markets are not so efficient, however, when individuals must calculate costs and benefits over a long period and do so with limited information. In such instances, people may display too short a time horizon; to say the same thing another way, they may be myopic and discount the future too heavily. For example, a society may collectively decide that some parents and children are prone to discount too heavily the benefits from education. Based on this rationale (among others), governments legislate, first, that parents educate their children until they reach a stipulated age and, second, that employers not engage children below a stipulated age as paid workers. Pensions are a more controversial example. Citizens may collectively decide that they do not trust themselves, acting as individuals, to make good decisions about provisions for old age. Using public myopia as a rationale, people may vote for a government that obliges its working-age citizens to set aside more of their income than they would in a free market.

The myopia argument amounts to government's claiming that it knows better how to evaluate the future.

The argument so far suggests that social policy can, by adjusting the lifetime pattern of investment and consumption, improve overall efficiency. But examined more closely, the logic is not so straightforward. To say, for example, that mandatory saving for pensions increases efficiency entails a circular argument. It is only true if one accepts that the appropriate discount rate for determining future pension income is less than the rate that people would use if left to make their own decisions. Why should government substitute its preferred low discount rate for the higher discount rate that many people would prefer? Like the merit good argument, the myopia argument amounts to government's claiming that it knows better how to evaluate the future than do the individuals concerned.

Despite the paternalism of this rationale, people do mistrust themselves when it comes to irreversible decisions with implications far into the future. The majority are willing to empower government to implement major mandatory pension programs. The ultimate legitimacy of such government intervention depends on citizens' willingness to ratify the results via elections and the inability of dissidents to persuade the courts that any fundamental individual rights have been thwarted.

Notice, however, the difference between myopia about pensions and the use of pensions for income redistribution. All Canadians over 65 receive a transfer from Ottawa under the Old Age Security (OAS) program, soon to become the seniors benefit (SB). This is a pay-as-you-go public pension plan in which the working generation pays taxes to provide defined pensions to the elderly. The rationale for this social program is primarily redistributive; the majority want to establish a floor for the income of *all* older citizens. On the other hand, the essential rationale for the Canada and Quebec Pension Plans was as an offset to myopia, a way to oblige working Canadians to undertake more saving and accordingly provide them with more income on retirement. The plan was established offline as a self-financing program. Unfortunately, in practice the program entails an overwhelming bias toward older workers who contributed relatively little to it; thereby, it has become, in effect, a second redistributive pay-as-you-go pension.

GOVERNMENT FAILURES

◆ ◆ ◆

Policy analysis should never be reduced to the disabused realism of Machiavelli. But any credible defense of the welfare state cannot rest simply on an analysis of market failures and collective goals. To borrow the Marxist notion of an intellectual dialectic, a credible defense must be a synthesis in which government failures are the antithesis of market failures.

The logic here is that economics is the study of rational agents (individuals, firms, or associations such as trade unions) seeking to maximize something—perhaps individual well-being or profits—in the context of market exchanges. Much politics amounts to the same thing and governments, like markets, can fail. The agents are not the same (interest groups, rather than firms) and the institutional rules defining political exchange differ from those governing exchanges in economic markets, but both markets and politics entail agents seeking to maximize something. To the extent politics is rational goal-seeking behavior subject to various institutional rules, no one should be surprised that, in many political markets, failure is as significant a problem as in economic markets.

What follows is a summary of five central themes in the study of government failures.

Rent Seeking by Interest Groups
Wherever market failures exist, the potential exists for government intervention to increase efficiency and create net benefits. Even the most conservative political theorists allow, for example, that government should establish a legal system and enforce contracts, creating an economic environment much better than a state of

anarchy. The question immediately arises, who reaps the net benefits (or *rents*) from government intervention?

Groups of people joined together to pursue explicitly identified common interests are the natural building blocks of politics. The essence of democracy is to enable people to participate in relevant interest groups, and the art of democratic politics is to reconcile conflicting interest group claims. The process is unstable, however, and particular interest groups frequently capture more of the net benefits than they should under any reasonable definition of the public good. The ultimate democratic check against such *rent seeking* by interest groups is citizens' ability to change governments via elections.

Bureaucratic Supply

The larger the organization, the more information is relevant to any managerial decision. Given onerous information costs, one strategy in large organizations—and governments are very large organizations—is to apply relatively simple rules in all cases. When the Model T dominated the automobile industry, Henry Ford allegedly told his managers that customers could have any color they wanted provided it was black.

Applying simple rules to complex social services results in less than optimum policy, so bureaucracies may develop complex rules that strive to maintain horizontal and vertical equity among citizens (that is, they strive to treat similar cases in similar ways and dissimilar cases in dissimilar ways). But codifying and applying complex rules creates new problems. Here, the problem is high transaction costs in interpreting rules and in modifying them as demands change.

Another strategy in large, for-profit firms is to decentralize managerial authority and motivate managers and workers to make efficient decisions via productivity-related compensation systems. Governments can also seek to motivate their workers by compensating them at levels above those for private sector workers with comparable skills. This strategy has important limits, however. At some point, citizens legitimately object that it has become a rationale for rent seeking by public sector workers at the expense of taxpayers.

In a market economy, an important constraint on firm size is that transaction costs rise as size increases. Other factors, such as engineering scale economies, may militate in favor of large size, but the high costs of decisionmaking in a large firm frequently enable the smaller and more nimble competitors to succeed. In discussing the welfare state, the analogue is that smaller jurisdictions can usually deliver more efficient social policy than

large ones because the problems of bureaucratic supply are less intractable.

Moral Hazard

Moral hazard refers to the potential that an insured individual will not exercise due caution in avoiding compensable losses. It is first cousin to adverse selection, which also arises in insurance markets. The essence of an insurance contract is to transfer the cost of some undesirable random event from the insuree to the insurer. Adverse selection arises when an insuree hides information relevant to assessing risk; moral hazard arises when an insuree behaves in a manner that the insurer would find inappropriate on the part of an uninsured person. On occasion, the two concepts merge. If a driver, when buying car insurance, fails to acknowledge that she enters her car in local stock car races, that is adverse selection. If she takes up stock car racing after she is insured, that is moral hazard.

Both adverse selection and moral hazard are present to varying degrees with all insurance contracts. I have treated adverse selection as a market failure because universal government insurance programs are one means of overcoming it. Although moral hazard is also present in private insurance markets, I list it here as a government failure because it is often an acute problem with government-run social insurance programs. It may not be severe immediately after the program is introduced, but after many years people are likely to adapt their behavior to the changed incentives.

An important example of moral hazard has arisen in Canada with unemployment insurance (UI) ... [with] the increasing share of claims accruing to repeat users who [have] adapted their employment patterns to UI regulations.

Median Voter Problems

Median voter problems arise when the majority opt for policies conferring small per capita benefits on the majority that are paid for by inefficient, large per capita costs imposed on a minority. For example, the majority may prefer a highly progressive income tax under which very high marginal tax rates affect only a few wealthy taxpayers. As already mentioned (see note 2), the evidence indicates that marginal tax rates above, say 50 percent, generate unacceptably high avoidance and evasion costs.

Median voter problems are particularly acute when the benefits of inefficient public policy are easily identified by recipients and the costs less so. Take, for example, workers' compensation, which is one of the oldest of social insurance programs (originating with Bismarck in late-nineteenth-century Germany). An efficiently run program can eliminate serious adverse selection problems that arise in a tort-based private insurance market. Both workers and their employers benefit because the former obtain reasonable certainty of compensation in the event of injury, and the latter get protection against a large compensation claim that could bankrupt a small firm. Unfortunately, workers' compensation boards (WCBs) across Canada have been subject to median voter problems over the past two decades. In an attempt to increase WCB revenues, certain provinces have extended coverage to additional, usually low-risk sectors at premiums above actuarially fair levels for them. The beneficiaries of this extended coverage are the majority of employers and workers[6] in sectors that were previously covered, while the losers are those in the newly inducted sectors (Thomason 1995).

Game Playing

[C]oordinated social policy can overcome inefficient free riding in the market for charity. Inefficient game playing also exists within government.

For an example relevant to social policy, return to the case of WCBs. A trend over the past two decades has been for government administrators to delegate most WCB policy decisions to quasi-autonomous boards composed of equal numbers of business and labor representatives (Bogyo 1995), the rationale being that if both sides have an interest in the system's success, let them administer it as they see fit. Both sides do indeed have a shared interest, but they also have conflicting interests over allocating costs and benefits. In many jurisdictions, labor representatives have argued for extending coverage to new sectors at rates above actuarial levels (see the previous discussion of median voter problems) and have lobbied for excessively generous benefits to injured workers (thereby creating moral hazard problems). Employer representatives have resisted increasing premiums to actuarially justified levels (a logical interest group behavior provided the resulting deficit can be shifted onto the general taxpaying population). The result, in several jurisdictions, has been rapidly increasing unfunded WCB liabilities. Vaillancourt (1995, 73) estimates the total net debt of Canadian provincial WCB systems at $15.8 billion as of 1992; the worst offender was Ontario with a debt of $11.0 billion.

By delegating management to labor and employer representatives, governments have transformed WCBs into chicken games. Both employer and labor representatives want their WCBs to succeed, but they have a strong incentive to undertake pre-emptive moves to place the costs of the system on the other side. Recall the prototype chicken game with the teenagers hurtling toward one another. Unfortunately, the girl friends cannot always dissuade their boy friends, and head-on collisions occur. Analysts who have examined the Ontario WCB in recent years are unanimous that it is inefficiently run and headed for financial disaster. No one is yet sure how to avoid the head-on collision.

CONCLUSION

◆ ◆ ◆

The welfare state is a massive work-in-progress with many flaws.... But I hope that from this chapter readers gather a better appreciation of why the welfare state remains relevant in an age when the ideology of liberal capitalism has seemingly triumphed.

... Relatively free competitive markets are institutions essential to realizing the full potential of industrial technology. But capitalism and a minimal state cannot create a decent life for the majority; well-run government social programs are essential. With all due respect to the importance of liberal thought in western culture, Adam Smith was partly wrong. He launched a theoretical discussion (one that is ongoing two centuries later) of why "the butcher, the brewer, or the baker" contribute to our well-being. Yet simultaneously, we need to understand when and how those "who trade for the public good" can make a positive contribution.

Notes

1. Occasionally, some subset of consumers of a public good or service find it sufficiently important to supply it voluntarily themselves. In south Asian cities, operators of private bus lines want traffic control at congested intersections to increase the efficiency of their buses, and the publicly supplied service leaves much to be desired. On occasion, the bus companies pay individuals to act as informal traffic controllers. This is an example of a privately supplied public good. Once supplied, all vehicles—rickshaws, cars, trucks, as well as the buses—benefit.

2. While $1.33 may be the *average* gross cost per $1.00 of tax revenue, the cost of raising an *additional* $1.00 by increasing marginal tax rates is far more than $1.33. During the 1990s, for example, the British Columbia government introduced new income tax surcharges. The combined federal-provincial income tax rate on incremental income above $60,000 now exceeds 50 percent. Kesselman (1995) cites estimates that this surtax may cause more than $60.00 in lost productivity per $1.00 of revenue raised. His figure may be too high, but it illustrates an important problem. As marginal tax rates rise, they induce increasing amounts of inefficient tax-avoidance activity. As a rule of thumb, the economic costs from setting marginal income tax rates above 50 percent almost certainly exceed any redistributive benefit (provided the government is reasonably egalitarian with the expenditures financed by revenues raised at lower rates).

3. Indeed, Joseph Stiglitz (1994) emphasizes information asymmetry as the core market failure to justify government intervention in private markets and, on occasion, government supply of goods and services.

4. As described in the next section, there are also rationales for public education that are based on the desire for redistribution, on certain externalities, and on a "merit goods" argument.

5. This argument has important limits. The well-educated citizens of Germany voted for the Nazis, whose ultimate impact on European prosperity was disastrous. The illiterate majority of India may not have voted for particularly efficient economic policies, but apart from the communal violence at the time of partition in 1947, they have demonstrated a greater tolerance for cultural differences than Europeans during the twentieth century.

6. WCB premiums take the form of a payroll tax on employers. In the first instance, such premiums affect employers and not workers. But over time, employers adjust their wage offers on the basis of total costs of hiring workers. Hence, the incidence of WCB premiums ultimately falls on both employers and workers, regardless of the formal imposition on employers only.

Terms & Concepts

adverse selection	merit goods	opportunity costs
experience goods	moral hazards	paternalism
externalities	myopia	public goods
gross costs	net costs	rent seeking
information asymmetry	nonexcludable items	transaction costs
median voter problems	nonrivalrous items	

Questions

1. According to this article, why should governments run, or not run, education systems? Use Richards's terms in your explanation.

2. Explain the kinds of market failures that are directly relevant to the development of public social policy.

3. There are "virtuous rationales" for governmental social policy. If this is the case, why then are the rationales for social policy "never simple"? Use clear examples to support your argument.

4. Richards argues that "a credible defense" of the welfare state "must be a synthesis in which government failures are the antithesis of market failures." What does this mean, and why is this point of view particularly relevant today?

5. What key *political* elements interfere with market forces, and why are rents and transaction costs often so high?

Unit Three   Discussion Questions

1. Do any of the belief systems discussed seem to explain our world better than other systems do? Do belief systems really matter anyway, as we go about our daily lives?

2. Do some ideologies seem to fit together whereas others seem opposed? Is liberalism, say, more compatible with feminism than with conservatism? Is nationalism more compatible with neo-conservatism than with liberalism?

3. In what ways do ideas matter? Can they be a force for political change, or are they merely indicators or symptoms of other political and economic conditions?

4. In the continuing contest of political ideologies, do you think any one or more will prevail? Will the future belong to nationalism, liberalism, or some other combination of belief systems?

Annotated Bibliography

Abu-Laban, Yasmeen. "The Politics of Race and Ethnicity: Multiculturalism as a Contested Arena." In *Canadian Politics*, 2nd ed., edited by James P. Bickerton and Alain-G Gagnon. Peterborough, Ont.: Broadview, 1994, 242–63. An examination of the concept of multiculturalism in Canada.

Arblaster, Anthony. *The Rise and Decline of Western Liberalism*. Oxford: Basil Blackwell, 1984. An acclaimed critical analysis of liberalism from its early development to its 20th-century forms.

Ball, Terrence, and Richard Dagger. *Political Ideologies and the Democratic Ideal*. New York: HarperCollins, 1991. This reader provides a historical foundation for traditional ideologies, as well as their current derivatives, and includes analysis of various "liberation ideologies."

Betz, Hans-Georg. *Radical Right-Wing Populism in Western Europe*. New York: St. Martin's Press, 1994. An analysis of the recent rise of populism in France, Italy, and Germany.

Brooks, Geraldine. *Nine Parts of Desire: The Hidden World of Islamic Women*. New York: Doubleday, 1995. A fascinating exploration of the private and public roles of women in Islamic countries.

Bissoondath, Neil. *Selling Illusions: The Cult of Multiculturalism in Canada*. Markham, Ont.: Penguin, 1994. A provocative critique of Canadian multiculturalism and affirmative action.

Boyd, Susan, ed. *Challenging the Public-Private Divide: Feminism, Law, and Public Policy*. Toronto: University of Toronto Press, 1997. A collection of essays exploring feminist interpretations of the state and public policy and how they interact with the private sphere.

Carens, Joseph, ed. *Is Quebec Nationalism Just?: Perspectives from Anglophone Canada*. Montreal: McGill-Queen's University Press, 1995. On the whole, this is a favourable examination of Quebec's policies on such matters as language and immigration.

Dworkin, Ronald. *A Matter of Principle*. Cambridge, Mass.: Harvard University Press, 1985. An examination of the balance struck between liberty and equality in liberalism.

Eisler, Riane. *The Chalice and the Blade: Our History, Our Future*. San Francisco: Harper and Row, 1988. A thought-provoking sociocultural investigation of gender relations in the past, present, and future.

Elshtain, Jean Bethke. *Democracy on Trial*. Concord, Ont.: Anansi, 1993. A fervent plea for the renewal of American civil society.

Etzioni, Amitai, ed. *Rights and the Common Good*. New York: St. Martin's Press, 1995. A comprehensive collection of essays by leading communitarian scholars, including Christopher Lasch, Benjamin Barber, and Mary Ann Glendon.

Flanagan, Tom. *Waiting for the Wave: The Reform Party and Preston Manning*. Toronto: Stoddart, 1995. An insider's account of the tension between pragmatism and ideology in a populist party.

Folkertsma, Marvin J., Jr. *Ideology and Leadership*. Englewood Cliffs, N.J.: Prentice-Hall, 1988. A look at the political ideas and beliefs that inspired leaders such as Roosevelt, Martin Luther King, Stalin, Mao, Hitler, and the Ayatollah Khomeini.

Frum, David. *Dead Right*. New York: New Republic Books; Basic Books, 1994. A sweeping, polemical attack on the state by a leading neoconservative.

Fukuyama, Francis. *The End of History and the Last Man*. New York: Free Press, 1992. A much-discussed work on what Fukuyama considers the triumph of liberal democracy.

Gilligan, Carol. *In a Different Voice*. Cambridge, Mass.: Harvard University Press, 1982. An important and frequently cited contribution to the debate surrounding gender difference.

Gray, John. *False Dawn: The Delusions of Global Capitalism*. London: Granta, 1998. A collection of polemical essays exploring the limits and perils of global capitalism.

Gray, John. *Enlightenment's Wake: Politics and Culture at the Close of the Modern Age*. London: Routledge, 1995. An engaging set of essays on the future of liberalism, conservatism, and social democracy in Western societies.

Havel, Václav. *Summer Meditations*. Translated by Paul Wilson. Toronto: Viking, 1992. A collection of essays on the political and spiritual dimensions of life after Communism by the dissident Czech playwright who became president, first, of Czechoslovakia, and then the Czech Republic.

Hubbard, Ruth. *The Politics of Women's Biology*. New Brunswick: Rutgers, 1990. Hubbard, who decided to write about science after becoming a respected biologist, describes what she sees as the patriarchal nature of science. Scientific inquiry, she claims, has been part of the power structure that has subjugated women.

Ignatieff, Michael. *Blood and Belonging: Journeys into the New Nationalism*. Toronto: Viking, 1993. A study of nationalism in several contemporary locations, including Yugoslavia, Germany, and Quebec.

Kamenka, Eugene. "Nationalism: Ambiguous Legacies and Contingent Futures." *Political Studies* (special issue, 1993). In a special issue of this journal, Kamenka offers a sobering analysis of the past and future of nationalism.

Limbaugh, Rush. *The Way Things Ought to Be*. New York: Pocket Books, 1994. The full ferocity of the "new" conservatism in the United States is evident in this volume.

Loney, Martin. *The Pursuit of Division: Race, Gender, and Preferential Hiring in Canada*. Montreal: McGill-Queen's University Press, 1998. A trenchant critique of feminist and multiculturalist claims of systemic discrimination and the need for preferential hiring policies.

Minogue, Kenneth. "Ideology After the Collapse of Communism." *Political Studies* 41, 4 (1993). An attempt to redefine *ideology* and limit the use of the term.

Pateman, Carole. "Feminism and Democracy." In *Democratic Theory and Practice,* edited by Graeme Duncan. Cambridge: Cambridge University Press, 1983. A classic essay by one of the foremost feminist critics of liberal democracy. Pateman believes that liberal democratic politics purposefully and wrongly limit the political participation of women and citizens of lower socioeconomic status.

Phillips, Derek L. *Looking Backward: A Critical Appraisal of Communitarian Thought*. Princeton, N.J.: Princeton University Press, 1993. A critical examination of the historical evidence of "community" and its relevance in the current era.

Radcliffe Richards, Janet. *The Sceptical Feminist: A Philosophical Inquiry*. London: Penguin, 1980. The author traces the nature of gender inequality, identifies its causes, and critically assesses the arguments justifying it.

Richards, John, Robert D. Cairns, and Larry Pratt, eds. *Social Democracy Without Illusions*. Toronto: McClelland & Stewart, 1991. A collection of useful essays on some of the key questions facing Canadian social democrats.

Rorty, Richard. "The Intellectuals at the End of Socialism," *Yale Review* 80, 1–2, (April 1992). A leading scholar discusses the role of left-wing intellectuals and the collapse of the Left.

Rosenblum, Nancy, ed. *Liberalism and the Moral Life*. Cambridge, Mass.: Harvard University Press, 1989. A collection of essays laying out the key debates in which liberalism is currently embroiled.

Sandel, Michael, ed. *Liberalism and Its Critics*. New York: New York University Press, 1984. A collection of articles examining the assault on American liberalism.Sandel, Michael J. *Democracy's Discontent: America in Search of a Public Philosophy*. Cambridge, Mass.: Belknap Press, 1996. A communitarian critique of modern, "procedural," individualistic liberalism.

Sigurdson, Richard. "Preston Manning and the Politics of Postmodernism in Canada." *Canadian Journal of Political Science* 27, 2 (June 1994). Hyper-modernism meets the retro-right, and globalization encounters parochialism.

Smith, Anthony. *National Identity*. London: Penguin, 1991. A concise and balanced review of ethnic and other forms of nationalism.

Walker, Connor. "Beyond Reason: The Nature of the Ethnonational Bond," *Ethnic and Racial Studies* (July 1993). An interesting discussion of a vital topic.

Young, Iris Marion. *Justice and the Politics of Difference*. Princeton, N.J.: Princeton University Press, 1990. A critical examination of the relationship between universal citizenship and group differences based on gender, ethnicity, and race.

Unit Four

Citizenship and Democracy

◆ ◆ ◆

Consider a paradox of Canadian politics. Canadians value democratic principles and tell pollsters that theirs is one of the best countries in which to live. Yet they are quite cynical about Canadian politicians and the political process. Over half of Canadians express little or no confidence in Parliament, and over a third believe politicians have lower than average ethical standards.[1] This is an odd state of affairs in a regime allegedly composed of self-governing citizens—that is, people who collectively govern themselves and shape the polity. Despite the democratic character of the Canadian state, Canadians compare themselves very favourably with those who hold political office.

On reflection, the paradox can be explained in terms of the nature of Canadian democracy. It is a representative democracy spanning a continent, with a federal constitution and a highly developed welfare state. Governing at the dawn of the 21st century is difficult, and Canadians may be forgiven for their frustrations. Furthermore, the principle of political representation does put citizens at one remove from the levers of power and responsibility, and so the system itself creates a distinction between government and the governed. One might also add that the history of political thought reveals an abiding suspicion of full-blown democracy, a suspicion that has led some to advocate contrivances to keep popular participation in government under strict control.[2]

Nonetheless, participation in democratic government is almost univer-sally considered desirable. In fact, to a great degree, democratic citizenship *is* participation.

Citizenship is a legal as well as sociological matter. Citizenship is a legal status in that citizens of a state are entitled to exercise the full measure of rights, ranging from political and legal rights to social welfare entitlements. How one gains citizenship varies from state to state. Generally, one becomes a citizen of a country by being born there. However, there have been conspicuous exceptions to this rule. Until 1999, the Federal Republic of Germany operated under a 1913 citizenship code that defined citizenship on the basis of ethnicity. This code effectively deprived over seven million residents of non-German ethnic background (either guest workers or their descendants) of the rights of citizenship.

In most cases, those not born in a country can be naturalized as citizens by making an application and satisfying certain conditions, for example, living in the country for a minimum period, demonstrating a knowledge of the country's history and politics, and pledging allegiance to the country and its constitution. Such conditions are always a matter of political debate. Some argue that conditions should be stringent, especially when the host country boasts a generous welfare state. Others maintain that rigorous condi-

Photo courtesy of Canapress.

Material inequalities in advanced democracies raise questions about the rights and obligations of citizenship.

tions are unacceptably exclusive in an age in which cultural pluralism ought to be affirmed.

When the discussion of citizenship shifts from rights to obligations, the sociological dimension of citizenship comes to the fore. Citizenship is a matter of membership, belonging, and identification, a fact clearly evident in the pomp and ritual associated with citizenship ceremonies. What can be expected of a citizen? What sacrifices of time and energy must citizens make? How exactly are the rights and duties of citizenship expressed in 21st-century democracies?

Several articles in this unit consider the issues of participation and belonging, as well as the rights of citizenship. They explore how people participate and in what ways democratic citizenship is hampered.

---

1. See Maureen Mancuso et al., *A Question of Ethics: Canadians Speak Out* (Toronto: Oxford University Press, 1998). For a comparative perspective see Neil Nevitte, *The Decline of Deference: Canadian Value Change in Cross-National Perspective* (Peterborough, Ont.: Broadview, 1996).

2. An excellent example of this suspicion of democracy is *The Federalist Papers,* a compilation of late 18th-century news articles written by James Madison, Alexander Hamilton, and John Jay, all of whom would have influenced the ratification of the American Constitution. The Fathers of Confederation, especially Canada's first prime minister, were no less suspicious of popular government.

The Decline of Civil Society: How Come? So What?

Robert D. Putnam

Editors' Note*

This provocative article takes us out of the world of global economics and political institutions and moves us into the world of social groups and "the dense fabric of civic life." Putnam's initial claim, based on longitudinal studies of Italian regions, is that the denser this fabric, the better governmental performance (and public services) will be. "When choirs sing, governments hum along," so to speak.

Of course, it isn't quite as simple as this, as the rest of this lecture, published under the auspices of the Canadian Centre for Management Development, makes clear. Translated into the North American context, Putnam's thesis is that the more we bowl or watch TV alone, lead private lives, neither stimulate nor create our social capital, and

fail to establish norms of reciprocity, the worse our condition will become, collectively and individually.

Without a flourishing and reasonably healthy civil society, there will be adverse consequences for our minds, our health, and our achievements, and there are all sorts of clear signs that North America's civil society is moving further and further away from the democratic ideal. It's easy to read Putnam's argument and think he's right. Blame the younger generation; blame this one for the way things have developed; blame television and films; blame our lack of trust; blame our lack of real conversations and meaningful interactions. It's a "civic plague" out there all right, and we will have to deal with the consequences. Yet just when the reader is

likely to become seriously depressed, Putnam surprises us with an optimistic conclusion.

Of course, it is difficult to capture what is meant when we write and speak about such things as communities. As members of all sorts of communities—professional, social, familial, local, provincial, national—what does having a sense of community entail for those of us who live, say, in a Canadian city? Is it mere civic pride, or does it and should it encompass action as well as feeling, and if so, action on behalf of whom or what? Putnam challenges us to think about such matters. His theme is that we need to "connect." He reminds us that civil societies have faced such challenges before and have coped. One hopes he is right.

◆ ◆ ◆

It is a great pleasure to be here and an honour to be asked to deliver the 1996 John L. Manion Lecture.[1] This evening I want to share a mystery with you, a detective story that I have been working on for the last several years. Please forgive me, though, if I begin with a brief autobiographical note which will help to explain how I came to this evening's topic.

Several years ago, I was engaged in a very academic study of a very obscure topic—the character, quality, and performance of local government in Italy. Over a twenty-

year period, with a number of colleagues, I measured the effectiveness of different regional governments. As a political scientist I am interested in why some governments work better than others. If you are a botanist and want to study plant development, you might take genetically identical seeds and plant them in different pots of soil, then water them differently to see how they grow and how their growth is a function of their physical environment. If you are a political scientist and you want to study the development of public institutions, you would

*We wish to acknowledge the assistance received from the Canadian Centre for Management Development, under whose auspices the John L. Manion lecture was delivered.

From a speech given by Prof. Robert D. Putnam to the Canadian Centre for Management Development in 1996. Reprinted by permission of the author. This article also appears in Prof. Putnam's upcoming text, *Bowling Alone: The Collapse and Revival of American Community,* to be published in 2000 by Simon and Schuster.

take the same paper organization and set it in different social, economic and cultural contexts to see how the institution is influenced by its environment. Normally, political science is not an experimental science, so it is not possible for political scientists to do this kind of research.

Yet in 1970 the Italians laid the basis for this kind of research by creating an entirely new set of regional governments across the peninsula of Italy. These governments all had the same powers on paper and looked essentially identical. They all had substantial resources. (They all now spend approximately ten percent of the GNP of Italy, about the same level as the American states.) So these were potentially quite powerful, quite important, institutions. They were genetically identical because they all looked the same on paper, but the pots of soil—the regions into which they were introduced—were quite different. Some of them were quite wealthy and economically advanced, some were quite backward, some were Catholic, some were controlled by Communists. The research question was simple: What happened to these genetically identical institutions as they developed in these different contexts?

For twenty years my colleagues and I very carefully explored the performance of these governments. We examined their budgets; we explored their administrative arrangements and administrative efficiency; we counted the number of day-care centres or irrigation projects they produced; we measured their "street-level" responsiveness to citizen inquiries.

Why do some governments work better than others? What were the secret ingredients?

We discovered that some of these regional governments were, and are, quite efficient and effective, but others were, and are, clear disasters. I have never had the pleasure of experiencing the efficiency of Canadian government, but I do have experience of the government of the Commonwealth of Massachusetts, and I can assure you that many of these Italian regional governments are much more efficient, much more effective, creative and innovative than the government of Massachusetts. Still others are disasters—corrupt, inefficient, never answer their mail. So the questions were: Why is this so? Why do some governments work better than others? What were the secret ingredients, the secret elements, in the soil?

We had lots of ideas. We thought it might be that richer, more economically advanced regions could afford better governments. We thought it might be related to education. (It's a conceit of educators to think that maybe we make a difference.) We thought it might be related to the political party system. We had lots of ideas, many hypotheses. We did not, however, guess what turned out to be the best predictors of government performance—choral societies and football clubs! And rotary clubs, and reading groups, and hiking clubs, and so on! That is, some of these communities had dense networks of civic engagement. People were connected with one another and with their government. It wasn't simply that they were more apt to vote in regions with high-performance governments, but that they were connected horizontally with one another in a dense fabric of civic life.

A norm of reciprocity had evolved in these regions, the type of reciprocity that makes a community work and, of course, also makes governments work much more effectively and efficiently. These regions had this dense civic fabric, this tradition, this habit of connecting with one's neighbours and with community institutions. These regions were also wealthier, more economically advanced. For a long time we thought this was so because *wealth* produced choral societies. We conjectured that people in economically advanced, more affluent places could afford to take the time to become engaged in community affairs, while the poor sickly peasants didn't have much opportunity to join a choral society. We thought wealth produced choral societies.

We had it, however, exactly backwards. It was not wealth that had produced choral societies, it was—at least in the Italian case—the choral societies that had produced wealth. That is, two identical regions one hundred years ago were equally backward, but one happened to have a tradition of civic engagement and it became wealthier and wealthier. We discovered to our amazement that this pattern of civic connectedness was a crucial ingredient, not only in explaining why some institutions work better than others, but also, at least partly, in explaining levels of economic well-being.

SOCIAL CAPITAL

◆ ◆ ◆

I want to introduce here some social science jargon, for which I apologize but which may be helpful in our subsequent discussion—*social capital*. We all know what *physical* capital is—it is some physical object that makes you more productive than you would be if you didn't have it. A screwdriver, for instance. You save up your nickels and dimes and you invest in a screwdriver so that you can repair more bicycles more quickly than you could without the screwdriver. That is physical capital. Then, about twenty years ago, economists began talking about *human* capital to refer to an analogy between a screwdriver and a degree from the University of Toronto. If you save up your money and go to college or to auto mechanics school, you can be more productive and more efficient than you would be if you lacked that training. That is human capital.

Now we are talking about *social* capital to refer to the features in our community life that make us more productive—a high level of engagement, trust, and reciprocity. If you are fortunate enough to live or work in a community or an organization like that, you can be more productive than you would be in a different context. This kind of social capital turned out to be crucial, at least in part, in explaining economic development, institutional performance, and so on. And that is the end of my preface. The question was why some governments work better than others, and the answer was choral societies—that is, social capital.

THE DECLINE IN TRUST

♦ ♦ ♦ *Social institutions*

When I finished the research in Italy several years ago and came back to the United States, I began to worry, as a citizen, about a problem that concerns most people in the United States now—a sense that our institutions are not working as well as they once did. There are many metrics of this, many measures. One convenient measure is the answer to the pollsters' question that has been asked for thirty or forty years: Do you trust the government in Washington to do what is right most of the time?

When I was growing up in the fifties and sixties, if you asked Americans if they trust the government to do what is right most of the time, 75 percent would have said yes. That answer now seems antique. Last year, to the same question, about 20 percent of Americans said that they trust the government to do what is right most of the time. And that reflects a steady thirty-year decline, not linked to any particular administration or any particular party.

Trust has been down under Democrats and under Republicans, in periods of prosperity as well as in peri-

ods of economic hard times. And it is not only distrust of government that has grown, and certainly not just the federal government. It is also a distrust of state and local government, a distrust and lack of appreciation, and lack of approval, of the performance of most of the institutions in our society. Trust in business is down, trust in churches is down, trust in medicine is down. Trust in—I am sorry to have to say this—trust in universities is down. We have this feeling that none of our institutions is working as well as it did twenty or thirty years ago.

The degree of this decline in confidence in public institutions is greater in the United States than in any of the advanced industrial democracies, at least to my knowledge. And the length of time during which this decline has occurred is greatest in the United States, but there are many other advanced industrial countries with similar trends. Everyone in the room is more expert on Canadian politics and government than I am, but I have the impression that there has been a similar decline, not so deep, more modest (that is the Canadian way of doing things)—but still the trend is here. I am not talking about this particular government, but about a general sense that civic institutions are no longer working as well. The trends are down in Sweden, in Japan, in Italy, in Britain, and in many of the advanced industrial countries.

THE DECLINE IN CIVIC ENGAGEMENT

♦ ♦ ♦

This evening I will focus on the United States because this is the case I know best, and it is where I have done my research. I began to wonder whether there could be a connection between this problem that worries me as a citizen—the performance of our institutions—and what I have been studying as a scholar, namely social capital. So several years ago I began investigating trends in social capital, trends in civic engagement in the United States over the past twenty or thirty years. What I found at first surprised me and then, increasingly, distressed me—and now, frankly, it has become a matter of grave concern to me.

What I found is that over this period there has been a substantial decline in many forms of civic engagement in the United States. The simplest example, and the one most familiar to Americans, is that we are voting less, about 25 percent less, than we were a generation ago. But this decline turns out to be relatively more modest than some of the other metrics of civic engagement, and it is certainly not the most important one. I mention it only because it is the most visible. There are other examples within the domain of politics and government. Pollsters, for instance, have been asking Americans every year for the last twenty or twenty-five years if they have been to any meeting within the last year at which there has been a discussion of town or school affairs. The results show a decline in this type of civic engagement of nearly 40 percent over the last twenty years. And there are similar declines in other measures of civic deliberation. We are not just voting less, we are exchanging ideas with one another less about public affairs.

There has been a substantial decline in many forms of civic engagement in the United States.

What I want to emphasize most is that this decline is not only true of politics—we Americans are connecting with one another and with our communities much less in many other spheres. Consider, for a moment, participation in community organizations. In the United States, the most common and most important of these are religious organizations. Since roughly half of all memberships are religious, roughly half of all philanthropy is religious, and roughly half of all volunteering is in a religious context—the trends in American religious activity and religious behaviour can tell us a great deal. Depending to some extent on what measures are used, there is evidence of a decline of about 20 percent, perhaps even 25 percent, in the number of Americans, for example, who say that they went to church last Sunday.

I want to pause here for just a second to report on a rather unkind recent sociological study in which pollsters asked people the standard question, Did you go to church last Sunday? and then went to see whether those who said yes were actually in the pews. I have two unfortunate things to report. First of all, we fib a lot about whether we went to church. Roughly twice as many of us say we were there as actually were. And there is also some evidence that we are fibbing more than our parents did. So these poll numbers, if anything, underestimate the degree to which there has been a decline in attendance at church, but not in every single congregation or in every denomination. Some have been gaining, some have been declining. Evangelical religion has been growing over this period, but not enough to

offset the really catastrophic collapse in attendance at the mainline religious organizations—Methodist, Lutheran, Episcopal, and Catholic as well. The decline in participation in religious organizations has been significant.

This is true also of trade unions. A generation ago the most important kind of affiliation for many working-class Americans, especially working-class men, was membership in trade unions. However, membership in trade unions is off by about 50 percent, or perhaps close to 60 percent, over this period. Thus, we are not going to church or the union lodge as often as we did in the past.

There are similar trends in many other kinds of civic organizations. Take, for example, what I have come to call the "animal" clubs—men's organizations. This is not a slur; it reflects the fact that I have discovered in the course of doing this research that most American men's clubs are named for animals—the Lions Club, the Moose Club, the Elks Club and the Eagles Club—and, of course, there are a few others like the Masons. All of these groups have experienced a decline of between 20 and 50 percent in membership over this period. In fact, the trend over this whole century is quite interesting. Over most of the century, it appears, rising numbers of American men belonged to such organizations (and the same pattern applies to women's organizations). More American men, proportionately, apparently belonged to "animal" clubs in 1960 than in 1950, and more in 1950 than in 1940. This was the trend over the whole of this century until suddenly, silently, inexplicably, all of them began to experience plateauing, followed by a steadily and then more rapidly declining membership over the last 20 to 25 years. There are other examples as well: volunteering for the Red Cross is off by more than 50 percent over this same period, and there are similar declines in adult volunteers for Boy Scouts and other community organizations.

BOWLING ALONE: THE DECLINE IN "CONNECTEDNESS"

◆ ◆ ◆

In many ways, therefore, we are connecting less. This does not mean, of course, that every single organization in America has lost members. That is not true. To take one example, membership in professional organizations has risen substantially, though hardly more than the number of Americans in professional and higher managerial jobs, so the "density" of such membership in the relevant portion of the population has not grown. On the other hand, some organizations have boomed. I happen to belong to the most rapidly expanding organization in America, one that has gone, over the same period, from about 300 thousand to 34 million members. This organization is called the AARP, the American Association of Retired Persons. I belong to this organization because when you turn fifty in America, and if you have a driver's licence, you get a letter in the mail asking you if you would like to join the AARP. Thinking that I might get a discount at motels or something, I signed up for the AARP, and I am an active member in good standing. My total membership activity each year consists of the 36 seconds that it takes to write a cheque for eight dollars, and then I flip through the pages of *Modern Maturity* magazine!

This is the general rule. Organizations in which membership means moving a pen, writing a cheque, are exploding. Organizations in which membership means being there, knowing another member, are stagnant or declining. (I don't know any other members of the AARP even though there are 34 million of us. Actuarially, I must know another member, of course, but I wouldn't know that I know another member because we never meet.) It is not that there are no lobbies—there are important big lobbies that have grown during this period. But the organizations in which you commit with other people are the ones that have experienced a decline in connectedness.

Here is some evidence that I hope will knock your socks off—membership in bowling leagues has dropped! (I can see that it didn't. Well, that is because you don't realize how important bowling is in America.) Bowling is big in America. More Americans bowled last year than voted last year. And bowling is up, up by 10 percent over this last decade or so. But bowling leagues, bowling with teams, is off by 40 percent over the same period. You will wonder how a professor knows such strange facts. The answer is that I happened to run into the man who owns one of the largest chains of bowling alleys in America who said, "You know, Professor Putnam, you happened on a major economic problem in our industry." It turns out that if you bowl in a league, a team, you drink four times as much beer and you eat four times as many pretzels—the money in bowling is made in beer and pretzels, not in balls and shoes. So this man is very much worried about the decline in league bowling, even though the numbers of people coming in the door are the same, or actually up. He is worried about the decline in league bowling because of the bottom line.

I, also, am worried about the decline in league bowling, and to explain why, I need to describe how team bowling works. If you bowl in a league in the United States, there are two teams with five people on a team—ten people. At any given time, two people are at the lane bowling and the other eight are sitting in a semicircle of benches at the back of the lanes drinking their beer, eating their pretzels, and talking. They are mainly talking about whether O.J. did it, but occasionally they talk about bond issues, or whether the garbage is being picked up properly, or how the local schools are performing. What I mean—and this is why I use bowling teams as a serious example—is that this is yet another occasion that we once had, but no longer have, for sustained conversation with other people we know well about shared interests and community affairs.

This is not to say that we are not talking about politics in America. We are *shouting* about politics in America! We have this talk radio plague (I hope it hasn't arrived in Canada) in which a caller says, "Hi, I'm Ted from Toledo ..." and then he goes on. I don't know Ted, I don't even know whether Ted *is* Ted, and I don't know if he is taking responsibility for his views in the way that my bowling league partner is. If you and I see each other every two weeks at the bowling alley and you say something crazy, you are taking responsibility for your views because you have to come back and face me again next week. This is fundamentally what has been happening to American democracy: we are less and less able to have serious discussions with people we know well. I don't mean highbrow academic discussions, I just mean having conversations with your neighbours about how things are going. I mean taking responsibility for your views. This is what this decline in social capital means. It is not just in a formal context, and it is not just in bowling leagues, or churches, or unions. It is a decline in informal connections.

This absence of civic conversation is characteristic not only of formal organizations but also of informal ties. For example, over the last thirty years American sociologists have asked people to keep a time budget of how they spend every minute of a particular day (so many minutes brushing their teeth, and so on). Therefore, we know how Americans have been spending their time over these thirty years and how this has been changing. In fact, the pattern has remained pretty constant. We spend about exactly the same number of minutes on most of our activities, such as commuting, as people did thirty years ago. This is somewhat surprising, but despite all the gains in technology, the number of hours spent commuting seems to have been constant for most of the century.

Against this pattern of basic consistency over time in how we spend our day is the fact that we are spending about 25 percent less time in ordinary conversation with other people and about 50 percent less time than we did thirty years ago in organizational meetings. And we know our neighbours less well. Over the past twenty or twenty-five years the number of people who say they never spend a social evening with a neighbour has doubled. It is not only in voting, it is not only in politics, it is not even only in a formal organizational context. It is in many different ways that we are no longer connecting with one another.

We trust one another less.

Furthermore—and this is in some sense the crux of the matter—we trust one another less. A generation ago if you asked Americans if they trust other people, nearly two thirds would have said yes. Today, if you asked that same question of Americans, nearly two thirds would say no. We are losing those habits of reciprocity and trust that are characteristic of communities with high levels of social capital.

SEARCHING FOR AN EXPLANATION

◆ ◆ ◆

The best predictor that people will become engaged in their communities is their level of education. More education means more engagement. Over this thirty-year period we have had a massive increase in the average education levels of the American public as more people have gone to college, yet over exactly the same period we have dropped out. We have disconnected from our neighbours and from our community organizations. Why? This is not some kind of natural sociological trend that has been going on for the last one hundred, two hundred or five hundred years—it has been happening in my lifetime, in our lifetimes. What might have caused this trend?[2]

Demographic Factors

Dual-income families may have separated us as large numbers of women moved into the labour force. But I have to be careful when I discuss this hypothesis: our mothers were doing a lot of social capital building (that

is jargon for taking the kids to the Little League). Our wives and daughters are working to help with the family income and for their own professional satisfaction, but nobody is carrying out the tasks that our mothers did. That, at least, is the hypothesis.

The evidence on the issue of women in the labour force is mixed. It is true that the declines in civic engagement are slightly greater among women than among men, but they are greatest among women who *do not* work outside the home. The category of Americans in which the decline has been greatest is that of "traditional moms"—married mothers who are not working outside the home. A generation ago, more than three-quarters of such women belonged to the PTA; now the figure is less than half. In fact, the level of civic engagement is now slightly higher among women who are working outside the home than among those who stay at home. None of this is evidence from a controlled experiment. We can't be completely sure whether the women who a generation ago would have been the joiners were disproportionately the women who went into the labour force, but it is certainly possible that the most civically inclined women have moved into the labour force, thus raising the level of civic activity among the employed female population and leaving behind those who are less likely to be engaged. It is a complicated question.

The trends, by the way, are down among men too. You could, of course, assume that this is because the men are picking up the slack at home, leaving less time for the animal clubs. I don't know about Canada, but this is not true in the United States. All the evidence suggests that men are not picking up the slack.

Divorce and other changes in the family structure might also have played a role. It is certainly true that the divorce rate has gone up and the number of people living alone has also increased quite substantially. It is statistically true that people who live alone are less likely to be connected to other people and are actually less likely to trust other people. This set of changes in the family structure is very likely an important contributor to the decline in community involvement.

Economic Factors

How about economic trends? Well, one key fact is that civic engagement is down at every level of the income hierarchy. The trends are down among rich folks, down among poor folks and down among the middle class. Indeed, one of the most striking things about this pattern of findings is that the trends are down in all parts of America. These various measures of civic engagement are down among highly educated people and they are down among high school dropouts; they are down at all levels of the educational and income and social hierarchy; they are down among blacks and down among whites; they are down on the east coast, down on the west coast, and down in middle America. This does not mean that each of these groups has the same absolute level of engagement—it means that the trends are down in each of them.

Age Factors

Indeed, there is only one exception, one set of categories, in which the trends are quite different, and that is age. Let us imagine that we line up all American adults according to their year of birth. At one end are the people who were born in the last years of the nineteenth century. Then there are the people who were born in the first years of this century, those born in 1910, 1920 and in the 1930s, the 1940s, the 1950s, the 1960s and the 1970s.

As we move along this line we ask each person a set of questions designed to measure their level of civic engagement—Did you vote last time? Do you read a newspaper? How many groups do you belong to? Do you trust other people?—all those measures of social capital. And what we find is that as we move along the line, beginning with birthdates at the end of the last century and in the first years of this century, the levels of civic engagement are quite high and unevenly rising— until we get to the people who were born in the early 1930s, when they are down a little bit, and for the next *forty years* of birth cohorts there is a steady, dramatic drop. By the time we get to the people who were born in the 1970s and who are just now coming of age, the average level of civic engagement is dramatically less than the level of civic engagement among their grandparents who were born in the 1920s. Their grandparents are twice as likely to vote and three times as likely to read the newspaper, and they belong to twice as many groups. They are also twice as likely to be trusting of other people. Thus, there are great differences by generation.

You might assume that this is because old folks are more engaged and young people have not yet had a chance to get engaged, but that is not a major part of the story. Most evidence suggests that habits of civic engagement are formed when you are fifteen or twenty. People who are now in their late sixties, seventies and eighties are much more civically involved than the younger generations. For their entire lives they have been holding up the civic structure of America, and those who are holding up more than their fair share are retiring. The last of this long civic-minded generation will be retiring next year. They are being replaced in the population by their children and grandchildren who are much less civically engaged. Unless we do something about this, the situation will get a lot worse.

Suburbanization, Architecture and Mobility

Suburbanization, the consequence of freeways, is certainly a plausible guilty-looking suspect, although I have to say that I have not yet been able to find any evidence. The average level of civic engagement or social trust is not lower in American suburbs than in the cities. In general, it is not true that suburbs are more fragmented or more isolating than central cities.

Architecture may also be an important part of the story—verandas and front porches, balconies and barbecues in the back yard. A town in California has recently been debating an ordinance—the Front Porch Ordinance—which would require, as a matter of zoning, that all new houses have front porches. The theory, I suppose, is that "if you build it, they will come." Architecture is important, and an earlier generation of urban planners have something to answer for in the design of our communities.

I thought that residential mobility might be a very prominent suspect, but actually this is a suspect in the United States that I can completely acquit, because it is simply not true that people are more mobile than their parents or grandparents. In fact we are less mobile. The number of people who move each year, whether we are talking about moving across the street or moving across the country, is actually significantly lower now. And this trend toward declining geographical mobility has been ongoing for nearly fifty years in the United States.

The Influence of Government

Governments also may have had a role in the destruction of social capital. Some conservative commentators and politicians claim that "big government" has caused this decline—that the reason people are not going to the PTA is because of the number of bureaucrats who go to the meetings. It is certainly true, in my view, that in the United States there have been some very important instances of government destroying social capital. Take, for example, the urban renewal programs in American central cities in the 1960s: a one-sentence summary for what they did was to renew physical capital and destroy social capital. There were brand new wonderful buildings and people lived in better homes, but they didn't have the same neighbours that they once did, nor did they know their new neighbours. We destroyed large numbers of quite well-functioning communities.

So some government programs have actually destroyed social capital. But it is difficult for me, frankly, to believe (and that is why I talk about bowling leagues) that the reason people are no longer going to gardening clubs or bowling leagues, the reason they no longer know their neighbours, is because of big government. Let me mention just two bits of evidence that seem to me not completely consistent with the idea that this basic trend is due to big government. One is that across the American states there is virtually no correlation between levels of social capital and the size of the government. That is, the citizens in the states that have larger governments and more welfare spending are no less likely to belong to civic groups or to trust other people.

Among the OECD countries, those that have the highest levels of social trust on average and the highest levels of civic engagement (group membership, for example) tend to be the very countries with the largest welfare states—Sweden, Norway, Denmark, for example. Actually, in that global perspective the United States and Canada are at almost exactly the same point. We have, in the aggregate, almost exactly the same levels of group membership and social trust. And we are still, I would say, in the United States and in Canada too, pretty high in comparison to most other countries—that is, there is a higher level of social capital in the U.S. even after this twenty- or thirty-year decline. I am not saying that America has no civic spirit left; what I am saying is that compared to where we were a generation ago, we have less. My best guess is that only a small part of this decline is due to government policies.

The Prime Suspect

Then what has caused this decline in social trust, in civic engagement, in "connectedness"? In general, this is a case, like the Agatha Christie novel *Murder on the Orient Express*, in which there are multiple culprits. The most reasonable conclusion from the available evidence, however, is that *a prime suspect is television*.

The timing is right. Television has hit America like a lightning bolt—the fastest infusion of any technological innovation in history. In 1949 less than ten percent of American homes had television; by 1959 more than ninety percent of American homes had television. It came like a lightning bolt and has had a continuing reverberation, so that by now the data say that the average American spends four hours a day watching television. That is not counting the hours that the set is on in the other room, but only the hours spent in front of it. There are some things you can do while you are watching television, but you cannot bowl and you cannot go to the PTA.

The main effect of the introduction of television—and this, by the way, is not unique to the United States—has been to make us more homebodies and more isolated. And whereas in the very first period all the family was sitting around the hearth watching television together, now, with the number of multi-set homes skyrocketing, we are just watching alone. And what we are watching is simulated social capital. We are watching the most popular television show in America, a show called *Friends*. Well, *Friends* is about social capital, but it is not *real* social capital. Like the program set in a Boston bar called *Cheers*, where "everybody knows your name," a lot of what you watch on television is designed to make you think that you actually have these good buddies you see every week—but they don't see you.

The statistical evidence is that for every hour you spend reading a newspaper you are substantially more likely to vote, more likely to trust other people, more likely to join a group. For every hour you spend in front of the television you are statistically substantially less likely to vote, less likely to join a group, and less likely to trust other people. So, although television is not the only part of the story, I think that it is a large part of the problem.

What about the Internet and "computer-mediated communication"? The net effect of the electronic revolution has been to make our communities, or what we experience as our communities, much wider geographically, and much thinner sociologically. Every day I can easily communicate with people in Germany and Japan, but I don't know the person across the street, and the fact that I don't know the person across the street would astonish my father more than the fact that I am talking to people across the globe every day. Place-based social capital is being replaced by function-based social capital. That is what the electronic revolution does.

For some purposes, function-based social capital is just as good, but for some purposes it is not. My friends abroad are great, and perhaps it is less likely there will be a war because I talk to them every day—but that does not do any good for the crime rate in my neighbourhood. I doubt that electronic communication has caused civic disengagement, for the computer came two or three decades into the change. On the other hand, we have to find ways in which we can use this electronic network structure to create *real* communities with *real* face-to-face interaction, not just phosphorous-to-phosphorus interaction.

WHY DOES IT MATTER?

◆ ◆ ◆

Does it matter that we are less civically engaged? Well, I don't want to spend a lot of time on this question but I do want to address it briefly because the decline in social capital matters a lot—and not just in the absence of warm cuddly feelings. Take, for example, the performance of your schools. If you are worried about the quality of schools in your community, you might have one of two strategies. You could pay ten percent more on schools, better teachers, more books in the library, and so on. Or you could increase by ten percent the number of parents who are engaged with their children's education. Evidence suggests that this latter strategy may be more effective for improving the quality of schools. I am not saying that we should not be spending money on schools (my wife is a public school teacher so I have a vested interest in paying teachers well!). What I am saying is that the decline in the number of parents in America who are engaged with their children's education is almost certainly a very important reason why our schools are not functioning as well as they should.

Crime is another example. If you are worried about crime in your neighbourhood, you might have one or two strategies: you could increase by ten percent the number of cops on the beat, or you could increase by ten percent the number of neighbours who know one another's first name. The latter is quite probably the more effective crime-fighting strategy. I am not saying that we don't want cops on the beat; I am saying that the fact that we don't know our neighbours as well as our parents knew theirs is an important explanation of why Americans are so worried about crime nowadays. There are many such examples.

Social capital also matters for your physical health. There are some really interesting studies, some fascinating studies, about the health effects of social connections. Even when controlling for whether you jog or not, how old you are, what gender you are and all the risk factors, your chance of dying (well, your chance of dying is high!)—your chance of dying over the next year is cut in half by joining one group; it is cut in a quarter by joining two groups. It is not that people who are healthy join. These studies measure a person's group membership today and then record how long that person survives. So it is not reverse causality, but rather that there are apparently some physiological effects of connecting with other people.

Part of it also is that the social connections provide a kind of safety net (if you go to church every Sunday and then one day you slip in the bathtub, someone will notice, but they won't if you don't). And another part of it is that we get feedback from other people about the state of our health. Not only the health of our communities, but also our own personal health is affected by this decline in civic engagement.

WHAT CAN BE DONE?

◆ ◆ ◆

I have described the tremendous civic plague that has come across the United States over the last thirty years. I think it is the key to many of our institutional problems. However, even though what I have said so far seems deeply pessimistic, in fact I am not at all pessimistic. But in order to explain why, I would like to offer a brief image of American history.

A short-form version of what I have said so far this evening is that technological and economic and social change over the last thirty years has led to a slow but cumulatively dramatic change in the way we connect, or do not connect, with one another. Much of our social capital has vanished as a result of technological, economic and social change.

One hundred years ago, exactly, America was in a very similar situation. The industrial revolution—the thirty-year period between 1865 and 1895—saw technological developments that transformed where and how people spent their lives. There were massive waves of immigration and, of course, urbanization. All of this had the effect of rendering obsolete a huge stock of social capital (that is just a jargony way of saying that people left their friends behind in Appleton when they moved to Chicago or elsewhere and didn't have friends or connections in their new town). Our country, in the 1890s, showed it: high rates of crime; widening economic gaps; a great sense of political corruption—a saturnalia of political corruption, as one person at the time described it; a sense that the institutions were not working and that people were disconnected from their communities. And then, in a very brief period of time, historically speaking, we created an entirely new set of institutions.

If you look at the dates at which they were created, almost all of the major civic institutions of the United States today—the Red Cross, the YWCA, the Boy Scouts, the NAACP, the Urban League, many labour unions, the Sons of Italy, the Sons of Norway, parent-teacher associations, the Rotary Club, the Sierra Club, the Knights of Columbus and many others—almost all of them were formed between 1880 and 1910, an astonishingly concentrated period. We had a social capital deficit as a country created by great technological and economic change, and at that point we could have said, "Whoa, wait a minute, stop! Everybody back to the farm. It was much nicer there. We knew everybody." And similarly today we could say, "It was much nicer back in the '50s. Would all women please report to the kitchen and turn off the TV on the way." But that is *not* what I am suggesting we should do. I am suggesting the contrary.

Our responsibility now is to create. It is not to complain about what has happened to all the Elks Clubs or bowling leagues, but to be as socially inventive as those people a century ago who created the Red Cross, the Boy Scouts and the PTA. We must figure out what the new institutions will be that fit the new way we are living our lives, while re-creating genuine bonds of community. This is, in my view, a central challenge of our times.

Notes

1. This Lecture draws on material first reported in the following articles by Dr. Putnam: "Bowling Alone: America's Declining Social Capital," *Journal of Democracy,* vol. 6, no. 1 (January 1995), pp. 65–78; and "Tuning In, Tuning Out: The Strange Disappearance of Social Capital in America," in *P.S.: Political Science and Politics,* vol. 28, no. 4 (December 1995), pp. 1–20.

2. [Editor's Note: The following portion of the Lecture is based on a dialogue with the audience about possible sources of the decline in civic engagement.]

Terms & Concepts

birth cohorts
connectedness
fabric of civic life

norm of reciprocity
residential mobility
simulated social capital

social capital

Questions

1. Putnam's Italian research reverses the usual chain of expected causes and effects. Why?

2. He calls upon us to create (and re-create) genuine bonds of community. Where should we start, and how do we do it—or are we already at work on new forms of civic reconstruction and action?

3. Are U.S. forms of civic engagement likely to be markedly different from Canada's, and if so, why?

4. What connections exist between federalism as a form of government and the development of civil societies? Does federalism help or hinder civic engagement?

Rethinking
Civil Society

Larry Diamond

Editors' Note

In the 1970s, the term *civil society* was not part of the technical vocabulary political science students acquired in their studies. Although, as Diamond points out, the theoretical origins of the term's meaning go back to early liberal thinkers, the political culture of democracies was not a major subject of discussion or analysis until after World War II, when political scientists, in trying to understand the success of totalitarianism within the Western cultures of Germany and Italy, spawned the first modern cross-national examination of political culture.[1] However, that study focused on the political attitudes of the citizens, not on "organized social life that is voluntary, self-generating, self-supporting, autonomous from the state, and bound by a legal order or set of shared rules" (Diamond's definition of civil society). More than any other event, the end of the Cold War and the consequent democratization of much of Eastern Europe brought the term *civil society* to the fore. Communist states, being totalitarian, harboured virtually no voluntary autonomous associations. Those states that had a memory of civil society from pre-Communist rule or that had maintained at least some segments of civil society were most successful in their transformation. Applying a similar analysis to Third World states, the strength or weakness of civil society may also be strongly correlated to the success or failure in transforming authoritarian regimes to democracies.

The discussion of civil society by political scientists and practitioners, like Czech Republic President Václav Havel, has also reverberated in democracies. Is the decline in political participation and interest leading to a decline in civil society, and does this erosion of one of its fundamental features not endanger democracy itself? Larry Diamond provides the reader with a thorough explanation of the concept of civil society and of its relevance to democratic systems, whether they are just emerging or well established.

◆ ◆ ◆

In this third wave of global democratization, no phenomenon has more vividly captured the imagination of democratic scholars, observers, and activists alike than "civil society." What could be more moving than the stories of brave bands of students, writers, artists, pastors, teachers, laborers, and mothers challenging the duplicity, corruption, and brutal domination of authoritarian states? Could any sight be more awe-inspiring to democrats than the one they saw in Manila in 1986, when hundreds of thousands of organized and peaceful citizens surged into the streets to reclaim their stolen election and force Ferdinand Marcos out through nonviolent "people power"?

In fact, however, the overthrow of authoritarian regimes through popularly based and massively mobilized democratic opposition has not been the norm. Most democratic transitions have been protracted and negotiated (if not largely controlled from above by the exiting authoritarians). Yet even in such negotiated and controlled transitions, the stimulus for democratization, and particularly the pressure to complete the process, have typically come from the "resurrection of civil soci-

---

1. Gabriel A. Almond and Sidney Verba, *The Civic Culture* (Princeton, N.J.: Princeton University Press, 1963).

From *Journal of Democracy* (July 1994): pp. 4-17. © 1994 The Johns Hopkins University Press and National Endowment for Democracy. Reprinted with permission.

ety," the restructuring of public space, and the mobilization of all manner of independent groups and grassroots movements.[1]

If the renewed interest in civil society can trace its theoretical origins to Alexis de Tocqueville, it seems emotionally and spiritually indebted to Jean-Jacques Rousseau for its romanticization of "the people" as a force for collective good, rising up to assert the democratic will against a narrow and evil autocracy. Such images of popular mobilization suffuse contemporary thinking about democratic change throughout Asia, Latin America, Eastern Europe, and Africa—and not without reason.

In South Korea, Taiwan, Chile, Poland, China, Czechoslovakia, South Africa, Nigeria, and Benin (to give only a partial list), extensive mobilization of civil society was a crucial source of pressure for democratic change. Citizens pressed their challenge to autocracy not merely as individuals, but as members of student movements, churches, professional associations, women's groups, trade unions, human rights organizations, producer groups, the press, civic associations, and the like.

It is now clear that to comprehend democratic change around the world, one must study civil society. Yet such study often provides a one-dimensional and dangerously misleading view. Understanding civil society's role in the construction of democracy requires more complex conceptualization and nuanced theory. The simplistic antinomy between state and civil society, locked in a zero-sum struggle, will not do. We need to specify more precisely what civil society is and is not, and to identify its wide variations in form and character. We need to comprehend not only the multiple ways it can serve democracy, but also the tensions and contradictions it generates and may encompass. We need to think about the features of civil society that are most likely to serve the development and consolidation of democracy. And, not least, we need to form a more realistic picture of the limits of civil society's potential contributions to democracy, and thus of the relative emphasis that democrats should place on building civil society among the various challenges of democratic consolidation.

WHAT CIVIL SOCIETY IS AND IS NOT

◆ ◆ ◆

Civil society is conceived here as the realm of organized social life that is voluntary, self-generating, (largely) self-supporting, autonomous from the state, and bound by a legal order or set of shared rules. It is distinct from "society" in general in that it involves citizens acting collectively in a public sphere to express their interests, passions, and ideas, exchange information, achieve mutual goals, make demands on the state, and hold state officials accountable. Civil society is an intermediary entity, standing between the private sphere and the state. Thus it excludes individual and family life, inward-looking group activity (e.g., for recreation, entertainment, or spirituality), the profit-making enterprise of individual business firms, and political efforts to take control of the state. Actors in civil society need the protection of an institutionalized legal order to guard their autonomy and freedom of action. Thus civil society not only restricts state power but legitimates state authority when that authority is based on the rule of law. When the state itself is lawless and contemptuous of individual and group autonomy, civil society may still exist (albeit in tentative or battered form) if its constituent elements operate by some set of shared rules (which, for example, eschew violence and respect pluralism). This is the irreducible condition of its "civil" dimension.[2]

Civil society is an intermediary entity, standing between the private sphere and the state.

Civil society encompasses a vast array of organizations, formal and informal. These include groups that are: (1) *economic* (productive and commercial associations and networks); (2) *cultural* (religious, ethnic, communal, and other institutions and associations that defend collective rights, values, faiths, beliefs, and symbols); (3) *informational and educational* (devoted to the production and dissemination—whether for profit or not—of public knowledge, ideas, news and information); (4) *interest-based* (designed to advance or defend the common functional or material interests of their members, whether workers, veterans, pensioners, professionals, or the like); (5) *developmental* (organizations that combine individual resources to improve the infrastructure, institutions, and quality of life of the community); (6) *issue-oriented* (movements for environmental protection, women's rights, land reform, or consumer protection); (7) *civic* (seeking in nonpartisan fashion to improve the political system and make it more democratic through human rights monitoring, voter education and mobilization, poll-watching, anticorruption efforts, and so on).

In addition, civil society encompasses "the ideological marketplace" and the flow of information and ideas. This includes not only independent mass media but also institutions belonging to the broader field of autonomous cultural and intellectual activity—universities, think tanks, publishing houses, theaters, film production companies, and artistic networks.

From the above, it should be clear that civil society is not some mere residual category, synonymous with "society" or with everything that is not the state or the formal political system. Beyond being voluntary, self-generating, autonomous, and rule-abiding, the organizations of civil society are distinct from other social groups in several respects. First, as emphasized above, civil society is concerned with *public* rather than private ends. Second, civil society *relates to the state* in some way but does not aim to win formal power or office in the state. Rather, civil society organizations seek from the state concessions, benefits, policy changes, relief, redress, or accountability. Civic organizations and social movements that try to change the nature of the state may still qualify as parts of civil society, if their efforts stem from concern for the public good and not from a desire to capture state power for the group per se. Thus peaceful movements for democratic transition typically spring from civil society.

A third distinguishing mark is that civil society encompasses *pluralism* and diversity. To the extent that an organization—such as a religious fundamentalist, ethnic chauvinist, revolutionary, or millenarian movement—seeks to monopolize a functional or political space in society, claiming that it represents the only legitimate path, it contradicts the pluralistic and market-oriented nature of civil society. Related to this is a fourth distinction, *partialness,* signifying that no group in civil society seeks to represent the whole of a person's or a community's interests. Rather, different groups represent different reasons.

Civil society is distinct and autonomous not only from the state and society at large but also from a fourth arena of social action, *political society* (meaning, in essence, the party system). Organizations and networks in civil society may form alliances with parties, but if they become captured by parties, or hegemonic within them, they thereby move their primary locus of activity to political society and lose much of their ability to perform certain unique mediating and democracy-building functions. I want now to examine these functions more closely.

THE DEMOCRATIC FUNCTIONS OF CIVIL SOCIETY

◆ ◆ ◆

The first and most basic democratic function of civil society is to provide "the basis for the limitation of state power, hence for the control of the state by society, and hence for democratic political institutions as the most effective means of exercising that control."[3] This function has two dimensions: to monitor and restrain the exercise of power by democratic states, and to democratize authoritarian states. Mobilizing civil society is a major means of exposing the abuses and undermining the legitimacy of undemocratic regimes. This is the function, performed so dramatically in so many democratic transitions over the past two decades, that has catapulted civil society to the forefront of thinking about democracy. Yet this thinking revives the eighteenth-century idea of civil society as *in opposition* to the state and, as I will show, has its dangers if taken too far.[4]

Civil society is also a vital instrument for containing the power of democratic governments, checking their potential abuses and violations of the law, and subjecting them to public scrutiny. Indeed, a vibrant civil society is probably more essential for consolidating and maintaining democracy than for initiating it. Few developments are more destructive to the legitimacy of new democracies than blatant and pervasive political corruption, particularly during periods of painful economic restructuring when many groups and individuals are asked to sustain great hardships. New democracies, following long periods of arbitrary and statist rule, lack the legal and bureaucratic means to contain corruption at the outset. Without a free, robust, and inquisitive press and civic groups to press for institutional reform, corruption is likely to flourish.

Second, a rich associational life supplements the role of political parties in stimulating political participation, increasing the political efficacy and skill of democratic citizens, and promoting an appreciation of the obligations as well as the rights of democratic citizenship. For too many Americans (barely half of whom vote in presidential elections), this now seems merely a quaint homily. A century and a half ago, however, the voluntary participation of citizens in all manner of associations outside the state struck Tocqueville as a pillar of democratic culture and economic vitality in the young United States. Voluntary "associations may therefore be considered as large free schools, where all the members of the community go to learn the general theory of association," he wrote.[5]

Civil society can also be a crucial arena for the development of other democratic attributes, such as tolerance, moderation, a willingness to compromise, and a respect for opposing viewpoints. These values and norms become most stable when they emerge through experience, and organizational participation in civil society provides important practice in political advocacy and contestation. In addition, many civic organizations (such as Conciencia, a network of women's organizations that began in Argentina and has since spread to 14 other Latin American countries) are working directly in the schools and among groups of adult citizens to develop these elements of democratic culture through interactive programs that demonstrate the dynamics of reaching consensus in a group, the possibility for respectful debate between competing viewpoints, and the means by which people can cooperate to solve the problems of their own communities.[6]

A fourth way in which civil society may serve democracy is by creating channels other than political parties for the articulation, aggregation, and representation of interests. This function is particularly important for providing traditionally excluded groups—such as women and racial or ethnic minorities—access to power that has been denied them in the "upper institutional echelons" of formal politics. Even where (as in South America) women have played, through various movements and organizations, prominent roles in mobilizing against authoritarian rule, democratic politics and governance after the transition have typically reverted to previous exclusionary patterns. In Eastern Europe, there are many signs of deterioration in the political and social status of women after the transition. Only with sustained organized pressure from below, in civil society, can political and social equality be advanced, and the quality, responsiveness, and legitimacy of democracy thus be deepened.[7]

Civil society provides an especially strong foundation for democracy when it generates opportunities for participation and influence at all levels of governance, not least the local level. For it is at the local level that the historically marginalized are most likely to be able to affect public policy and to develop a sense of efficacy as well as actual political skills. The democratization of local government thus goes hand in hand with the devel-

opment of civil society as an important condition for the deepening of democracy and the "transition from clientelism to citizenship" in Latin America, as well as elsewhere in the developing and postcommunist worlds.[8]

Fifth, a richly pluralistic civil society, particularly in a relatively developed economy, will tend to generate a wide range of interests that may cross-cut, and so mitigate, the principal polarities of political conflict. As new class-based organizations and issue-oriented movements arise, they draw together new constituencies that cut across longstanding regional, religious, ethnic, or partisan cleavages. In toppling communist (and other) dictatorships and mobilizing for democracy, these new formations may generate a modern type of citizenship that transcends historic divisions and contains the resurgence of narrow nationalist impulses. To the extent that individuals have multiple interests and join a wide variety of organizations to pursue and advance those interests, they will be more likely to associate with different types of people who have divergent political interests and opinions. These attitudinal cross-pressures will tend to soften the militancy of their own views, generate a more expansive and sophisticated political outlook, and so encourage tolerance for differences and a greater readiness to compromise.

A sixth function of a democratic civil society is recruiting and training new political leaders. In a few cases, this is a deliberate purpose of civic organizations. The Evelio B. Javier Foundation in the Philippines, for instance, offers training programs on a nonpartisan basis to local and state elected officials and candidates, emphasizing not only technical and administrative skills but normative standards of public accountability and transparency.[9] More often, recruitment and training are merely a long-term byproduct of the successful functioning of civil society organizations as their leaders and activists gain skills and self-confidence that qualify them well for service in government and party politics. They learn how to organize and motivate people, debate issues, raise and account for funds, craft budgets, publicize programs, administer staffs, canvass for support, negotiate agreements, and build coalitions. At the same time, their work on behalf of their constituency, or of what they see to be the public interest, and their articulation of clear and compelling policy alternatives, may gain for them a wider political following. Interest groups, social movements, and community efforts of various kinds may therefore train, toughen, and thrust into public notice a richer (and more representative) array of potential new political leaders than might otherwise be recruited by political parties. Because of the traditional dominance by men of the corridors of power, civil society is a particularly important base for the training and recruitment of women (and members of other marginalized groups) into positions of formal political power. Where the recruitment of new political leaders within the established political parties has become narrow or stagnant, this function of civil society may play a crucial role in revitalizing democracy and renewing its legitimacy.

Seventh, many civic organizations have explicit democracy-building purposes that go beyond leadership training. Nonpartisan election-monitoring efforts have been critical in deterring fraud, enhancing voter confidence, affirming the legitimacy of the result, or in some cases (as in the Philippines in 1986 and Panama in 1989) demonstrating an opposition victory despite government fraud. This function is particularly crucial in founding elections like those which initiated democracy in Chile, Nicaragua, Bulgaria, Zambia, and South Africa. Democracy institutes and think tanks are working in a number of countries to reform the electoral system, democratize political parties, decentralize and open up government, strengthen the legislature, and enhance governmental accountability. And even after the transition, human rights organizations continue to play a vital role in the pursuit of judicial and legal reform, improved prison conditions, and greater institutionalized respect for individual liberties and minority rights.

Civil society is a particularly important base for the training and recruitment of women ... into positions of formal political power.

Eighth, a vigorous civil society widely disseminates information, thus aiding citizens in the collective pursuit and defense of their interests and values. While civil society groups may sometimes prevail temporarily by dint of raw numbers (e.g., in strikes and demonstrations), they generally cannot be effective in contesting government policies or defending their interests unless they are well-informed. This is strikingly true in debates over military and national security policy, where civilians in developing countries have generally been woefully lacking in even the most elementary knowledge. A free press is only one vehicle for providing the public with a wealth of news and alternative perspectives. Independent organizations may also give citizens hard-won information about government activities that does not depend on what government *says* it is doing. This is a vital technique of human rights organizations: by contradicting the official story, they make it more difficult to cover up repression and abuses of power.

The spread of new information and ideas is essential to the achievement of economic reform in a democracy, and this is a ninth function that civil society can play. While economic stabilization policies typically must be implemented quickly, forcefully, and unilaterally by elected executives in crisis situations, more structural economic reforms—privatization, trade and financial liberalization—appear to be more sustainable and far-reaching (or in many postcommunist countries, only feasible) when they are pursued through the democratic process.

Successful economic reform requires the support of political coalitions in society and the legislature. Such coalitions are not spontaneous; they must be fashioned. Here the problem is not so much the scale, autonomy, and resources of civil society as it is their distribution across interests. Old, established interests that stand to lose from reform tend to be organized into formations like state-sector trade unions and networks that tie the managers of state enterprises or owners of favored industries to ruling party bosses. These are precisely the interests that stand to lose from economic reforms that close down inefficient industries, reduce state intervention, and open the economy to greater domestic and international competition. The newer and more diffuse interests that stand to gain from reform—for example, farmers, small-scale entrepreneurs, and consumers—tend to be weakly organized and poorly informed about how new policies will ultimately affect them. In Asia, Latin America, and Eastern Europe, new actors in civil society—such as economic-policy think tanks, chambers of commerce, and economically literate journalists, commentators, and television producers—are beginning to overcome the barriers to information and organization, mobilizing support for (and neutralizing resistance to) reform policies.

Finally, there is a tenth function of civil society—to which I have already referred—that derives from the success of the above nine. "Freedom of association," Tocqueville mused, may, "after having agitated society for some time,... strengthen the state in the end."[10] By enhancing the accountability, responsiveness, inclusiveness, effectiveness, and hence legitimacy of the political system, a vigorous civil society gives citizens respect for the state and positive engagement with it. In the end, this improves the ability of the state to govern, and to command voluntary obedience from its citizens. In addition, a rich associational life can do more than just multiply demands on the state; it may also multiply the capacities of groups to improve their own welfare, independently of the state. Effective grassroots development efforts may thus help to relieve the burden of expectations fixed on the state, and so lower the stakes of politics, especially at the national level.

FEATURES OF A DEMOCRATIC CIVIL SOCIETY

◆ ◆ ◆

Not all civil societies and civil society organizations have the same potential to perform the democracy-building functions cited above. Their ability to do so depends on several features of their internal structure and character.

One concerns the goals and methods of groups in civil society. The chances to develop stable democracy improve significantly if civil society does not contain maximalist, uncompromising interest groups or groups with antidemocratic goals and methods. To the extent that a group seeks to conquer the state or other competitors, or rejects the rule of law and the authority of the democratic state, it is not a component of civil society at all, but it may nevertheless do much damage to democratic aspirations. Powerful, militant interest groups pull parties toward populist and extreme political promises, polarizing the party system, and are more likely to bring down state repression that may have a broad and indiscriminate character, weakening or radicalizing the more democratic elements of civil society.

A second important feature of civil society is its level of organizational institutionalization. As with political parties, institutionalized interest groups contribute to the stability, predictability, and governability of a democratic regime. Where interests are organized in a structured, stable manner, bargaining and the growth of cooperative networks are facilitated. Social forces do not face the continual cost of setting up new structures. And if the organization expects to continue to operate in the society over a sustained period of time, its leaders will have more reason to be accountable and responsive to their constituency, and may take a longer-range view of the group's interests and policy goals, rather than seeking to maximize short-term benefits in an uncompromising manner.

Third, the internally democratic character of civil society itself affects the degree to which it can socialize participants into democratic—or undemocratic—forms of behavior. If the groups and organizations that make up civil society are to function as "large free schools" for democracy, they must function democratically in their internal processes of decision-making and leadership selection. Constitutionalism, representation, transparency, accountability, and rotation of elected leaders within autonomous associations will greatly enhance the ability of these associations to inculcate such democratic values and practices in their members.

The more pluralistic civil society can become without fragmenting, the more democracy will benefit.

Fourth, the more pluralistic civil society can become without fragmenting, the more democracy will benefit. Some degree of pluralism is necessary by definition for civil society. Pluralism helps groups in civil society survive, and encourages them to learn to cooperate and negotiate with one another. Pluralism within a given sector like labor or human rights, has a number of additional beneficial effects. For one, it makes that sector less vulnerable (though at the possible cost of weakening its bargaining power); the loss of repression of one organization does not mean the end of all organized representation. Competition can also help to ensure accountability and representativeness by giving members the ability to bolt to other organizations if their own does not perform.

Finally, civil society serves democracy best when it is dense, affording individuals opportunities to participate in multiple associations and informal networks at multiple levels of society. The more associations there are in civil society, the more likely it is that they will develop specialized agendas and purposes that do not seek to swallow the lives of their members in one all-encompassing organizational framework. Multiple memberships also tend to reflect and reinforce cross-cutting patterns of cleavage.

SOME IMPORTANT CAVEATS

◆ ◆ ◆

To the above list of democratic functions of civil society we must add some important caveats. To begin with, associations and mass media can perform their democracy-building roles only if they have at least some autonomy from the state in their financing, operations, and legal standing. To be sure, there are markedly different ways of organizing the representation of interests in a democracy. Pluralist systems encompass "multiple, voluntary, competitive, nonhierarchically ordered and self-determined ... [interest associations] which are not specially licensed, recognized, subsidized, created or otherwise controlled ... by the state." Corporatist systems, by contrast, have "singular, noncompetitive, hierarchically ordered, sectorally compartmentalized, interest associations exercising representational monopolies and accepting (de jure or de facto) governmentally imposed limitations on the type of leaders they elect and on the scope and intensity of demands they routinely make upon the state."[11] A number of northern European countries have operated a corporatist system of interest representation while functioning successfully as democracies (at times even better, economically and politically, than their pluralist counterparts). Although corporatist arrangements are eroding in many established democracies, important differences remain in the degree to which interest groups are competitive, pluralistic, compartmentalized, hierarchically ordered, and so on.

While corporatist-style pacts or contracts between the state and peak interest associations may make for stable macroeconomic management, corporatist arrangements pose a serious threat to democracy in transitional or newly emerging constitutional regimes. The risk appears greatest in countries with a history of authoritarian *state corporatism*—such as Mexico, Egypt, and Indonesia—where the state has created, organized, licensed, funded, subordinated, and controlled "interest" groups (and also most of the mass media that it does not officially own and control), with a view to cooptation, repression and domination rather than ordered bargaining. By contrast, the transition to a democratic form of corporatism "seems to depend very much on a liberal-pluralist past," which most developing and postcommunist states lack.[12] A low level of economic development or the absence of a fully functioning market economy increases the danger that corporatism will stifle civil society even under a formally democratic framework, because there are fewer autonomous resources and organized interests in society.

By coopting, preempting, or constraining the most serious sources of potential challenge to its domination (and thus minimizing the amount of actual repression that has to be employed), a state-corporatist regime may purchase a longer lease on authoritarian life. Such regimes, however, eventually come under pressure from

social, economic, and demographic forces. Successful socioeconomic development, as in Mexico and Indonesia, produces a profusion of authentic civil society groups that demand political freedom under law. Alternatively, social and economic decay, along with massive political corruption, weakens the hold of the authoritarian corporatist state, undermines the legitimacy of its sponsored associations, and may give rise to revolutionary movements like the Islamic fundamentalist fronts in Egypt and Algeria, which promise popular redemption through a new form of state hegemony.

Societal autonomy can go too far, however, even for the purposes of democracy. The need for *limits* on autonomy is a second caveat; paired with the first, it creates a major tension in democratic development. A hyperactive, confrontational, and relentlessly rent-seeking civil society can overwhelm a weak, penetrated state with the diversity and magnitude of its demands, leaving little in the way of a truly "public" sector concerned with the overall welfare of society. The state itself must have sufficient autonomy, legitimacy, capacity, and support to mediate among the various interest groups and balance their claims. This is a particularly pressing dilemma for new democracies seeking to implement much-needed economic reforms in the face of stiff opposition from trade unions, pensioners, and the state-protected bourgeoisie, which is why countervailing forces in civil society must be educated and mobilized, as I have argued above.

In many new democracies there is a deeper problem, stemming from the origins of civil society in profoundly angry, risky, and even anomic protest against a decadent, abusive state. This problem is what the Cameroonian economist Célestin Monga calls the "civic deficit":

> Thirty years of authoritarian rule have forged a concept of indiscipline as a method of popular resistance. In order to survive and resist laws and rules judged to be antiquated, people have had to resort to the treasury of their imagination. Given that life is one long fight against the state, the collective imagination has gradually conspired to craftily defy everything which symbolizes public authority.[13]

In many respects, a similar broad cynicism, indiscipline, and alienation from state authority—indeed from politics altogether—was bred by decades of communist rule in Eastern Europe and the former Soviet Union, though it led to somewhat different (and in Poland, much more broadly organized) forms of dissidence and resistance. Some countries, like Poland, Hungary, the

Czech lands, and the Baltic states, had previous civic traditions that could be recovered. These countries have generally made the most progress (though still quite partial) toward reconstructing state authority on a democratic foundation while beginning to constitute a modern, liberal-pluralist civil society. Those states where civic traditions were weakest and predatory rule greatest—Romania, Russia, the post-Soviet republics of Central Asia, and most of sub-Saharan Africa—face a far more difficult time, with civil societies still fragmented and emergent market economies still heavily outside the framework of law.

Civil society must be autonomous from the state, but not alienated from it.

This civic deficit points to a third major caveat with respect to the positive value of civil society for democracy. Civil society must be autonomous from the state, but not alienated from it. It must be watchful but respectful of state authority. The image of a noble, vigilant, organized civil society checking at every turn the predations of a self-serving state, preserving a pure detachment from its corrupting embrace, is highly romanticized and of little use in the construction of a viable democracy.

A fourth caveat concerns the role of politics. Interest groups cannot substitute for coherent political parties with broad and relatively enduring bases of popular support. For interest groups cannot aggregate interests as broadly across social groups and political issues as political parties can. Nor can they provide the discipline necessary to form and maintain governments and pass legislation. In this respect (and not only this one), one may question the thesis that a strong civil society is strictly complementary to the political and state structures of democracy. To the extent that interest groups dominate, enervate, or crowd out political parties as conveyors and aggregators of interests, they can present a problem for democratic consolidation. To Barrington Moore's famous thesis, "No bourgeois, no democracy," we can add a corollary: "No coherent party system, no stable democracy." And in an age when the electronic media, increased mobility, and the profusion and fragmentation of discrete interests are all undermining the organizational bases for strong parties and party systems, this is something that democrats everywhere need to worry about.[14]

DEMOCRATIC CONSOLIDATION
◆ ◆ ◆

In fact, a stronger and broader generalization appears warranted: the single most important and urgent factor in the consolidation of democracy is not civil society but political institutionalization. *Consolidation* is the process by which democracy becomes so broadly and profoundly legitimate among its citizens that it is very unlikely to break down. It involves behavioral and institutional changes that normalize democratic politics and narrow its uncertainty. This normalization requires the expansion of citizen access, development of democratic citizenship and culture, broadening of leadership recruitment and training, and other functions that civil society performs. But most of all, and most urgently, it requires political institutionalization.

Despite their impressive capacity to survive years (in some cases, a decade or more) of social strife and economic instability and decline, many new democracies in Latin America, Eastern Europe, Asia, and Africa will probably break down in the medium to long run unless they can reduce their often appalling levels of poverty, inequality, and social injustice and, through market-oriented reforms, lay the basis for sustainable growth. For these and other policy challenges, not only strong parties but effective state institutions are vital. They do not guarantee wise and effective policies, but they at least ensure that government will be able to make and implement policies of some kind, rather than simply flailing about, impotent or deadlocked.

Robust political institutions are needed to accomplish economic reform under democratic conditions. Strong, well-structured executives, buttressed by experts at least somewhat insulated from the day-to-day pressures of politics, make possible the implementation of painful and disruptive reform measures. Settled and aggregative (as opposed to volatile and fragmented) party systems—in which one or two broadly based, centrist parties consistently obtain electoral majorities or near-majorities—are better positioned to resist narrow class and sectoral interests and to maintain the continuity of economic reforms across successive administrations. Effective legislatures may sometimes obstruct reforms, but if they are composed of strong, coherent parties with centrist tendencies, in the end they will do more to reconcile democracy and economic reform by providing a political base of support and some means for absorbing and mediating protest in society. Finally, autonomous, professional, and well-staffed judicial systems are indispensable for securing the rule of law.

These caveats are sobering, but they do not nullify my principal thesis. Civil society can, and typically must, play a significant role in building and consolidating democracy. Its role is not decisive or even the most important, at least initially. However, the more active, pluralistic, resourceful, institutionalized, and democratic is civil society, and the more effectively it balances the tensions in its relations with the state—between autonomy and cooperation, vigilance and loyalty, skepticism and trust, assertiveness and civility—the more likely it is that democracy will emerge and endure.

Notes

1. Guillermo O'Donnell and Philippe C. Schmitter, *Transitions from Authoritarian Rule: Tentative Conclusions about Uncertain Democracies* (Baltimore: Johns Hopkins University Press, 1986), ch. 5.

2. This conceptual formulation draws from a number of sources but has been especially influenced by Naomi Chazan. See in particular Chazan, "Africa's Democratic Challenge: Strengthening Civil Society and the State," *World Policy Journal* 9 (Spring 1992): 279–308. See also Edward Shils, "The Virtue of Civil Society," *Government and Opposition* 26 (Winter 1991): 9–10, 15–16; Peter Lewis, "Political Transition and the Dilemma of Civil Society in Africa," *Journal of International Affairs* 27 (Summer 1992): 31–54; Marcia A. Weigle and Jim Butterfield, "Civil Society in Reforming Communist Regimes: The Logic of Emergence," *Comparative Politics* 25 (October 1992): 3–4; and Philippe C. Schmitter, "Some Propositions about Civil Society and the Consolidation of Democracy" (Paper presented at a conference on "Reconfiguring State and Society," University of California, Berkeley, 22–23 April 1993).

3. Samuel P. Huntington, "Will More Countries Become Democratic?" *Political Science Quarterly* 99 (Summer 1984): 204. See also Seymour Martin Lipset, *Political Man* (Baltimore: Johns Hopkins University Press, 1981), 52.

4. Bronislaw Geremek, "Civil Society Then and Now," *Journal of Democracy* 3 (April 1992): 3–12.

5. Alexis de Tocqueville, *Democracy in America*, 2 vols. (New York: Vintage Books, 1945 [orig. publ. 1840]), 2:124.

6. Maria Rosa de Martini and Sofía de Pinedo, "Women and Civic Life in Argentina," *Journal of Democracy* 3 (July 1992): 138–146; and Maria Rosa de Martini, "Civic Participation in the Argentine Democratic Process," in Larry Diamond, ed., *The Democratic Revolution: Struggles for Freedom and Pluralism in the Developing World* (New York: Freedom House, 1992), 29–52.

7. Georgina Waylen, "Women and Democratization: Conceptualizing Gender Relations in Transition Politics," *World Politics* 46 (April 1994): 327–354. Although Waylen is correct that O'Donnell and Schmitter speak to the dangers of excessive popular mobilization during the transition, her criticism of the democracy literature as a whole for trivializing the role of civil society is unfairly overgeneralized and certainly inapplicable to work on Africa. Moreover, accepting her challenge to treat civil society as a centrally important phenomenon in democratization does not require one to accept her insistence on defining democracy to include economic and social rights as well as political ones.

8. Jonathan Fox, "Latin America's Emerging Local Politics," *Journal of Democracy* 5 (April 1994): 114.

9. Dette Pacsual, "Organizing People Power in the Philippines," *Journal of Democracy* 1 (Winter 1990): 102–109.

10. Tocqueville, *Democracy in America*, 2: 126.

11. Philippe C. Schmitter, "Still the Century of Corporatism?" in Wolfgang Streeck and Schmitter, eds., *Private Interest Government: Beyond Market and State* (Beverly Hills: Sage Publications, 1984), 96, 99–100.

12. Ibid., 126. See 102–108 for the important distinction between societal (democratic) and state corporatism.

13. Célestin Monga, "Civil Society and Democratization in Francophone Africa" (Paper delivered at Harvard University, 1994). This paper will appear in the same author's forthcoming French-language work, *Anthropologie de la colère: Société et démocratie en Afrique Noire* (Paris: L'Harmattan, 1994).

14. Juan J. Linz, "Change and Continuity in the Nature of Contemporary Democracies," in Gary Marks and Larry Diamond, ed., *Reexamining Democracy: Essays in Honor of Seymour Martin Lipset* (Newbury Park, Calif.: Sage Publications, 1992), 184–190.

Terms & Concepts

corporatism

democratic consolidation

democratic corporatism

partialness

pluralism

state corporatism

Questions

1. Can civil society, as defined by Diamond, exist in a nondemocratic society?

2. What activities are you involved in that would qualify as being part of civil society?

3. How do your civil society activities contribute to the functioning of your democratic governments (local, provincial, federal)?

4. How does civil society contain the power of democratic governments?

5. Is civil society declining in Canada? If so, what effects does this have on Canada's democracy?

15

Conserving Communities

Wendell Berry

Editors' Note

However common are the pastoral scenes of rural farming life in pickup truck commercials and other icons of North American culture, the reality is that rural life is rapidly and decisively shrinking in vitality and importance relative to the throbbing urban industrial centres. In the early part of this century, 32 million farmers lived on farms in the United States. By 1991, the number was only 4.6 million, less than 2 percent of that country's population. In Canada, most young people growing up on the farm know that they must leave it to gain a livelihood elsewhere. Small communities move from being living things to becoming the subjects of museum displays. Grain elevators in small towns strung along railway lines are toppled almost as quickly as stands of trees in the leaseholds managed by transnational forestry companies. As Michael Broadway's article (Chapter 20) makes clear, the cattle industry is no longer a decentralized collection of small-scale ranches and processing facilities. Instead, we see massive feedlots and even larger integrated processing facilities, monuments to rural industrialization.

In this article, Wendell Berry reflects on local communities and the tender balance they create between humankind and the natural environment. While the word *community* is frequently invoked to describe almost any collection of human beings, Berry insists that its most compelling use is in the context of the local geographical community of people tied together by time, land, and economic satisfaction of human need. Berry is keenly aware of the economic and political forces driving globalization, and of the insistence that the decline of rural communities is both inevitable and good (because cities and industrial agribusinesses are more "efficient"). But he sees massive costs stemming from what he calls the "absentee economy." To the trite slogan "Think globally, act locally," Berry responds, "Think locally, act locally."

◆ ◆ ◆

As we all know, we have much to answer for in our use of this continent from the beginning, but in the last half century we have added to our desecrations of nature a deliberate destruction of our rural communities.... If you have eyes to see, you can see that there is a limit beyond which machines and chemicals cannot replace people; there is a limit beyond which mechanical or economic efficiency cannot replace care.

I am talking here about the common experience, the common fate, of rural communities in our country for a long time. It has also been, and it will increasingly be, the common fate of rural communities in other countries. The message is plain enough, and we have ignored it for too long: the great, centralized economic entities of our time do not come into rural places in order to improve them by "creating jobs." They come to take as much of value as they can take, as cheaply and as quickly as they can take it. They are interested in "job creation" only so long as the jobs can be done more cheaply by humans than by machines. They are not interested in the good health—economic or natural or human—of any place on this earth. And if you should undertake to appeal or complain to one of these great corporations on behalf of your community, you would discover something most remarkable: you would find that these organizations are organized expressly for the evasion of responsibility.

The ideal of the modern corporation is to be (in terms of its own advantage) anywhere and (in terms of local accountability) nowhere.

They are structures in which, as my brother says, "the buck never stops." The buck is processed up the hierarchy until finally it is passed to "the shareholders," who characteristically are too widely dispersed, too poorly informed, and too unconcerned to be responsible for anything. The ideal of the modern corporation is to be (in terms of its own advantage) anywhere and (in terms of local accountability) nowhere. The message to country people, in other words, is this: Don't expect favors from your enemies.

And that message has a corollary that is just as plain and just as much ignored: The governmental and educational institutions from which rural people should by right have received help have not helped. Rather than striving to preserve the rural communities and economies and an adequate rural population, these institutions have consistently aided, abetted, and justified the destruction of every part of rural life. They have eagerly served the superstition that all technological innovation is good. They have said repeatedly that the failure of farm families, rural businesses, and rural communities is merely the result of progress and efficiency and is good for everybody.

You cannot have a postagricultural world that is not also postdemocratic, postreligious, postnatural.

We are now pretty obviously facing the possibility of a world that the supranational corporations, and the governments and educational systems that serve them, will control entirely for their own enrichment—and, incidentally and inescapably, for the impoverishment of all the rest of us. This will be a world in which the cultures that preserve nature and rural life will simply be disallowed. It will be, as our experience already suggests, a postagricultural world. But as we now begin to see, you cannot have a postagricultural world that is not also postdemocratic, postreligious, postnatural—in other words, it will be posthuman, contrary to the best that we have meant by "humanity."

In their dealings with the countryside and its people, the promoters of the so-called global economy are following a set of principles that can be stated as follows. They believe that a farm or a forest is or ought to be the same as a factory; that care is only minimally necessary in the use of the land; that affection is not necessary at all; that for all practical purposes a machine is as good as a human; that the industrial standards of production, efficiency, and profitability are the only standards that are necessary; that the topsoil is lifeless and inert; that soil biology is safely replaceable by soil chemistry; that the nature or ecology of any given place is irrelevant to the use of it; that there is no value in human community or neighborhood; and that technological innovation will produce only benign results.

These people see nothing odd or difficult about unlimited economic growth or unlimited consumption in a limited world. They believe that knowledge is property and is power, and that it ought to be. They believe that education is job training. They think that the summit of human achievement is a high-paying job that involves no work. Their public boast is that they are making a society in which everybody will be a "winner"—but their private aim has been to reduce radically the number of people who, by the measure of our historical ideals, might be thought successful: the independent, the self-employed, the owners of small businesses or small usable properties, those who work at home.

The argument for joining the new international trade agreements has been that there is going to be a one-world economy, and we must participate or be left behind—though, obviously, the existence of a one-world economy depends on the willingness of all the world to join. The theory is that under the rule of international, supposedly free trade, products will naturally flow from the places where they can be best produced to the places where they are most needed. This theory assumes the long-term safety and sustainability of massive international transport, for which there are no guarantees, just as there are no guarantees that products will be produced in the best way or to the advantage of the workers who produce them or that they will reach or can be afforded by the people who need them....

We can't go on too much longer, maybe, without considering the likelihood that we humans are not intelligent enough to work on the scale to which we have been tempted by our technological abilities. Some such recognition is undoubtedly implicit in American conservatives' long-standing objection to a big central government. And so it has been odd to see many of these same conservatives pushing for the establishment of a supra-national economy that would inevitably function as a government far bigger and more centralized than any dreamed of before. Long experience has made it clear—as we might say to the liberals—that to be free we must limit the size of government and we must have some sort of home rule. But it is just as clear—as we might say to the conservatives—that it is foolish to complain about big government if we do not do everything we can to support strong local communities and strong community economies.

We humans are not intelligent enough to work on the scale to which we have been tempted by our technological abilities.

But in helping us to confront, understand, and oppose the principles of the global economy, the old political alignments have become virtually useless. Communists and capitalists are alike in their contempt for country people, country life, and country places. They have exploited the countryside with equal greed and disregard. They are alike even in their plea that it is right to damage the present in order to make "a better future."

The dialogue of Democrats and Republicans or of liberals and conservatives is likewise useless to us. Neither party is interested in farmers or in farming or in the good care of the land or in the quality of food. Nor are they interested in taking the best care of our forests. The leaders of these parties are equally subservient to the supranational corporations. Of this the North American Free Trade Agreement and the new revisions to the General Agreement on Tariffs and Trade are proof....

... A new political scheme of opposed parties, however, is beginning to take form. This is essentially a two-party system, and it divides over the fundamental issue of community. One of these parties holds that community has no value; the other holds that it does. One is the party of the global economy; the other I would call simply the party of local community. The global party is large, though not populous, immensely powerful and wealthy, self-aware, purposeful, and tightly organized. The community party is only now becoming aware of itself; it is widely scattered, highly diverse, small though potentially numerous, weak though latently powerful, and poor though by no means without resources....

The natural membership of the community party consists of small farmers, ranchers, and market gardeners, worried consumers, owners and employees of small shops, stores, community banks, and other small businesses, self-employed people, religious people, and conservationists. The aims of this party really are only two: the preservation of ecological diversity and integrity, and the renewal, on sound cultural and ecological principles, of local economies and local communities....

If the members of a local community want their community to cohere, to flourish, and to last, these are some things they would do:

1. Always ask of any proposed change or innovation: What will this do to our community? How will this affect our common wealth?
2. Always include local nature—the land, the water, the air, the native creatures—within the membership of the community.
3. Always ask how local needs might be supplied from local sources, including the mutual help of neighbors.
4. Always supply local needs *first*. (And only then think of exporting their products, first to nearby cities, and then to others.)
5. Understand the unsoundness of the industrial doctrine of "labor saving" if that implies poor work, unemployment, or any kind of pollution or contamination.
6. Develop properly scaled value-adding industries for local products to ensure that the community does not become merely a colony of the national or global economy.
7. Develop small-scale industries and businesses to support the local farm and/or forest economy.
8. Strive to produce as much of the community's own energy as possible.
9. Strive to increase earnings (in whatever form) within the community and decrease expenditures outside the community.
10. Make sure that money paid into the local economy circulates within the community for as long as possible before it is paid out.
11. Make the community able to invest in itself by maintaining its properties, keeping itself clean (without dirtying some other place), caring for its old people, teaching its children.
12. See that the old and the young take care of one another. The young must learn from the old, not necessarily and not always in school. There must be no institutionalized "child care" and "homes for the

aged." The community knows and remembers itself by the association of old and young.

13. Account for costs now conventionally hidden or "externalized." Whenever possible, these costs must be debited against monetary income.

14. Look into the possible uses of local currency, community-funded loan programs, systems of barter, and the like.

15. Always be aware of the economic value of neighborly acts....

16. A rural community should always be acquainted with, and complexly connected with, community-minded people in nearby towns and cities.

17. A sustainable rural economy will be dependent on urban consumers loyal to local products. Therefore, we are talking about an economy that will always be more cooperative than competitive.

These rules are derived from Western political and religious traditions, from the promptings of ecologists and certain agriculturists, and from common sense. They may seem radical, but only because the modern national and global economies have been formed in almost perfect disregard of community and ecological interests.

How might we begin to build a decentralized system of durable local economies? Gradually, I hope. We have had enough of violent or sudden changes imposed by predatory interests outside our communities. In many places, the obvious way to begin the work I am talking about is with the development of a local food economy. Such a start is attractive because it does not have to be big or costly, it requires nobody's permission, and it can ultimately involve everybody. It does not require us to beg for mercy from our exploiters or to look for help where consistently we have failed to find it. By "local food economy" I mean simply an economy in which local consumers buy as much of their food as possible from local producers and in which local producers produce as much as they can for the local market.

The obvious way to begin the work I am talking about is with the development of a local food economy.

Several conditions now favor the growth of local food economies. On the one hand, the costs associated with our present highly centralized food system are going to increase. Growers in the Central Valley of

---

Consumers are increasingly worried about the quality and purity of their food, and so they would like to buy from responsible growers close to home.

California, for example, can no longer depend on an unlimited supply of cheap water for irrigation. Transportation costs can only go up. Biotechnology, variety patenting, and other agribusiness innovations are intended not to help farmers or consumers but to extend and prolong corporate control of the food economy; they will increase the cost of food, both economically and ecologically.

On the other hand, consumers are increasingly worried about the quality and purity of their food, and so they would like to buy from responsible growers close to home. They would like to know where their food comes from and how it is produced. They are increasingly aware that the larger and more centralized the food economy becomes, the more vulnerable it will be to natural or economic catastrophe, to political or military disruption, and to bad agricultural practice....

What we have before us, if we want our communities to survive, is the building of an adversary economy, a system of local or community economies within, and to protect against, the would-be global economy. To do this, we must somehow learn to reverse the flow of the siphon that has for so long been drawing resources, money, talent, and people out of our countryside with very little if any return, and often with a return only of pollution, impoverishment, and ruin. We must figure out new ways to fund, at affordable rates, the development of healthy local economies. We must find ways to suggest economically—for finally no other suggestion will be effective—that the work, the talents, and the interest of our young people are needed at home.

Our whole society has much to gain from the development of local land-based economies. They would carry us far toward the ecological and cultural ideal of local adaptation. They would encourage the formation of adequate local cultures (and this would be authentic multiculturalism). They would introduce into agriculture and forestry a sort of spontaneous and natural quality control, for neither consumers nor workers would want to see the local economy destroy itself by abusing or exhausting its sources. And they would complete at last the task of freedom from colonial economies begun by our ancestors more than two hundred years ago.

Terms & Concepts

adversary economy
community party
global party

local community
local food economy
old political alignments

one-world economy
postagricultural world

Questions

1. Berry's vision of the future, if our course does not change, is that it will be "posthuman." What does he mean?

2. What is the global economy's effect on local community?

3. What political ideology, if any, is most consistently represented in Berry's article? Is there a party in Canada that supports the notion that local community should be protected?

4. Berry argues that local community is good and should be revived by a new political formation, the "local community party." What is the composition of this party, and what are its prospects?

The Federal Citizen

Richard Vernon

Editors' Note

Federalism is associated mainly with detailed and technical constitutional provisions setting out divisions of powers, fiscal arrangements, residual clauses, and constitutional amending formulae. The failed 1992 Charlottetown Accord, which proposed a reorganization of Canadian federalism, led many Canadians to become amateur constitutional critics, even as they tired of talk of interpretive clauses, vetoes, third orders of government, and qualified majorities. Canadians know (and sometimes regret) that federalism is central to their political condition.

Richard Vernon shifts our attention from institutional forms and constitutional clauses to the questions of attachment, identity, and belonging. These matters are truly fundamental; they guide to a great degree the politics of constitutional reform in Canada. As Alan C. Cairns has argued, federal and provincial governments in Canada have long battled for the hearts of Canadians. Each order of government has attempted to demonstrate how *it* is primarily responsible for Canadians' well-being.[1] Provincial governments concede that their residents are Canadians, but that they are Canadians who live in Alberta, Newfoundland, or Ontario. The federal government, for its part, insists that though Canadians live in provinces, they are Canadians above all.

As Quebec nationalists often put it, "Canada is my country, but Quebec is my home." For Canadian nationalists, this statement is maddening, because it means that a Canadian's sense of belonging is attached to a province (or, for the nationalists, a nation), not to the country.

Vernon asks whether we have to choose. Federalism's essence, he argues, is that our attachments as citizens can be dual or coordinate, not singular or hierarchical. Pointing to themes evident elsewhere in this volume, Vernon claims that federalism accommodates and requires multiple, coordinate objects of political belonging.

◆ ◆ ◆

Federalism has traditionally been defined in terms of constitutional law as a system in which powers are divided between central and regional authorities, each governing directly and independently within its own defined sphere, and neither being able to modify the division of powers unilaterally.[1] From time to time, indeed, social scientists appear to have felt uneasy about relying upon constitutional law for their categories, and thus have been led to criticize the traditional definition. Should we not, as some have argued, adjust our categories to the realities of social and political process, not constitutional forms?[2] But to interest oneself in federalism is necessarily to interest oneself in a constitutional category, for it is in constitutional terms that the other-

1. Alan C. Cairns, "The Governments and Societies of Canadian Federalism," in Douglas E. Williams, ed., *Constitution, Government, and Society in Canada: Selected Essays by Alan C. Cairns* (Toronto: McClelland & Stewart, 1988), 141–70.

From Olling and Westmacott, eds., *Perspective on Canadian Federalism* (Scarborough: Prentice-Hall, 1988). Reprinted by permission of the author.

wise disparate polities termed "federal" are related. It may or may not be the case that all the polities termed "federal" are acted upon by some common social or political factor that makes them all federal. But even if they are all acted on this way, what *defines* them as federal has to be distinguished from what *explains* their federal character. Finally, even if we are looking for explanations of why some polities are federal, it would be quite wrong to suppose that constitutional features are mere effects and not causes, for it is plainly the case that constitutions can exercise important influences over politics and, in the longer run, over society too.

For these reasons, then, anxiety about relying upon a constitutional definition is largely misplaced. Such a definition is adequate to the task. A federation, as opposed to a unitary state, is a regime of coordinate authority, in which some division of jurisdiction between centre and region is constitutionally protected.

All that is proposed here is a change of, so to speak, a tactical nature. Instead of looking at federalism from the top down, in terms of the imposition of authority, we may look at it from the other angle, that is, from the perspective of its members, and define it in terms of coordinate *citizenship*. A federation is a system in which each participant enjoys a constitutionally protected membership in two polities, one regional and one central. This does nothing to the substance of the above definition. It merely changes perspectives on it from that of *obeying* to that of *belonging*. But this switch of perspective may be of some use in bringing to light an intriguing question. Can the concept of citizenship lend itself to dual political allegiance?

Can the concept of citizenship lend itself to dual political allegiance?

The theme of citizenship has been an important one in Western political thought. It has always had strongly hierarchical implications, in the sense that "citizens" have been viewed as people with a single overriding object of loyalty. Machiavelli (in the *Discourses*) and Rousseau (in *Emile*) propose somewhat caricatured examples. Machiavelli recommends Brutus as a model citizen, because he sacrificed his sons to save Rome, while Rousseau admires the story of the Spartan mother who cared nothing for her children's lives, as long as Sparta won the battle. The citizen, as described in such classical texts, is not attractive as a friend, still less as a

parent. But even in less overdrawn pictures, citizens are required to be alive to the general interests of a political community and to set particular interests aside when necessary. They are supposed to attach importance to their membership in a political community, at the expense sometimes of their membership in families or professional or regional communities; and they are supposed to define their own interests, at least in certain contexts, in terms of the interests of the political community to which they belong. It is this, traditionally, that has distinguished the "citizen" from the mere "subject." While subjects are "subjected" to law in a manner no different from that of a foreign visitor, citizens see membership in a community as something that in part defines who and what they are and arrange their priorities accordingly.

Now it is this aspect of citizenship that places federalism in an interesting light and may also render it problematic. The citizen, as viewed by political theorists, sets the general above the particular and ranks his or her attachments. To be a citizen is to put one's priorities in strict order. But to be a *federal* citizen, as we at once see, must be different. A federal citizen has *two* official loyalties. This is simply not the same as having one official loyalty and all sorts of other unofficial loyalties—loyalties to be set aside, when necessary, in order to be a good citizen, as theorists such as Machiavelli and Rousseau so vividly recommend. Federal constitutions explicitly provide that neither provincial nor national authorities are supreme over the other, that obligations are owed to each within their defined spheres. Because authority is divided in this way, the citizen too is divided.

What is the point of drawing attention to this notion of divided loyalty?[3] It may provide a basis for explaining why federalism matters, what difference it makes, and why it might be worth having. It helps to explain what federalism might have to do with widely accepted values such as democracy and freedom—a question which is often raised, but which is remarkably hard to answer. It also helps to explain why some recent Canadian debates about the *mode* of federalism are important. They are debates about how to make sense of the difficult notion of competing civic loyalties in a specific political context.

But this is to run ahead of the argument. First, I must explain why federalism needs defending at all; second, I must explain why a "competing civic loyalties" argument is better than other proposed defences; and finally, I must attempt to show how this rather abstract idea connects with political debate.

I

♦ ♦ ♦

Why, first of all, does federalism require a defence? The answer is simple: federalism has been declared to be quite pointless. Here fashions in criticizing federalism have changed. For an earlier generation of critics, federalism was malign because it impeded central planning, hindered firm political action, prevented national majorities from enjoying their due, and defended local prejudices and tyrannies. An eloquent statement of such a view is Harold Laski's "The Obsolescence of Federalism" (1939),[4] prompted by economic depression and the (federal) state's inability to respond effectively.

Similar sorts of objections were provoked by the protection apparently afforded by federalism to racist policies in American states and to Nazism in pre-war Germany. Federalism gets in the way of urgently needed change. But more recent criticisms attribute no efficacy to federalism at all, not even the efficacy in doing the evil which earlier critics saw in it. Their spirit is well conveyed by the subtitle of an essay by W.H. Riker: "Does Federalism Exist and Does It Matter?"[5] In particular, recent critics have attempted to discredit the idea that federalism has any connection with freedom, which they take to be the value which is supposed to give federalism its point. They have certainly succeeded in casting doubt upon the case that they believe has been made for federalism. What are their arguments?[6]

Federalism is a system in which governing powers are constitutionally dispersed between different governmental levels. If federalism has a point, it must be shown that such a dispersal of power promotes some significant and widely shared value. The first and most obvious possibility is that a federal arrangement, in dispersing power between national and provincial governments, thereby limits the power of national majorities to do as they wish, and thus protects minorities. Interest- or opinion-groups which have no hope of becoming a national majority may become a provincial majority or at least a minority strong enough that provincial majorities must reckon with them. Thus, a structure of government assigning powers to provincial majorities or their representatives certainly enhances the position of such groups. But unfortunately for the argument, if it is wrong to give national majorities power over provincial minorities, it must also be wrong to give provincial majorities power over provincial minorities, which is what federalism does. It subjects black minorities to white majorities in white majority states, even though

the cause of black minorities may be supported by a national majority. In such cases it is hard indeed to suppose that the federal dispersal of power is an instrument of freedom. But we cannot disapprove of the federal dispersal of power when we dislike the consequences and approve of it when we like the consequences, just as we cannot (consistently) deny national majorities the right to impose upon minorities while constitutionally confirming the right of provincial majorities to do exactly the same thing.

If it is wrong to give national majorities power over provincial minorities, it must also be wrong to give provincial majorities power over provincial minorities.

Alternatively, we could seek to defend federalism, not in terms of protecting minority freedom, but in terms of protecting a whole society's freedom against the undue concentration of power, the abuse of power, or both. A famous maxim of political science is that power can be checked only with power. What better way of checking power than by multiplying governments, so that they restrain and limit one another? They will do so, however, only if they have opposed interests or values. If they act in concert they will not check one another. If they do check one another, that may be because they reflect a diversity of interests or values in society—a diversity which, if there were no federal system, would probably find political reflection by other means (such as the party system). So if "the real cause for the existence of liberty is the pluralist structure of society"[7] and not a federal constitution, then the significance of the federal constitution is clearly limited. And when a national mood of fear or anger overrides social pluralism—anti-communist paranoia, for example—governments act concertedly and liberties receive no protection from the federal system.

But surely there are some arguments for decentralization? Of course there are. There are arguments based upon the efficiency of service provision, which is likely to be improved if there is a mixture of governmental levels rather than a single distant central distributor. There are values based upon the merits of democratic participation, which is often thought to be enhanced by the provision of relatively small and relatively homogeneous units. There are arguments based upon the preservation of local cultures, to which political decentralization may offer one route. There are, doubtless, many other arguments too. All of them, however, run into a serious difficulty: the objection that unitary states, too, can be decentralized. Here the example of Britain, a (politically) decentralized but (constitutionally) unitary state, is frequently cited and clearly is instructive. In the British political tradition local self-government and the limitation of central power are themes often stressed. The British process of state formation is often contrasted with the French case, in which the state grew by systematically demolishing local powers instead of coming into counterpoise with them. But it is plainly not federalism that explains this difference; it is explained by a complex of political factors. Observers impressed by this fact have made the claim that decentralization does not require federalism at all. "All that is needful," J.S. Mill wrote, "is to give a sufficiently large sphere of action to the local authorities."[8]

A possible reply, however, is that only a federation can give adequate constitutional protection to the subnational governments. The Greater London Council can be abolished at will by the British Parliament, but the Province of Ontario cannot be abolished by the Canadian Parliament. At any given point, in other words, there may be as much decentralization in some unitary states as in some federations. But over time, the chances of preserving the powers provinces have in a federation are better than the chances of preserving the powers subordinate governments have in a unitary state. Such a view has been attributed to the American founders,[9] and also to Proudhon. It is not obviously unreasonable. If it is true that federations arise when smaller territories desire some unity but fear complete absorption into a unitary state, then some such view must presumably be held by the inhabitants or leaders of the smaller territories, or else they would have no reason to choose federation. But the view is not in any unqualified sense true. A federal constitution has not protected subnational governments in the U.S.S.R.; and in cases where subnational governments *have* retained their powers, they have done so, not only because of the federal constitution, but because of many other contributing factors (including, of course, those factors which incline political actors to accept constitutional provisions!). The claim, then, needs to be weakened: federation may be one of the ways in which subnational autonomies are protected, though it is neither (always) a necessary nor (ever) a sufficient condition.

> *Federation may be one of the ways in which subnational autonomies are protected, though it is neither (always) a necessary nor (ever) a sufficient condition.*

II

♦ ♦ ♦

One approach to defending federalism, currently popular and apparently promising, must be mentioned here, if only to be rejected. This is an approach based on the logic of social choice. Let us suppose that a political society (like an economy) is made up of individuals who make choices and want to get as many as possible of the things they choose. What scale of organization will best enable them to get what they choose? Here we seem to face a dilemma. Relatively small organizations will, of course, be relatively more responsive to any individual's choices—in a group of ten, each counts for one-tenth; in a group of one million, each counts for only one-millionth. To this we may add further consideration that the smaller the groups which make decisions, the better the chance of homogeneity, so that the choices of one group of like-minded citizens are less likely to be constantly thwarted by the choices of other groups with different interests. So for these reasons, organizations should be small.

But that is only half the picture. The smaller the organization, the smaller its jurisdiction. If we draw the boundaries narrowly, we shall be less able to exercise control over events which impinge upon the community from outside its boundaries. The smaller the organizations, the more of them there will be, and thus there will be more "externalities," that is, effects generated by one community's choices which spill over into another community's life. And the more fragmented decision-making is, the more likely we are to encounter unwanted policy results which only concerted common action could avert. Each community may derive benefits from its own polluting industries which far outweigh the costs specifically attributable to its own pollution, but the benefits may be outweighed by the costs imposed by *everyone's* pollution cumulatively. So organizations should be large, permitting allowance to be made for such cumulative costs.

The outcome of this logic, as was argued by the authors of a study of *Size and Democracy* in 1973, is a "complex federated polity" in which small and large political organizations coexist.[10] When responsiveness is essential and diversity precludes consensus, we assign powers to small organizations. Where "externalities" abound or where joint action is essential, we assign powers to large organizations. Such a view has more recently been elaborated by Vincent Ostrom and offered specifically as a reply to Riker's critique.[11] Ostrom's argument is more refined and detailed than the mere sketch offered above and should be consulted by anyone who is interested in the spirited construction of ingenious defences. But the trouble is, it is not really a defence of *federalism*. It is a defence of a system in which "citizens confront several purveyors of public goods and services" so that they can "search out an appropriate mix of public goods and services." That says nothing, however, about the constitutional form of such a system. It thus misses the point of the objection: whatever is claimed for decentralization can also be claimed for a unitary state. The point is made by Ostrom's appeal to examples such as the "fragmented" but (he claims) exemplary management of water use in Southern California. While the United States is a federal system, the State of California is a unitary system, and the West and Central Basin Replenishment District is not a partner in a federal arrangement but (legally speaking) the creature of a superior government. And if such agencies *are* to be regarded as components of "federalism," then logically it could make no difference if the states themselves were merely creatures of the federal government, so that we no longer had federalism in the relevant (constitutional) sense.

Worse than that, the "federalism" defended in the above way ideally demands fluid boundaries, defined by intersecting preferences, and redefined constantly as salient issues shift. While it would be satisfying to suppose that the division of jurisdiction in any actual federation might more or less correspond to this model, it would in fact be entirely irrational to do so. The provinces of Canada may or may not correspond to relatively homogeneous communities of interest. They may be too small: a unified Atlantic region might fit the social choice model better than four provinces. They may be too big: Northern Ontario and Metro Toronto should be separate actors, not subsumed under one province. It may also be that more than two levels of organization are needed to give optimal expression to the distribution of choices, as Ostrom indeed says.[12] But there is no evidence that federal regimes are more hospitable to multiple levels of organization than unitary regimes are. Indeed, confronted with a predatory federal centre, provinces may seek to concentrate power jealously and to minimize the autonomy of sub-provincial (municipal) organizations.[13] So if the "federalism" defended by social choice theorists demands multiple, functionally defined jurisdictions, then it provides us with a critique rather than a defence of what federalism is generally taken to be.

The social choice approach ... treats the citizen only as a consumer *of quantifiable goods.*

It may be revealing, though, to ask what is wrong with the social choice approach, and whether there is some general reason why it leads us away from understanding federalism. The answer, surely, is that it treats the citizen only as a *consumer* of quantifiable goods. Anything quantifiable can vary indefinitely in quantity, and any desire to consume can vary indefinitely in relation to other desires. Here we scarcely have a promising basis for any constitutional arrangement, least of all for federalism. If federalism is to be defended as constitutionally protected decentralization, we remove any possibility of using an economic model to defend it. For if economic models derive their persuasive power from their flexibility in relation to shifting preferences, federalism derives whatever persuasive power it has from its resistance to shifting preferences, and from its protection of a distribution of power against whatever majorities happen to want.

III
♦ ♦ ♦

Now it is perfectly true that the consumption of desired things is an integral part of politics. Politics *is* about who gets what, when, and how. Any view of politics which neglects this fact is doomed to hopeless irrelevance. Politics *is* consumption. But that is not all it is. It is also a matter of self-identification, that is, of declaring not merely what one wants but who one is. To vote (or work) for a nationalist party, or for a provincialist party such as the Parti Québécois, or for a class party such as the British Labour Party is to declare something about how one sees oneself and which of the various identifications one might adopt is most salient. And this is prior to the act of wanting: what one takes oneself to *be* is logically prior to determining the salience of various possible wants and desires. A sort of spurious realism attaches to the idea that wants are somehow primary or given, that reflection on self-identification is a luxury of dubious political importance. What seems to be realism is actually nothing more than excessive neatness. Wants affect what one decides to be; what one decides to be governs what one wants. There is a two-way process, and any desire to reduce it to a one-way process displays impatience with the complexity of human motivation.[14]

Where, then, should one look? Let us examine very briefly three texts which establish a connection between federalism and the process of self-definition, where membership involves determining where one belongs, and which of one's attachments have priority. That, it was suggested above, is the point of introducing the notion of federal *citizenship*. A citizen, ideally viewed, is concerned, not simply with identifying the rules which he or she is subject to, but wants to view himself or herself as a participant in a political community, and thus attaches value to belonging to one community rather than another. The three texts to be briefly discussed may help to illustrate the importance of this point in justifying federalism's significance.

A citizen ... wants to view himself or herself as a participant in a political community....

---

1. For a defence of federalism it is natural to turn first to *The Federalist,* written during the constitutional debates in the United States in the 1780s and an unrivalled statement of American political philosophy.[15] However, to turn to *The Federalist* is to be disappointed, for there is rather little about federalism in it. The object of the authors, Madison, Hamilton, and Jay, is to make a case for a more unified constitution than the original Articles of Confederation had provided, and their best known and most powerful arguments would serve to justify a unitary state as well as a federation.

Take, for example, the famous argument of Letter 10. A democracy, by which Madison means a direct democracy, can exist only in a small society, but in a small society minorities are constantly imperilled by "factions" or self-interested majorities. A larger society places more obstacles in the path of factious majorities: "Extend the sphere, and you take in a greater variety of parties and interests; you make it less probable that a majority of the whole will have a common motive to invade the rights of other citizens."

Madison's argument concerns the extent of political organization, not its form. Something a little more promising follows at once: "The influence of factious leaders may kindle a flame within their particular States, but will be unable to kindle a general conflagration through all the States." This part of the argument entails local political autonomy as well as sheer diversity. But we have seen that local autonomy arguments are not necessarily federalism arguments, and it is interesting to note that when the same argument is used later by Tocqueville, it is intended to support, not federalism, but simply administrative decentralization.

What, then, are the specifically federalist arguments of *The Federalist*? In Letter 17, Hamilton speaks of the state governments as a "counterpoise ... to the power of the Union," and this might seem a natural argument for theorists of checks and balances to use. The division of powers between State and Union, on such an argument, could be defended in the same way as the separation of powers between branches of government, or between upper and lower branches of the legislature.

Such a connection is hinted at in Madison's Letter 51, perhaps the fullest statement of his pluralistic point of view: "In the compound republic of America, the power surrendered by the people is first divided between two distinct governments, and then the portion allotted to each, subdivided among distinct and separate departments. Hence a double security arises to the rights of the people. The different governments will controul each other; at the same time that each will be controuled by itself." But very little is made of this, and one cannot fail to gather the impression that if federalism is important for this reason, it is not very high on Madison's list of priorities. Even in Letter 17, where Hamilton speaks of "counterpoise," the context is the extremely limited one of persuading states that there is no risk of federal encroachment on their powers—a task quite different from that of explaining why (if at all) it is a good thing that states should *have* any powers. At best, it explains why "local" (that is, state) government is necessary: "It is a known fact of human nature that its affections are commonly weak in proportion to the distance or diffuseness of the object," and there is thus a necessary place in political schemes for objects of local attachment.

But this notion of "affection" points towards a different line of argument, premised not upon balance but upon *competition*. People will have affections for various objects, and the affections that they have for nearer objects will normally be stronger than their affections for more distant objects. "The operations of the national government ... will be less apt to come home to the feelings of the people; and, in proportion, less likely to inspire a habitual sense of obligation and an active sentiment of attachment." But something may intervene to change this normal pattern: maladministration, tyranny, or corruption.

Hamilton offers two examples. The first is that of feudal Europe, where power was divided between a sovereign and his feudatories (or barons). Being "immediate lords" of their subjects rather than a distant sovereign whose power was mediated through subordinates, barons generally enjoyed a more secure authority. For short periods, a "vigorous" sovereign "of superior abilities" could redress the balance, and in the long run, the barons' oppression of their subjects was so intolerable that the latter formed an alliance with the king against the barons. "Had the nobles, by a conduct of clemency and justice, preserved the fidelity and devotion of their retainers and followers, the contests between them and the prince must almost always have ended in their favour." The second example, that of the decline of the clans of Scotland after the Act of Union, adopts a similar tack. Hamilton then goes on to compare with these examples the federal situation, the same in displaying "the rivalship of power." Here we have at least a plausible defence of federalism: by systematically dividing loyalties, it sets authorities in competition for the affection of followers. If it does so, then presumably it will enhance at least one democratic value, that of the responsiveness of government to opinion. Civic efficacy is greater, *The Federalist* in effect claims, when the objects of civic affection are multiple and thus potentially in contestation.

Here we have at least a plausible defence of federalism: by systematically dividing loyalties, it sets authorities in competition for the affection of followers.

---

2. It is *not* natural to turn for illumination to *The Principle of Federation*, a book written in 1863 by P.-J. Proudhon, better known as an anarchist than as a federal thinker.[16] What he proposes is in detail too radical, too eccentric, and still too imbued with anarchist feeling to serve as a guide to the modern federal state. Whereas Madison and Hamilton were arguing for the *aggregation* of thirteen semi-independent states into a closer union, Proudhon was arguing for nothing less than the *dis*aggregation of France into (about) eighteen provinces and for the replacement of nation-states by "federations." But although this conclusion takes him far afield, his *principle* does tell us something about federalism.

Nothing could be more misleading than the assumption that Proudhon, because he believed in the disaggregation of large units into small ones, is therefore the victim of a cult of smallness. What he is against is the cult of monism or the exaggerated belief in unity. Like so many French thinkers of both the left and right, he believed that the centralization of the French state had been carried to absurd lengths, thanks in part to the French Revolution. "In the social contract as imagined by Rousseau and the Jacobins the citizen divests himself of sovereignty, and the town and the Department and province, absorbed by central authority, are no longer anything but agencies under direct ministerial control."[17] But it is not Proudhon's intention to set against this vision of the indivisible sovereign state a counter-vision of an indivisible town or province. His is a thesis of the systematic divisibility of power. No level of government is to assume a dominant position on the horizons of individuals' lives.

Higher levels of government, Proudhon believed, must keep their hands off local administration, which is not only something better accomplished locally, but also a realm of action in which civic virtues are best displayed; the centralized state reduces the citizen to a passive and pathetic role, leaving him nothing to do but "perform his little task ... relying for the rest upon the providence of government,"[18] while the federal state cultivates local initiative. In that sense it is the local or provincial government that is the agent of freedom, if freedom is taken to mean activity rather than passivity, self-assertiveness rather than dependence. But in at least two other senses the federal state itself is the agent of freedom. For one thing, if it is to keep its hands off administration, it has a correspondingly dignified role as "prime mover and general director" and as "the highest expression of progress." It is thus the state that expresses and gives direction to freedom in the sense of a society's capacity to initiate, to change its own circumstances, and to achieve common objectives. For another thing, the locality or province, no less than the state, can become oppressive to the individual, and it is necessary to set a federal state above it in order to act as a guarantor of individual rights. In Proudhon's account the idea of "freedom" takes on rich and complex forms, and it would be instructive to compare his account with the rather mechanical and impoverished view of freedom which critics of federalism tend to adopt.

The extraordinary interest of Proudhon's argument does not lie, as I have noted above, in the details of what he has to offer—details which are open to innumerable criticisms. His argument is interesting because he believes in "citizenship" but not in "cities"; that is, he values above all else the sort of virtues that citizens are supposed to display—self-sacrifice, responsibility, concern for shared goals—but he does not want these virtues to be directed towards any single focus. Indeed, he believed that if civic loyalty is directed towards any single object it will be destroyed, that citizenship is compatible only with multiple loci of attachment. Perhaps more than any other theorist, he exemplifies the value of what has recently and aptly been called "agnosticism about community";[19] that is, Proudhon does not believe that any level of organization inherently expresses one's sense of who one is and what one belongs to, and that this sense can best be realized when feelings of belonging are in competition. To the extent that one is obliged to choose one obligation over another, one is less free to choose between potentially rival attachments, and, consequently, to choose one identity rather than another. To the extent that "the federal principle" leaves open the question of priority, permitting individuals to balance one attachment against another, it permits more scope, Proudhon believes, for self-determination.

3. The third example is a remarkable essay entitled "Nationality" by Lord Acton,[20] a British liberal of the Victorian period, published one year before Proudhon's *Principle of Federation*. Acton's concern is scarcely with federalism as we know it. Although he mentions Switzerland and the United States he also offers a passionate defence of "the British and Austrian multiracial empires." That, of course, at once distances him rather sharply from Proudhon, for whom "federalism" and "empire" were antitheses. Yet the interesting thing is that, despite enormous distance of what we might call an ideological kind, Acton's liberal imperialism is remarkably in tune with Proudhon's socialist anarchism.

Like Proudhon, Acton dreads above all the creation of single, supreme, and unqualified loyalties, and values federalism precisely because it sets loyalties in perma-

nent competition. Like Proudhon, too, he sees the pernicious source of undivided loyalty in the democratic principle of the French Revolution, which sought to represent political society as the expression of an undivided common will. On the French democratic view, Acton complains, "nationality is founded on the perpetual supremacy of the collective will, of which the unity of the nation is the necessary condition, to which every other influence must defer, and against which no obligation enjoys authority, and all resistance is tyrannical.... Whenever a single definite object is made the supreme end of the state, be it the advantage of a class, the safety or the power of the country, the greatest happiness of the greatest number, or the support of any speculative idea, the State becomes for the time inevitably absolute."

Acton contrasts this absolutist view with a liberal one. Instead of requiring submission to a "single definite object," liberals seek to establish conditions under which multiple and various desired objects can coexist, liberty being a precondition for the pursuit of diverse ends. Liberty is possible only when one end is not supposed to be all-inclusive or all-important. That is why it is so necessary to separate ends, to divide loyalties, and to ensure that political structures do not wholly coincide with other objects of loyalty. "The presence of different nations under the same sovereignty is similar in its effect to the independence of the Church in the State. It provides against the servility which flourished under the shadow of a single authority, by balancing interests, multiplying associations, and giving to the subject the restraint and support of a combined opinion. In the same way it promotes independence by forming definite groups of public opinion, and by affording a great source and centre of political sentiments, and of notions of duty not derived from the sovereign will."

Here Acton's argument plainly shares something with Madison as well as with Proudhon. Acton is Proudhon-like in demanding recognition of a diversity of wills which resists subsumption under a general will. He is Madison-like in demanding an association which is "the vastest that can be included in a state." But Acton's introduction of the church-state analogy introduces a wholly new dimension. Madison and Proudhon speak of the division of interests and of the advantage of separating interest-representing mechanisms. Acton speaks, also, of the advantage of separating *kinds* of interests, so that states do not become overbearing in the sort of attachment that they invite or demand. To fuse the state and the nation, in other words, is to do much the same as to fuse the state and the church. It is to overload politics with aspirations and passions which appropriately belong elsewhere. Federalism, then, is the means of confining politics to its proper scope, by setting other loyalties in a position of rivalry with loyalty to state.

Here, then, we have three different approaches, written in quite different political contexts and with quite different ideological assumptions, that nevertheless have something important in common: they promote federalism because it divides civic loyalty. The arguments are not the same, of course. *The Federalist*—to the extent that it *is* federalist—wants to enhance the responsiveness of government to shades and diversities of opinion that could simply vanish in a majoritarian unitary state. Proudhon wants to cultivate a certain kind of moral responsibility, which he believes can be cultivated only where responsibilities are both specific and tangible, and not swamped by the demands of a (fictitious) "people." Acton wants to protect a certain style of politics by excluding from politics those obsessive and redemptive passions which churches, but not states, can sustain. These arguments are so interesting, and so richly diverse, that one suspects that a very much better case could be made for federalism than the case which critics of federalism delight in overturning.

IV

♦ ♦ ♦

There could then be reasons why citizenship should be divided. But *how* can citizenship be divided? How can something traditionally thought to be exclusive by its very nature, come to be directed to two objects at once? Such a thing may go against the grain of one's expectations. It did so in the Canadian case. It was the belief of Sir John A. Macdonald, among many others, that provincial identities would wither away as the Canadian state gained increasing saliency as a focus of political attention and an outlet for political ambition.[21] But as one careful examination of political loyalties in Canada concludes, "citizens generally see no need to 'choose sides'—to renounce either their federal or their provincial loyalties or identities."[22] The authors continue: "The perceptions of citizens and the policies of governments ... reflect a balance of unity and diversity, of convergence and divergence, of loyalties to larger and smaller units.... The tension and conflict so obvious to any observer indicate that no one view, no one loyalty, no one identity has any predominance, nor is it likely to in the near future."

One way of explaining this situation is as follows. Provincial and federal loyalties share something in that they are political loyalties. They entail legal obligations, the legitimate use of coercion, the official expression of conflict, and the symbolism of sovereignty. But although they are similar in type, they can differ in content. Some official powers can belong to one level, others to another level. So just as in private life people can readily adjust to the existence of authorities in different spheres—children, for example, expecting instructions of one kind from parents, another kind from teachers—so federal citizens adapt to dual political allegiances. There are, as it were, two states, occupying themselves with distinct areas of each individual's life. If the division of powers has been appropriately settled, the provincial state will concern itself with matters of primary concern to a region, while the federal state will concern itself with matters of general interest. This is what has been termed "interstate" federalism—a federalism which divides powers between two states or political systems, each of which has its own political life, neither impinging in any primary way upon the other.[23]

Just as in private life people can readily adjust to the existence of authorities in different spheres ... so federal citizens adapt to dual political allegiances.

What is called "intrastate" federalism, however, contains a different and more complex relationship between the two levels of identification, which are pictured as parts of a single political system. The stress does not fall on the independence of provinces as (partially) self-governing entities, and thus upon the division of responsibilities which gives them this status: rather, the stress falls upon the fact that provinces retain *an identity as political actors in federal politics*. If Canada were a unitary state, Ontario could simply vanish as a distinct interest or a distinct voice in national policy-making. In a Canadian federation of an "intrastate" kind, on the other hand, Ontario's interests and views must be taken into account in formulating what the Canadian general interest *is*.

One could say that intrastate federalism is a form of democratic theory in which the constituencies are regional ones, as opposed to professional or social or economic ones. In pluralist democracy as once understood in the United States, policies reflected the interplay of "groups" with varied demands and varying degrees of leverage, whereas in intrastate federalist democracy the crucial interplay occurs among provincial demands, perhaps with the difference that provincial demands are already more likely than "group" demands to represent aggregation, compromise, and democratic legitimation. They are already the demands of citizens, citizenship finding its locus not merely at one level, as in pluralist democracy, nor in two separate realms, as in interstate federalism, but in two realms, one of which is embraced by the other.

Are provinces or provincial governments to be represented at the federal centre? The difference is enormous.

Here, though, we evidently face a choice. Are provinces or provincial governments to be represented at the federal centre? The difference is enormous. Provincial governments, as political elites, have some political objectives which non-elites do not share. Even if provincial governments perfectly reflect provincial majorities, it makes a difference whether or not a federal government can mobilize "dispersed majorities," or majorities lacking decisive strength in any one province. Even with respect to reflecting the views of provincial majorities, a federal government can change those views by manipulating alternatives or offering inducements, if it is able to bypass provincial governments and seek the support of provincial opinion directly. A version of intrastate federalism permitting federal government to do that is evidently more "centralist" in its potential. It gives federal government itself the possibility of becoming the outlet for important provincial demands, thus undercutting the claim of provincial governments to be the sole voice of provincial interests. Conversely, of course, a version of intrastate federalism in which provincial governments were the sole voice of provinces would tend to be highly decentralist. The federal government would be constrained in its role of national government not only by the federal division of powers but also by the fact that, even in exercising its *own* powers, it would be impeded by the opposition of provincial governments with interests different from its own and from

each other's. In the latter case, *federal* citizenship would seem to be quite attenuated. Federal politics would be intergovernmental politics, and federal citizenship would be expressed only in a periodic national vote which of necessity could exercise only remote influence with respect to any given issue.

It is in the "centralist" version of "intrastate" federalism, then, that the idea of divided citizenship is pushed to the most interesting lengths. Here we have a situation in which, ideally viewed, two distinct kinds of judgment are made systematically available to every citizen, perhaps, even, with respect to one and the same issue. First, one is required to judge which of two or more outcomes is preferable in relation to one's own interests, when set in the context of other (*provincial*) interests with which one's own interests may be highly interdependent. Second, one is required to judge which of two or more outcomes is preferable when set in the context of other (*national*) interests, where even more complex sets of interdependencies exist. This would seem to require great sophistication—certainly more that Machiavelli required Brutus to exercise, or Rousseau required the Spartan mothers to exercise in condemning their children in the name of a single unambiguous standard. Yet it appears not altogether unrealistic to expect such sophistication.

These three conceptions of federal citizenship naturally affect conceptions of federalism itself and are notably prominent in discussions of constitutional change. *How* they affect constitutional proposals is a question which, although intriguing, goes beyond the scope of this paper.[24] All that can be said here is that assessments of any given federation, and proposals for amending its constitution, may helpfully be examined in the light of the broad themes mentioned above: democratic responsiveness, the openness of choice of identification, and the preservation of politics from (unqualified) nationalism. If none of these themes find any reflection in political fact, then we may have to agree that federalism makes no difference. If one or more of them *do* find concrete expression, then the federal character of a polity will have to be taken as seriously as its democratic, its liberal, or its pluralist character, for its federal character bears upon the most fundamental issue that can be raised about it—namely, what it means to be a citizen within it.

Notes

1. A clear and careful definition is provided by Peter W. Hogg: "In a federal state governmental power is distributed between a central (or national or federal) authority and several regional (or provincial or state) authorities, in such a way that every individual in the state is subject to the laws of two authorities, the central authority and a regional authority.... The central authority and the regional authorities are 'coordinate,' that is to say, neither is subordinate to the other." *Constitutional Law of Canada*, revised edition (Toronto: Carswell, 1985), 80.

2. See especially W.S. Livingston, *Federalism and Constitutional Change* (Oxford: Clarendon, 1956).

3. For an exploration of this theme in the Canadian context, see Edwin R. Black, *Divided Loyalties: Canadian Concepts of Federalism* (Montreal: McGill-Queen's, 1975).

4. *The New Republic*, vol. 98, May 3, 1939, 367–9.

5. *Comparative Politics* 2 (1969), 135–46.

6. The following arguments are assembled from three sharply critical texts: Franz Neumann, "On the Theory of the Federal State," in *The Democratic and the Authoritarian State* (New York: Free Press, 1957), 216–32; William H. Riker, *Federalism: Origins, Operation, Significance* (Boston: Little, Brown, 1964); Preston King, "Against Federalism," in R. Benewick et al., eds., *Knowledge and Belief in Politics* (London: Unwin, 1973), 151–76.

7. Neumann, op. cit., 220.

8. J.S. Mill, *Utilitarianism, On Liberty and Considerations of Representative Government* (London: Dent, 1910), 375.

9. See Martin Diamond, "The Ends of Federalism," in Daniel J. Elazar, ed., *The Federal Polity* (New Brunswick, N.J.: Transaction, 1974), 129–52.

10. Robert A. Dahl and Edward R. Tufte, *Size and Democracy* (Stanford: Stanford University Press, 1973), 137.

11. "Can Federalism Make a Difference?" in Elazar, *Federal Polity*, 197–237.

12. Ibid., 204–5.

13. See for example Neumann, "Theory of the Federal State," and for a Canadian case, Robert A. Young, "Remembering Equal Opportunity: Clearing the Undergrowth in New Brunswick," *Canadian Public Administration* (forthcoming).

14. For a fluent and wide-ranging discussion, see Charles Taylor, "Alternative Futures: Legitimacy, Identity and Alienation in Late Twentieth-Century Canada," in Alan Cairns and Cynthia Williams, eds., *Constitutionalism, Citizenship and Society in Canada* (Toronto: University of Toronto Press, 1985), 183–229.

15. The edition I have used is *The Federalist Papers* by Alexander Hamilton, James Madison and John Jay (New York: Bantam, 1982).

16. See Richard Vernon, ed. and trans., *The Principle of Federation* by P.-J. Proudhon (Toronto: University of Toronto Press, 1979).

17. Ibid., 59.

18. Ibid., 60.

19. See Reginald Whitaker, "Federalism and Democratic Theory," Institute of Intergovernmental Relations, Queen's University (Discussion Paper #17), 1983, 45.

20. In Acton's *Essays in the Liberal Interpretation of History* (Chicago: University of Chicago Press, 1967), 131–59. A more recent discussion sharing something with Acton's is P.E. Trudeau, *Federalism and the French Canadians* (Toronto: Macmillan, 1968).

21. See for example Gordon Stewart, "The Origins of Canadian Politics and John A. Macdonald," in R. Kenneth Carty and W. Peter Ward, eds., *National Politics and Community in Canada* (Vancouver: University of British Columbia Press, 1986), 15–47.

22. David J. Elkins and Richard Simeon et al., *Small Worlds: Provinces and Parties in Canadian Political Life* (Toronto: Methuen, 1980), 308.

23. See Alan C. Cairns, "From Interstate to Intrastate Federalism in Canada," Institute of Intergovernmental Relations, Queen's University (Discussion Paper #5), 1979.

24. Discussions include Alan C. Cairns, "Recent Federalist Constitutional Proposals: A Review Essay," *Canadian Public Policy* 5 (1979): 348–65.

Terms & Concepts

coordinate citizenship
decentralization
dual political allegiance
federalism

general will
interstate federalism
intrastate federalism
membership

pluralist democracy
social choice theory
subnational governments
unitary state

Questions

1. What are the virtues of the federal citizen?

2. What is the difference between intrastate and interstate federalism?

3. How do federal constitutions preserve politics from what Vernon calls "(unqualified) nationalism"?

4. What are the political and institutional implications of hierarchical and coordinate arrangements of political allegiances and identities?

5. Do you think Canadians have as sophisticated a sense of citizenship as Vernon thinks is required in a federation?

Time and News: The Media's Limitations as an Instrument of Democracy

Thomas E. Patterson

Editors' Note

Gwynne Dyer, expatriate Canadian journalist and military historian, noted in *The Human Race,* a video series originally broadcast on CBC in September 1994, that rulers of ancient empires with illiterate populations and without modern means of mass communication had to instill obedience through terror. News of incidents of terror can be counted on to spread rapidly by word of mouth, which is why the Russian revolutionary Trotsky, leading the Red Army into a brutal civil war in a semifeudal country, considered it a powerful tool. The flip-side of these observations is that mass communication and literacy make it possible to rule by persuasion, with the occasional dose of authority and coercion as backup. In totalitarian regimes, mass communication was used to control and indoctrinate; thus, its means were monopolized by the state. This is becoming increasingly difficult to achieve in our electronic age.

In a democracy, mass communication is a two-way process. It serves as a conduit through which citizens and interest groups can channel their demands to government. But it is also the public's main source of information about government and government policies. Mass communication, in turn, becomes a forum through which citizens make their demands as well as their evaluations of government performance. To do this job freely, mass media, the principal agents of mass communication, are either in private hands or, in the case of public broadcasters, at least at arm's length from the government.

Although the mass media have an undeniably important function in democracies, are they up to the task? Many observers have investigated alleged partiality, either toward the political Left (as when journalists are accused of having left-wing sympathies) or the Right (for example, ownership is concentrated in the hands of conservative billionaires who determine editorial direction). Patterson takes a more structural approach by focusing not on choices of either journalists or owners, but on the constraints imposed by the time sensitivity of commercial media. And just as the media have two-way functions, so does time sensitivity. On the one hand, it gives us a relatively limited or poorly chosen selection of news to frame our demands to government and evaluate its performance. We might call this mal-information. More dangerously, it can create major issues from good stories that are artificial or inconsequential. These issues may then become the basis for citizen demands and focus the scarce resources of government on fictitious or minor problems. We might call this effect perverse information.

Finally, Patterson also links the negative framing of political news reporting with our increasingly dim perception of politics. Increasingly, political candidates slavishly follow public opinion in their pursuit of public office, while poorly informed citizens reflexively accuse them of sleaze, unwillingness to lead, and (paradoxically) unwillingness to do what the people wish. We may indeed wonder about the future of democracy.

As political parties and representative institutions have weakened under the strain of post-industrialism, the news media have been expected to fill the void. The media are asked to give order and direction to democratic processes that are built increasingly upon entrepreneurial leaders, floating voters, and freewheeling interest groups.

Can the media carry this burden? Can they organize public opinion and debate in a meaningful way? Many journalists apparently believe they can. Our study of journalists in five Western democracies found that they regard "news reports" as a more accurate expression of public opinion than "parliamentary debates" (Patterson and Donsbach, 1992). This perception was particularly strong in the continental European countries of Germany, Sweden and Italy but also characterized the views of U.S. and British journalists (see Table 17.1).

Table 17.1   The News and Legislative Debate as Expressions of Public Opinion, as Perceived by Journalists in Five Democracies (all figures in percent)

How good as expression of public opinion?	Journalists from:				
	US	UK	Germany	Sweden	Italy
Parliamentary Debate					
Excellent/good (%)	42	42	16	8	21
Fair/Poor (%)	58	58	84	92	79
The News					
Excellent/good (%)	60	64	56	45	58
Fair/poor (%)	40	36	44	55	42

Note: Surveys were conducted by the author in 1990–1993 and were based on random samples of about 275 journalists in each country. About half the respondents were print journalists and half were broadcast journalists. The survey question read as follows: "In principle, a democracy rests upon the wishes of the governed. However, it is not easy to determine precisely what the people want. In your judgment, how good is each of the following as an expression of public opinion?"

Many scholars also assume that the press[1] can carry the burden. They argue, usually in a qualified way, that the media have the capacity to give order and direction to public opinion and debate (see, for example, Rosen, 1992).

Yet the news media were not designed for this responsibility. Of course, the press has traditionally had a duty to inform the public. But this obligation has always been balanced against the media's economic needs. The commercial media's primary objective is "to attract and hold a large audience for advertisers"

(Jamieson and Campbell, 1992: 4). Moreover, the recent view that the media can somehow compensate for the defects in political institutions requires more of the press than has been asked of it in the past. The press is no longer expected just to keep an eye out for wrongdoing and to help citizens stay abreast of current affairs. It is also expected to take a lead role in setting the public agenda, organizing public discussion, and instructing citizens on the values at stake in policy problems and issues—functions that have traditionally been the responsibility of political institutions.

The news media are poorly suited to the role of organizing public opinion and debate.

The thesis of this article is that the news media are poorly suited to the role of organizing public opinion and debate. This function requires an institution that is capable of seeing the larger picture—of looking at reality whole and not in small pieces—and which has incentives that lead it to articulate society's needs and values in rough proportion to their magnitude. The press has neither of these characteristics. It has its special strengths, but they do not include these strengths.

Among the factors that limit the capacity of the media to organize public opinion and debate, perhaps none is more important than the impact of time on the news process. Time shapes the news agenda in ways that make it an inadequate substitute for the agendas created by properly functioning political institutions.

TIME HORIZONS
◆ ◆ ◆

Time affects the work of every institution, but few so substantially as the news media. Philip Schlesinger describes the news media as a "time machine" (Schlesinger, 1977: 336).

News time is deliberately shortsighted. The *New York Times'* James Reston described reporting as "the exhilarating search after the Now" (Taylor, 1990: 25). The latest news abruptly replaces the old. In May and early June of 1994, for example, front-page stories in the American press spoke of a showdown pending with North Korea over its production of weapons-grade plutonium. News reports projected a "day of reckoning" that would be President Clinton's "moment of truth." Then suddenly, the issue disappeared from the headlines, not because it had been resolved but because it was displaced by the breaking story that Nicole Brown Simpson had been murdered in Los Angeles (example from Fallows, 1994: 32).

Journalists respond less to the pressing demand of issues than to the relentless churn of the news cycle. Each day is a fresh start, a new reality. Novelty is prized, as is certainty. Journalists must have a story to tell, and it must be a different one than yesterday's. The speed of the news cycle and the relentless search for fresh stories steer the journalist toward certain developments and away from others. There is no precise rule for determining which developments will actually make news, but the day's major stories nearly always derive from "hard events"—developments that have taken a clear and definable shape within the past twenty-four hours (Schudson, 1986: 8).

Without a hard event to lend it form and immediacy, an issue is likely to go unreported. For example, although few developments in the post-war era had a bigger impact on U.S. politics than the northward trek of southern blacks, it was rarely mentioned in the news. As African-Americans in the late 1940s and 1950s moved into the northern cities by the hundreds each day, white people, pushed by racial fears and pulled by the lure of the suburbs, moved out in equally large numbers. Within a few decades, the political, social, and economic landscape of urban America had been substantially altered—a transformation which was rarely the subject of news coverage. A *Newsweek* columnist wryly noted that a ribbon should have been stretched across the Mason-Dixon line as the one-millionth African-American crossed it on the way north; the breaking of the ribbon would have given the media a "peg" on which to hang the story of urban America's radical transformation (example from Patterson, 1993: 403).

In the late 1960s, the U.S. press finally got the peg it required. America's cities erupted in riots when pent-up frustration and anger in the African-American community turned to rage. It was a scene, and a story, that was repeated in 1992, when the Rodney King verdict precipitated the Los Angeles riots. In both cases, the news coverage flared with the rioting and then quickly receded when the violence died out. In the two weeks immediately after the three-day Los Angeles riots in 1992, race relations in the nation's cities were a daily subject on the nightly television newscasts. Within a month, however, the issue had virtually disappeared from the news (Center for Media and Public Affairs, 1992: 6).

There are always critical problems facing a nation and the world, but the emphasis they receive from the media depends on the degree to which they conform with the requirements of the daily news cycle. Abrupt developments are regarded as more newsworthy than chronic conditions. For this reason, society's biggest problems do not routinely dominate media coverage. A new twist may thrust a long-standing problem into the limelight, but major problems tend not to change much from one day to the next. And because they are relatively static, they fall in the category of "old news" (Robinson and Sheehan, 1983: 148).

If a hard event is "big" enough, it can have a transcending effect on news coverage. In a study of German news coverage, Hans Mathias Kepplinger and Johanna Habermeier (1995) found that key events alter the normal criteria for news selection. But this alteration also distorts reality. The researchers found, when a key event occurs, that journalists report more often on past events and place more emphasis on new events, making both appear similar to the key event, thus giving the "false impression" that episodes of the kind represented by the key event are growing in frequency and magnitude, even when their rate is unchanged. This process serves the media's need for additional material on the issue raised by the key event but does not illuminate the actual situation.

[Journalists] are required to view the world as constantly changing in important ways from day to day.

In *Thinking in Time*, Richard Neustadt and Ernest May (1986: 251) assert that sound judgment requires an understanding that the present and the future have no place to come from but the past. Therefore, what matters in the present for the future are those substantial breaks in continuity which are significant enough to represent alterations in normal patterns. Time constraints make it difficult for journalists to render this type of judgment. Their job requires that they focus on the obtruding developments that make today different from yesterday. They are in the business of producing news, which is to say that they are required to view the world as constantly changing in important ways from day to day.

Of course, journalists are not fully imprisoned by each day's events, and they have gained an added measure of freedom from the emergence of interpretive journalism, a style of reporting that gives them opportunities to range across time in the telling of a story (Patterson, 1994: chap. 2; Westerståhl and Johansson, 1986: 137). The older descriptive style largely restricts the journalist to relating the five W's of a day's event: who said what to whom, when, and where. This style cast the journalist in the narrow role of reporter. The newer interpretive style requires the journalist to act also as an analyst. The journalist is thus positioned to extend the boundaries of a story in ways the descriptive style does not allow (Andersen and Thorson, 1989: 272). And in fact, news stories now contain more references to the past and future than they once did (see Figure 17.1).

Figure 17.1   Time in U.S. News Coverage (*Newsweek* Magazine), 1960s and 1990s, as Percent of Total News Content

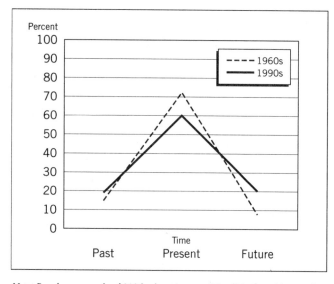

Note: Based on a sample of 233 lead stories on public affairs from *Newsweek* magazine during a three-year period in the early 1990s. News content was judged as past if it referred to historical or discontinuous past developments; as present if it referred to current or ongoing developments; and as future if it referred to possible developments in the weeks, months, or years ahead.

Nevertheless, interpretive reporting asks of journalists what they are normally incapable of doing. When the journalist Bill Moyers claims that the media are now required to deliver "truth as much as news" (Lichter and Smith, 1994: 86), he is claiming a standard of performance that journalists infrequently achieve. The older descriptive model is demanding enough. The journalist seeks to give the audience a precise account of an event,

a process subject to errors of observation. But the journalist's goal is a modest one—factual accuracy. The truth demanded by the interpretive form is much more elusive, and the news media are poorly designed to deliver it on a daily basis.

The main effect of interpretive journalism has been to enlarge the voice of the journalist and, with that, to shrink the time horizon for policy action (see Figure 17.2). The critic James Fallows notes that the news has become "an endless stream of emergencies," presented with an "artificial short-lived intensity" (Fallows, 1994: 32). Reviewing the first two years of the Clinton presidency, Fallows identified 30 such news events, a few of which (Bosnia and Rwanda) were real tragedies while most (Travelgate and Paula Jones) were not, but all of which were presented by the media as "right-now" emergencies. The life of most of these crises lasted exactly as long as their newsworthiness, which is to say not very long. The effect, says Fallows, "is to make the week the fundamental unit of political measurement."

In the world of politics, issues flow from societal problems and people's values and are thus deeply embedded in the social fabric. In the world of news, issues have shallower roots; they flow from events of the

Figure 17.2   Urgency of Future Action as a Theme in U.S. News Magazine Coverage (*Newsweek* Magazine), 1960s and 1990s

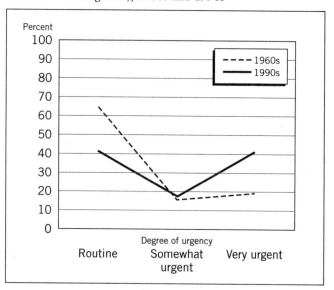

Note: Based on a sample of 233 lead stories on public affairs from *Newsweek* magazine during a three-year period in the early 1990s. Judgments about degree of urgency surrounding future action in regard to reported events were based on statements made both by reporters and those quoted in stories. In the 1990s as compared with the 1960s, a sense of urgency was more frequently communicated through reporters' statements.

moment. Although the news has been compared to a mirror held up to society, it is actually a highly selective account of the day's obtruding events. There are always critical problems facing the nation, but whether they play a large or small part in the news, and do so in a true or distorted form, depends significantly on how they mesh with the time horizon established by the news cycle.

The 1947 Hutchins Commission on Freedom of the Press concluded that journalistic values create an agenda that lacks depth and proportion (Leigh, 1947: 90–96). The journalist Walter Lippman's judgment was harsher. The limits on news, he said, quoting from Isocrates, cause it "to make of moles mountains, and of mountains moles" (Lippmann, 1965: 220).

RUNNING TIME

◆ ◆ ◆

Political time has greater variation and is more complex than news time. Although some political processes and developments are short-lived, most extend for weeks or months and some stretch out for years and beyond.

Political time has greater variation and is more complex than news time.

A few news stories also get sustained play. Among the dozens of issues on the news agenda each week, there are always a few that were there when the week began. If the typical story lasts only a day, the biggest ones invariably last longer. "Stories that matter are stories that persist and take different turns over days or weeks or longer," says Michael Schudson. "With an important [event], as time passes, the story grows, the ripples spread out into the past and the future, the reverberations to past and future become the new context for the story" (Schudson, 1986: 5).

These "running stories" often make headlines even on days when there is no hard event to drive them. Most running stories have an anticipated conclusion, as in the case of an election campaign, court case, legislative session, or economic cycle. The movement toward resolution makes the event a "timely" topic even on days when nothing really new is happening. This time-flexibility is reflected in the way running stories are told. The typical news story is narrated in the past tense. The running story, in contrast, is told through a journalistic version of the "continuous present" tense. The running story also allows the journalist to slip frequently into the future tense through speculation about the event's outcome and impact (Schudson, 1986: 5–8).

It might be thought that experience in the reporting of the same story would make journalists' accounts ever more precise. This is exactly what happens in some cases. But novelty rather than precision is what drives the journalist's search for news. The running story allows the journalist to work across time, but the connection of past and present even within the same story pales alongside any break in their continuity. If such breaks are ordinarily nothing more than small or momentary deviations, the journalist is conditioned to see them differently. Even if they appear tiny on the surface, they may hide a larger truth.

The result, frequently, is a distortion of both the events being covered and the larger reality of which they are a part. Crime coverage in the United States, for example, doubled in 1993 from its previous level, driven in part by several high-profile murder cases, including the arrest of serial killer Joel Rifkin who murdered eighteen women in New York, the parent-killing trial of the Menendez brothers, the kidnap-murder of 12-year-old Polly Klaas in California, and a crazed gunman's shooting spree on a Long Island commuter train that killed six people and wounded nineteen. These running stories spawned a larger running story: the breakdown of civility. News reports on gang fights, drug busts, and other manifestations of a disorderly and dangerous society filled the headlines and the newscasts. Crime was the most heavily covered national issue in 1993, overshadowing all others, even the timely topics of health care reform, the economy, and Bosnia.

The image of an America awash in murder and mayhem had a dramatic impact on public opinion. In the previous decade, no more than 5 percent of Americans had believed at any time that crime was the nation's biggest problem. By early 1994, however, more than 40 percent of Americans said crime was the top issue. Politicians also got caught up in the frenzy. Lawmakers rushed to enact harsh new sentencing policies, and they appropriated more funds for new prison construction than at any time in the nation's history.

This frenzy, however, is comprehensible only in the context of the media's version of reality. For the fact is, the actual level of crime in America was *declining* during this time period. According to U.S. Justice Department statistics, the rate of violent crime dropped by nearly 3 percent in 1993.

Was crime coverage the exception? Are news images of society normally highly accurate? Scholars have addressed this question by comparing media coverage of social conditions with statistical indicators of these conditions. The results are disheartening. In a study of U.S. television news, for example, Lichter and Smith compared economic coverage with the course of the domestic economy in the period 1982–87, when the economy moved from recession to early recovery to steady growth to vigorous expansion. They discovered that "as the economy improved, economic news actually grew more pessimistic, moving from a five-to-one negative ratio in the first year of the study to a seven-to-one negative ratio in the last" (Lichter and Smith, 1994: 84).

A Swedish study by Westerståhl and Johansson produced a similar finding. They examined the Swedish media's coverage of seven major policy areas, including the economy, crime, and defense. They found that in practically no case was there "any correspondence between the factual and reported development" (Westerståhl and Johansson, 1986: 141).

Of course, the news media are not always off the mark. Nevertheless, running stories on complex social trends are only slightly more accurate indicators of actual conditions than would be expected on the basis of chance alone, a situation that can best be explained by the role of time in news judgments. The most recent developments nearly always overshadow longer-term ones. Lichter and Smith concluded that the media's "interpretations tend to be episodic, shallow and formulaic, focusing on the most obvious short-term effects.... Linkages rarely go beyond the simplistic level of ... [the] explanation that 'the dropping dollar got a lift today, and that pushed stock prices up on Wall Street" (Lichter and Smith, 1994: 82). They found that although economic indicators were cited in nearly half of all stories on the economy, journalists tended to cite them as standalone items on the days that the government released them. In fewer than 10 percent of the cases was the reference placed in the context of a general analysis of economic conditions.

Journalists also have difficulty correcting faults in the broader themes that emerge during the coverage of a running story. Any such story has a past and a future, and journalists gradually construct a general theme that binds together what has happened with what is likely to happen. With their eye fixed on the events of the moment, however, journalists have difficulty recognizing when small day-to-day changes have accumulated to the point where the theme is outmoded. An example is the claim of America's economic decline that became the theme of news reporting during the late 1980s. The U.S. economy was compared unfavorably to those of Germany and Japan, a storyline buttressed by references to trade imbalances, rising deficits, and a weak dollar. The theme persisted until 1995, a full two years *after* the U.S. economy had begun to outperform Germany's and Japan's.

The pattern of news coverage in this case is the rule, not the exception (Westerståhl and Johansson, 1986; Lichter and Smith, 1994). The pressures of time are a primary reason. The purpose of broad themes, their time-saving function, is to free the journalist from having to rethink anew each day the underlying patterns of complex phenomena. Yet the very existence of a theme, and the intricacy of the process it summarizes, leads the journalist to interpret new information in ways that fit with the theme. Gradually, however, the theme becomes outdated and serves only as misrepresentation. If journalism is not the only activity for which this is so, journalism, by its nature, is more poorly designed than most to detect the error. The crush of time, which compelled the creation of a time-efficient theme in the first instance, prevents its easy detection in the second. In the world of news, the conventional wisdom of the moment overrides any studied assessment of social conditions.

TIME FRAMES

◆ ◆ ◆

The power of the press to a large degree works through its ability to "frame" events. Framing, as Robert Entman notes, is the process by which journalists select certain aspects of reality and thrust them to the forefront, thus promoting a particular perspective on this reality (Entman, 1989).

The power of the press to a large degree works through its ability to "frame" events.

Framing is an inescapable part of news reporting. The news would be a buzzing jumble of facts if journalists imposed no structure on their stories. They need a framework within which to select and order their observations. Yet framing is also discretionary; stories can be told in a number of different ways. It is in this respect that time substantially affects how journalists frame their stories. Journalists rely heavily on those frames that quickly yield stories they can use. These frames, unfortunately, better serve journalists' immediate story needs than they do the public's long-term information needs.

In his book *Is Anyone Responsible?*, Shanto Iyengar (1991) notes that most news stories are based on episodic frames, which focus on particular events, cases, or individuals. Episodic framing is more prevalent than thematic framing, which places events or issues in a larger context. Iyengar demonstrates that these two frames differ in more ways than just their focus and frequency. They also affect how news audiences interpret reality and judge issues of accountability.

In controlled experiments, Iyengar found that viewers exposed to episodic frames tend to concentrate on the individuals involved, make few connections to larger forces in society ("the big picture"), and deny accountability to anyone but the individuals in the story. A general effect is to turn potentially public and enduring stories into essentially private and momentary ones.

In contrast, thematic framing encourages viewers to confront larger questions of cause and effect, to consider how public policy and social conditions might be related, and to take a longer view of policy problems and solutions. However, because of the media's preference for hard events, thematic frames are infrequently invoked. An extreme example is U.S. network coverage of terrorism during the 1980s: there were hundreds of stories on individual acts of terrorism and almost none on the political and social forces underlying terrorist activity. Iyengar concludes: "In the long run, episodic framing contributes to the trivialization of public discourse and the erosion of the electoral accountability. [E]pisodic reporting ... provides a distorted picture of public affairs. The portrayal of recurring issues as unrelated events prevents the public from cumulating the evidence toward any logical, ultimate consequence" (Iyengar, 1991: 143).

A larger body of research has documented a second framing tendency that generates an impression that politics is ephemeral: the inclination of journalists to depict politics as a struggle between top leaders for competitive advantage rather than as an issue of public policy (see for example, Patterson, 1994; Semetko, et al., 1991; Seymour-Ure, 1974). In the strategic frame, questions of policy, rather than being at the center of public life, are a backdrop to political ambition and tactics (Weaver, 1973: 69).

For the journalist, the strategic frame has two time-connected advantages over the policy frame. First, the daily give and take among political leaders is more easily observed and understood than are policy conditions, alternatives, and preferences. Reporters are aware, of course, of the long-term policy forces affecting short-term political action, but these are more difficult and time-consuming subjects to understand (Owen, 1991; Lang and Lang, 1968). The second advantage of the strategic frame is that it is a reliable source of fresh new material. The strategic game, James David Barber notes, "is a naturally structured, long-lasting dramatic sequence with changing scenes" (Barber, 1978: 117–118). Policy problems and issues do not change much from day-to-day, but the political game is constantly in motion.

Of course, political infighting has an impact on policy outcomes and has grown in importance as the burden of mobilizing support is carried more by entrepreneurial politicians and less by political parties (Ansolabehere, Behr and Iyengar, 1992: 3). Nevertheless, the day-to-day strategic game looms much larger in the news than it does in the political life of the country. It is not simply that the press neglects lasting policy issues in favor of the strategic game; these issues, even when covered, are subordinated to the drama of the current phase of the conflict between opposing elites. In this sense, the press "depoliticizes" issues, treating them more as the backdrop to daily political rituals than as objects of serious debate or expressions of society's values (Levy, 1981).

Although citizens have an interest in the strategic game, it is less important to them than are issues of policy. One study found that news stories framed in the context of strategy are substantially less likely than those framed in policy terms to draw a reaction from either television viewers or newspaper readers (Patterson, 1980: 86–89). Another study found that when news stories "discussed serious social problems," people were inclined to advocate action to address them, but when stories discussed strategic maneuvering, they tended to have less involved reactions, including feelings of resignation about politicians' behavior (Graber, 1988: 203–206).

Journalists justify their use of the strategic frame by arguing that it alerts the public to the self-serving actions of political leaders (Walsh, 1996). This argument is a component of "critical" reporting, which holds that the press should look beyond politicians' words and focus on their motives and designs. American reporters since Watergate have operated on this premise, and European journalists have also increasingly adopted a critical perspective. Westerstähl and Johansson note, for example, that Swedish print and broadcast journalists "strive to ensure that ... the behaviour of the holders of power [is] under constant supervision" (Westerstähl and Johansson, 1986: 137).

Critical reporting, however, demands a level of time and knowledge that journalists do not routinely possess. It is no simple matter to divine a politician's immediate motives or uncover instances of gross wrongdoing or ineptitude. As a result, the media in practice has resorted to less demanding forms of scrutiny. A common technique is to use a politician's opponents to discredit his motives or performance. Rather than engaging in the time-intensive method of "digging" for disconfirming evidence, the journalist uses the time-efficient method of "calling" upon an opponent to ask for a discrediting retort. The critical element is supplied, not by a careful assessment of a politician's claim, but by the insertion of a counter-claim (Steele and Barnhurst, 1995: 16; Sabato, 1991). "This has become a routine procedure among modern journalists," note Westerstähl and Johansson. "Instead of straight news, they prefer, on supposedly professional grounds, to support a controversy. This development or degeneration of critical journalism explains, in our view, the high rate of criticism in the news" (Westerstähl and Johansson, 1986: 146–147).

Critical reporting has indeed resulted in a dramatic increase in negative framing (see Figure 17.3). News of politics is increasingly the story of wayward or inept leadership. In Sweden, for example, the amount of negative news tripled in the decade after the onset of critical journalism (Westerstähl and Johansson, 1986). In the United States, negative coverage of political leaders and institutions has also nearly tripled in recent decades (Patterson, 1994).

The impact of negative framing on public opinion has been substantial: the sharp rise in negative news has been accompanied by a correspondingly sharp increase in public cynicism and mistrust of government. It would be inaccurate to conclude that the high levels of public alienation in Western democracies are solely a function of negative framing, but studies indicate that the negative coverage has contributed to the public's dissatisfaction with its political leaders and institutions (Patterson, 1994; Westerstähl and Johansson, 1986; Robinson, 1976; Lichter and Noyes, 1997; Just, et al., 1996).

Figure 17.3   Good News and Bad News in U.S. Newscoverage (*Newsweek* Magazine), 1960s and 1990s, as Percent of Total News Content

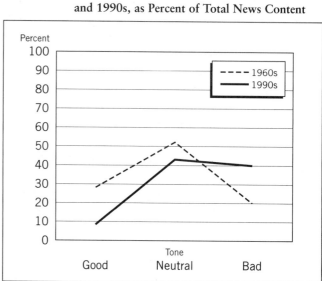

Note: Based on a sample of 233 lead stories on public affairs from *Newsweek* magazine during a three-year period in the early 1990s. Each story was judged overall as positive, neutral, or negative based on the substance and tone of its content.

POLITICAL TIME

◆ ◆ ◆

The news media are a much less reliable source of information than their advocates believe. The idea that the news agenda can somehow substitute for the agendas established through the proper workings of political institutions requires one to ignore the media's highly refracted version of reality. Yet the pervasiveness of the media makes it difficult for citizens and policymakers to ignore media images. In Western democracies, the politics of time is increasingly the politics of news time, often with adverse consequences for policy and opinion.

In Western democracies, the politics of time is increasingly the politics of news time, often with adverse consequences for policy and opinion.

Real time and near real-time news are the consequences of the modern media's capacity to transmit information from almost anywhere in the world instantaneously. The analyst Paul Virilio argues that "there is no politics possible at the speed of light," since events come and go so quickly that there is no time for reflection or deliberation (cited in Keenan, 1997). Yet if today's news media are characterized by their electronic wizardry, their incapacity as an instrument of public opinion and debate resides less in their technology than in the mindnumbing confines of the 24-hour news cycle.

In searching for a critique of news-centered politics, my thoughts are drawn, not to technology-based arguments, but to the late V.O. Key's indictment of party politics in the Old American South (Key, 1949: 302–310). It was the late 1940s, and there was no effective two-party competition in the South, only a form of factionalism that excluded blacks and shifted abruptly from one election to the next. "Although it is custom to belittle the contributions of [political] parties," Key wrote, "their performance seems heroic alongside that of pulverized factionalism."

Key described a type of politics that was based "on transient squabbling." Issues came and went with lightning speed as and when they served a faction's needs. There was "no discussion," only "attacks" and "disassociation." At times within this framework, campaigns were "but personal rivalries uncomplicated by substantial social and economic issues. The issue becomes one of who is the 'best man' or the 'most competent' man." Campaigns were "often the emptiest sorts of debates over personalities."

The carriers of these messages had "not a semblance of ... responsibility." Free of accountability for the actions of government, they could serve "as critic." The attacks were "erratic" and "chaotic," characterized more by "disorganization" than any identifiable sense of "collective interest" or clear notion of "public choice."

Within this framework of competition the voters were "whipped from position to position by appeals irrelevant to any fundamental interest." They were allowed "fitful rebellions" but no real "voice." They were forced to keep up with "a loose, catch-as-catch-can politics" in which there was a low premium on "general-policy orientations." And in the end, the voters were the losers. They were "confused" over their choices and forced to function "in a sort of state of nature."

The chaotic agenda of old-style southern politics is not unlike that of new-style media politics. In neither case is the agenda a reasonable basis for political action. Walter Lippmann reasoned that the thin texture of the news disqualified it as a platform of mass politics. "The press is no substitute for [political] institutions," Lippmann wrote. "It is like the beam of a searchlight that moves restlessly about, bringing one episode and then another out of darkness into vision. Men cannot do the work of the world by this light alone. They cannot govern society by episodes, incidents, and interruptions" (Lippmann, 1965: 221).

Note

1. The terms "news media" and "press" are used interchangeably in this article and refer to both print and broadcast media.

References

Andersen, K., and S. J. Thorson (1989). "Public Discourse or Strategic Game? Changes in Our Conception of Elections." *Studies in American Political Development*, 3: 263–278.

Ansolabehere, S., R. Behr, and S. Iyengar (1992). *The Media Game: American Politics in the Television Age*. New York: Macmillan.

Barber, J.D. (1978). "Characters in the Campaign: The Literary Problem." In *Race for the Presidency* (J.D. Barber, ed.), pp. 111–146. Englewood Cliffs, NJ: Prentice-Hall.

Center for Media and Public Affairs (1992). "Clinton's the One." *Media Monitor*. Washington, DC, November.

Entman, R. M. (1989). *Democracy Without Citizens*. New York: Oxford University Press.

Fallows, J. (1994). "Did You Have a Good Week?" *The Atlantic Monthly*, 274(6): 32–33.

Graber, D. (1988). *Processing the News*. New York: Longman.

Iyengar, S. (1991). *Is Anyone Responsible?* Chicago: University of Chicago Press.

Jamieson, K.H., and K. Campbell (1992). *The Interplay of Influence: Advertising, Politics, and the Mass Media.* Belmont, CA: Wadsworth.

Just, M., A. Crigler, D. Alger, T. Cook, M. Kern, and D. West (1996). *Crosstalk.* Chicago: University of Chicago Press.

Keenan, T. (1997). "Live Feed: War, Humanitarianism, and Real-Time Television." Unpublished fellowship proposal, Department of English, Princeton University.

Kepplinger, H.M., and J. Habermeier (1995). "The Impact of Key Events on the Presentation of Reality." Unpublished paper, Institut für Publizistik, Johannes Gutenberg-Universität Mainz.

Key, Jr., V.O. (1949). *Southern Politics.* New York: Knopf.

Lang, K., and G.E. Lang (1968). *Politics and Television.* Chicago: Quadrangle.

Leigh, R. (1947). *A Free and Responsible Press.* Chicago: University of Chicago Press.

Levy, M. (1981). "Disdaining the News." *Journal of Communication,* 31: 24–31.

Lichter, S.R., and R.E. Noyes (rev. ed.) (1997). *Intentions Make Bad News.* Lanham, MD: Rowman & Littlefield.

Lichter, S.R., and T.J. Smith (1994). "Bad News Bears." *Media Critic,* 81–87.

Lippmann, W. [1922] (1965). *Public Opinion.* New York: Free Press.

Neustadt, R.E., and E.R. May (1986). *Thinking in Time: The Uses of History for Decision Makers.* New York: Free Press.

Owen, D.M. (1991). *Media Messages in American Presidential Elections.* Westport, CT: Greenwood.

Patterson, T.E. (1980). *The Mass Media Election.* New York: Praeger.

Patterson, T.E. (1993). *The American Democracy* (2nd ed.). New York: McGraw-Hill.

Patterson, T.E. (1994). *Out of Order.* New York: Knopf.

Patterson, T.E., and W. Donsbach (1992). "Journalists' Perceptions of Public Opinion: A Cross-National Comparison." Unpublished manuscript, presented at the annual meeting of the International Communication Association, Miami.

Robinson, M. (1976). "Public Affairs Television and the Growth of Political Malaise: The Case of 'The Selling of the Pentagon'." *American Political Science Review,* 70: 409–432.

Robinson, M., and M. Sheehan (1983). *Over the Wire and on TV.* New York: Russell Sage Foundation.

Rosen, J. (1992). "Politics, Vision, and the Press: Toward a Public Agenda for Journalism." In *The New News v. The Old News* (J. Rosen and P. Taylor, eds.), pp. 3–33. New York: Twentieth Century Fund Press.

Sabato, L. (1991). *Feeding Frenzy: How Attack Journalism Has Transformed American Politics.* New York: Free Press.

Schlesinger, P. (1977). "Newsmen and Their Time Machine." *British Journal of Sociology,* 28: 336–350.

Schudson, M. (1986). "What Time Means in a News Story." Gannett Center for Media Studies, Occasional Paper No. 4, New York.

Semetko, H., J.G. Blumler, M. Gurevitch, and D.H. Weaver, with S. Barkin and G.C. Wilhoit (1991). *The Formation of Campaign Agendas.* Hillsdale, NJ: Lawrence Erlbaum.

Seymour-Ure, C. (1974). *The Political Impact of Mass Media.* Beverly Hills, CA: Sage.

Steele, C.A., and K.G. Barnhurst (1995). "The Growing Dominance of Opinionated Journalism in U.S. Presidential Campaign Television Coverage, 1968 and 1988." International Communication Association, Albuquerque. Unpublished Manuscript.

Taylor, P. (1990). *See How They Run: Electing the President in an Age of Mediacracy.* New York: Knopf.

Walsh, K.T. (1996). *Feeding the Beast.* New York: Random House.

Weaver, P. (1973). "Is Television News Biased?" *Public Interest,* 69.

Westerståhl, J., and F. Johansson (1986). "News Ideologies as Molders of Domestic News." *European Journal of Communication,* 1: 137.

Acknowledgment. The author wishes to thank research assistants Matthew Malady, Sandy Morris, and Rebecca Stern for their invaluable help in preparing the original data presented in this article.

Terms & Concepts

descriptive journalism
episodic frames
interpretive journalism
negative framing

news cycle
running time
strategic frames
thematic frames

time frames
time horizons

Questions

1. Compare the Sunday edition of a seven-day-a-week newspaper with the Monday edition of a six-day-a-week newspaper. On what pages of the Monday paper do you find the front-page stories of the Sunday paper? Which front-page stories are more important?

2. What is the difference in performance of the political functions of a private and a public broadcaster? Why is there a difference?

3. Is television or the newspaper the better medium for the political functions of the media? What makes one more suitable than the other?

4. Patterson argues that "time shapes the news agenda." In what ways, and with what effects?

5. Given the vital political functions of the media in a democracy, what can be done to improve their performance in carrying out these functions?

Unit Four   Discussion Questions

1. You have just been appointed minister of immigration and citizenship for Canada. You have reflected on the state of citizenship and democracy and Canada. What recommendations, if any, would you make to your Cabinet colleagues on changes to immigration and citizenship rules? Why?

2. Federalism in many countries is about divided loyalties. Some argue that for this reason federalism is an inherently unstable form of government. Do you agree?

3. How does political ideology affect citizenship? For example, do feminists weigh the obligations and benefits of citizenship differently than, say, conservatives? What implications does nationalism have for citizenship?

4. What is required of citizens in order for democratic self-government to function, if not flourish? Should such requirements be encouraged or enforced?

5. Can federal constitutional arrangements accommodate or handle the territorially dispersed social and cultural diversity of countries like Canada? If not, what, if anything, can be done to fix this shortcoming?

Annotated Bibliography

Achbar, Mark, ed. *Manufacturing Consent: Noam Chomsky and the Media*. Montreal: Black Rose Books, 1994. This is the companion volume to the video series of the same name.

Atkinson, Michael, ed. *Governing Canada: Institutions and Public Policy*. Toronto: Harcourt Brace Jovanovich, 1993. Intended as a textbook, it contains excellent essays on a broad range of topics, all of continuing importance.

Bogart, W.A. *Courts and Country: The Limits of Litigation and the Social and Political Life of Canada*. Toronto: Oxford University Press, 1994. A discussion of the relationship between law and political culture in Canada, as well as the limits of litigation in achieving social change.

Burgess, Michael, and Alain-G. Gagnon. *Comparative Federalism and Federation: Competing Traditions and Future Directions*. Toronto: University of Toronto Press, 1993. A comparative discussion of federalism, federation, and federal principles.

Cairns, Alan C. *Charter versus Federalism: The Dilemmas of Constitutional Reform*. Montreal: McGill-Queen's University Press, 1992. Investigates, in vintage Cairns style, the deep divisions and difficulties encountered over the past 25 years.

Cairns, Alan C., and Cynthia Williams, eds. *Constitutionalism, Citizenship, and Society in Canada*. Toronto: University of Toronto Press, 1985. A widely read collection of essays by leading Canadian scholars.

Campbell, Robert M., and Leslie A. Pal. *The Real Worlds of Canadian Politics*, 3rd ed. Peterborough, Ont.: Broadview, 1994. Provides five in-depth case studies, including the 1993 federal election and the defeat of the Charlottetown Accord.

Carens, Joseph, ed. *Is Quebec Nationalism Just?* Montreal: McGill-Queen's University Press, 1995. A series of essays on what is actually taking place inside Quebec regarding rights, roles, rules, and citizenship. Largely favourable in its conclusions.

Carty, R.K., ed. *Canadian Party Systems: A Reader*. Peterborough, Ont.: Broadview, 1992. There are several excellent readers on the market; this one is particularly strong on historical developments as well as current issues.

Dobrowolsky, Alexandra. "Of 'Special Interest': Interest, Identity, and Feminist Constitutional Activism in Canada," *Canadian Journal of Political Science* 31 (1998), 707–42. This essay explores different explanations of feminist involvement in constitutional change in Canada.

Elshtain, Jean Bethke. *Democracy on Trial*. Concord, Ont.: Anansi, 1993. A fervent plea for the renewal of American civil society.

Epp, Charles R. *The Rights Revolution: Lawyers, Activists and Supreme Courts in Comparative Perspective*. Chicago: University of Chicago Press, 1998. A study of the causes of the "rights revolution" in several countries, including Canada.

Etzioni, Amitai, ed. *Rights and the Common Good*. New York: St. Martin's Press, 1995. A comprehensive collection of essays by leading communitarian scholars, including Christopher Lasch, Benjamin Barber, and Mary Ann Glendon.

Gagnon, Alain-G., and A. Brian Tanguay, eds. *Canadian Parties in Transition*, 2nd ed. Scarborough, Ont.: Nelson Canada, 1995. A new edition of a comprehensive collection of essays by well-known scholars. Clear and well organized.

Ginsberg, Benjamin, and Martin Shefter. *Politics by Other Means: Politicians, Prosecutors, and the Press from Watergate to Whitewater,* 2nd ed. New York: W.W. Norton, 1999. An examination of how scandal is replacing electoral politics in the United States.

Greene, Ian, and David P. Shugarman. *Honest Politics: Seeking Integrity in Canadian Public Life.* Toronto: Lorimer, 1997. This book examines the ethical requirements of Canadian democratic politics from an institutional perspective.

Gutmann, Amy, ed. *Freedom of Association.* Princeton, N.J.: Princeton University Press, 1998. A first-class collection of essays by renowned scholars on the political theory of associational rights and obligations of democratic citizens.

Heard, Andrew. *Canadian Constitutional Conventions.* Toronto: Oxford University Press, 1991. A comprehensive review of constitutional conventions and how they operate in Canada.

Kaplan, William, ed. *Belonging: The Meaning and Future of Canadian Citizenship.* Montreal: McGill-Queen's University Press, 1993. A wide-ranging collection of essays by Canadian academics and social commentators.

King, Anthony. "Overload: Problems of Governing in the 1970s," *Political Studies* 23, 2–3 (1974), 284–96. This is a classic article outlining the "state overload" thesis. Still very useful.

Kymlicka, Will. *Multicultural Citizenship.* Oxford: Clarendon Press, 1995. This book attempts to reconcile a liberal vision of society with the need to recognize rights of minority cultures within democratic societies.

Kymlicka, Will. *Recent Work in Citizenship Theory.* Ottawa: Multiculturalism and Citizenship Canada, 1992. An excellent review of the academic literature on the nature and meaning of citizenship.

Lijphart, Arend. "Democracies: Forms, Performance, and Constitutional Engineering," *European Journal of Political Research* 25, 1 (January 1994), 1–17. A recent contribution from the political scientist who first developed the idea of "consociational" democracy.

Mancuso, Maureen, Michael M. Atkinson, André Blais, Ian Greene, and Neil Nevitte. *A Question of Ethics: Canadians Speak Out.* Toronto: Oxford University Press, 1998. This timely book examines survey evidence of what Canadians consider the bounds of acceptable political conduct, from conflicts of interest and patronage to lying and personal morality.

McRoberts, Kenneth. *Misconceiving Canada: The Struggle for National Unity.* Toronto: Oxford University Press, 1997. A sustained critique of Pierre Elliott Trudeau's attempt to refashion Canadian citizenship and identity to quell Quebec nationalism and assert the dominance of the federal order of government in Canada.

Morgan, Edmund S. *Inventing the People: The Rise of Popular Sovereignty in England and America.* New York: W.W. Norton, 1988. A classic dissection of the constitutional fictions we erect and defend and on which our system is based. Brilliantly argued.

Nevitte, Neil. *The Decline of Deference: Canadian Value Change in Cross-National Perspective.* Peterborough, Ont.: Broadview, 1996. Nevitte offers an empirical analysis of how Canadian social and political attitudes are more participatory and less deferential and trusting of their political and social elites.

Offe, Claus. *Contradictions of the Welfare State.* Edited by John Keane. Cambridge, Mass.: MIT Press, 1984. Capital cannot live with the welfare state but cannot live without it either. Important critical essays by a leading post-Marxist scholar.

Patterson, Thomas E. *Out of Order.* New York: Knopf, 1993. An attack on the cynicism of the press and its recent manifestations. Thomas argues for a more complex view of issues in the press.

Price, David E. *The Congressional Experience: A View from the Hill.* Boulder, Colo.: Westview, 1992. An insider's view of how Congress really works. An excellent example of "participant observation."

Resnick, Philip. *Twenty-First Century Democracy.* Montreal: McGill-Queen's University Press, 1997. A provocative set of essays on the prospects for democracy beyond the nation-state.

Seidle, F. Leslie, ed. *Equity and Community: The Charter, Interest Advocacy and Representation.* Montreal: Institute for Research on Public Policy, 1993. A collection of essays exploring the effect of the Canadian Charter of Rights and Freedoms on political culture and the articulation of interests in Canadian society.

Smiley, Donald V. *The Federal Condition in Canada.* Toronto: McGraw-Hill Ryerson, 1987. Still one of the best analyses written on the subject.

Sniderman, Paul, Joseph F. Fletcher, Peter H. Russell, and Philip E. Tetlock. *The Clash of Rights: Liberty, Equality, and Legitimacy in Pluralist Democracy.* New Haven: Yale University Press, 1996. A comprehensive study of Canadians' opinions on the politics of rights in the Charter era.

Taras, David. *Power and Betrayal in the Canadian Media.* Second Edition. Peterborough, Ont.: Broadview, 2000. A wide-ranging discussion of trends that weaken the political functions of the media.

Thomas, David M., ed. *Canada and the United States: Differences That Count.* Peterborough, Ont.: Broadview, 1993. A collection of 19 essays on Canadian–American differences.

Tuohy, Carolyn J. *Policy and Politics in Canada: Institutionalized Ambivalence.* Philadelphia: Temple University Press, 1992. A sophisticated discussion of policy and institutions, with in-depth case studies.

Verney, Douglas. *Three Civilizations, Two Cultures, One State: Canada's Political Traditions.* Durham: Duke University Press, 1986. A sweeping historical analysis of Canada's traditions and contradictions.

Unit Five

Political Institutions

◆ ◆ ◆

Political institutions continue to fascinate us. This is particularly true of political executives, specifically prime ministers, premiers, or presidents. We also focus considerable attention on electoral matters, periodically on Parliament (notably question period), and we certainly discuss political parties. Much of the debate is media linked. If it bleeds (politically), it leads.

At the same time, we should recognize that a great deal that is institutional—and of fundamental import—escapes us and also escapes media scrutiny and analysis. All of the articles in this section attempt to fill such gaps in our understanding. We expect a great deal of our leaders and of our institutions, even though there is a continuing denigration of the role of politicians and of the state itself. Anger and dissatisfaction with our institutions have been widespread, and trust levels have dropped, even as demands on governments escalate.

This section of *Braving the New World* has been extensively revised to incorporate a new article on the changing role of the Supreme Court and the controversies surrounding its deliberations; a revised look at our ongoing electoral challenges; a post-impeachment update of president–prime minister comparisons; and an analysis of the interface between "local" and "global," written especially for this edition.

There appears to have been a return to a politics of constitutional conservatism (about which we wrote in the first edition) as memories of such issues as the Charlottetown Accord fade. Yet change, and sometimes very significant change, still goes on, as several of the essays in this section illustrate. What is also made evident is that our institutional system is unique and has some extraordinary features: we certainly get odd electoral results; Quebec's place in Confederation remains problematic; secession has been sanctioned under certain circumstances; the balance between judicial and political power continues to alter; and crucial referendums have been and probably will continue to be held.

Tampering with institutions is never easy, and Canadians have been prepared to discuss all sorts of ideas, in all sorts of reports, but most of it comes to nought. Perhaps this is just as well. Recent Italian experience shows how difficult successful institutional change can be. Two general elections ago, a first-past-the-post system was introduced in Italy for 75 percent of the lower house seats, with the remaining 25 percent being allocated, under proportional representation, as before. The aim was to reduce instability and paralysis and to import Britain's version of stable government. A recent referendum attempted to remove even this 25 percent category, but it failed to pass. British-type stability has not arrived—the number of parties has increased, and now there is concern about

From imperial to federal diet: In 1999, the newly renovated Reichstag building in Berlin finally housed a stable, democratic legislature.

Photo courtesy of Canapress.

the effect of a first-past-the-post system on turnout and on voter alienation.

Such cases are instructive because they raise, as always, the question of the extent to which institutions can be transplanted into other polities. (Perhaps British electoral stability has relatively little to do with the electoral system.) As Tim Parks asked in a review of a new book on national and institutional reflections, are institutions "intimately related to history, race or what is more vaguely referred to as 'national character'?"[1] This is dangerous terrain to venture into, and we do not wish to suggest, as some have, that there is an underlying "native soil" intertwining of race and place, which sets limits to our institutions and actions. Such views can lead to national and provincial stereotyping that is deeply suspect. Yet the fact remains that whatever institutional innovations or alterations we make, they will have to operate within a uniquely Canadian context and will be driven, as are our current institutions, by the ways in which we make them work—in other words, by the ways in which we behave and by our own expectations.

---

1. Tim Parks, review of *Voltaire's Coconuts* by Ian Buruma, *London Review of Books* (May 27, 1999).

The Institutional Expression of Multiple Identities: The Electoral Reform Debate

Roger Gibbins and Loleen Youngman Berdahl

Editors' Note

Most Canadians take their electoral system for granted. They have an intuitive sense of how it operates but are only vaguely aware of its particular virtues and vices. Although the debate on institutional reform has become a veritable national sport in Canada in the last 15 years, the electoral system has not been one of the footballs kicked around. Politicians and royal commissions have preferred to tinker with the current system. Obviously, the beneficiaries of the current system—the people who are elected—have no incentive to change the rules, and populists have sought to remove political power from representatives altogether in the name of direct democracy.

As Roger Gibbins and Loleen Youngman Berdahl point out, there are new forces that may cause Canadians to take a fresh look at electoral reform. Among these is the burgeoning consciousness of ethnic, racial, and gender diversity. Increasingly, groups defined by demographic characteristics (rather than by territory or province) consider legislative assemblies illegitimate if they do not mirror the demographic composition of the population as a whole. This view implies that non-Aboriginals, for example, cannot represent or speak for Aboriginals. Therefore, Parliament must have Aboriginal MPs, or, alternatively, Aboriginal peoples must be represented in some other institutional context.

"Mirror representation" has obvious common sense and political appeal. There are, however, also some problems. How do we prevent an endless proliferation of demands for group representation? How do we know that a representative from a certain group will indeed know and act on the wishes of that group? Is it desirable to assume that only Aboriginals can represent Aboriginals, or women only women? Will this cause people to refuse even to try to understand others? Underlying the complex and at times tedious debate about the details of electoral reform are some fundamental questions about representation, citizenship, and the recognition of diversity in a political community.

◆ ◆ ◆

Political scientists have long recognized that political institutions are not neutral in their effects. Each set of arrangements has its own set of biases, strengths, and weaknesses. Electoral systems are an example of a biased political institution. Even in the abstract, there is no perfect electoral system: each has its flaws.[1] Some electoral systems foster consensus, others adversity. Some promote unity, others diversity. There is no one "best" electoral system that could be successfully imposed on each and every society; rather, electoral systems must be assessed according to the particular tensions and needs of an individual country.

Although electoral law may seem to some a minor political institution, it is in fact a vital factor in representative democracy. By aggregating votes in a particular fashion, electoral law determines who and what are represented. In addition, the electoral law serves as the primary link between the representatives and the citizens. These two functions enable electoral law to direct a country's history. What might Canada's party system have been, for example, if proportional representation were used instead of single-member plurality ("first-past-the-post") elections? What sort of policies might have emerged out of such a party system? Although it is impossible to answer such questions, it does appear safe to hypothesize that a different electoral system may have led to a very different political reality.

Electoral law also sends normative statements to the population, indicating which types of political interests are considered important enough to represent legislatively. Proportional systems are designed to ensure representation of all significant political parties according to their electoral weight, suggesting that the important societal interests are articulated and promoted by parties. Plurality and majoritarian systems, in contrast, are designed to ensure the representation of territorial units, with the apparent assumption that interests are largely linked to territory. Even within electoral systems, districting decisions send normative messages. Requiring strict population equality between electoral districts tells the electorate that each vote is given precisely the same weight—in other words, that the individual is the unit to be represented. In contrast, allowing for variations in district size to account for geography, community of interest, or other factors indicates that the community and society are the units represented.

Canada is among a handful of countries using the "first-past-the-post" (FPTP) electoral system. In many ways, the FPTP system limits the institutional expression of the multiple identities that individuals bring to political life. First, electoral constituencies are defined by geography; there are no constituencies that group voters by gender, ethnicity, language, or other demographic characteristics. In this respect, territorial identifications have an institutional trump over all others. Second, because only one representative is elected in any given constituency, that representative is inherently limited in mirroring the multitude of political identities on the basis of which his or her constituents seek expression. Finally, the ballot itself precludes any complexity of expression. While voters may bring a complex host of identities and interests into the voting booth, in the final analysis all of these must be expressed through a single X, printed with a blunt pencil on a piece of paper.

These constraints would not be particularly problematic if voters were concerned only about bringing territorial identities into the electoral process. However, Canadians have a host of political identities—relating to political ideology, ethnicity, and partisanship—that lack territorial definition. When these multiple identities are considered, the FPTP system seems too restrictive. Territorial constituencies, single-member representation, and a simple X do not capture the complexity of multiple political identities in contemporary Canada. Concerns about such representational issues have led to debate about the electoral system.

Territorial constituencies, single-member representation, and a simple X do not capture the complexity of multiple political identities.

THE EVOLUTION OF THE ELECTORAL REFORM DEBATE

◆ ◆ ◆

Professor Alan C. Cairns established the fundamentals for the first round of the electoral reform debate. Writing in 1969, Cairns argued that Canada's first-past-the-post, single-member plurality system distorts the translation of votes into seats in a number of important ways.[2] First, it tends to overreward the party winning the largest share of the popular vote, and thus inflates the size of parliamentary majorities in the House. Second, the system tends to penalize minor parties with diffuse national support, a primary example being the CCF/NDP and its persistent failure to win a share of seats commensurate with its share of the popular vote. Third, the system tends to overreward parties with concentrated regional support; the primary historical example is provided by the Social Credit party, whose Alberta base consistently generated more seats than one would expect from the party's share of the popular vote. Fourth, and most relevant to the present analysis, Cairns argued that the major parties are more broadly reflective of the national electorate with respect to their popular vote than they are with respect to the regional distribution of their seats in the House of Commons. Simply put, the national electorate inadvertently produces regionalized parliamentary parties, and therefore regionalized national governments. In this way, the electoral system works to fragment rather than integrate the national party system and political community.

Cairns's critique of the electoral system gained strength over the next 15 years. In western Canada, the Liberals won a reasonable share of the popular vote but were unable to convert that vote into elected MPs. Across the four general elections held from 1972 to 1980, for example, the Liberals received 25.6 percent of the regional popular vote but came away with only 8.6 percent of the western Canadian seats in the House of Commons.[3] The Liberal nadir came in 1980 when the party won a majority government but in the process captured only two seats (2.6 percent) in western Canada with 23.4 percent of the regional vote. While the Liberals were struggling for a reasonable seat return in the West, the Conservatives were hampered by the same lack of success in Quebec where in the four general elections from 1972 to 1980 the party averaged only two seats (2.7 percent) although it received, on average, 16.2 percent of the provincial popular vote.[4]

Neither Quebec nor the West, it should be stressed, suffered any loss of representation in the House of Commons itself, for proportional representation for the regions was guaranteed by the formula used to determine the provincial distribution of seats. The problem was that the electoral system did not ensure adequate regional representation within the winning party, *and thus within the government of the day*. Proposals for electoral reform, therefore, sought to ensure that the national parties would have elected members from across the country even in those circumstances where the FPTP system would not yield such results. The proposals generally incorporated some form of proportional representation, usually tacked onto conventional single-member districts, to guarantee that a party forming the national government would never lack elected representation from across the country.

The electoral system was to be reformed to guarantee what the parties themselves apparently could not guarantee, and that was broadly representative government.

In short, the electoral system was to be reformed to guarantee what the parties themselves apparently could not guarantee, and that was broadly representative government. When, in the absence of reform, the Progressive Conservatives provided just such a government in 1984 and again in 1988, electoral reform disappeared as a matter of public interest and debate. Then,

the 1993 federal election reopened the reform debate for many Canadians by illustrating once more how the electoral system can distort the translation of party shares of the popular vote into seats in the House. The most dramatic evidence was provided by the Progressive Conservatives, who captured 16 percent of the national popular vote but won only two seats (0.7 percent) in the House of Commons. The distortions were not limited to the Tory debacle. The NDP won 6.9 percent of the national popular vote, but only nine (3.1 percent) seats. In Quebec, the sovereigntist voice of the Bloc Québécois was amplified by the electoral system when 49.2 percent of the vote garnered 72 percent of the provincial seats for the Bloc, enough to form Her Majesty's Loyal Opposition in the House. In the four western provinces the voice of the Reform Party was amplified in a similar fashion: 38.2 percent of the vote resulted in 60.7 percent of the regional seats. And, in Ontario, the Liberals swept all but one of the province's 99 seats with only 52.8 percent of the vote. Similar distortions occurred in the 1997 election.

The 1993 and 1997 elections thus resurrected concerns about the impact of the electoral system on partisan representation. However, current considerations about electoral reform are not limited to concerns about partisanship. Over the 1990s, the electoral reform debate has evolved to include "descriptive" representation issues. Although partisanship issues remain paramount, the representation of nonterritorial and nonpartisan identities, such as gender, race, and ethnicity, are also often raised in contemporary electoral system debates. This additional dimension dramatically shifts the debate from representation of regions within the national government to representation of *all* Canadian diversity within Parliament. It is often argued that elected legislatures should serve as a "portrait of the nation," reflecting not only its political parties and regional interests but also its social, ethnic, racial, and gender compositions. Of particular concern to date is the underrepresentation of Aboriginal peoples, visible minorities, and especially women, who constitute over 50 percent of the population but less than 25 percent of the MPs in the present House.

The debate, then, has expanded in at least two respects: it moves away from territory as the primary focus of representation, and it shifts attention from the composition of the government, and the attendant composition of legislative parties, to the composition of the legislature itself. In these respects, the new debate poses a more vigorous challenge to the institutions of

Canadian federalism; the challenge is not only to more effectively accommodate the traditional territorial and linguistic cleavages within the Canadian political community but, at the same time, to accommodate a growing number of nonterritorial interests and concerns. We would suggest that the debate also brings into play more radical and comprehensive notions of electoral reform, ones that tackle not only the formal electoral process itself but also the means by which parties nominate candidates and finance their internal operations.

To understand why more radical notions of electoral reform may be brought into play, we must take a moment to explore the arguments lying behind the new debate. Although there are no legal restraints barring women, Aboriginal peoples, and visible minorities from Canadian legislatures, systemic discrimination has limited these groups' electoral and representational success.[5] In other words, apparently neutral, nondiscriminatory features of the political process operate to exclude some groups from entering politics. For example, the long working hours and travel required of an elected representative are not occupational qualifications put in place to discriminate against women intentionally, but these factors nonetheless discourage women from considering a political career, especially women with child-care responsibilities. Although the representativeness of the House of Commons and provincial legislatures has improved in the past decade, progress has been slow. For example, the Canadian Advisory Council on the Status of Women predicts that if change continues at its current pace, men and women would not have equal numerical weight in the House until 2038.[6]

But why should legislative institutions attempt to mirror Canadian society in their composition? More specifically, why should they attempt to do so beyond capturing the regional composition of the electorate? One argument in favour of descriptive representation is based on the assumption that a legislature is undemocratic unless it reflects the major divisions in society. Kathy Megyery articulated this argument in one of the research studies for the Royal Commission on Electoral Reform and Party Financing (the Lortie Commission, tabled in 1991): "A system that does not, over time, come closer to adequately representing its citizenship calls into question the legitimacy of its democratic institutions."[7] The argument, then, is that improving demographic representation in legislative bodies would not only counter inequalities in the broader political order but would also strengthen the democratic legitimacy of the political community.

A second argument for descriptive representation states that there are specific social benefits to mirroring demographic diversity in legislatures. An individual from an underrepresented or disadvantaged group can identify with an MP on the basis of physical similarities (for example, gender or race) and for this reason perceive him- or herself as being more adequately represented. Descriptive representation thereby enhances a group's sense of identification with the political community, increases its opportunities for participation in decision making, and provides potential career opportunities for group members.[8] Descriptive representation, in this sense, is closely linked to the idea of identity politics and its assumption that voters desire representatives who possess characteristics similar to their own.[9]

The final and undoubtedly most controversial argument is that descriptive representation will alter or influence the functioning of politics. This argument assumes that different groups or subsets of society have "distinctive values, attitudes and concerns which may have an impact on legislative behavior and the content of public policy."[10] If, in other words, the composition of legislative assemblies is altered, the values, operating styles, and policies of those assemblies will also change. It is assumed that institutions are shaped by the nature of their incumbents and can therefore be transformed by changing their composition.[11]

All of these arguments run up against the inability of the existing electoral system to provide effective accountability for new forms of group representation. The central problem is that group representation by its very nature transgresses territorial boundaries and therefore does not sit comfortably with the present system of territorial representation and its geographically defined constituencies. If an MP claims to speak for "women," she does so on behalf of all women, not just those in her own constituency. Thus, a legislator claiming to represent group interests other than those of a territorial constituency is not subject to reelection or dismissal by the group he or she claims to represent. The critically important electoral link between the representative and the represented is severed, as a consequence.

To summarize, contemporary electoral reform debate has two dimensions. The first is continuing concern about the representation of regions within the government of the day. The second is concern about the representation of nonpartisan, nonterritorial diversity within the House of Commons. These concerns have led to a variety of electoral reform proposals.

OPTIONS FOR ELECTORAL REFORM

◆ ◆ ◆

There are at least five options for electoral reform that have been raised in Canadian debate. Three of the five options deal only with issues of descriptive representation, while the remaining two are seen as a solution to both descriptive and regional partisan representation.

Reforms to the Party Nomination System

Before an individual can serve as a legislative representative, he or she must first be nominated by a political party in a constituency and then be elected to represent that constituency. (It is an extremely rare event when an individual is elected as an independent candidate, without the endorsement and support of a political party.) Thus, it is a two-stage struggle to achieve a legislative seat.[12] In the 1993 general election, women constituted only 23 percent of all major party candidates, a proportion still well in excess of the number of Aboriginal or visible minority candidates.[13] It is not surprising, therefore, that women are numerically underrepresented in the House of Commons. It is also not surprising that the nomination process has come under increasing critical assessment by those interested in promoting a more proportionate representation of women in legislative assemblies.

The Lortie Commission on electoral reform and party financing cites two structural barriers to women's entry to politics: the cost of the nomination process and the lack of party support for women seeking nomination, a lack linked, in turn, to the decentralized nomination system used in Canada.[14] The cost of contesting a party nomination is a major difficulty for potential women and minority candidates. Nomination costs for competitive urban ridings can exceed $50 000,[15] and pre-writ election spending and the costs of the party nomination contest are neither regulated by federal legislation nor reimbursed from public funds. Financing nomination campaigns can be a significant problem for female, Aboriginal, and visible minority candidates since these groups are more likely to come from nontraditional career backgrounds, have less financial security, and have more difficulty getting bank loans to finance an inherently risky political career. In addition, women have less access to business contacts, corporate donors, and moneyed networks than do men,[16] and it can be assumed that Aboriginals and visible minorities encounter the same barriers.

> *Financing nomination campaigns can be a significant problem for female, Aboriginal, and visible minority candidates.*

The second problem encountered by potential women and minority candidates is the decentralized nomination system currently in place. Canadian political parties allow local constituency organizations to select the party nominee; although the party leader typically has a veto power with respect to nominations, this power is seldom used. Nor is the party leader often active in the recruitment of constituency candidates. (An exception to this was the Liberal party's strategy of recruiting women and male "star" candidates for the 1993 campaign, a strategy that required the active intervention of leader Jean Chrétien.) In the context of the present discussion, the decentralized nomination system is important because it restricts more centralized control over the nomination process, control that is seen as undemocratic by local party members and the public. (Certainly, the 1993 Liberal strategy met with such criticism.) This means, in turn, that parties are unable to establish effective quotas for the number of female and minority candidates; parties must hope but cannot ensure that 301 independently conducted constituency nominations will yield a party slate that is broadly representative of the national electorate.

The Lortie Commission made a number of recommendations to address the problems posed by the nomination process for the representation of women, Aboriginals, and visible minorities. To lower the financial burden of contesting party nominations, the Lortie Commission recommended that (1) employers be required to grant employees leaves of absence if the latter seek nomination and if they are elected, (2) spending limits be imposed on all candidates seeking party nomination, (3) tax receipts be granted for contributors to nomination campaigns, and (4) child-care expenses "incurred by the primary caregiver" while seeking nomination be tax deductible.[17] The commission also recommended the establishment of formal search committees in registered political parties to promote the nomination of "broadly representative candidates."[18] To encourage the nomination of female candidates in competitive seats, the commission proposed financial incentives: "We recommend ... the reimbursement of each registered political party with at least twenty percent female MPs be increased by an amount equivalent to the percentage of its women MPs up to a maximum of 150 percent."[19] The commission suggested that this measure should be eliminated once the overall percentage of female MPs equals or surpasses 40 percent.

It should be noted that these recommendations have never been debated in the House of Commons. Nor do they address the problem of local party control over the nomination process. Although the central party offices may be motivated to nominate more female and minority candidates, the incentive structures must also be changed at the constituency level. Incentives may include offering financial rewards to constituency associations that nominate women or minority candidates; such rewards could be provided by the national party organizations or by differential public reimbursements for campaign costs. Steps could also be taken to create nomination procedures that encourage greater participation by women and minorities. For example, in 1993 the NDP required that each nomination be contested by an equal number of men and women; as a result, 38 percent of the NDP candidates were women. However, as the electoral fortunes of the NDP illustrate, increasing the representativeness of candidates does not alone lead to a more representative House.

Reforms within the present nomination system may prove to be the ... most likely means available to encourage descriptive representation.

Reforms within the present nomination system may prove to be the least controversial and therefore most likely means available to encourage descriptive representation. Such reforms would not require changes to the formal election process itself, and thus would avoid some of the anxieties associated with more radical forms of electoral reform. However, reforms to the nomination process may entail further public regulation of the internal affairs of political parties, an intrusion of the state into the private sphere that will not go unchallenged. Of more importance for the present discussion, such reforms alone would not *ensure* the selection of women and minority candidates, nor would they *ensure* greater mirror representation within legislative assemblies. Moreover, as representation within those assemblies would continue to be based on territorial constituencies, the accountability of group representatives would remain a problem.

Affirmative gerrymandering is the redrawing of electoral boundaries in a manner that increases the voting power of a minority group or interest.

Affirmative Gerrymandering

Affirmative gerrymandering is the redrawing of electoral boundaries in a manner that increases the voting power of a minority group or interest. This technique is used in the United States, where electoral lines have been redrawn to increase the concentration of minority groups such as blacks, Hispanics, and Asians within specific electoral districts.[20] The 1982 amendment to the U.S. Voting Rights Act prohibits the "dilution of the minority vote" by any device, including the drawing of electoral boundaries. Any minority group that constitutes at least 5 percent of the state population is allowed to seek the protection of the law to ensure that its vote is not diluted. Similar legislation could be passed by the Canadian Parliament. Appeals for affirmative gerrymandering could also be made through the courts by invoking section 3 (voting rights) and section 15 (equality rights) of the Charter. Prior legal cases invoking section 3 have established the precedent that electoral boundary commissions should respect "communities of interest" when constructing boundaries. Perhaps, then, a minority group could reasonably argue that it represented a community of interest that should be reflected in the design of constituency boundaries.

However, notwithstanding these possible legislative and constitutional avenues to affirmative gerrymandering, this approach is unlikely to provide a solution to Canada's representation problems. First, affirmative gerrymandering would do nothing to increase the representation of women in legislative assemblies. Women and men are evenly distributed throughout the country; short of creating separate male and female districts, the redrawing of electoral boundaries would do little if anything to increase the number of elected women. Second, it is by no means clear that affirmative gerrymandering would increase other forms of social diversity within the House and the provincial legislatures. Part of the problem stems from the territorial distribution of Aboriginal peoples and visible minorities. For the most part, neither has sufficient territorial concentration to make affirmative gerrymandering possible (Indian reserves and Alberta Métis settlements are a clear exception).[21]

Furthermore, the lower turnout and voter eligibility of minority groups (many minorities counted in the census are not Canadian citizens) means that even a constituency with a large minority *population* may not contain enough minority *voters* to elect a minority representative.

Federalism presents a third obstacle to affirmative gerrymandering. Although a group may constitute a significant minority in the country as a whole, it may be distributed across a number of provinces in a manner that cannot be accommodated by affirmative gerrymandering. However, the constitution would have to be amended before constituencies crossing provincial boundaries could be created. If affirmative gerrymandering were to be used to ensure the representation of minority interests, other important communities of interest would have to be broken up. Affirmatively gerrymandered districts are usually spread out geographically, and thus may fragment the representation of various territorial and economic interests held to be important by the electorate. For these reasons, affirmative gerrymandering holds little potential for addressing representational problems within the Canadian federal state.

Reserved Representation

Reserved representation ensures the selection and election of minority candidates by creating separate seats for minority groups. This system is used in the New Zealand Parliament to ensure Maori representation, and it has been recommended by the Lortie Commission as a means to improve Aboriginal representation in Canada.[22] Some have also argued that separate constituencies should be established for men and women to ensure equal representation of the sexes in Parliament.[23] Both ideas were floated in the recent constitutional debate, when various formats for an elected Senate were under discussion.

Reserved representation ensures the selection and election of minority candidates by creating separate seats for minority groups.

Under the Lortie Commission plan, Aboriginals would have the option of registering as either Aboriginal voters or "regular" voters. If the number of Aboriginal persons registering within a province as Aboriginal vot-

ers were large enough to merit the creation of an Aboriginal seat, then a reserved Aboriginal riding would be created, in which only Aboriginal candidates could run and only Aboriginal voters could vote. Such a system of reserved representation would ensure Aboriginal representation within Parliament. It could also provide an important means of electoral empowerment to the large and amorphous urban Aboriginal population, a population that may lie beyond the reach of Aboriginal self-government.

Not surprisingly, the Lortie recommendations and the larger principle of reserved Aboriginal constituencies are not without their problems.[24] First, the dispersion of Aboriginal peoples across Canada, and the dispersion of *specific* Aboriginal peoples, means that many provinces would have insufficient numbers to merit an Aboriginal seat. This problem, of course, becomes more acute if we think not of Aboriginal seats but rather of status Indian, Métis, and Inuit seats. Second, the creation of reserved seats would be based on the number of registered *voters*; in all other Canadian ridings, district sizes are measured by the total *population* within the riding. In reserved seats, the representation of children, nonvoters, and those ineligible to vote would be neglected. A third problem with the Lortie recommendations is that they would require Aboriginal voters to publicly declare their identification; no other group in Canada is required to do so, nor is such a requirement desirable. Such a system may also require voters to prove their Aboriginal status, which could be a controversial requirement, given the lack of constitutional guidance in matters of Aboriginal status. Finally, the pressure for Aboriginal representation in the House of Commons is not coming from within the Aboriginal community. Rather, it stems from the attempt by other underrepresented groups to be inclusive when discussing electoral reform. The focus of Aboriginal communities at present, and quite likely for some time to come, is on the design and implementation of Aboriginal self-government. Reserved representation in federal institutions is seen, at best, as a supplement to the far more important self-government initiative.

The greatest general problem of reserved representation is the assumption that a single identification—for example, gender or Aboriginal status—is the most important identification to the voter and that it remains so across time. Establishing gender-based constituencies, for example, would assume that gender identification takes precedence over racial, linguistic, territorial, or other political identifications. Even if this might be the case at a single point in time, one's primary identification may change over a lifetime and, indeed, may change in the time period between elections. Thus, gender-based or ethnicity-based constituencies lack flexibility; they lock voters into a single political identity. Although it might be argued that the present system of territorial representation does the same thing, the creation of reserved constituencies based on other criteria would compound rather than resolve the existing problem.

At present, there is no evidence of significant public support for reserved representation, or at least for the application of this principle beyond Aboriginal peoples. Although reserved seats for women and visible minorities would ensure descriptive representation, in Parliament, it would be far too radical a departure from the existing Canadian political culture to be acceptable unless all other avenues of representational reform were to be blocked.[25] Fortunately, more conventional avenues of reform are available.

Electoral Reform and Proportional Representation

As discussed, Canada's FPTP electoral system has been criticized for its failure to ensure regional representation in the national government. In addition, comparative studies indicate that the FPTP system is not advantageous to women's legislative recruitment, nor is it a reliable vehicle for ensuring descriptive representation. Simply put, it is difficult to achieve descriptive representation at the constituency level when there is only one elected representative who must be male *or* female, a visible minority *or* not, an Aboriginal *or* not. It is equally difficult to ensure descriptive representation within legislative assemblies when the membership of those assemblies is determined by the outcome of elections in single-member constituencies. The composition of the assembly is determined in a manner more analogous to a "crap shoot" than to anything else. It is also difficult for political parties to impose gender and racial quotas within the context of single-member constituencies and the decentralized nomination process.

Given this critique, it is important to note that Canada's use of the FPTP system is becoming increasingly idiosyncratic. Although Britain and the United States also use the FPTP system, the majority of Western democratic states employ more complex balloting and/or districting. The proportional representation (PR) list system, which produces a more nuanced legislative "portrait of the nation," is widely used. The PR-list system's use of multimember constituencies loosens the FPTP constraints on descriptive representation. The PR-list system does not allow voters to distinguish between

candidates. Parties select a slate or list of rank-ordered candidates for multimember constituencies. Voters cast one vote for the party of their preference. Theoretically, if a party receives 30 percent of the vote, it should receive 30 percent of the seats, although the precision of proportionality varies with constituency size. Because of centralized party control over the candidate lists, the PR-list system is open to gender and racial quotas. Whereas voters cannot rank candidates by gender or race or by any other social or ideological characteristic, the parties can. Moreover, the parties can ensure that particular candidates are elected by placing them at the top of their list.

Canada's use of the FPTP system is becoming increasingly idiosyncratic.

Other electoral system alternatives include the single transferable vote (STV) and alternative vote (AV) systems. The STV system does not enforce the proportional representation of political parties, as nothing in the formula requires proportionality. Rather, the system attempts to accurately reflect the attitudes of the electorate by selecting the preferred *candidates* rather than the preferred parties.[26] The system is designed to serve the electors rather than the political parties, and electors are free to cross party lines when listing their preferences. Thus, a voter who chooses to vote not on the basis of party but on the basis of environmentalism would rank candidates according to their "greenness." A voter could also rank candidates by their support for or opposition to feminism, by their more general ideological orientation, or by any other criteria, including demographic characteristics. The AV system also uses preferential ballots; however, like the FPTP, the AV system is based on geographic representation and uses a single-member district.

These alternatives to the FPTP system have some appeal for those who support electoral reform. For example, the PR-list system would eliminate the regional overrepresentation of parties and would allow for quotas to ensure diversity in the House. However, the adoption of the PR-list system would weaken accountability. The chances of being elected would depend almost entirely on where a candidate was placed on the party list, and thus candidates are likely to be more responsive to party rather than constituency demands. A second and related criticism is that voters would be encouraged in such a system to vote on the basis of party alone; the individual characteristics of the representatives would diminish in importance. To balance these criticisms, many proponents of electoral reform advocate a mixed system in which half of all candidates are selected by the FPTP method, and the other half by the PR-list method. This solution is seen by some to combine the best features of each system.

Such electoral alternatives have long been of considerable attractiveness to those acquainted with the intricacies of electoral reform, and they are (or at least should be) of growing interest to those concerned with the lack of descriptive representation in Canadian legislative assemblies. At the same time, they have never found significant support among voters or the mainstream parties. The FPTP system currently used for the House of Commons and provincial legislatures has proven to be extremely resistant to fundamental reform, and there is little evidence that either the public or the partisan mood is about to change.

Senate Reform

This is neither the time nor the place to discuss Senate reform in any detail. It is important to note, however, that because a reformed Senate is almost certain to be an elected Senate, any discussion of Senate reform will force us to engage in a debate on electoral reform. It will be difficult to engage in any substantive public debate on Senate reform without coming to grips with how a reformed Senate would serve both regional representation and nonterritorial interests and communities. If a balance is to be found between these two representational concerns, it will be found in adopting a method of election for the Senate that is quite different from that used at present for the House of Commons. In turn, electoral innovation with respect to the Senate may touch off a more wide-ranging and fundamental public debate on electoral reform to the House than we have witnessed to date.

In short, a debate on Senate reform will require a parallel debate on the role that elections should play in the democratic politics of the 21st century. Canadians will have to address how a reformed upper house can be expected to meet a cacophony of regional and nonterritorial interests. We will need to reconsider the issue of constituencies—whether our political interests should be aggregated within provincial, multimember constituencies quite different from those used to elect MPs, or indeed whether the representation of nonterritorial interests requires that the nation itself be treated as one large constituency. We will be forced to consider ballot formats that are more in line with the complex political identities of contemporary citizens, identities that cannot be adequately expressed or captured by a single X scrawled once every four or five years on the federal ballot. It will be a debate that will tax our political imaginations, but also one that could also lead to a vigorous articulation of a new sense of political community.

A debate on Senate reform will require a parallel debate on the role that elections should play in the democratic politics of the 21st century.

CONCLUSIONS

◆ ◆ ◆

Despite the many arguments for change, the electoral system has proved even more resistant than the constitution to reform. Certainly, there is no partisan imperative for reform. The Liberal, Bloc, and Reform parties all profit from the system, at least to a degree, and the two parties that are the current clear losers, the Conservatives and the NDP, are marginalized as partisan actors on the national stage; their complaints will not find a significant audience. This does not mean, however, that the electoral system is immune to change. A renewal of the Senate reform debate; an intensification of concern over the representation of women, ethnic minorities, or Aboriginal peoples in the House of Commons; populist pressure to institute recall mechanisms; or exposure to electoral reform initiatives in other countries could ignite a renewed electoral reform debate in Canada.

Should electoral reform once again climb up the national agenda, the debate will be very different than it was in the late 1970s and early 1980s. The underpinnings of the electoral reform debate have been transformed in a variety of important ways. Questions of regional representation must share ground with a growing and much more complex debate surrounding gender, ethnic, and Aboriginal representation. This new debate, in turn, is likely to lead to more radical reform proposals than we have encountered to date, proposals that will embrace multimember and proportional representation systems with greater enthusiasm than in the past and that may challenge the territorial definition of political constituencies. Populist measures designed to constrain representative government will further cross-cut and confuse the earlier emphasis on territorial representation. Although western Canadians were the major players in the electoral reform debates of the recent past, other players are likely to come to the fore when the debate reopens.

In this new and potentially contentious debate, it is by no means clear that western Canadians will have a regionally distinct perspective. To the extent that they do, it will be one anchored in a regional commitment to an elected Senate. In fact, the most probable scenario for successful electoral reform is one that brings together Senate reformers and feminists. By themselves, neither Senate reformers nor feminists are likely to generate enough public enthusiasm for electoral reform to occur, but together they just might pull it off.

Notes

1. See William Riker, *Liberalism against Populism* (San Francisco: W.H. Freeman, 1982).
2. Alan C. Cairns, "The Electoral System and the Party System in Canada, 1921–1965," *Canadian Journal of Political Science* 1 (1968), 55–80.
3. It is important not to attribute all of the Liberals' woes in western Canada to the perverse effects of the electoral system. For a discussion of how the Liberals were also the architects of their own misfortune, see David E. Smith, *The Regional Decline of a National Party: Liberals on the Prairies* (Toronto: University of Toronto Press, 1981).
4. For a discussion of the adverse impact of the electoral system on both Conservative fortunes in Quebec and internal politics within the national party, see George C. Perlin, *The Tory Syndrome: Leadership Politics in the Progressive Conservative Party* (Montreal: McGill-Queen's University Press, 1980).
5. Royal Commission on Electoral Reform and Party Financing, *Reforming Electoral Democracy,* Volume 1 (Ottawa: Minister of Supply and Services, 1991), 97.
6. Marina Jimenez, "Slow Going on the Long Road to Ottawa," *Saskatoon Star Phoenix* (August 14, 1993), D3.
7. Kathy Megyery, ed., *Women in Canadian Politics—Towards Equity in Representation* (Toronto: Dundurn Press, 1991), xvii.
8. Jerry Perkins and Diane L. Fowlkes, "Opinion Representation versus Social Representation; or, Why Women Can't Run as Women and Win," *American Political Science Review* 74 (1980), 92.
9. Hanna Pitkin, *The Concept of Representation* (Berkeley: University of California Press, 1967), 78.
10. Pippa Norris and Jodi Lovenduski, "Women Candidates for Parliament: Transforming the Agenda?" *British Journal of Political Science* 19 (1989), 107.
11. A moment's reflection reveals why this argument is controversial. It assumes that Parliament is where policy decisions are actually made; that the representative in Parliament sharing the characteristic of the group (be it gender, ethnicity, or sexual orientation) will act in ways that reflect the interests of that group; and that the group in question has an identifiable, coherent political identity to be given effect in Parliament. There is reason to question each of these assumptions.
12. Lynda Erickson, "Women and Candidacies for the House of Commons," in Megyery, *Women in Canadian Politics,* 110.
13. Although the number of women candidates can be easily determined, the number of candidates who are visible minorities is less easily determined. Therefore, the assumption that the number of visible minority and Aboriginal candidates for the major parties was low must at this point be treated as precisely that—an assumption.
14. Royal Commission on Electoral Reform and Party Financing, *Reforming Electoral Democracy,* 107. We assume that these barriers also work in a similar fashion for Aboriginal peoples and visible minorities.
15. Janine Brodie, "Women and the Electoral Process in Canada," in Megyery, *Women in Canadian Politics,* 40.
16. Ibid., 46.
17. Royal Commission on Electoral Reform and Party Financing, *Reforming Electoral Democracy,* 93, 117–19.
18. Ibid., 121.
19. Ibid., 273.
20. Affirmative gerrymandering has also been proposed as a means to increase the voting power and elected representation of gays and lesbians in the United States. To be effective, however, this would require some geographic concentration of the gay and lesbian population, something that does not seem to be characteristic of the Canadian scene.
21. Affirmative gerrymandering may be easier with respect to provincial constituencies than with respect to federal constituencies, given that the former are smaller in terms of both population and geographic scope.
22. See Robert A. Milen, ed., *Aboriginal Peoples and Electoral Reform in Canada* (Toronto: Dundurn Press, 1991).
23. See Christine Boyle, "Home Rule for Women: Power-Sharing Between Men and Women," *Dalhousie Law Journal* 6 (1983), 790–809.
24. For an expanded discussion, see Roger Gibbins, "Electoral Reform and Canada's Aboriginal Population: An Assessment

of Aboriginal Electoral Districts," in Milen, ed., *Aboriginal Peoples and Electoral Reform,* 153–84.

25. There is reason to think that the idea of reserved representation is not wholly popular among Aboriginal peoples either. Prior to the creation of the new territory of Nunavut, a referendum was held on the advisability of a new dual-member electoral system, which would ensure that two members, one male and one female, would be elected in each constituency. The referendum was defeated. The only woman subsequently elected to the Nunavut Assembly under the FPTP system was an opponent of the referendum proposal.

26. W.J.M. Mackenzie, *Free Elections* (London: George Allen & Unwin Ltd., 1958), 69.

Terms & Concepts

affirmative gerrymandering
Canadian Advisory Council on the Status
    of Women
constituency
descriptive representation
electoral reform
first-past-the-post electoral system
Her Majesty's Loyal Opposition

incumbents
Lortie Commission
mirror representation
multiple political identities
nonterritorial representation
party nomination
political identities
PR-list

proportional representation
regionalized national governments
regionalized political parties
reserved representation
Senate reform
single and multimember constituency
single transferable vote
territorial representation

Questions

1. What do Gibbins and Youngman Berdahl mean by the phrase "multiple political identities"?

2. Describe some common reform proposals to enhance the representativeness of legislative assemblies. What problems are associated with each?

3. What role should political parties have in determining the slate of candidates they support in elections? Should constituency associations or the party leadership be able to select candidates? Should voters in an election be given the opportunity to select the party and candidates of their choice separately, or should both preferences be combined in one vote?

4. To what extent can and should the members of a legislative assembly mirror the sociodemographic features of the electorate? What criteria should be used to select the groups for mirror representation?

5. Should all political parties be expected to appeal to the whole population of Canada—that is, to all territorial and nonterritorial groups equally? Should they be encouraged to do so? Forced to do so? If so, by whom? What implications would such a policy have, for example, for a feminist party seeking to advance women's concerns?

Politics and the Courts: Contending Theories of Judicialized Politics in Canada

Thomas M.J. Bateman

Editors' Note

As the Supreme Court of Canada noted in the *Reference Re: Secession of Quebec*, reprinted in Chapter 25 of this volume, democratic political institutions must be tempered by constitutional constraints to avoid what political thinkers have called "the tyranny of the majority." Democracies are premised on the idea of majority rule, and majorities can easily oppress minorities. When politics becomes a numbers game, those without the numbers get nervous and can suffer at the hands of the democratic majority.

Constitutional rights are an auxiliary precaution employed to protect minorities. Rights place limits on what governments can legitimately do. They define a sphere of liberty for citizens. They allow people to participate in political life regardless of the political ideas they hold or the particular characteristics they possess. Institutionally, charters or bills of rights are interpreted by courts exercising judicial review. Judicial review refers to the examination of laws and state conduct in light of their constitutionality. If a law or an official action is found to be inconsistent with a constitutional right, the

courts have the authority to declare that law or conduct invalid and of no force or effect. In this way, legislative institutions are subject to constitutional constraint.

This essay explores the politics of the Canadian Charter of Rights and Freedoms and suggests that the judicial enforcement of constitutional rights is a complicated and controversial political matter. The controversy is not simply due to the fact that constitutional review requires unelected judges to override the will of elected parliamentarians. It also has to do with the indeterminate meaning of Charter rights.

◆ ◆ ◆

Charters of constitutional rights are a popular means of constraining democratic government. To the two-hundred-year-old American Bill of Rights may be added charters in such disparate countries as Japan, India, Germany, and South Africa. Even the communist countries found it irresistible to include sets of citizen rights, though they were typically breached, not observed. Groups in Britain and Australia clamour for such a constitutional instrument in those countries. Others argue that Britain is, in effect, bound by a char-

ter by being a signatory to the European Convention on Human Rights.[1] We live in the heyday of charters of rights as instruments for the protection of democratic minorities.

Do charters of rights really offer the uncomplicated protection of minorities? Do they operate above the political fray, commanding the support of all, regardless of political commitment and ideological persuasion? Canada entrenched the Canadian Charter of Rights and Freedoms (hereafter the Charter) in its constitution in

1982. The circumstances of this high political act were deeply controversial and remain so today. Contrary to the simple argument for charters of rights outlined above, the Canadian Charter is subject to many interpretations, each of them growing out of strongly held political commitments. It turns out that the Charter is not above the political fray. And the assertion of rights in courts against acts of government has attracted no end of political comment.

This essay suggests that the Charter is subject to a number of plausible political interpretations. What are the Charter's purposes? Who benefits from the Charter? Who loses? What are the effects of the Charter on the political system, on democratic life in Canada? This essay will discuss several different answers to these questions. Each interpretation is plausible, and each can be challenged on the basis of the evidence. The unifying theme throughout is that the Charter is a deeply political document that represents a unique way of contesting political priorities in Canada.

THE CHARTER AS AN INSTRUMENT OF NATIONAL UNITY

◆ ◆ ◆

For most of his political career, Pierre Elliott Trudeau sought to make Canada home to Quebeckers. Nationalism to Trudeau was a retrograde political instinct, the sign of emotionalism, weakness, and lack of confidence in the talents and possibilities of a people. Worse, it spawned political repression: those who dared to question nationalist orthodoxy, who were on the outside of nationalist consciousness, were subject to the heavy hand of the state. In Quebec of the 1940s and 1950s, Quebec's nationalist elite feared dangerous communists lurking in the shadows of the labour union movement and cunning Jehovah's Witnesses stealing the sheep of the Catholic flock. The young civil libertarian Trudeau sided with outsiders against the government of the day. His lifelong liberalism and his later support for the Canadian Charter had their beginnings in the Premier Maurice Duplessis's mid-century persecution of minorities in Quebec.

Trudeau found the association of Quebec nationalism and civil rights violations more than accidental. Nationalism, he thought, was inherently intolerant precisely because it prizes the national group over individual persons. An entrenched Charter would have other foundations. In an essay reflecting on his political life,

Trudeau wrote that "the very adoption of a constitutional charter is in keeping with the purest liberalism according to which all members of a civil society enjoy certain fundamental, inalienable rights and cannot be deprived of them by any collectivity (state or government) or on behalf of any collectivity (nation, ethnic group, religious group or other).... It follows that only the individual is the possessor of rights."[2] Nationalism in general, and Quebec nationalism in particular, needed to be dissolved by the application of universal, pan-Canadian individual rights.

Trudeau's constitutional vision took shape in the 1960s when he became minister of justice and then Liberal prime minister. An entrenched Charter would guarantee a pan-Canadian set of individual rights that would protect anyone from his or her government, federal or provincial. Further, an entrenched Charter would be a potent symbol of Canadian identity, uniting all Canadians in their joint possession of the same constitutional status as rights-bearers. Thus, the Charter would establish, Trudeau hoped, a pan-Canadian political identity transcending every Canadian's provincial identity. Trudeau was a philosophical friend of federalism but loathed provincial premiers' tendencies to run their provinces like petty fiefdoms, of which the separatist Quebec government of René Lévesque was only one major historical example. The Charter would counter stubborn Canadian territorialism.

In this regard, three additional points are important. First, the entrenchment of a charter of rights would give institutional expression to Canadian national unity by vesting the Supreme Court of Canada—the final court of appeal with the power to interpret all laws, federal and provincial, and whose members are appointed by the prime minister—with final authority to establish Canada-wide constitutional standards for all laws and official conduct.

When nonterritorial interest groups of various kinds became pitted against premiers representing territorial communities, the public relations war was won by the Charter Canadians.

Second, the circumstances of the Charter's entrenchment in 1982 conspired to reduce the status of provinces in the Canadian federation. For reasons just described, most provincial premiers opposed patriation[3] of the constitution, especially when amendments like entrenchment of the Charter were to be made by the British Parliament before the constitution was brought fully under Canadian sovereign control. Trudeau's political manoeuvring was artful. As discussions developed, it became obvious that a coterie of nonterritorial groups of Canadians, the so-called Charter Canadians[4]—groups defined by ethnicity, race, gender, language, and disability—favoured the Charter for the same reasons that many Canadians found it either attractive or at least innocuous: the Charter protects people's rights, and what can be wrong with rights? When nonterritorial interest groups of various kinds became pitted against premiers representing territorial communities, the public relations war was won by the Charter Canadians. The premiers were unable to explain their opposition to the entrenchment of rights without appearing to be against rights.

Third, the paradox in Trudeau's Charter nationalism was that for all his criticism of nationalism in general and Quebec nationalism in particular, Trudeau sought a Canadian nationalism, albeit a nationalism founded on liberal individualist principles. In his political universe, Canadian liberal nationalism became a counteridentity to Quebeckers' primary attachment to Quebec.

The nationalist interpretation of the Charter resonates with most Canadians, especially those outside Quebec. Canadians are generally happy with the Charter and consider it part of what it means to be Canadian. Pierre Trudeau's vision has in part been realized.

If the Charter was to act as a solvent of Quebec nationalism, it has failed miserably.

However, if the Charter was intended to act as a solvent of Quebec nationalism, it has failed miserably. Indeed, the patriation exercise, achieved without the Quebec government's political consent, has been interpreted in Quebec as a provocation, revitalizing what was even by 1981 a sputtering separatist movement. Contrary to Trudeau's best judgment, the Charter and the circumstances of its entrenchment have helped widen the divide between Quebec and the rest of Canada.[5] And the Charter's effect on Canadian federalism has been mixed. It has stimulated further attempts to redress and even reverse what was done in 1982. The Meech Lake and Charlottetown accords were widely seen as attempts to blunt the sharp edges of the Charter. In addition, the courts have been careful not to interpret the Charter to

eradicate the federal principle from the Canac tutional order.[6] Furthermore, as the federal g   ....ent has reduced its role in fiscal federalism, the provinces' prominence in the federation has only increased. We have today a pan-Canadian Charter nationalism resting alongside a decentralized federalism and a vibrant Quebec nationalism, an outcome Pierre Trudeau would neither have foreseen nor desired.

THE CHARTER AS LIBERAL CONSTITUTIONALISM

◆ ◆ ◆

Pierre Trudeau is not only an anti-nationalist; he is also a philosophical liberal. Liberals are predominantly concerned with the protection and advancement of the status of individual persons, with the improvement in social conditions for individual persons, and with the setting of those conditions that expand the scope of individual freedom. These are general principles so commonly held that we easily dismiss them as platitudes. They are part of the intellectual air we breathe, and like the air we breathe are unquestioned and taken for granted. Liberals in the modern world are democrats—not because democracy is necessarily good in itself, but because this form of government is considered most congenial to liberal political aims.

In fact, liberals have a curious relation to government. Government is a good; it establishes order, enforces common rules for the pursuit of individual goals, and at bottom guarantees life. It is the critical antidote to fear, one of the most primordial human motivations.[7] Yet for liberals, the state is as much an enemy as a friend. It can lose control of itself by infringing citizens' liberties, often in the name of worthy public purposes. The paradigmatic case is the criminal law. No one questions the basic legitimacy of the criminal law: thieves, rapists, drunk drivers all present real dangers to others, and the state is in the best position to punish those who harm others. But in its zeal to punish wrongdoing the state may deal harshly with the accused. And in the contest between the criminally accused and the state, the accused is at a grave disadvantage. The state operates prisons, employs a battery of prosecutors, and most often has the support of public opinion in the pursuit of crime control. The criminally accused are an embattled minority, as described in the introduction to this essay. In the pursuit of the public interest the state may trample the liberties it is meant to protect.

A judicially enforced charter of rights operates as a check on government excesses. It protects a set of legal rights that ensure that accused persons have a fair trial, know their rights, are tried within a reasonable time, are not subject to unreasonable search and seizure, are not subject to cruel and unusual punishment, and so on. If these rights are violated the accused is entitled to a remedy that the courts consider fitting. Whereas the state polices its citizens, the courts armed with the Charter police the state. For liberals, none if this is undemocratic. A distinction must be drawn between the momentary, impassioned public will and the "long-term public will."[8] The Charter implements the long-term public will, though it may clash with the public's short-term impulse.[9]

Some liberal scholars have argued that the Canadian Charter asks courts not so much to interpret particular provisions but rather to require governments to *justify* any limitations they place on people's exercising their rights.[10] They look with particular approval upon the Supreme Court's 1986 decision in *R. v. Oakes*.[11]

Police caught David Edwin Oakes in possession of a small quantity of a prohibited drug. Possession was a crime under the Narcotic Control Act. But the Act went further. It provided that a person who is proven beyond a reasonable doubt to be in possession of a prohibited drug will also be considered to be in possession for the purpose of trafficking in that drug, a more serious offence carrying a more serious punishment. The provision reflected Parliament's concern with stemming the traffic in banned drugs but hardly seemed fair. An accused was presumed to be trafficking on the basis of having been found in possession only. This provision ran against fundamental principles of the criminal law, that the innocent shall not be punished and that one should be presumed innocent until proven guilty. Section 11(d) of the Charter protects just these principles. The offending provision of the Narcotic Control Act gave accused persons an out. It provided that once convicted of possession, if the accused can prove on a balance of probabilities that he or she was not in possession for the purpose of trafficking, he or she will be acquitted of the more serious offence.

For the Supreme Court, allowing Oakes to prove that he was innocent was no help. This meant that an accused could submit to the court evidence questioning the trafficking charge and raise a reasonable doubt as to his guilt, yet fail to introduce enough evidence to establish his innocence on a balance of probabilities. In the end, the accused would be convicted of trafficking even though there was a reasonable doubt as to his guilt. In Oakes's case, the Court found that the reverse onus provision violated section 11(d): the right to be presumed innocent until proven guilty. But the case did not end there, for the Charter begins with the following provision:

> 1. The *Canadian Charter of Rights and Freedoms* guarantees the rights and freedoms set out in it subject only to such reasonable limits prescribed by law as can be demonstrably justified in a free and democratic society.

Now the Court had to consider whether the government's infringement or limitation of the right set out in section 11(d) was nonetheless reasonable within the terms of section 1. Section 1 allows a government to justify a law that limits a Charter right. For liberals, this is a crucial element in Charter jurisprudence. Governments often act in the public interest, for example by fighting the illegal drug trade. But they can easily go too far and trample the rights of criminally accused. The public is no help in this event, since it is frightened by crime and is encouraged by the press to assume that if someone is arrested on a charge, that person must be guilty.

To make a long story short, the Court in the Oakes case held that section 1 requires governments to show that a law serves a legitimate purpose and that the legislative means it chooses to attain that purpose are tailored as narrowly as possible to that end. Rights may be limited but only to the smallest degree consistent with attaining a legitimate public purpose, and legitimate purposes are defined in terms of what is consistent with a "free and democratic society," referred to in section 1.[12] The state may use only "the least drastic means." In this case, the government went too far in presuming that someone in possession of narcotics is in possession for the purpose of trafficking.

LOOKING AT THE CHARTER FROM THE LEFT AND THE RIGHT

◆ ◆ ◆

Part of the sales pitch for the Charter was that its entrenchment would facilitate "progressive" social change. Liberal pluralist societies embrace a teleology in which the tide of history sweeps in the direction of greater individual freedom, knowledge, tolerance, and civilization. To be judged an anachronism is to receive one of the cruelest insults that a liberal can hurl. And to oppose the Charter's entrenchment in 1982 was to invite the charge. Charterphiles—those who saw great progressive promise in the entrenchment of the Charter—have, by their oft-expressed hopes, invited others to test their progressive hopes empirically. Has the Charter indeed ushered in a more progressive age?

Part of the sales pitch for the Charter was that its entrenchment would facilitate "progressive" social change.

But what is progressive and what is retrograde? Criminal laws prohibiting the willful promotion of hatred ostensibly support tolerance and multicultural harmony. This is a good thing. But it also limits free speech, and progressives have long thought free speech also to be a good thing. Can prosecutors and judges know exactly what it means to "promote hatred"? Is it possible that whatever is currently considered politically incorrect will attract the state's attention? Would the existence of such a law discourage people from speaking for fear of prosecution? And what of the effect of the prosecution of hatemongers? Does this not, as anti-Semite Ernst Zundel once said, give hatemongers free publicity? Does this tell them that their ideas are foolish and detestable, or that there must be something truthful and accurate in them to trigger such an extreme state reaction? As civil libertarian Alan Borovoy says, if someone calls your mother a whore, you do not debate the point. On the other hand, should society sit idly by while hatemongers and xenophobes attract attention, support, and credibility through the broadcasting of vile falsehoods?[13]

In the abstract, rights are benign things. When applied to specific disputes in which opposing forces have much to gain and lose by a particular interpretation of rights, consensus breaks down and rights become deeply contested. It is often thought that whereas the less politically aware and astute general public is inconsistent, ignorant, and prejudiced about rights in a liberal society, society's elites—senior civil servants, judges, politicians, and high political party officials—have a better understanding of rights, of their proper application, and of even-handed tolerance. This is the theory of democratic elitism. But in a study of Canadians' attitudes toward rights and the Charter, a team of political scientists suggests that there is no obvious "right" or "progressive" way to understand rights.[14] Members of the general public *and* of Canada's political, legal, and administrative elite interpret the meaning and applica-

tion of rights depending on who is exercising them and the context in which they are being exercised. In this basic, empirical sense, rights are objects of political contest, and their content derives from the clash of opposing interests and ideologies arising from particular circumstances in time and place.

It should be no surprise, then, that commentators from various points on the ideological spectrum disagree on the meaning and impact of the Charter. Some observers on the political Left looked forward to the progressive potential of the Charter, hoping that it would provide a new political and constitutional mechanism for the fight for economic and social equality, personal liberty, and select group rights. From the Left's perspective, a good society is one in which economic power is evenly distributed among all members of society and everyone has the material means to live well and participate freely in society's governance. A good society also avoids imposing on all persons a single standard of the ideal citizen. The problem with liberalism, says one critic, is that while it trumpets the worth of the individual person, in practice "the liberal individual takes on a very male, heterosexual, European, educated, middle-class character in its orientation, interests, and relation to the world."[15]

Rights are objects of political contest.

Has the Charter delivered on its progressive promise? Critics on the Left say no. Instead, the Charter has become merely a tool appropriated by wealthy, resourceful interests in society to buttress and *further legitimate* positions of privilege they already occupy. Instead of using the Charter to break new ground in the advancement of the progressive agenda, marginal groups, argue the leftists, have been forced to participate in the rearguard defence of legislative gains being challenged by others in court.

On the economic front, the Left has always seen unions as critical instruments in the pursuit of justice for workers. Collective labour action was responsible for better working conditions, better wages, more secure jobs, and the possibility of retirement for people who would otherwise have to work until their death. But in Charterland, union rights are no match for individual rights. Courts have refused to interpret freedom of association rights in section 2(d) to include the right to bargain collectively. While the courts have conceded that picketing is expression, they consider it economic expression and therefore a weaker right than other expression rights.[16] And does the constitution protect people's rights to a basic standard of living? No, said the Supreme Court: section 7 of the Charter does indeed say that everyone has the right to life, liberty, and security of person, but these rights are not to be interpreted in economic terms.[17]

However, say those on the Left, entrenched corporate economic interests do well by the Charter. Retail businesses can use freedom of religion to force governments to allow them to open on Sundays, as if businesses have religious sensibilities that need constitutional protection. And when governments are too aggressive in limiting businesses' ability to advertise, the courts back up their demands for freedom from government control. Bans on cigarette advertising, for example, were substantially vetoed by the Supreme Court in 1995.[18]

How can this be? The law is indeterminate, left-wing critics contend. Charter provisions are vague generalities whose specific meaning in particular cases is a matter of judicial fiat. Precedents are no help, because judges can choose from among a variety of precedents those they wish to follow. Judges drive the meaning of Charter rights, and it so happens that they come from the same privileged backgrounds as those representing the powerful economic groups whose cases they hear. Litigation is also very expensive and time consuming. Because of the vagaries of the litigation process, any litigant may lose one case. But for the big, powerful players, any one loss is no problem. As repeat players, their stock is in the doctrinal orientation of courts, not in the outcome of any one case. For the little guy, though, the stakes in one case are too high to risk losing.[19] More fundamentally, leftist critics contend that charters of rights are liberal documents containing a bias against state activity of all kinds, even that which advances people's welfare against oppression, the source of which may be in the private sector.

The right-wing critique of the Charter appears as a mirror image of that of the Left. Where the Left sees a Charter dominated by the rich bourgeois seeking to entrench themselves by keeping the marginalized out, observers on the Right fear that the Charter has become the institutional vehicle for radical, egalitarian identity politics that could not be implemented via conventional, majoritarian political channels. The best way to set out the Right's critique is to examine the ideas of Rainer Knopff and F.L. Morton, whose "Court Party" thesis epitomizes the reservations those on the Right have about Charterland.[20]

> *Observers on the Right fear that the Charter has become the institutional vehicle for radical, egalitarian identity politics.*

Revolutions are always carried out by and operate in favour of elites, Knopff and Morton maintain; the Charter revolution is no exception. The black-letter law of the Charter is nearly empty of meaning. Judges give it form. But judges themselves are pushed by other groups and individuals who envision a postmaterialist society along the progressive lines outlined above. The Charter, in other words, by itself is nothing. What is important is the constellation of interests and groups arrayed around it, each of which has either material interests or an ideological vision to be advanced by the "correct" approach to interpreting the Charter. Lawyers, law professors, feminists, homosexuals, judges, Aboriginal activists, church groups, activists for criminals' legal rights, groups representing (or claiming to represent) the categories listed in section 15 of the Charter—all form a sort of "party" of like-minded persons arranged around a branch of government, a constitutional document, and in some cases, particular Charter provisions. According to Knopff and Morton, all prefer the courts to the other branches of government as vehicles for political change—hence, they call this collective the Court Party.

According to Knopff and Morton, the beauty of Charter litigation for the Court Party is precisely that it is an elite political process not easily understood by the general public. Political programs without the popularity to command the necessary support to succeed in the legislative realm can be pursued with greater effect in the courts. This is social transformation by stealth. Legislatures would not be able to extend voting rights to the criminally convicted, but courts have done so. Legislatures have found it difficult to extend homosexual rights, but courts have done so. Legislatures have defined crimes in a way to communicate the seriousness of the charge and to make convictions relatively easy to procure. Courts have reversed these initiatives. Legislatures have tailored state benefits with an eye to the costs of extending benefits too widely. Courts have used the section 15 anti-discrimination provision to extend state benefits to excluded groups, whether or not there was evidence that the government deliberately excluded those groups from its legislative scheme.

Left- and right-wing "Charterphobes"[21] think, for their own reasons, that legislatures are better than courts and that the Charter is undemocratic.[22] Courts have not been unaware of this criticism. In an early case, the Supreme Court said,

> It ought not to be forgotten that the historic decision to entrench the Charter in our Constitution was taken not by the courts but by the elected representatives of the people of Canada. It was those representatives who extended the scope of constitutional adjudication and entrusted the courts with this new and onerous responsibility. Adjudication under the Charter must be approached free of any lingering doubts as to its legitimacy.[23]

Fair enough, but the Court could hardly have picked a poorer case in which to defend its democratic legitimacy. In the *B.C. Motor Vehicles Reference*, the Court was asked to interpret section 7 of the Charter in an expansive manner. There was evidence that the drafters of the Charter intended a restrained interpretation for that section. The Court essentially ignored the drafters' intentions and adopted a more sweeping interpretation. How far, then, can democratic legitimacy go when the meaning the Court attributes to the Charter defies the meaning the democratically elected legislature intended for it? On this answer, the Right and Left critics are agreed.

On the other hand, the critiques of the Charter from Right and Left both suffer from the same malady. There are judicial decisions supporting each view; accordingly, there are decisions conflicting with each view. Each is hard-pressed to explain away the unhelpful decisions. How can those on the feminist Left trivialize the Supreme Court's invalidation of Canada's abortion law in 1988? How can the Charterphobic Right dismiss the Supreme Court's limited interpretation of union rights under section 2 and social or economic rights under section 7? Indeed, not only does the whole set of Charter decisions at *any* level in the judicial hierarchy contain a diversity of results favourable to no one particular ideological worldview, but at the appeal level, court decisions are often divided, betraying ideological diversity in the same appeal panel on the same case. The judges are divided because any group of reasonable people would be divided on what is the best result in cases involving complex policy and moral implications.[24] Instead of seeing the Charter as one or another ideological Trojan horse, it may be more accurate to imagine it as a field of battle on which opposing forces contend for advantage, one small manoeuvre at a time.

THE CHARTER DIALOGUE

◆ ◆ ◆

A final way to interpret the Charter is less ideological and more institutional in character. Constitutional scholar Peter Russell some time ago argued in a classic article that the Charter's main effect will likely be to judicialize politics and politicize the judiciary. In other words, the Charter will narrow the institutional distance separating the courts from the conventional parliamentary realm of parties, interest groups, ideological competition, and majoritarian prompting.[25] His prophecy has been borne out.

There is evidence of the courts and legislatures participating in a kind of inter-institutional dialogue. Legislatures often respond to court decisions. Courts, in striking down legislation, often signal to legislatures that a legitimate public purpose can be achieved in other, less intrusive ways. Sometimes, legislatures respond to an unfavourable court decision by implementing substantially the same policy as was struck down, this time prefacing an amendment with a preamble stating clearly Parliament's purpose in enacting a policy. As two observers put it,

> Where a judicial decision is open to legislative reversal, modification, or avoidance, then it is meaningful to regard the relationship between the Court and the competent legislative body as a dialogue. In that case, the judicial decision causes a public debate in the Charter values to play a more prominent role than they would if there had been no judicial decision. The legislative body is in a position to devise a response that is properly respectful of the Charter values that have been identified by the Court, but which accomplishes the social or economic objectives that the judicial decision has impeded.[26]

The Charter dialogue operates as an infusion of the concept of separation of powers into the Canadian parliamentary system, which, but for its federal character, has otherwise been highly centralized. The dialogue, in this view, permits more points of access to the political system and allows a policy to be subject to review by more than one institutional logic. The notion of dialogue takes seriously the convergence of the judicial and legislative realms. Increasingly, each institution is familiar and comfortable with the discourse historically associated with the other. Each anticipates the other's response.

The Charter dialogue operates as an infusion of the concept of separation of powers into the Canadian parliamentary system.

The Charter dialogue demands a certain sophistication among Canadians. They must be able to tolerate the rigidities and delays the dialogue involves. They must also be aware of attempts by members of the elected branches of government to skirt their political responsibilities and avoid making tough decisions, hiding behind the aura of Charter rights in explaining their inaction. Confronted with an issue that hotly divides the electorate, politicians have frequently deferred to the courts with relief. One robust interpretation of the Charter dialogue is that it permits a more liberal use of the notwithstanding clause. To date, there appears to be little support for this use, especially among elites in Canada outside of Quebec.[27] The romance of rights retains its grip, a fact that suggests that the Charter dialogue may resemble a one-sided conversation in which the courts do most of the talking and the legislature does a great deal of listening.[28]

CONCLUSION

◆ ◆ ◆

Constitutional innovations are experiments. Often an innovation will have unforeseen consequences. Sometimes an innovation will succeed, and at other times it will be a dud. The Canadian Senate, most will agree, has turned out to be a dud, despite the intentions of its founders in 1867.

The entrenchment of the Charter is likewise an experiment, one whose effects have not conclusively been discerned. Indeed, given the number of conflicting interpretations examined above, it is not even clear what *purposes* were set for the Charter. And as with much scientific experimentation, sometimes we doctor the data to have to the experiment prove what we want it to prove. It says much about our turbulent political era that we cannot even agree on the purposes the Charter was designed to serve, much less the effects it will ultimately have. It is tempting, as a result, to consider the Charter a part of the mélange of political purposes, hopes, and fears that pervade other parts of the Canadian political landscape. The Charter functions as a new constitutional-political setting in which the contests of the age are fought.

Notes

1. Legislation recently passed in Britain gives domestic British courts the authority to review domestic legislation for its consistency with the European Convention. While courts are not authorized to exercise judicial review in the full sense—that is, to declare domestic laws inoperative when they are held to be inconsistent with the Convention—they are obliged to declare that laws, though still in force, are incompatible with the Convention. See Kate Malleson, "A British Bill of Rights: Incorporating the European Convention on Human Rights," *Choices: Courts and Legislatures* 5 (1999), 21–42.

2. Pierre Elliott Trudeau, "The Values of a Just Society" in Thomas S. Axworthy and Pierre Elliott Trudeau, eds., *Towards a Just Society: The Trudeau Years* (Markham, Ont.: Viking, 1990), 363–4. See also Pierre Elliott Trudeau, *Federalism and the French Canadians* (Toronto: Macmillan, 1968).

3. *Patriation* is a peculiar Canadian term referring to Canada's assumption of complete control over its constitutional development in 1982. Prior to that date, Canada's constitution was also a piece of British legislation amendable by a bill passed by the British Parliament. Canada had to make a formal request of the British when it wanted its constitution amended. In 1982 the Canadian constitution was "brought home," severing entirely the constitutional link between Canada and its former colonial master.

4. See Alan C. Cairns, "Citizens (Outsiders) and Governments (Insiders) in Constitution-Making: The Case of Meech Lake" in Alan C. Cairns, *Disruptions: Constitutional Struggles from the Charter to Meech Lake,* edited by Douglas E. Williams (Toronto: McClelland & Stewart 1991), 108–38.

5. Kenneth McRoberts, *Misconceiving Canada: The Struggle for National Unity* (Toronto: Oxford University Press, 1997), and Guy Laforest, *Trudeau and the End of a Canadian Dream* (Montreal: McGill-Queen's University Press, 1995).

6. See, for example, *R. v. S.(S.)* [1990] 2 S.C.R. 254, in which the Supreme Court declared that in matters of differential provincial application of laws, even of federal laws like the Criminal Code, the principles of federalism should be respected.

7. Judith Shklar, "The Liberalism of Fear," in Judith Shklar, *Political Thought and Political Thinking,* edited by Stanley Hoffman (Chicago: University of Chicago Press, 1998), 3–20.

8. Barry L. Strayer, "Life Under the Canadian *Charter*: Adjusting the Balance Between Legislatures and Courts" *Public Law* (1987), 366.

9. The Supreme Court applied this notion in a case that had to do with the admissibility of illegally obtained evidence in a criminal trial. The Court had to interpret section 24(2) of the Charter, which requires that improperly obtained evidence is to be excluded if the admission of it would "bring the administration of justice into disrepute." This standard requires judges to have recourse to public opinion—but not unvarnished public opinion. The Supreme Court in *R. v. Collins* [1987] ISCR.215 stated that the views of the reasonable person about the effects of admission of improperly obtained evidence are to be discerned. The reasonable person is usually the average person in the community, but only when that community's current mood is reasonable.

10. David Beatty, *Constitutional Law in Theory and Practice* (Toronto: University of Toronto Press, 1995), 17.

11. *R. v. Oakes* [1986] 1 S.C.R. 103.

12. Lorraine Eisenstat Weinrib, "The Supreme Court of Canada and Section One of the *Charter*" *Supreme Court Law Review* 10 (1988), 469–513.

13. All of these issues were canvassed in *R. v. Keegstra* [1990] 3 S.C.R. 697. The Supreme Court upheld the Criminal Code's anti-hate provisions in this case. Another anachronistic Criminal Code provision used to prosecute hatemonger Ernst Zundel was struck down by the Court in *R. v. Zundel* [1992] 2 S.C.R. 731.

14. Paul M. Sniderman, Joseph F. Fletcher, Peter H. Russell, and Philip E. Tetlock, *The Clash of Rights: Liberty, Equality, and Legitimacy in Pluralist Democracy* (New Haven: Yale University Press, 1996).

15. Allan C. Hutchinson, *Waiting for Coraf: A Critique of Law and Rights* (Toronto: University of Toronto Press, 1995), 94.

16. *Retail, Wholesale, and Department Store Union, Local 580 et al. v. Dolphin Delivery* [1986] 2 S.C.R. 573; *Reference Re Public Service Employee Relations Act* [1987] 1 S.C.R. 313; *Public Service Alliance of Canada v. The Queen* [1987] 1 S.C.R. 424; *Retail, Wholesale and Department Store Union v. Saskatchewan* [1987] 1 S.C.R. 460.

17. *Finlay v. Canada* [1990] 1 S.C.R. 1080.

18. *RJR-MacDonald Inc. v. Canada* (Attorney-General) [1995] 3 S.C.R. 199.

19. See Peter McCormick, *Canada's Courts* (Toronto: Lorimer, 1994). Occasionally, litigants may have their litigation expenses covered by interest groups that will sponsor a case if it serves a larger political goal consistent with the group's aims. In other countries, litigation expenses in constitutional challenges are avoided. The German Constitutional Court, for example, must consider challenges to laws initiated by citizens following a simple complaints procedure. A small fraction of complaints actually make it to a formal court proceeding, but the number of citizen complaints vastly outnumbers challenges initiated by members of legislative assemblies. Erhard Blankenburg, "Changes in Political Regimes and Continuity of the Rule of Law in Germany" in Herbert Jacob, Erhard Blenkenburg, Herbert M. Kritzer, Doris Marie

Provine, and Joseph Sanders, *Courts, Law & Politics in Comparative Perspective* (New Haven: Yale University Press, 1996), 309.

20. See Rainer Knopff and F.L. Morton, *Charter Politics* (Scarborough, Ont.: Nelson Canada, 1992); Rainer Knopff and F.L. Morton, "The Supreme Court as Vanguard of the Intelligentsia: The Charter Movement as Postmaterialist Politics" in Janet Ajzenstat, ed., *Canadian Constitutionalism, 1791–1991* (Ottawa: Canadian Study of Parliament Group, 1991), 54–78; and F.L. Morton, "The *Charter* Revolution and the Court Party" *Osgoode Hall Law Journal* 30 (1992), 627–51.

21. The term is from Richard Sigurdson, "Left- and Right-Wing Charterphobia: A Critique of the Critics," *International Journal of Canadian Studies* 6–7 (1993), 95–115. See also his "The Left-Legal Critique of the *Charter*: A Critical Assessment," *Windsor Yearbook of Access to Justice* 13 (1993), 117–55.

22. It should be noted, though, that some on the Left are more ambivalent about the virtues of legislatures than are those on the Right. Critics like Hutchinson and Mandel point to the manner in which legislatures are responsive to moneyed interests and how even the electoral process is geared to the financially advantaged. For them, there is no easy political choice to be made between courts and legislatures as vehicles for the realization of the left-wing political agenda.

23. *Reference Re B.C. Motor Vehicles Act* [1985] 2 S.C.R. 486, at 497. Also, Brian Dickson, "*The Canadian Charter of Rights and Freedoms*: Dawn of a New Era?" *Review of Constitutional Studies* 2 (1994), 1–19. More generally, see Ian Greene, Carl Baar, Peter McCormick, George Szenblowski, and Martin Thomas, *Final Appeal: Decision-Making in Canadian Courts of Appeal* (Toronto: Lorimer, 1998), chapter 1.

24. Christopher Manfredi, *Judicial Power and the Charter: Canada and the Paradox of Liberal Constitutionalism* (Toronto: McClelland & Stewart, 1993), 83.

25. Peter H. Russell, "The Political Purposes of the Canadian Charter of Rights and Freedoms" *Canadian Bar Review* 61 (1983), 31–54.

26. Peter W. Hogg and Allison A. Bushell, "The Charter Dialogue Between Courts and Legislatures (Or Perhaps the Charter of Rights Isn't Such a Bad Thing After All)" *Osgoode Hall Law Journal* 35 (1997), 79–80.

27. Two perennial exceptions to this are former premiers Peter Lougheed and Alan Blakeney, who participated in the patriation debate in the early 1980s, opposed the Charter's entrenchment, then later agreed to it as long as it included section 33. They still believe that occasional use of section 33 would best preserve the "creative tension" between courts and legislatures. Robert Fife, "Ex-Premiers Call for Use of Charter's 'Safety Valve,'" *National Post* (March 1, 1999), A1, A2. See also, Manfredi, *Judicial Power and the Charter*, chapter 7. It should be noted that while the Supreme Court has lately seized upon the idea of dialogue to deflect criticisms of its activism, it has often insisted that the courts are the guardians of the constitution. The principles of dialogue and

judicial guardianship are in obvious tension, and the Court has not said anything to resolve it.

28. For a lively discussion of this issue, see the collection of commentaries in *Policy Options* (April 1999).

Terms & Concepts

Charter Canadians
Charter dialogue
Charterphobes

Court Party
judicial deference
liberal nationalism

patriation
section 1
section 33

Questions

1. What were Pierre Trudeau's reasons for advocating the entrenchment of the Charter?

2. What effects has the Charter had on the role of courts in Canadian politics?

3. Does the Charter enhance or impair democratic government in Canada?

4. Should governments use the Charter's section 33 notwithstanding clause more often?

Global Goes Local: The North American Meatpacking Industry

Michael Broadway

Editors' Note

Most of us know little or nothing about the agribusiness industry and the changes taking place within it. Food simply appears in supermarkets. The circumstances surrounding its development, production, and distribution are hidden from view, and many of us are not sure we even want to know how our food arrives on the table, as long as the price is right. Michael Broadway is able to demystify certain aspects of these processes by analyzing what has been going on in the meatpacking business.

The data in the tables in this essay are graphic and startling: they encapsulate the revolution that has overtaken the agribusiness industry—in this case the beef-packing industry—and reveal unprecedented changes in the scale and type of operations. Michael Broadway makes these figures come alive; he shows how and why the industry has changed so much and the consequences of the meatpacking revolution. These consequences are not only an increase in the interdependency and integration of the U.S. and Canadian markets, though this is an important result. There are also, quite clearly, environmental and social problems created that are long term and significant for both the communities directly involved and for the governments that are supposed to provide regulatory frameworks.

The live cattle and beef industry sectors "are perhaps the most integrated market of the major agricultural commodities."[1] In 1987, prior to the Canada–U.S. Trade Agreement, Canada exported 262 000 cattle to the United States. By 1996 this figure had grown to almost 1.5 million. Not surprisingly, this increase has caused an angry reaction among U.S. producers, who blame not Canadian ranchers but the multinational conglomerates who dominate the industry.

In his essay, commissioned for this volume, Broadway gives us a case in which global really does meet local, and local loses. It also involves an industry in which "Fordist" assembly line practices have reappeared, except that now we have a "disassembly" line instead.

◆ ◆ ◆

Globalization has become a fashionable term among academics and politicians to describe the increasing economic interdependence between countries. It can take many different forms. Manufacturing plant closures in southern Ontario during the late 1980s and early 1990s were attributed to the implementation of the Canada–U.S. Free Trade Agreement (FTA) and the decision by U.S.-based companies to close branch plants. At the same time in southern Alberta, a U.S.–based agribusiness company began operating a beef slaughter facility in High River, which would eventually employ over 1800 workers. These and other investment decisions are the product of companies constantly seeking lower-cost production sites and acquiring

---

1. Linda M. Young and John S. Marsh, "Integration and Interdependence in the U.S. and Canadian Live Cattle and Beef Sector," *The American Review of Canadian Studies* 28, 3 (Autumn 1998), 351.

Article prepared for this publication.

new markets. At the end of the 20th century this movement of capital has been greatly enhanced by technological innovations in communications and trade agreements that have opened new markets.

Globalization is not a new process. It dates back to the beginnings of merchant capitalism and European colonialism. Canada's agricultural sector was "globalized" from its early beginnings, supplying distant markets with commodities. Its staples economy in the 18th and 19th centuries was based on the export of salted fish and fur, and later lumber and wheat, to England in exchange for manufactured goods. At the end of the 20th century a more complex pattern has emerged with the increasing concentration of agricultural production and inputs among transnational agribusiness corporations. Agriculture's transformation from a market orientation to an industrialized sector aims to deliver crops and livestock at the lowest possible cost using economies of scale and substituting capital for labour. Agricultural industrialization is the product of three fundamental structural forces: intensification, concentration, and specialization. Intensification refers to the rising level of capitalization required by agriculture, concentration is associated with the emergence of fewer but larger units producing more output, and specialization is the tendency for farmers to produce a single crop or livestock type.

The effects of globalization and agricultural industrialization are well illustrated by the Canadian beef-packing industry. As late as the 1970s, the industry was owned largely by Canadian companies that operated small plants scattered across the country in population centres. At the end of the 1990s, most of the old urban-based plants have shut down and have been replaced by plants in rural areas. The industry has consolidated in Alberta under the control of two foreign agribusiness firms: Cargill of Minneapolis, Minnesota, and IBP of Dakota City, Nebraska. Each company operates a large-capacity slaughter plant in southern Alberta. During this period of structural change, cattle feeding has also consolidated in the province owing to its extensive supplies of pasture land and cattle feed. This chapter identifies the consequences for rural communities of a "globalized" beef processing system in Canada. First, the processes underlying the globalization of agriculture and the restructuring of Canada's beef industry are identified, then the social, economic, and environmental implications of these processes for local communities are discussed.

GLOBALIZATION AND AGRICULTURAL TRADE

◆ ◆ ◆

Globalization has been part of the capitalist world economy since the age of European exploration. Wealthy merchant capitalists helped fund voyages of discovery in pursuit of spices and other goods. This process eventually led to the establishment of colonies and the production of agricultural commodities for colonial powers in exchange for manufactured goods. The pattern of trade from peripheral to core regions was gradually altered with the incorporation of some peripheral regions into the core. Europe's hegemony over agricultural trade eventually passed to the United States in the 20th century. Within the United States a highly productive energy and capital intensive system of agriculture evolved during the 19th and 20th centuries which became the model for agricultural development in Europe and the post-colonial world. This industrial form of agriculture requires continual inputs of fertilizers, hybrid seeds, pesticides, machinery, and oil and has led to the integration of industry and agriculture into agribusiness firms. By the 1990s these companies have become transnational in scope, controlling the exchange of inputs and commodities across national boundaries. Agribusiness firms are driven by the twin imperatives of increasing market share and lowest cost production. As a result, they search the globe for new markets and cheaper access to sources of labour, land, and commodities, while negotiating favourable incentives from foreign governments for their investment. Cargill Incorporated epitomizes these trends, trading and processing commodities with over 80 000 employees in 72 countries. In Canada the company, through its subsidiary Cargill Limited, is involved in grain handling and merchandising, manufacturing and distributing fertilizer, and meatpacking.

The increased globalization of agriculture has been made possible by technological innovations in transport and data transmission and by the removal of trade barriers. Improvements in refrigerated transport and in packaging have enabled the shipment of perishable products over vast distances. In the 1960s, mobile refrigerated containers were developed for intermodal transfer between ships and road/rail transport. Most recently, controlled atmosphere technologies have been developed that allow operators to lower the respiration rate of produce by monitoring and adjusting levels of oxygen, carbon dioxide, and nitrogen within a container. This adjusted environment slows the rate of ripening, retards discoloration, and maintains the produce's freshness.

Accompanying these developments in container technology have been increases in the capacity of container vessels, which have led to a lowering of unit shipping costs and have made it cheaper to ship goods over longer distances.

The electronic transmission of information via the Internet has facilitated the linking of potential buyers with sellers. In the beef industry, processors and feeders have instant access to cattle and feed prices, which allows them to make informed purchasing decisions. It also enables a processor to identify a niche for a particular quality of beef in a distant market and then communicate the precise genetic and feeding requirements to a cattle feeder. Negotiations on delivery and other conditions can also be conducted via e-mail. These types of transactions are already occurring in Europe, where pork and chicken meat are produced for niche markets that specify feed ingredients, additives, and other conditions.

The FTA, the North America Free Trade Agreement (NAFTA), and the General Agreement on Tariffs and Trade (GATT), which was concluded in 1994, are based on the premise that increasing trade stimulates economic growth. In the case of agriculture, all three agreements aim to increase market access by having countries reduce tariffs, lower export subsidies, and withdraw domestic price supports. In North America the agreements have had the effect of boosting agricultural trade and reinforcing the trend toward greater market integration. NAFTA is credited with increasing beef exports from Canada to the United States by over 15 percent between 1994 and 1997. At the same time, government support for agricultural programs has declined. The 1995 Canadian federal budget cancelled the Western Grain Transportation Program, which provided farmers in the western provinces with an annual half-billion-dollar subsidy for the cost of shipping their grain to export terminals. The same budget also reduced the amount of federal assistance for farm safety-net programs.

Critics of these trade agreements note that they lessen the authority of sovereign governments to regulate food production and threaten sustainable agriculture. In the beef industry, the European Union has banned the import of U.S. beef produced with growth hormones, citing potential health hazards. The U.S. government and beef industry have challenged the legality of the ban under GATT, and the World Trade Organization has ruled that the ban should be lifted. Proponents of sustainable agriculture argue that free trade is leading to a global system of specialized produc-tion and crop monoculture which depends on chemical inputs and shipping food long distances to market. Such a system threatens the environment by depleting soil nutrient levels and increasing soil erosion and energy consumption. At the same time, the increased use of chemicals to control pests and replenish soils leads to a reduction in biodiversity and to increased groundwater contamination, which threatens human health. Despite such concerns, the prevailing trend at the dawn of the 21st century is toward a global industrialized agri-food production system characterized by regional specialization and large capital inputs. The following section illustrates how the forces of globalization have resulted in the restructuring of Canada's beef industry.

HISTORICAL BACKGROUND

◆ ◆ ◆

Until the 1980s, Canada's beef-packing industry was market oriented. Cattle were raised on the prairies and shipped by rail to be slaughtered in multispecies plants at railroad terminals across the country. The industry was dominated by three companies: Canada Packers, Burns Meats, and Swift Canadian, a subsidiary of U.S.-based Swift & Co. The three companies accounted for an estimated 63 percent of the cattle slaughtered in Canada during the 1950s, with Canada Packers having the largest share of the slaughter market. The plants were vertically integrated and produced a variety of fresh and processed meats, as well as lard and other byproducts. Work was labour intensive and well paid. Cattle were slaughtered on the top floor and carcasses were moved down to lower floors by gravity feed chutes for further processing. Workers' hourly wages at Canada Packers' main plant in Toronto between 1939 and 1949 were almost the same as those of employees at nearby steel plants. In 1946 the United Packinghouse Workers of America and the three leading packers signed an industry-wide master contract. The contract regulated industry wages and working conditions throughout Canada, with packing companies following the terms established by Canada Packers. This system of wage negotiations lasted until 1984.

The 30 years following World War II were marked by industry-wide expansion. Demand for meat products increased and the industry responded by hiring more workers. From 1946 to 1976 the number of employees rose from 22 536 to 33 237. Most of this expansion occurred in Ontario and Quebec among small facilities employing fewer than 20 employees. But in 1976 per capita meat consumption started to decline as a result of health-related concerns, cost factors, and competition from other protein sources, most notably poultry. By the early 1980s the industry was confronted with major problems of overcapacity. In 1983 Alberta's cattle slaughter facilities ran at approximately 26 percent of capacity. At the same time as the industry began to deal with this problem, the effects of lower-cost beef producers from the United States began to be felt. The combined effect of these two forces would lead to a massive restructuring of the industry and the adoption of an industrialized meat production system.

RESTRUCTURING AND CANADA'S MEATPACKING INDUSTRY

◆ ◆ ◆

In the United States the structural forces of intensification, concentration, and specialization have led to the concentration of production among new low-cost meatpacking companies. IBP (formerly known as Iowa Beef Packers), founded in 1961, is the company widely credited with revolutionizing the industry with its cost-cutting innovations. Its first plant in Denison, Iowa, was located in a cattle-producing region and enabled the company to reduce transportation costs and the shrinkage and bruising associated with shipping cattle long distances. The plant was a one-story structure, which allowed for greater automation and the development of a disassembly line. Under this system, workers are stationed along the line and are responsible for one task in the preparation of the carcass. The company, arguing that this work required less skill than work in older plants where workers were expected to perform a variety of tasks, refused to abide by the terms of the union master agreement and thus paid their workers lower wages and benefits. Later in the decade the company introduced boxed beef. Instead of shipping a carcass to its customers, the company removes fat and bone at the plant and prepares the meat according to retail specifications before vacuum packaging it. This type of packaging adds to the product's shelf life and reduces shrinkage caused by exposure to air. This innovation allowed IBP to ship more beef, and it appealed to the company's customers, since they could lower their own costs by not hiring their own butchers. The net effect of these cost-cutting innovations was to increase the demand for IBP products; the company responded by

constructing large-capacity slaughter plants in rural areas close to a supply of fed cattle on the High Plains. Its competitors either went bankrupt and shut down old inefficient plants or emulated IBP's rural industrialization strategy. ConAgra, a transnational food processor, acquired some of its U.S. meatpacking interests by purchasing bankrupt companies and reopening the plants at lower wage levels. Cargill entered the beef industry by purchasing another meatpacking company, Missouri Beef Packers, renaming it Excel and then following IBP's strategy by building the world's second largest beef-processing plant in Dodge City in southwest Kansas.

Beginning in the 1980s Canada's beef-packing industry underwent a similar structural transformation, with plant closures in urban areas and the construction of large-capacity slaughter plants in rural areas. In 1981 Swift Canadian closed plants in Calgary and Winnipeg and sold its remaining operations to Alberta-based Gainers. Canada Packers closed plants in Montreal, Hull, Charlottetown, Saint John, and Winnipeg, with the loss of nearly 2000 jobs, while Burns Meats closed facilities in Kitchener and Calgary.

Canada's beef-packing industry underwent a similar structural transformation.

Labour costs were reduced by breaking the power of the union to bargain on a national basis. In 1984 Burns Meats demanded that workers at its two oldest plants take a pay cut and accept bargaining on a plant-by-plant basis. The union rejected both requests and called a strike. The company responded by filing an unfair labour practice charge against the union, arguing that the union's insistence on national bargaining was a violation of its duty to bargain in good faith. This position was subsequently upheld by the Labour Relations Boards in Ontario, Manitoba, and Alberta. With the collapse of the union's master contract, other companies demanded concessions from their workers. Canada Packers, after a five-week national strike, was able to obtain a two-year wage freeze from its workforce and a lower rate of pay for its new hires. In Alberta, Lakeside Packers, of Brooks, used the national strike to break the union local. As soon as the strike began, the company hired replacement workers at 30 percent below the union rate, which translated to a $3.00–$3.80 per hour pay cut. This cost advantage led to increased demand for its products, and the company responded by adding a second shift. By the end of 1984 it had become Canada's largest single cattle plant.

The final element in the industry's restructuring was its takeover by transnational companies. In 1987 Cargill Limited announced plans to construct a state-of-the-art beef-processing plant 3 km north of High River in southern Alberta. It would be Canada's first fully integrated beef plant, encompassing slaughter, fabrication, and the preparation of byproducts. When it opened in 1989, it employed a nonunion labour force with starting wages at $4.00 an hour less than wages in surrounding unionized plants in Lethbridge and Calgary. The initial slaughter capacity was 6000 head a week using 410 production workers, which was significantly more efficient than older plants operating in other parts of the country. The entry of a low-cost producer set off a new round of plant closures. In southern Ontario between 1988 and 1990, a shortage of cattle, coupled with the high costs of transporting slaughter cattle and increased competition, resulted in 10 beef-packing plants either closing or shifting to hog production. The biggest round of plant closures occurred with the departure of Canada Packers from the industry. In 1990 the company was acquired by the transnational Hillsdown Holdings Ltd. and merged with Maple Leaf Mills Ltd. to form Canada's largest food processor, Maple Leaf Foods Inc. Two years later, Hillsdown closed the remaining Canada Packers beef plants as part of a strategy to increase profitability and stockholder dividends.

The final element in the industry's restructuring was its takeover by transnational companies.

The industry's restructuring was completed in 1994 when IBP purchased Lakeside Packers of Brooks and immediately announced plans to add a fabrication plant for the production of boxed beef. At the same time, Cargill announced plans to double its High River slaughter capacity to 1 million head a year by adding a second shift. The effect of these investments and plant closures was the increasing concentration of production at the national level and within Alberta. In 1991, 43 percent of the cattle slaughtered in Canada came from four plants, and by 1998 the corresponding figure was 75 percent (see Table 20.1). Even higher levels of concentration are found within Alberta.

Table 20.1   Distribution of Cattle Slaughtering Activity 1991, 1997

	1991		1997	
	Canada	Alberta	Canada	Alberta
Number of Plants	63	9	45	9
Average Kill	38 507	136 627	66 394	207 967
Top Four Plants	43%	78%	70%	98%

Source: *Livestock Market Review, 1997.* Ottawa: Agriculture Canada. Online. Available: http://www.agr.ca/misb/aisd/redmeat/98toce.html

ALBERTA'S ADVANTAGES

◆ ◆ ◆

Transnational capital in the beef industry has been attracted to Alberta by its plentiful supplies of beef cattle, favourable labour climate, and government incentives. Since the 1980s, successive governments have sought investment in the meatpacking industry as a means of increasing the value-added component of the province's cattle industry. Cattle have been raised on the province's extensive pastureland since European settlers arrived in the 19th century. The construction of the transcontinental railroad enabled the export of live cattle east and west. The large-scale shipment of cattle to southern Ontario continued until the construction of boxed beef plants in High River and Brooks. Boxed beef lowered shipping costs and enabled the construction of plants away from market locations. A 1993 study estimated the cost of shipping a full load of boxed beef (25 000 kg on a triple-axle trailer) from Calgary to Toronto at $29.91 a head, while the equivalent cost for a load of fed cattle was $112.50.[1] Therefore, access to fed cattle has become a primary consideration for the industry. Excel, in selecting High River, was able to obtain 80 percent of its cattle supply from within a 150 mile radius of the plant. Alberta is Canada's leading feedlot province because of extensive supplies of low-cost feed grains, most notably barley, good supplies of fresh water, and dry winters that are easy on cattle. The proportion of Canada's fed cattle produced within the province has increased from 46 percent in 1985 to 69 percent in 1998, while major declines have occurred in Ontario and Saskatchewan/Manitoba (see Table 20.2). During the same period the proportion of cattle slaughtered in Alberta has increased from 40 to 66 percent (see Table 20.3).

Table 20.2 Cattle on Feed in Canada (in thousands), 1985, 1998

| | 1985 | | 1998 | |
	Number	Percent	Number	Percent
British Columbia	70.1	3.0	38.7	1.1
Alberta	1061.2	46.1	2390.9	68.9
Saskatchewan/ Manitoba	428.0	18.6	340.0	9.8
Ontario	632.7	27.5	608.0	17.5
Quebec	72.3	3.2	50.3	1.5
Atlantic Provinces	35.6	1.5	40.1	1.2
CANADA	2299.8	100.0	3468.0	100.0

Source: Canadian Cattleman's Association (Calgary: Canfax, n.d.).

Table 20.3 Cattle Slaughtered in Federally Inspected Establishments, 1985, 1998

| | 1985 | | 1998 | |
	Number	Percent	Number	Percent
British Columbia	93 859	3.0	41 566	1.3
Alberta	1 270 408	40.2	2 084 962	66.5
Saskatchewan/ Manitoba	608 590	19.3	180 460	5.7
Ontario	839 729	26.6	566 209	18.0
Quebec	288 331	9.1	207 410	6.6
Atlantic Provinces	58 390	1.8	58 065	1.9
CANADA	3 159 307	100.0	3 138 672	100.0

Source: *Livestock Market Review, 1986, 1998*. Ottawa: Agriculture Canada. Online. Available: http://www.agr.ca/misb/aisd/redmeat/98toce.html

Alberta's "pro-business" environment was enhanced during the early 1980s by a series of defeats for organized labour. The provincial Conservative government believed that high wages and rigid workplace rules within the province's agricultural processing sector placed it at a competitive disadvantage. Therefore, in 1984, when strikebreakers were employed at Lakeside Packers and the union local was effectively destroyed, the government saw no need to intervene. Two years later, a bitter labour dispute at a Gainers meatpacking plant in Edmonton involving the use of strikebreakers led to a new Labour Relations Code for the province. The code gives the Cabinet the right to decertify a union engaged in illegal strikes. It also makes it harder for unions to obtain certification by removing the right of the Labour Relations Board to certify a union if the board finds that management has interfered with an organizing drive. At the same time, the province is seeking investors by emphasizing its low costs. A 1998 publication from the Department of Economic Development proudly boasts that Alberta has "the lowest overall taxes in Canada ... much lower wage costs than in the United States" and the lowest workers' compensation premiums in Canada.[2] These inducements have been rewarded by investments from such transnationals as Ralston Purina, ConAgra, Central Soya Ltd., and Archer Daniels Midland.

The provincial government's support for meatpacking during the 1980s included the provision of loan guarantees and outright grants to individual companies. In 1987 it provided Gainers Inc. with a $67 million loan package. Two years later, when the company defaulted, the government took over the company before eventually selling it to Burns Foods of Calgary in 1993. In 1990 the government provided Lakeside Packers with a $10 million loan and $6 million grant to finance modernization at their Brooks facility. Most controversially, from the perspective of Albertan-owned businesses, it provided Cargill with a $4 million grant for the construction of a waste-water treatment plant at its High River facility, at a time when the industry was already plagued by overcapacity. Officials at Alberta Agriculture justified the decision as part of their overall strategy to increase value-added manufacturing in the province and keep cattle from being exported to the United States. In short, since the 1980s successive provincial governments have pursued a variety of measures that have favoured agribusiness interests and helped the beef industry consolidate in the province. The impact of this strategy on rural communities is discussed next.

BEEF PACKING AND RURAL COMMUNITY CHANGE

◆ ◆ ◆

The physical and economic advantages of a rural prairie or High Plains location for the beef industry are readily apparent. But the small towns where the industry has located its processing facilities lack a major requirement for a manufacturing facility, namely access to a large pool of surplus labour. This deficiency is exacerbated by the industry's high employee turnover, which is attributable to the physically demanding nature of the work, relatively low wages, and high injury rate. Monthly turnover among the 1300 line workers at Excel's High River plant averaged 100 workers during the first six months of 1996, which meant that in the course of a full year nearly all the line workers will have been replaced. In Alberta, the meatpacking industry's rate of lost time owing to injury was triple the average for manufacturing during the early 1990s, and although the rate has since declined it remains above the manufacturing average. Indeed, work-related injuries were cited as a bargaining issue in a 1997 strike at the Excel plant. These conditions mean that the packers are engaged in a continual effort to recruit labour for their plants, and it is this strategy that has prompted the demographic and social transformation of small towns with packing plants. Accompanying these changes are significant environmental impacts related to the increased demand for fed cattle. The specific demographic, social, and environmental consequences of the consolidation of beef packing in Alberta are outlined below.

Packers are engaged in a continual effort to recruit labour for their plants.

a. Demographic Changes

In the United States, IBP and Cargill have recruited Latinos and Southeast Asians to staff their rural beef-packing plants. This influx of newcomers has boosted local populations. When two new beef-processing plants opened in Finney County, Kansas, during the early 1980s, it became the fastest-growing county in the state. In Alberta, the packers' recruitment efforts have produced very diverse labour forces. At Excel's High River plant, an estimated 80 percent of the line workers are visible minorities, with over 50 different languages and dialects represented. The leading groups consist of Southeast Asians, Iraqis, East Indians, and Somalis. But, unlike U.S. communities with beef-processing plants, High River has not experienced significant population growth after the plant opened owing to a shortage of affordable housing in the town. Instead, most line workers live in Calgary and commute to the plant.

Lakeside has hired nearly 2000 persons since December 1996. Over time, the labour-force characteristics have changed with different recruitment strategies. The company began by recruiting locally and specifically targeted female single parents. However, the physically demanding nature of the work meant that many of these workers soon quit, and the company widened its efforts to include Medicine Hat and Lethbridge. When this supply was exhausted, recruiters travelled to the Maritime provinces, seeking laid-off workers from the collapse of the cod fishery. In turn, an estimated 400 Maritimers have moved to Brooks. Lakeside has also worked with Calgary's Catholic Immigration Society to supply the plant with workers, with the leading groups consisting of Iraqis, Somalis, Ethiopians, Filipinos, Cambodians, and Bosnians. Population growth in Brooks during this period has been constrained by the absence of affordable housing; many workers have little choice but to live in Medicine Hat, a 70-minute drive southeast of Brooks, and commute to the plant by company bus. By spring 1999, Lakeside had become Medicine Hat's largest manufacturing employer, with nearly 1000 workers.

b. Social Changes

The sudden influx of population to small towns with packing plants has led to many of the same social problems experienced by western energy boomtowns during the 1970s, including increases in homelessness, crime, domestic violence, and child abuse. These problems have been attributed to the breakdown in the sense of community accompanying rapid population growth and high turnover; the stress of moving to a new location; and the influx of young adult single males, the demographic group with the highest incidence of crime and substance abuse. High River has, so far, remained immune to these social changes as most of the plant's labour force resides in Calgary. Brooks, by contrast, has experienced an increase in a variety of social problems. Many of the newcomers who have been drawn to the town by the prospect of employment at Lakeside arrive penniless and need accommodations. The company has responded to this need by providing ATCO trailer units that can accommodate up to 162 single men and women. The housing is located adjacent to the plant. It is surrounded by a chainlink fence and barbed wire, and its entryway consists of a guardhouse structure. Food is provided by a system of vouchers that workers exchange in the plant's cafeteria. Lakeside deducts the cost of rent, food, and any extra equipment the employee may have purchased from their pay. This means that many workers, even after they receive their first paycheque, have little to live on and are unable to save for a damage deposit for an apartment. Indigent newcomers may also be eligible for a one-time transitional assistance payment from Alberta Family and Social Services. Since Lakeside began recruiting, the demand for these payments has increased so much that the agency has had to hire additional caseworkers. The local branch of the Salvation Army also provides shelter and clothing assistance for newcomers.

Crime has increased in Brooks since Lakeside's expansion. The local RCMP detachment reports that the number of persons detained because they were intoxicated to the point of being a danger to themselves rose from 128 in 1996 to 398 in 1997. Meanwhile, the number of persons arrested for violating Alberta's liquor act jumped from 168 to 308. These increases are related to the influx of young adult single males, since this group has the highest proportion of heavy drinkers. Alcohol consumption is also a factor behind increases in domestic violence. Caseworkers at Alberta Family and Social Services reported that during the fall of 1997 they paid the airfare of a spouse or girlfriend who decided to return to the Maritimes to escape an abusive relationship two to three times a month. The doubling of child welfare caseloads from 45 in January 1997 to 90 at the end of the year provides further evidence of the overall rise in social disorders.

Brooks, like meatpacking towns south of the border, has attempted to address some of these problems. A women's crisis line was established in the summer of 1998. In the first six weeks of its operation, seven women sought assistance, and in each case either they or their partner worked at Lakeside. In the fall of 1998 a food pantry opened, while the issue of public intoxication has been addressed by a vigorous enforcement of existing regulations. These problems and the efforts to remediate them attest to the high social costs of this form of development incurred by workers, their family members, and communities.

c. Environmental

The environmental impacts of Alberta's increasing concentration of beef production deal primarily with cattle feeding. The province's share of Canada's fed cattle production has risen with its share of slaughtered cattle (see Tables 20.2 and 20.3). Cattle feeding is located in the southern portion of the province, owing to its relatively mild winter and the availability of barley feed. Economies of scale mean that large feedlots are more economical, so capacities have increased and production

has become concentrated among a few producers. As feedlots have expanded in size, environmental concerns dealing with dust, odour, and surface and groundwater contamination have grown, along with the effects of increased truck traffic. Lakeside's feedlot is located 5 km west of Brooks, and during the 1990s its capacity has increased from 25 000 to 75 000 heads. With the prevailing wind coming from the west, dust is carried into town during long dry spells, while odour is an omnipresent reminder of the industry. To promote growth and protect the health of cattle, hormones and antibiotics are used. Their usage is associated with the presence of volatile organic chemicals in manure, which are odorous in high concentrations and hazardous to human health. Increasing the size of feedlots creates major problems in terms of manure disposal. Good feedlot management requires that solid manure be piled into mounds to allow it to dry. It is stored until early spring and late fall, when it is applied to fields. However, there are limits to the capacity of soil to absorb the nutrients, and any excess quantity is likely to result in runoff and surface water contamination. Moreover, it is uneconomical to transport manure more than 19 to 24 km; thus, storing manure on-site increases the risk of contamination. Widespread public concern over these issues and rising opposition to the expansion of feedlots in the province's feedlot alley, north of Lethbridge, led the local health authority in 1998 to undertake a study of the industry's health effects.

CONCLUSIONS

◆ ◆ ◆

The primary objective of agribusiness is to provide food at the lowest cost. In pursuing this goal, agriculture has become industrialized using economies of scale and new technologies to increase output. At the same time, advances in transportation have allowed food to be shipped longer distances from producing regions to the consumer. These factors have combined to produce a globalized food production system characterized by increasing regional specialization. National governments have facilitated this process by removing trade barriers and domestic agricultural subsidies. In this new competitive global environment of open markets and capital mobility, governments attempt to attract investment by creating a pro-business environment. Alberta offers transnational agribusiness companies low taxes, low labour costs, and a weakened labour movement.

The social costs of this production system are evident in communities where beef-packing plants are located. These costs include increases in homelessness, crime, domestic violence, child abuse, and demands for social assistance. Local communities and their citizens lack control over the business practices of beef-packing companies, yet they must deal with the social consequences of the industry's presence. Similarly, residents of rural areas surrounding beef-packing plants have to deal with the environmental impact of an expanding feedlot industry that is fed by the increased demand for cattle. In short, the evidence from Alberta indicates that a globalized agri-food production system threatens the environment and the communities in which it operates.

Notes

1. Canadian International Trade Tribunal, *An Inquiry into the Competitiveness of the Canadian Cattle and Beef Industries* (Ottawa: Minister of Supply and Services, 1993), 21.

2. Province of Alberta, *Highlights of the Alberta Economy* (Edmonton: Alberta Economic Development, 1998), 1, 24, 25.

Terms & Concepts

Cargill
concentration
disassembly line
economies of scale
feedlots

Fordism
GATT
groundwater contamination
IBP
intensification

NAFTA
rural industrialization
specialization
staples economy

Questions

1. In an industrial/agricultural sector in which government intervention has been relatively unimportant and market forces have been dominant, what problems have arisen to which governments will have to pay increased attention?

2. What, presumably, are the benefits this industry brings to (a) the province of Alberta, (b) Canadian beef producers, and (c) consumers? How should we compare these benefits to the associated "externalities" that arise?

3. Can the forces of intensification, concentration, and specialization be resisted in the agricultural sector? Discuss and use another agricultural example in which these forces are also clearly at work.

4. How and why did well-paid work become low paid and marginalized?

5. How should we protect those working in, or affected by, the beef-packing industry, while accepting the fact that some major changes are likely to be here to stay?

The Grass Is Always Greener: Prime Ministerial vs. Presidential Government

Jennifer Smith

Editors' Note

Political executives, particularly prime ministers and presidents, fascinate us. To study a prime minister or a president is to investigate power, personality, intrigue, policy, and a political system in action. It is to examine how a political race was run, how public confidence was won or lost, what happened at moments of crisis, and how history will judge those who have ruled us. It is the stuff of popular novels, academic biographies, and journalistic exposés.

Jennifer Smith focuses on the very different legislative–executive relationships that exist in the Canadian parliamentary system and the United States' presidential system. It is no great surprise that, in spite of public interest in the subject of leadership, so little is known of the details of office and of the systems of government. The media deal with personalities, not the overall system. This will have changed somewhat with the extensive coverage of the impeachment hearings and Clinton's travails, and Smith has expanded her article to include a comparison of the rules and procedures (or lack of them) surrounding executive removal from office.

Canadian students, when asked who is the more powerful, a prime minister or a president, will usually pick the latter. As Smith points out, this may be due to the immense military power of the United States and to the president's foreign policy role. What such a superficial comparison does not do, however, is take into consideration the enormous constraints placed on a president compared with the powers of a prime minister backed by a majority government.

It can be argued that what really constrains a Canadian prime minister is the power of the provinces. An American president certainly does not have to face the equivalent of a regular First Ministers' Conference with state governors, nor does he have to deal with the equivalent of Quebec—not even Texas fills these shoes! But he (and one day she) does have to deal with Congress, with its powerful lower house, and an even more powerful Senate.

Smith emphasizes that, in terms of efficiency, the office of prime minister is "the clear winner." Note, however, her comments when we compare what she refers to as a more "democratic" standard. Canadians must pay a price for this untrammelled executive power. Americans, on the other hand, will have to wait a long time for such things as a comprehensive approach to universal health care, if indeed agreement is ever reached on this matter. So they pay a price too.

Reprinted by permission from *Canada and the United States: Differences that Count*, 2nd edition, David Thomas, ed., to be published by Broadview Press.

INTRODUCTION

◆ ◆ ◆

The word *execute* is derived from the Latin *exsequor*, which means "follow out." Thus the political executive is understood to follow out or to give effect to something. And that something is the will of the legislators as expressed in the laws. This is stated clearly in the American constitution, which requires that the president take care to execute the laws faithfully. It is also expressed in the doctrine of the president as chief clerk, according to which the president can act only when explicitly empowered to do so under the constitution or the laws of the Congress.[1] But there must be more to the executive than that, otherwise political executives around the world, including the American president, would hardly inspire the attention, envy, and fear that they sometimes do.

The American constitution supplies some clues about the more formidable side of the executive. For instance, the president is commander-in-chief of the army and navy and of the militia of the states, and he receives ambassadors from foreign countries. Here we have the executive in armour, the military might of the entire nation at his disposal, as well as the executive as statesman-diplomat, in charge of the conduct of foreign policy. The president is required to deliver an annual state-of-the-union address to the assembled members of Congress. This is an occasion on which he can sketch future policy initiatives, as well as review the record of the year past. Thus the modern executive is not merely the servant of the legislature but a powerful initiator of action in his own right.

It is instructive that in both cases—the executive as follower and the executive as initiator—it is essential to make reference to the legislature. The story of the modern executive in constitutional governments is largely about the executive–legislative relationship, and at bottom it revolves around the question of which is dominant. Obviously the answer will vary from one system of government to the next, but there are two main models: presidential and parliamentary. And there are two neighbouring countries—the United States and Canada respectively—which are leading examples of each.

Since the two models are so different, it might seem that to compare them is like comparing apples and oranges—not very fruitful, so to speak. Yet people do compare them in order to better understand them, indeed, often to determine which is the better, an endeavour normally inspired by a "grass is greener" sen-

timent and a pre-established standard of judgement. One of the most sensational examples in the history of political science is an essay published in 1884 by Woodrow Wilson, long before he became president of the United States. Wilson was troubled by the "clumsy misrule" of an overbearing Congress, and sought to make Congress more amenable to direction by the president. He thought he saw an answer in the parliamentary model, which often enables a prime minister and his cabinet to control the legislature.[2]

How ought we to compare the presidential apple and the prime ministerial orange? There are a number of possibilities, ranging from an historical account of the origins of the offices to a description of the way each functions today. In a short essay like this, the more direct approach is to begin with the obvious yet fundamental questions of political science: Who qualifies? How long? How chosen? What constitutional powers and limits? To simplify, we will consider these questions under the following headings: selection; term and removal; powers.

1. SELECTION

◆ ◆ ◆

The selection of a president and the selection of a prime minister are as different as night and day. In the case of the American president, the process is nightmarishly complicated and insufferably long. In the case of the Canadian prime minister, it is uncomplicated and short—although occasionally nasty and brutish. There are other differences. The American process is older; it is watched by the world; and it is governed by written rules. The Canadian event is watched only by Canadians, and there are almost no written rules. Let us give seniority its due and begin with the Americans.

The selection of a president and the selection of a prime minister are as different as night and day.

For a non-American, the rules of selection outlined in the constitution seem to belong to another era, as indeed they do, and it is hard to see how they square with what actually transpires. Yet they still provide the constitutional framework of the selection process. The framers of the American constitution were not happy with the idea of the Congress electing the president, since that would make for a weak executive dependent upon the favour of the legislative branch. But they were just as troubled by the idea of direct election by the people, since that would mean another kind of dependence—dependence on the whim of popular opinion. Moreover, they doubted that voters would know enough about the candidates to be able to exercise good judgement in choosing among them. In the end, they hit upon the expedient of the Electoral College.

The Electoral College remains a unique institution, since it has been copied by no other country in the world. It is basically a method of indirect election of the president, and it is state-based. Each state's membership is equal to the total of its share of senators and members of the House of Representatives, which means that currently there are 538 presidential electors who make up the Electoral College. Voters in each state elect their state's Electoral College electors, who in turn meet to elect a president and vice-president. The framers of the constitution thought that voters would choose politically knowledgeable electors who could be counted on to make better choices than the voters themselves. It was a sensible enough scheme in a pre-party era in which the conditions of transportation effectively kept communities isolated from one another. But it went awry with the development of political parties and became less appropriate as the communications infrastructure improved steadily.

The Electoral College ideal of independent electors quickly turned into the reality of partisan electors as political parties soon came to dominate the presidential selection process. Parties simply put up slates of electors in each state in compliance with the terms of the constitution. Once electors became partisans who could be counted on to register their respective parties' choices, their role in the process no longer mattered. What does matter is the outcome of the popular vote in each state, particularly since a winner-take-all system is in effect. The winning presidential candidate in a state—who, along with the vice-presidential candidate, makes up the party's "ticket"—almost always take all of that state's Electoral College votes, which in practice means the votes of the party's slate of electors.[3] To be elected president, the winning candidate needs a simple majority of the Electoral College votes of the states.

While the constitution governs the final race between presidential (and vice-presidential) candidates, it says nothing about how individuals become contenders. Thus presidential hopefuls normally face a two-phase process, the first phase of which is to gain the

nomination of a political party, today the Republican Party or the Democratic Party. As Ross Perot's participation in the 1992 presidential election demonstrates, it is possible to run as an independent—but it is also very difficult to win that way. The race to gain the party's nomination is long, expensive, and arduous. It takes over a year and is marked by a series of electoral contests, state by state. More than two-thirds of the states hold primaries, and the remainder hold caucus conventions.[4] The primaries and the caucus conventions serve two functions, one of which is to choose delegates to the national convention that each party holds in the summer months before the November election. At the national convention, delegates choose the party's presidential and vice-presidential candidates, but since most of them are committed, the outcome in recent years has been predictable. This points to the real function of the primary and caucus contests, which is to test the field of candidates.

At the beginning of the "presidential sweepstakes," the field of candidates tends to be large, since the main criteria for entry are skill at fundraising and overweening ambition, more or less in that order. Money—lots of it—continues to be an absolute *sine qua non*, since American campaigns rely heavily on media advertising. There is matching public financing available to candidates—the government will match individuals' contributions to their campaigns up to a limit of $250. But candidates who choose to accept these public monies must accept, as well, government-imposed spending limits on their campaign expenditures. According to information supplied by the Federal Elections Commission, in 1996 the candidates spent some $237 million during the primary season, whereas in 1992 the figure was $123 million for the same period.[5]

Prospective candidates work hard to win the early primary contests because, as the saying goes, money follows power. The losers continue to drop out, and as the contests draw to a close, a winner emerges. Technically, the winner has accumulated a majority of committed delegates, which is why the choice of the party convention is normally a foregone conclusion. Once the parties have nominated their presidential and vice-presidential candidates at the conventions, the second phase of the campaign opens, and the contenders face one another in the general election. Public financing is available again—a flat amount with no matching requirements—and if accepted spending ceilings apply. In 1992 it was $55.2 million apiece for the Republican candidate, President George Bush, and his Democratic challenger, William

Clinton. Independent candidate Ross Perot declined the aid of public monies, which meant that there was no limit on the amount of money that he could raise and spend. Perot spent a staggering $60 million of his own money on his campaign.[6] In 1996 the major-party candidates, Republican challenger Robert Dole and President Clinton, each received a grant of $61.8 million. Perot, also running again, decided to avail himself of the public monies on offer, which amounted to $29 million, a sum calculated on the basis of the 19 percent of the popular vote that he captured in his 1992 outing. He was also permitted to raise private funds to make up the difference between this figure and $61.8 million.[7] It must be pointed out that the public financing available to the candidates throughout the process makes up only part of the amounts spent directly and indirectly on their campaigns, since the political parties are spending too, as are interest groups of all stripes. It is estimated that in 1996, the campaign spending of the presidential and congressional candidates, the political parties, and interest groups exceeded $2 billion.[8]

It is worth pausing to consider the implications of the primary, which is another unique American institution. Primaries vary in kind from state to state, but essentially they are open electoral contests. They test the candidates' popular appeal among registered voters of the party, not just the party notables. As a result, they encourage "outsiders," candidates whose main assets are financial and organizational, not long years of faithful party service. This effect is heightened by the fact that public financing is targeted toward the candidates themselves, rather than dispensed through the parties. Furthermore, because the primaries are so closely watched, they also favour candidates who play well to the world's most sophisticated media. President Clinton is a good example of a long-shot candidate with the right stuff. At the start of the 1992 presidential sweepstakes, he was a little-known governor of an obscure state (Arkansas), certainly not a Washington insider or a Democrat with national experience and a national profile. But he had a strong organization and demonstrated skill in communicating to voters through the media, and he eventually won enough Democratic primaries to pull ahead of his opponents and secure the party's nomination. As president, of course, he has had to learn on the job, which is another way of saying that the selection process is no guarantee of experience in office.

On the other hand, it is not a bar to experience either. Since the World War II, a number of vice-presidents have made the jump to the office of president, and not simply because presidents have been assassinated or driven out of office. Richard Nixon and George Bush are examples of two-term vice presidents who gained the party's nomination for president and campaigned successfully for the office. President Clinton's vice-president, Albert Gore, currently is regarded as the front-runner for the Democratic party's presidential nomination in 2000.

The fact that the primary system is so wide open to prospective candidates points to a significant difference between the American and Canadian systems. Whatever else it is, the Canadian route to the prime ministership is still very much a party process dominated by party notables and party activists. It is true that in recent years, some political parties have experimented with processes that are designed to broaden the base of the vote to include all members of the party, not just the delegates sitting in convention, and we will consider them below. In the meantime, however, it is instructive to review the convention process that has been used for a long time and may well continue to be used. As in the American case, the nomination phase is capped by a party leadership convention, but en route to it there is nothing like a primary system in operation. Instead, delegate-selection meetings are held in each riding, a riding being the Canadian equivalent of a congressional district. The meetings are open to party members only, and the purpose is to select a slate of delegates to the convention. For the most part these delegates are committed to a particular candidate.

The Canadian route to the prime ministership is still very much a party process dominated by party notables and party activists.

Skirmishes among the candidates and their supporters at the riding meetings are not unknown. Organizers work hard to get their supporters out, some of them newly minted partisans, and unregulated amounts of money are spent to this end. However, in the Canadian case the amounts involved are in the range of thousands of dollars, not millions of dollars. Setting aside transportation and organization costs, there is little to spend money on at the riding meetings, and not much time to spend it in, since this phase of the process is completed within two or three months. Moreover, in addition to riding delegates, there are a significant number of *ex officio* delegates who attend the leadership conventions of the national parties. Generally speaking, they include party officials, all former and serving elected representatives at both levels of government, and senators. The New Democratic Party sets aside a share of delegate seats for union representatives.

The divergence between the Canadian and American systems widens at the convention itself, for often there is nothing predictable about the Canadian event at all, one reason being the significant number of *ex officio* delegates, many of whom are uncommitted. The decision-making rules at the convention require that the candidate with the fewest votes after each ballot be dropped, and balloting continues in this fashion until one of the candidates gains a majority of the votes cast. Finally, and again in contrast to the American system, at the conclusion there are two prizes—the party leadership *and* an obedient party. For the party in power—the governing party—there is an additional prize: the office of prime minister.

This last point was demonstrated by the 1993 leadership convention of the federal Progressive Conservative Party. Prime Minister Brian Mulroney indicated his intention not to run again early in the year, an announcement that immediately set the stage for a convention to choose his successor. In accordance with the unwritten rules of parliamentary government, Governor General Ramon Hnatyshyn, the vice-regal representative of the Queen (the British monarch being the Queen of Canada), appointed the new Conservative leader chosen at the party convention, Kim Campbell, to be his chief privy counsellor, and asked her to form a government, that is, to name a new cabinet. Canadians did not have an opportunity to decide the fate of the new prime minister and her government until she advised the Governor General to adjourn the House of Commons and drop the election writ, the election being set for 25 October 1993. In a remarkable election, Canadian voters issued a "thumbs down" for the governing Conservatives, returning only two of their candidates to the House of Commons, and instead handed the opposition Liberals a majority of the seats in the Commons. Accordingly, their leader, Jean Chrétien, became prime minister.

There have been some innovations in the method used to select party leaders, particularly at the provincial level, and most recently in the contest in 1998 for the leadership of the federal Progressive Conservative Party. Basically, the idea has been to shift from a convention system to a direct-democracy system in which advanced technology is used to give effect to the principle of one party member, one vote. The process begins with the nomination of candidates, who then campaign by signing up as many party members as possible to vote for them on the appointed day. In the time between the nomination deadline and the vote, the party organizes some candidate debates in an effort to enable the candidates to communicate their platforms to party members and to generate some interest in the contest among the media and the public. On the day of the vote, registered party members use state-of-the-art telecommunications to post their vote from their homes, a process that, like the voting process at conventions, continues until one of the candidates gains a majority of the votes cast.[9] It is too early to give authoritative observations on the significance of this type of selection process, but one thing is certain—voting day is a media bust. The old-fashioned convention might be elitist, but it has often been a source of considerable excitement and a wonderful way for the winning candidate to gain national media exposure and recognition among voters. The newer affairs feature rather desultory convention floors and a voting process that seems curiously abstract because it takes place, unseen, in people's homes. It remains to be seen what process the governing federal Liberals will choose when Prime Minister Chrétien decides to step down.

2. TERM AND REMOVAL

◆ ◆ ◆

For Americans, the constitution issues some clear guidelines on the term of office and the removal of a president. Looking to fix the president's term differently from those of members of Congress, the framers decided on four years and unlimited re-eligibility.[10] Subsequently there developed a convention, based on the precedent set by the first holder of office, George Washington, that a president would seek to serve no more than two terms. The precedent held until Franklin Roosevelt won re-election to a third (1940) and then a fourth term (1944), arguing wartime exigencies. A Republican-dominated Congress, unhappy about this string of successes as well as the New Deal policies that the Roosevelt administrations had sponsored, passed a constitutional amendment imposing a two-term limitation. The twenty-second amendment was ratified in 1951.

Removal is a matter of impeachment. To impeach an official means to vote to bring charges against him in what amounts to a political trial. The eighteenth century was the heyday of impeachment trials in England, so it is understandable that the framers would have turned to the practice in their search for a method of early removal from office. It is applicable to the president, vice-president, and civil officers of the United States, including members of the cabinet and federal judges, but not members of the Congress.[11] The grounds are "Treason, Bribery, or other high Crimes and Misdemeanors." Congress does the impeaching. The House of Representatives is empowered to decide whether to proceed against an individual, which involves drawing up and voting on articles of impeachment, or the charges. Should the House vote to impeach, it is responsible for prosecuting the case before the Senate, where a conviction requires a vote of two-thirds of the members present.

The constitutional provisions on impeachment seemingly have an antique ring to them. In Britain the last impeachment was the trial of Warren Hastings, which began in 1787 and ended in 1795, when he was acquitted by the House of Lords. In the case of American presidents, there was only one such proceeding in the nineteenth century, which was triggered when the House of Representatives voted to impeach Andrew Johnson, who had moved from the office of vice-president to president when President Abraham Lincoln was assassinated in 1865. A recalcitrant southerner from the point of view of the northern-dominated "Radical Congress," Johnson escaped an impeachment conviction in the Senate by exactly one vote. In our century, President Richard Nixon, a Republican, skated rather close to an impeachment in the wake of the Watergate scandal, named after the hotel that housed the headquarters of the Democratic National Committee, whose files were rifled during a break-in. The burglars, who were caught, turned out to be linked to the White House and engaged in a variety of illegal actions undertaken to enhance the prospects of the president's re-election in 1972, allegedly with the knowledge of the president himself.[12] The House Judiciary Committee began work on impeachment proceedings, including drawing up articles of impeachment. However, before the articles were put before the House for a vote, President Nixon resigned his office. Thus he was not impeached. President Clinton has not been so fortunate.

President Clinton is the second president in the history of the United States to be impeached by the House of Representatives. In his case, the immediate cause of the impeachment was not rooted in the high politics of public-policy disagreements, or even the low politics of shady campaign tactics, but instead in personal (mis)behaviour involving a relationship with a young woman who was not his wife—Monica Lewinsky, a White House intern. Kenneth Starr, a special prosecutor appointed under the Ethics in Government Act[13] in 1994, was already investigating charges that President Clinton and his wife, Hillary Rodham Clinton, had participated in illegal activities in connection with their partnership in a real estate company while Clinton was governor of Arkansas. Starr turned his attention to the Clinton–Lewinsky relationship on the basis of evidence that had arisen in the course of a sexual harassment action brought against the president by a former Arkansas state employee. The president had denied the relationship during court proceedings. Subsequently, in testimony videotaped for a federal grand jury that Starr convened as part of his investigation, the president admitted to an inappropriate relationship, but not to much else.

In September 1998 Starr presented a massive report of the findings of his investigations to the House of Representatives, which turned the matter over to the House Judiciary Committee. In October the committee decided to open an impeachment inquiry, and following the mid-term congressional elections, in which the Republicans, incidentally, fared poorly, it began hearings, with Kenneth Starr as the first witness. The committee also posed a lengthy series of questions to the president, to which he responded at the end of November in televised testimony. Lawyers for the president were given an opportunity to make his case before the committee, and for that purpose they called witnesses—academics and former senior government officials—who argued that the offences in question were not the crimes against the state that the framers of the constitution regarded as impeachable actions. On the basis of these hearings and the findings in the Starr Report, the House Judiciary Committee, voting on party lines, eventually approved four articles of impeachment and sent them to the full House. In the articles, the president was accused of perjuring himself in legal proceedings, obstructing justice, and abusing the powers of his office. Voting in late December, the House approved only two of the articles, one on perjury and the other on obstruction of justice, and again the voting was largely on party lines. Thus, President Clinton was impeached by the House of Representatives.

Impeachment is no small thing. Indeed, it is a political disaster for a president. The only thing worse is a conviction at the conclusion of the political trial in the

Senate that the impeachment triggers. And it must be stressed that it *is* a political trial, not a judicial one. Moreover, it is a political trial governed by the few rules set out in the constitution and by precedents developed in earlier cases by the Senate itself. Accordingly, the House managers, led by the Republican chair of the House Judiciary Committee, Henry Hyde, argued their case before the Senate, which for the purposes of such a trial is presided over by the Chief Justice of the Supreme Court, in this case, William Rehnquist. The president's lawyers responded by denying the validity of the charges. They also argued again that even if valid, the charges involved behaviour that did not fit the category of impeachable offences. Throughout the proceedings the Senate had to make procedural and other decisions on the fly, as it were, perhaps the most important being the question of witnesses. In the end, the Senate permitted the House managers to call three witnesses, including Monica Lewinsky, but instructed that the testimony be taken in the form of closed-door depositions, thereby avoiding the spectacle of "live" witnesses at the bar of the Senate. The president's lawyers declined to call any witnesses of their own.

As indicated earlier, a two-thirds vote of the Senate is required for an impeachment conviction. It is a stiff requirement, but suitably stiff given the fact that a conviction has the effect of *overturning the result of an election,* since a president who is convicted must resign the office. As the proceedings drew to a close, it was clear that the two-thirds vote was not there. Indeed, there was not even a majority. Ten Republican senators joined the Democratic senators to defeat the perjury charge by 55 to 45, while the vote on the charge of obstruction of justice was 50–50.[14] The outcome reflected the fact that the impeachment proceedings were conducted within the horizon of public opinion, which was on the side of the president throughout. During the months that passed since the first revelations of the Lewinsky–Clinton relationship, a steady and substantial majority held that the president's wrongdoings were insufficient grounds to remove him from office.[15] Thus the institutional verdict to acquit matched the public verdict, which was a fitting democratic conclusion to this highly unusual and unhappy episode in American political life.

There are reasons other than an impeachment conviction for which the office of president might become vacant, and efforts have been made to ensure that the constitution covers them. The Twenty-Fifth Amendment, ratified in 1967, establishes rules governing the succession in the event of presidential resigna-

tion, death, or disability. Essentially the vice-president assumes the office, which is the major purpose of the position of vice-president, and then appoints a new vice-president. The tricky part of the amendment is the determination of presidential disability, particularly if there is disagreement among the principals themselves. The rules are cumbersome and seem to have been neglected altogether in the confusion immediately following the attempted assassination of President Reagan in 1981. Secretary of State Haig thought he was in charge and said so in a White House press conference, a claim dismissed by others in the administration. In the end, with the president recovering nicely in hospital from the gunshot wound, the rules of the Twenty-Fifth were never invoked.

Where the Americans rely on written rules, the Canadians rely largely on unwritten ones, and the result is a startling contrast. What prime ministerial term? The only applicable written rule stipulates that no House of Commons shall continue longer than five years, which fixes the outer boundary of a government's term. But a prime minister can call an election anytime within the five years. At least he can if he is in control. The other side of the equation is the House of Commons, and it is important to remember that in parliamentary systems, a prime minister and his government must have the confidence of the chamber, that is, the support of a majority of the members. If the prime minister's party forms the majority, which is often the case, there is no problem of confidence. The practice of party discipline ensures majority support. However, if his party is in a minority, the prime minister needs the support of members of other parties, which renders his position and that of his government less secure.

Where the Americans rely on written rules, the Canadians rely largely on unwritten ones, and the result is a startling contrast.

On the question of removal, guiding precedents are lacking and legal rules are non-existent. In Canada, no sitting prime minister has been forced openly by his party to resign. It could happen, of course, but probably only if the senior ministers resigned en masse in order to force the issue. Such a circumstance would signal serious internal upheaval within the governing party and might leave the Governor General in the position of having to decide whether to ask the leader of the official opposition party in the House of Commons to form a government or instead to dissolve Parliament and set an election date. Crises of this sort, which are not so difficult to imagine despite never having happened, raise the delicate issue of the "reserve" powers of the Crown, Canada being a constitutional monarchy.[16] However, although it is intriguing, the issue can hardly be settled here, and so it is best to focus on the usual practice that is followed when a prime minister becomes an electoral liability, in the party's eyes if not his own. He decides to leave, possibly after some encouragement by those close to him whom he trusts, and the party gets an opportunity to choose a successor who, it is hoped, will lead the troops to another election victory. This is precisely what happened when Prime Minister Mulroney decided early in 1993 not to lead his party in a third general election. Alternatively, there is the current prime minister, Liberal leader Jean Chrétien, who is well into his second term of office and showing no signs of wanting to relinquish it. Public-opinion polls show reasonable support, and he faces an array of opposition parties, which among them have managed only to carve up the anti-government vote. As long as these conditions prevail, the prime minister can call the tune, and Liberal prime-ministerial hopefuls must bide their time.

3. POWERS

◆ ◆ ◆

As far as powers are concerned, the contrast between the two executives deepens. In the American case, the applicable constitutional provisions are brief but clear. Article II, which is devoted to the office and powers of the president, opens by vesting executive power in him. What this might mean is amplified later in the Article, where the president is named commander-in-chief of the army and navy and of the militia of the constituent states. He is assigned a power to make treaties and to appoint ambassadors, senior officers of government, and Supreme Court judges, but only with the agreement of the Senate. He is empowered to receive ambassadors and officials from other countries.

In addition to these war and foreign policy powers, there are important domestic powers. The president heads the "executive Departments" (the public service) because he is empowered to appoint (with the agreement of the Senate), remove, and supervise senior officials. He appoints federal judges, again with the Senate's agreement. And in the elegant eighteenth-century prose char-

acteristic of the constitution, he is required to "take Care that the Laws be faithfully executed." He also has a power to grant pardons to individuals convicted of offences. On the legislative front, he is assigned the duty of addressing the Congress on the state of the union and recommending to it legislative measures that he finds necessary. Finally, his signature is required for bills to become law, which means that he has a veto power. The Congress can override the veto, but only by a two-thirds vote of each chamber.

A striking feature of the president's executive power is that the Congress manages to share in it. This is evident in the fact that the Senate must approve an array of important presidential nominations. Moreover, in Article I, which deals with the legislative branch, we find that the Congress is assigned the power to declare war and the all-important taxing and spending powers. The upshot is that Congress and the president need to cooperate in some fashion in order to govern.

Few presidents can be said to have dominated Congress, even when their party has possessed a majority of the seats in both houses. And certainly the current Republican-dominated Congress has President Clinton on the run, or at least tied up rather disastrously in impeachment proceedings. Still, most observers agree that in this century there has been a shift from a Congress-centred government to a president-centred government.[17] One reason is that Congress delegated significant legislative powers to the executive branch during the New Deal era of the 1930s, when President Franklin Roosevelt introduced major programmes to counter the effects of the Great Depression. Another is the impressive array of management resources available to the modern president: the White House Staff; the Executive Office of the President, which includes permanent agencies like the National Security Council and the Office of Management and Budget; and the departments of cabinet.

The American cabinet is an interesting institution for students of parliamentary government, since it functions differently from its parliamentary counterpart, despite having the same name. It includes the heads of all the major federal government departments[18] who, as mentioned above, are appointed by the president with the agreement of the Senate. Although the word denotes a collective, in fact the cabinet is not a collective body because it does not make decisions collectively. Indeed, presidents are not much inclined to hold cabinet meetings. Nor is the cabinet responsible to the Congress, although its members individually appear before congressional committees to answer questions about their respective departments, just as they answer to the president. Occasionally presidents arrive in office determined to work a "cabinet government"—President Jimmy Carter is an example— but the effort has always come to nothing. Instead, presidents seem to end up relying on the advice of a small number of individuals, perhaps cabinet secretaries of key departments like the State Department and the Treasury Department, perhaps senior White House staffers.

By contrast, in Canada the cabinet, of which the prime minister is the leading member, is very much a collective. As a result, it is not possible to talk about the "powers of the prime minister" without reviewing cabinet government. Although the constitution vests executive power in the Queen of Canada, and by implication her representative, the Governor General, the "real" executive is the cabinet, on whose advice the Governor General always acts.[19] The cabinet is responsible to the House of Commons for the advice that it tenders to the Governor General. It is important to notice that the advice covers purely executive matters as well as legislative matters. For example, since cabinet members are usually heads of government departments, they oversee the administration of the laws. Thus they exercise purely executive powers. But they also hold seats in the Commons, which means that they participate in the legislative branch as well. Thus they advise the Crown on proposed laws, and shepherd them through the House of Commons. The convention of party discipline, particularly when the cabinet's party is in the majority, permits the cabinet to dominate the legislature.

How does the prime minister fit into this picture? Since the written constitution is silent on the powers of the prime minister—indeed, the position is nowhere named in the document—it is essential to recall the selection process as described above. Asked by the Governor General to form a government because he or she is the leader of the party with the most seats in the House of Commons—not necessarily a majority—the prime minister's first notable power is in evidence in the construction of a cabinet. He not only appoints ministers—almost always from among party colleagues elected to the House of Commons—he can dismiss them at any time and without offering any reasons for doing so. He is in charge of the organization of the cabinet and the agenda of the cabinet. He controls senior civil servant appointments and appointments to central agencies. The latter include the Prime Minister's Office, the counterpart of the White House Staff, and the Privy Council

Office, which assists the cabinet. The prime minister also monopolizes the considerable patronage appointments available to the government, unlike an American president who, as noted earlier, must share so many senior appointments with the Senate.

The timing of elections is an especially important decision that the Canadian prime minister makes, subject to the five-year limitation noted earlier in the essay. Obviously, he will try to time the election to suit his party's prospects and his own. By contrast, an American president has to fight an election at a prescribed time, and it may not suit him at all. Consider the example of President Clinton's predecessor, George Bush. Between September 1990 and March 1991, polls recorded that approval rates of President Bush reached record highs, at one point over 90 percent of those polled. This was the period when the United States prosecuted the Gulf War against Iraq. Any prime minister in a comparable situation would want to take advantage of it by calling an election after an appropriate interval. President Bush had no such option. He watched his popularity sink from an all-time high in March 1992, to a low in November 1992, precisely when he had to fight the election.[20]

CONCLUSION

◆ ◆ ◆

At first glance the American presidency seems to be an immensely powerful office, a perception linked to the country's military and economic strength and fed by the omnipresent American media. On closer examination, it is evident that there are significant constraints on a president's powers. At bottom, these constraints arise out of the fact that the president faces institutional rivals whose political careers are not dependent on his. This is a result of the design of the American system of government, which is often described as one of separate branches (executive, legislative, and judicial) with shared powers.

The framers of the constitution found many ways to separate the branches, some of which we have noted, like term of office and selection. Members of the House of Representatives, senators, and the president have different terms of office, and are elected by different constituencies. For a member of the House it is a congressional district, for a senator it is a state, and for the president, the nation. Even minimum age requirements differ. For a representative it is twenty-five, for a senator it is thirty, and for a president, thirty-five. We might expect that political parties would hook these politicians together, and to some extent they do, but not in the fashion of parliamentary parties. And separateness is the reason. American representatives, senators, and candidates for president do not stand or fall together in electoral terms. Put another way, few presidents have "coat-tails" that congressional candidates can ride to office. Yet they share powers.

The constitutional fact of shared powers means that cooperation between the branches is required in order for the government to function. Power is diffused. The president needs to exercise powers of persuasion, not just over members of the opposing party but sometimes over members of his own. A Canadian prime minister at the head of a majority party faces nothing remotely comparable to this so long as he takes care to keep the caucus united behind him, a task for which he is well equipped in terms of the carrots (a cabinet appointment, a committee chairmanship, a senatorial appointment, or foreign travel on assignment) and the sticks (ultimately a refusal to sign a candidate's nomination papers at the election) at his disposal. Power is centralized, not diffused. So it is easy to see why Woodrow Wilson, looking for ways to enhance the office of president in relation to the Congress, was tempted by the parliamentary model.

How should we judge these two offices? As always, it depends on the standard of judgement. Wilson's standard was executive effectiveness, and in that race the office of prime minister is the clear winner. But if we use a democratic standard that emphasizes openness and consultation, the office of president is the clear winner.

Notes

1. William Howard Taft, *Our Chief Magistrate and His Powers* (New York: Columbia University Press, 1916), 138–45.

2. Woodrow Wilson, "Committee or Cabinet Government?" in Ray Stannard Baker and William E. Dodd, eds., *The Public Papers of Woodrow Wilson: College and State*, Vol. 1 (New York and London: Harper and Brothers, 1925), 128. See also Wilson's famous book, *Congressional Government: A Study in American Politics* (Boston and New York: Houghton Mifflin Company, 1885 and 1913).

3. It is up to the states to decide how their electors are chosen, and the general practice is a state-wide system. In other words, in each state the party chooses a slate of electors who are committed to the party's presidential and vice-presidential candidates. Occasionally states have devised systems allowing for a split vote, which Maine did in 1972 by requiring that electors be chosen by congressional district. That year the Republicans carried the districts and therefore the whole of the state's electoral votes anyway. Electors still meet in their respective state capitals about six weeks after the election to cast their votes formally. At this stage, there is always the possibility of the "faithless" elector. This occurred in the 1976 presidential election, when a Washington state elector pledged to Gerald Ford, the Republican party's candidate for president, but voted instead for Ronald Reagan, whom Ford had defeated at the party's nomination convention.

4. The caucus convention is a traditional method of choosing delegates to a party's national convention. It begins with meetings of party members that are held at the county level to choose delegates to a state convention, who in turn will select delegates to the national convention. The widely watched "Iowa caucuses" that are scheduled early in the primary season are an example of the genre in its initial "county meetings" phase.

5. In 1988, the figure was $210 million, which is almost twice as much as in 1992, although less than in 1996. However, the point is made that in 1988, no incumbents were running for re-election. The information is supplied by the Federal Elections Commission (FEC) on its Web site, 29 January 1999, "Financing the 1996 Presidential Campaign": http://www.fec.gov/pres96/presgen1.htm

6. Susan Welch, John Gruhl, Michael Steinman, and John Comer, *Understanding American Government*, 2nd ed., (Minneapolis/St. Paul: West Publishing Company, 1993), 247.

7. See "General Election Campaigns," www.fec.gov/pres96/presgen1.htm, January 1999, 2, 29.

8. See Theodore J. Lowi and Benjamin Ginsberg, *American Government: Freedom and Power,* 5th ed. (New York and London: W.W. Norton & Company, 1998), 508. Americans try to regulate campaign finances by limiting the amount of money that individuals and organizations can donate to the candidates and the political parties. Only in the case of the presidential election process is there an effort to limit the amount that the candidates and the political parties can spend, and to provide some public funding for the candidates and the parties. There are no spending limits in effect for congressional campaigns. The spending limits in effect for the presidential campaigns seem to be ineffective, since political organizers spend ever-increasing amounts of money at each campaign outing. Loopholes or gaps in the law are well exploited. For example, there is no limit on the amount of money that individuals and organizations can spend independently in support of or in opposition to the candidates and

the political parties, that is, without the knowledge or the approval (or disapproval) of the candidates and the parties. There is also the infamous "soft money" loophole, under which individuals and organizations can donate money to national party committees, which channel the money to state parties that spend it under often lax state laws. Soft-money expenditures are used for activities like voter-registration drives, direct mailings, and polling, and they need not be reported to the Federal Elections Commission. Canadian campaign finance law is completely different, since here the effort is made to limit spending during election campaigns, but not contributions. In other words, while the candidates and the political parties at the federal level and in many of the provinces face stringent expenditure limits, individuals and organizations can donate unlimited amounts of money to them, contributions that must be officially disclosed, of course. It must be noted, however, that spending during the nomination phase of the process is not regulated.

9. See Leonard Preyra, "Changing Conventions: Plebiscitarian Democracy and Party Leadership Selection in Canada" in Hugh G. Thorburn, ed., *Party Politics in Canada*, 7th ed. (Scarborough, Ont.: Prentice Hall, 1996), 213–24.

10. The Congress is the Senate and the House of Representatives. The phrase "member of Congress" is confusing because it might refer to a senator or to a member of the House.

11. The phrase "civil officers" includes federal judges, including judges of the Supreme Court, and cabinet officers. It excludes members of Congress and military and naval officers. Only one Supreme Court justice has been the subject of impeachment proceedings. Samuel Chase was the target of the victorious Jeffersonians in 1894, but they failed to get a conviction against him in the Senate. For a full discussion of impeachment see Raoul Berger, *Impeachment: The Constitutional Problems* (Cambridge: Harvard University Press, 1973).

12. The burglars were referred to as the White House "plumbers" because one of their tasks was to plug the holes through which information about the White House was leaked to the press and members of Congress.

13. It is worth noting that the Ethics in Government Act of 1978 was enacted by Congress in the years following the Watergate scandal in an effort to redress a perceived imbalance between an overpowered executive branch and a weak legislative branch. The Act authorizes the special prosecutor to investigate allegations of wrongdoing by executive branch officials.

When Congress decides to begin an investigation, a panel of federal judges is struck to appoint the prosecutor. The attorney general can remove a prosecutor only for reasons set out in the Act. Barring such a move, the special prosecutor more or less has carte blanche to pursue an investigation until he or she is satisfied that the task is accomplished.

14. "Prosecutors Fail to Get Even Simple Majority in Favour of Removal," *National Post*, 13 February 1999, A1.

15. "The Events, Trials, Politics and Popularity—Measured by Gallup Polls—of the 42nd President of the United States," *National Post*, 19 December 1998, A13.

16. The issue of the Governor General's reserve power is debated occasionally and essentially revolves around the question of whether she or he has any power that can be exercised independently of the advice of ministers. For example, can he or she act independently in the situation described in the text? Or, to use an example commonly found in discussions of the issue, can she or he refuse a prime minister's patently self-serving request for yet another election (the first not having handed him the majority he sought)? Most observers say no, but Canada's late, great constitutional expert, Senator Eugene Forsey, vigorously refuted the "rubber stamp theory of the Crown." See "Crown and Cabinet" in his *Freedom and Order: Collected Essays* (Toronto: McClelland & Stewart, 1974), 21–72. The best recent book on the role of the Crown in Canada's system of government is David Smith's *The Invisible Crown: The First Principle of Canadian Government* (Toronto: University of Toronto Press, 1995). In it Smith observes that "the problem of the reserve power today is not so much how to check the Crown's use of it as how to prevent the prime minister (or premier) from abusing it" (57).

17. Lowi and Ginsberg, 239–71.

18. There are fourteen departments, listed here in order of their establishment: State (1789); Treasury (1789); Defense (1789); Interior (1849); Agriculture (1862); Justice (1870); Commerce (1903); Labor (1913); Health and Human Services (1953); Housing and Urban Development (1965); Transportation (1966); Energy (1977); Education (1979); Veterans Affairs (1989).

19. This statement is subject to the caveat of the reserve powers, discussed earlier.

20. Lowi and Ginsberg, 264–65.

Terms & Concepts

Article II	diffusion of power	impeachment
caucus conventions	Electoral College	initiator
"coat-tails"	ex-officio delegates	primaries
collective responsibility	fixed terms	unwritten rules
confidence	follower	

Questions

1. What are the key differences between the Canadian and American cabinets?

2. Is the American system more "democratic" than the Canadian system?

3. What aspects of the executive–legislative relationship seem to make the office of prime minister more powerful than that of his or her American counterpart?

4. What reforms suggested over the past few years would move Canada far closer to the American model? Are there forces at work that seem to be pushing us toward a more American-style system?

5. How are the powers of each executive linked to the operations of the party system, and how did the Clinton impeachment hearings illustrate this point?

Unit Five   Discussion Questions

1. When we make institutional comparisons across political systems, what issues do we have to be particularly concerned about? Is the "import" or "export" of institutions easy?

2. Are our governments and financial institutions overloaded? If so, what should be done about this?

3. What new demands are being placed on political institutions, and how, to date, have our institutions responded or been altered to cope with such pressures? Has there been significant change?

4. In what ways do changes to our informal institutions, such as the media and political parties, affect and influence the operation of formal bodies, such as Parliament? Give examples.

Annotated Bibliography

Banting, Keith, George Hoberg, and Richard Simeon. *Degrees of Freedom: Canada and the United States in a Changing World.* Montreal: McGill-Queen's University Press, 1997. A collection of research papers examining political institutions in Canada and the United States.

Blakeney, Allan, and Sandford Borins. *Political Management in Canada.* Toronto: University of Toronto Press, 1998. An account of the mechanics of governance and administration from two collaborators who blend wide-ranging political experience and theoretical expertise.

Cook, Curtis, ed. *Constitutional Predicament: Canada After the Referendum of 1992.* Montreal: McGill-Queen's University Press, 1994. A collection of thoughtful essays by prominent Canadian political scientists.

Docherty, David C. *Mr. Smith Goes to Ottawa: Life in the House of Commons.* Vancouver: UBC Press, 1997. This study of Canadian parliamentarians indicates that while MPs with new ideas can have influence, the institutional norms of parliamentary government, including party discipline, are hard to resist.

Erickson, Lynda. "Might More Women Make a Difference? Party and Ideology Among Canada's Parliamentary Candidates," *Canadian Journal of Political Science* 30 (1997), 663–88. Erickson examines whether gender affects policy preferences of Canadian politicians and what influence the gender gap has relative to party position.

Heilbroner, Robert. *Twenty-First Century Capitalism.* Don Mills, Ont.: Anansi, 1992. The futurist-economist considers capitalism in the third millennium.

Huntington, Samuel P. *The Third Wave: Democratization in the Late Twentieth Century.* Norman: University of Oklahoma Press, 1991. A study of the causes and processes of democratization around the world.

Hutchinson, Allan C. *Waiting for Coraf: A Critique of Law and Rights.* Toronto: University of Toronto Press, 1995. Hutchinson offers a left-wing critique of Charter politics, arguing that radical democracy offers better hope for progressive political change.

Lane, Jan-Erik. *Constitutions and Political Theory.* Manchester: Manchester University Press, 1996. An accessible introduction to constitutions in comparative perspective, what they contain, and what purposes they are intended to achieve.

LeDuc, Lawrence, Richard G. Niemi, and Pippa Norris, eds. *Comparing Democracies: Elections and Voting in Global Perspective.* Thousand Oaks, Calif.: Sage, 1996. An indispensable collection of research papers examining all aspects of electoral democracy in dozens of countries.

Lemco, Jonathan. *Turmoil in the Peaceable Kingdom.* Toronto: University of Toronto Press, 1994. Lemco deals with the implications of Quebec sovereignty for Canada and the United States.

Moore, Christopher. *1867: How the Fathers Made a Deal.* Toronto: McClelland & Stewart, 1997. A fresh look at the principles and compromises that went into the Confederation settlement. It shows that some current constitutional and political issues occupied Canadians from the beginning.

Russell, Peter. *Constitutional Odyssey: Can Canadians Be a Sovereign People?* 2nd ed. Toronto: University of Toronto Press, 1993.

Savoie, Donald. *Governing from the Centre: The Concentration of Political Power in Canadian Politics.* Toronto: University of Toronto Press, 1999. Savoie's study of the operation of the federal government indicates that the prime minister and the prime minister's office—not

Cabinet or Parliament—is the heart of political power in Canada.

Smith, David E. *The Invisible Crown: The First Principle of Canadian Government*. Toronto: University of Toronto Press, 1995. A study of the continuing importance of the institution of the Crown (not to be confused with the royal family) for Canadian politics and government.

Ware, Alan. *Political Parties and Party Systems*. Oxford: Oxford University Press, 1996. A comprehensive account of political parties and their institutional settings in developed democracies.

Young, Robert A. *The Breakup of Czechoslovakia*. Kingston, Ont.: Institute of Intergovernmental Relations, 1994. Young explores the conditions necessary for a peaceful breakup.

———. *The Secession of Quebec and the Future of Canada*. Montreal: McGill-Queen's University Press, 1995. The author applies some of the observations gained from his comparative work on secessions to the possibility of Quebec secession.

Unit Six

Regimes and Change

◆ ◆ ◆

Changes in regimes have proceeded throughout the 20th century, but the pace of change in the last decade rivals that of the period following World War I. The collapse of the Soviet Union resulted in changes in the types—and number—of governments, both in its successor states and in its former satellites. A new category of "postcommunist state" is now part of the political vocabulary, denoting those countries struggling with the creation of civil societies, the rule of law, and the decentralization of economic activity after decades of near-totalitarian control. The postcommunist regime may be a transitional category, but for the foreseeable future it will remain useful. As Richard Rose argues in this unit, the transitions experienced by former communist states are unlike the transitions of other regimes.

In a more gradual process, several developing states, many of them in the NIC (newly industrialized countries) category, have also experienced political change. Although the shift has often been to democracy, this trend has been far from universal. The *caudillo* and man-on-horseback authoritarianisms of Latin America seem to have fallen by the wayside, and the authoritarianisms of clientelism and cronyism often found in Asia would also seem to be in retreat. A new postindustrial—and some say benevolent— authoritarianism seems to have developed in Singapore and is watched with interest by democracy's opponents and advocates alike. Islamic states, with Iran providing the most fascinating example,

are wrestling with modernization and the separation of state and religion.

The breakup of the Soviet Empire and globalization have both unleashed formerly dormant forces of nationalism. Many new flagpoles have been added to the United Nations Plaza as a result, and a few more may have to be ordered yet. Nationalism and various forms of globalization in many regions are locked in a mutual but unsteady embrace. Nationalism in Quebec seems to have been boosted by NAFTA, and in Scotland and Catalonia by the European Union. Transnational economic links make distinct regions less dependent on their putative national governments.

Regime change may, of course, allow many skeletons out of the closet. Nationalism is one. Others are the crimes of repression for which authoritarian and totalitarian regimes are well known. These crimes will continue to be uncovered and provide us with sobering studies of international and national reconciliations. Reconciliation is a matter for individual citizens and for whole societies. And it may be as difficult for peoples as for individual persons to practise.

This section reveals the depth of difficulties faced when we attempt to deal with changes going to the roots of political order. Canada's problems, by

Photo courtesy of Canapress.

Scotland is broadly recognized as a distinct society within the U.K. Policy powers have been devolved to the Scottish parliament and the Scottish National Party is a considerable political force.

international standards, are mere child's play, but the 1998 Secession Reference opinion of the Supreme Court of Canada, excerpted in this unit, indicates that even the most civil of societies finds it difficult to come to terms with historical grievances and arrive at amicable constitutional and political settlements.

The "New Authoritarianism" in East Asia

Meredith Woo-Cumings

Editors' Note

Political economy is a branch of political science concerned with the study of the relationship between state, government, and politics on the one hand and economic life and the distribution of economic goods on the other. One aim of political economists is to understand patterns of economic and political development in different societies, which involves examining the relationship among cultural, political, and economic variables.

Political economists have long debated the causes of Western countries' extraordinary economic wealth; some locate it in Western, individualistic religious traditions, whereas others point to Western liberal principles of the rule of law, independent courts, the limited state, and the right to private property. In any event, the conventional wisdom has been that Western-style economic prosperity requires Western-style culture and political institutions.

In the last 30 years, several Asian economic powerhouses have risen to challenge this orthodoxy. South Korea, Japan, Taiwan, Singapore, and, more recently, China, have experienced staggering growth rates, but without replicating Western modes of market-led development. Instead, governments in these countries have been intimately involved in economic coordination, in some cases picking the industries and the firms destined to lead export-driven growth. This involvement has provoked some observers to suggest that there is an Asian model of economic development that varies significantly from Western orthodoxy. In other words, there can be economic modernization that does not follow the same patterns as those in Western countries.

Although one cannot assume that all Asian countries operate in the same way—in fact, there are significant differences in the political economies of Japan, Taiwan, and Singapore—it is not inaccurate to say that the Asian experience suggests that a strong economic state has also meant, relative to the Anglo-American experience, a strong political state. Many Westerners are distinctly uncomfortable with the extent to which some Asian countries' laws constrain private and social life. Subtle (and sometimes overt) control of the political process allows governments to preside over economic development without fear of political instability. Thus, the Asian regimes have been labelled *soft* authoritarian states, meaning they are not as repressive as the earlier, more brutal versions seen in Latin America, but they are every bit as interested in political predictability.

This article pursues these themes. One is left wondering whether the Singapore model of an efficient, meritocratic, but less-than-democratic state open to world trade and foreign investment can be exported to other countries.

In April I was in Tokyo for a conference on regional institutions. At a public forum afterward I gave a brief talk on the Asian Development Bank, but the audience seemed less interested in this low-profile bank based in Manila than they were in the scandal of the month—namely, the imminent caning of Michael Fay in Singapore. Most of the questions I fielded concerned the incident, and like most callers to American radio talk shows, the audience in Tokyo cheerfully supported the Singaporean resolve to cane the American teenager for his alleged vandalism. It seemed the world had suddenly discovered draconian politics in the Shining City in the Pacific, and liked it.

Political discipline and economic performance have always gone hand in hand in East Asia. For most of the past three decades Japan and the "Four Tigers" (South Korea, Taiwan, Hong Kong, and Singapore) experienced rapid economic growth under either one-man or one-party rule, with colonial Hong Kong not even permitted to exercise the right of self-determination.

In the last few years much has changed: the military has turned over the government to civilians in South Korea, and the dominant parties are allowing for greater electoral competition in Taiwan and Singapore—even the redoubtable Liberal Democratic Party in Japan briefly suffered the humiliation of being the opposition. Yet the East Asian nations remain profoundly conservative, distrustful of changes that purport to do away with the political formula that has served them well in the race to get rich. Moreover, the increasingly confident elites of the region do not appreciate hectoring by the United States about the shortcomings of their political system, not to mention chastisement of their venerable culture.

Hence the authorities in Singapore proceeded to give the American youth the promised whipping. Meanwhile the leadership in Beijing, with the connivance of the American business establishment, mocked the China policy of President Bill Clinton's administration, taking the steam out of Secretary of State Warren Christopher's human rights crusade this spring.

TAILORING THE AUTHORITARIANS' NEW CLOTHES

◆ ◆ ◆

In the heyday of Pax Americana, when American parochialism worked as well as universalism and the reigning social science idea was modernization theory, scholars and policymakers believed in the redemption and ultimate democratization of the heathens. Authoritarianism in East Asia was seen as an aberration, soon to be eclipsed by liberalism. Not so today. In the summer 1993 issue of *Foreign Affairs,* Harvard professor Samuel P. Huntington presented a stylized version of the global divide after the cold war that emphasized the remarkable persistence of cultural and civilizational boundaries. He singled out "Confucian civilization," along with Islamic civilization, as the most resistant to the Western perspective and hence a threat in the next phase of global politics. (He threw China and North Korea into the Confucian camp, but not Japan—an interesting departure that would not occur to any East Asian specialist.) Leaders in Beijing could not have been pleased that America's premier strategic thinker portrayed China as the next evil empire. But the argument on civilizational autonomy would be to their liking, if only to justify their human rights record.

The Chinese have not shrunk from proclaiming that Singapore-style authoritarianism as their formula for political and ideological stability while carrying out paramount leader Deng Xiaoping's economic reform program, since Communism would not serve the purpose. Their preferred term is "New Authoritarianism," connoting both continuity and change, the former occurring in the political and the latter in the economic realm—a political means of holding all other things "equal" while pursuing economic growth.

The new authoritarianism presupposes an older version. Latin Americanists equate the old authoritarianism with the caudillo or oligarchic politics characteristic of economies that relied on the export of primary commodities, or with the populist regimes that wanted to foster a self-reliant, indigenous industrial base—the Peronistas being the classic example. The new authoritarianism, according to the Argentine political scientist Guillermo O'Donnell, developed to provide stability in the transition from self-reliance to an export-led system, holding together the rapidly developing, outward-looking, capitalist economy, with transnational actors and technocrats as administrative linchpins.

Deng presumably had in mind a similar combination of continuity and change. Old authoritarianism in China would refer to the inward-looking, state-centric economic development Mao Zedong pursued. New authoritarianism, Chinese style, would correspond to the state-centrism of an outward-looking and coastal-oriented economy, with emphasis on light industrial exports, market reforms, and reliance on the private sector.

Tracing this political trajectory in the newly industrialized economies of East Asia is perhaps problematic, but if the Chinese emulated anything it was not the bureaucratic authoritarianism of the militarists in Latin America but the strong states of South Korea and Taiwan, and the industrial might of Japan. Openly emulating Japan is difficult for anyone to do in postwar Asia, however, which is why the Beijing leadership has made Singapore the shining example of "New Authoritarianism" and its presumed economic payoffs.

If the political economy of the People's Republic before 1978 was based on the predictability of political and economic outcomes (repression combined with state planning), and if Western liberal democracy rests on the predictability of procedures (rule of law, a formal constitution, regular elections, and so on) but not the outcomes of politics and markets, then the new authoritarianism seems to offer a way to have one's cake and eat it too. Political predictability reins in the anarchic behavior of both the market and the polity, through state intervention in the market and political behavior, but it does not become a Stalinist smothering of market and polity. This approach is said to be workable because it appears to have worked already in the "mirror of the future" for China: Japan, Taiwan, Singapore, and South Korea.

The new authoritarianism seems to offer a way to have one's cake and eat it too.

The attractiveness of the newly industrializing country model also comes from a sense that East Asian countries have essentially the same political culture. On this score, a whole phalanx of Western political scientists is available to help Deng out, pulling the concept of "culture" from the dustbin of history and informing the world that the success of East Asian capitalist economies is based on the region's traditional culture. But they introduce a new twist: instead of Weber's notion in *The Religion of China* that Confucian society squashed capitalist activity and possessed no "ethic" conducive to commerce, Confucius is suddenly active, promoting aggressive Confucianism, samurai Confucianism, post-Confucianism, and maybe one day even appearing in an Adam Smith tie.[1]

EXPLANATIONS FOR A MIRACLE

◆ ◆ ◆

So what is this East Asian political economy? For all the sound and fury about the East Asian miracle, there is no comprehensive thesis. At the more coherent end is Chalmers Johnson's 1982 work, *MITI and the Japanese Miracle*, which employs an institutional analysis, including a genealogy of prominent bureaucrats' careers, to unlock the secret of Japanese neomercantilism. Johnson vigorously eschews any cultural argument in this book, since a better one already exists in the political economy of "late" development. The developmental state that emerges from his study, however, is an ideal-type of Japan; the book does not provide a structural understanding of how things came to be the way they are.

Other writers merely assert that the East Asian state guides industrialization, or—in the neoclassical attempt to account for the state—that it pursues "hand-waving" and other such gesticulations to influence market mechanisms. Still less impressive are the cultural determinists mentioned earlier, who find causality emanating from residual categories labeled aggressive Confucianism, or historical evolution in a region assumed to have a common "tradition," or the diffuse concept of "emergence," which harks back to the modernization literature.

It is probably Johnson's ideal-type, however, that comes closest to Beijing's notion of an authoritarian valhalla at the end of the developmental path. *MITI and the Japanese Miracle* does not just explicitly include capitalist nations in East Asia other than Japan, but goes on to assert that what is unique about the East Asian political economy is its combination of "soft authoritarianism" and high-growth economies. This can be termed "plan-rational authoritarianism"—a deeply seductive notion for former Stalinists accustomed to plan-irrational outcomes (as Johnson puts it). In other words, Johnson takes us perilously close to the Dengist notion of new authoritarianism.

The developmental juggernaut in East Asia exhibits the following characteristics, according to analyses by Johnson and others, including my own work:

◆ autonomy of the state
◆ state-exercised financial control over the economy
◆ coordinated or corporatized labor relations (which are or had better be tranquil, even if this is achieved by terrorizing labor)
◆ bureaucratic autonomy (especially for key economic bureaucracies)

- ◆ "administrative guidance," which pushes some industries over others
- ◆ the existence of special private-sector organizations, especially general trading companies and industrial conglomerates favored by government (whether zaibatsu, keiretsu, chaebol, or caifa)
- ◆ a limited role for foreign capital[2]

This is an ideal-type of a statist utopia that would make Adam Smith turn over in his grave: the state wields power over society and the market at home, and holds foreign interests at bay by means of its formidable gatekeeping power. Whether this describes the reality of the East Asian industrial countries is another question entirely, but it is no wonder the Chinese leadership likes a formula that combines political stability, control of the gates against the imperialists, and rapid growth. It is a "Great Leap Forward" without the costs.

There is one problem with this picture, of course: it is a portrait of a capitalist developmental state. It does not matter whether the cat is black or white, Deng once said, so long as it catches mice. But as he himself must have learned during the 1989 Tiananmen revolt, the color of the cat does matter. The aforementioned characteristics of East Asian political economy may not be goods that can be chosen as if off a supermarket shelf. They are closely linked, and together form the gestalt of late capitalist development.

Development in East Asia is a temporal phenomenon, which makes it hard to emulate in different times and other countries. It took place in the context of a kind of benign neglect by a hegemonic power—the United States—which has tolerated neomercantilist practices so long as they occur in the interstices of the world market or when America dominates a broad range of industrial markets. Japan enjoyed such benign neglect from about the turn of the century to the 1930s, and then again from the 1950s to about the mid-1980s. South Korea and Taiwan have had their chance from the 1960s to the 1990s, relying above all else on the vast American market. Seizing the opportunity created by United States sponsorship—in particular the decision to keep the American market open to East Asia's industrial commodities, in spite of increasing protectionist pressures—the capitalist states in East Asia built export powerhouses, while insulating their own markets and prevailing over their own societies. In the prophylactic realm they created, these states produced mechanisms that would serve as substitutes for—in economic historian Alexander Gerschenkron's formulation—"missing" prerequisites for an economic takeoff, the most impor-

tant of these being entrepreneurial segments and domestic capital for industrialization.

THE CONSEQUENCES OF CAPITALISM
◆ ◆ ◆

The example of China immediately makes clear the hazards of pursuing this model in a different time and place. As several analysts have recently pointed out, if the textile sector were not so heavily protected—especially with the quotas and other barriers in the American market—China would quickly become the world's premier textile exporter. In the protectionist 1990s, as opposed to the open 1960s, textiles probably cannot be a "leading sector" for China as they were for South Korea and Taiwan. China cannot rely overwhelmingly on exports, as have other newly industrialized East Asian countries that have—Japan excepted—paltry domestic markets. China's huge domestic market must be able to absorb not only its own manufactures but vast quantities of foreign imports as well, in part to assure continuing access to markets for its exports.

The 1960s and 1970s were also indulgent toward "soft authoritarianism," with much hortatory literature penned by political scientists touting the virtues of putting the military in the saddle of "political development." Paradoxically, China went from "hard" to "soft" authoritarianism just in time to get bashed for bashing Chinese students—a reprehensible and terrible action, but arguably not worse than what happened in South Korea in 1980 or Mexico City in 1968.

The East Asian newly industrialized countries, however, during the earlier periods erected a huge bureaucratic apparatus to incubate a nascent capitalist class. From this logic flowed a set of repressive policies that characterized prewar Japan and postwar South Korea and Taiwan: financial repression by the state, in the form of a non-market-determined, exceedingly low price for capital, so that large sums were transferred from savers to corporate borrowers; labor repression, so that a class could be broken and a new one created; discrimination against foreign commodities to protect domestic capital; and finally, repression of the popular sector, which is to say, democracy.

Thus in South Korea the historical task of the authoritarian state was the creation (not re-creation, as in more advanced capitalist countries) of a capitalist class. This was particularly urgent because Korea inherited a tiny capitalist class on liberation in 1945—

Japanese colonialism having been less interested in incubation than infanticide when faced with independent Korean capitalist development.

If the authoritarian state in South Korea is thus viewed as an entity that has jump-started not just a stagnant economy but an entire capitalist constellation—with the Korean conglomerates, the chaebol groups, the first major fruit—the implications of China's emulation of the South Korean political economy are highly interesting. They imply a transition from communism to capitalism, with the octogenarian Communists who cling to power in Beijing playing midwife to the birth not just of export-led growth but the capitalist classes their dictatorship of the proletariat was designed to quash.

What all this means is that authoritarianism in East Asia is an integral part of development strategy, useful not just for steadying societies in developmental flux but for creating the class that carried all before the modern world—the entrepreneurial class—and in the shifting of resources to that class. Authoritarian politics is not something genetically encoded in Confucian civilization, but a tried-and-true political arrangement in East Asia in its rush to industrialize.

Notes

1. See Kent Calder and Roy Hofheinz, Jr. *The Eastasia Edge* (New York: Basic Books, 1982); Lucian Pye, *Asian Power and Politics* (Cambridge: Harvard University Press, 1982); and Michio Morishima, *Why Has Japan Succeeded?* (New York: Cambridge University Press, 1982).

2. Chalmers Johnson, "Political Institutions and Economic Performance: The Government-Business Relationship in Japan, South Korea, and Taiwan," in Frederic Dexo, ed., *The Political Economy of the New Asian Industrialism* (Ithaca, N.Y.: Cornell University Press, 1987).

Terms & Concepts

caudillo politics
"Confucian civilization"
"Great Leap Forward"
hegemonic power
neomercantilist practices

"new authoritarianism"
oligarchic politics
plan-rational authoritarianism
prophylactic realm
protectionism

Singapore-style authoritarianism
soft authoritarianism
statist utopia

Questions

1. What are the differences between the "old" authoritarianism of Mao's China and the "new" authoritarianism China's leaders now wish to follow?

2. Why would Adam Smith supposedly "turn over in his grave" at the kind of economic regimes that have emerged in East Asia?

3. Can China expect to be able to practise a similar model of development to the one(s) others have been able to use so successfully?

4. What role does this kind of "soft," "new," or "plan-rational" authoritarianism imply for a state's bureaucracy?

Social Values,
Singapore Style

Goh Chok Tong

Editors' Note

In 1965 the young federation of Malaysia fell apart when Singapore was expelled in an extraordinarily rapid breakup. Upon leaving, Singapore faced enormous economic and social problems and "the situation seemed hopeless." Within five years Singapore was experiencing a boom; thirty years later it has become a world economic power. How was this accomplished?

Singapore is a society of amazing contradictions. It is a bastion of capitalism, yet government control is pervasive and citizens are part of an all-encompassing welfare state. There is "virtually no poverty, no homelessness, and no begging."[1] Does the Singapore system have any larger, more global significance, or is it so small and unique, so much the product of the efforts of one remarkable man, Lee Kuan-Yew, that it is destined to be a transitory and very local phenomenon?

Singapore offers a startling contrast to the liberal individualism of the West, as well as to both the corrupt, bureaucratic incompe-

tence of Eastern European communism and the frenzied, fanatical leader-worship we have seen in North Korea and Iran. In this speech, Singaporean Prime Minister Goh Chok Tong launches a sweeping attack on freedom, democracy, and liberalism, North American style. He does not apologize for what others have seen as Singapore's democratic shortcomings, which include the harassment of political opponents through defamation suits for criticizing the government. Instead, he focuses on the need for social equality and what he terms "the rule of law," ideas that he then ties to family values and social discipline and to a willingness to micromanage social and economic life.

Prime Minister Goh's speech raises an issue addressed by other readings in this collection, namely the relationship between universal human rights and cultural diversity. Singapore shrewdly deploys to its advantage arguments often heard in university classrooms: cultures are merely different; no cul-

ture is any better than any other; human rights are Western standards posing as universal ones; and to ask other cultures to respect human rights is to impose a form of Western imperialism. Critics of Singaporean politics have to come to terms with Goh's cultural relativism.

Does Singapore offer a model of "neo-authoritarianism" that might be followed by other countries, especially China? Is the price to be paid not only short-term constraints and a regime of coercion (the caning of foreigners being a notorious example of the latter) but also the long-term absence of a flourishing and sustainable democratic political culture? Or do we take our liberties as universal absolutes and place far too high a value on some of them while ignoring communal and family needs? Prime Minister Goh makes it absolutely clear that there is a price to be paid for everything and that he finds the price paid in the West far too high.

---

1. See Stan Sesser, *The Lands of Charm and Cruelty* (New York: Alfred A. Knopf, 1993). Chapter One contains a readable discussion of what keeps Singapore Inc. so successful and the price paid for that success.

From a transcript reproduced in *Current History* magazine, December 1994 (pp. 417–22).

Four years ago, I could not have predicted that we would do so well. Last year's growth of 9.9 percent was extraordinary. Its momentum has carried over to this year. We grew by 10.5 percent for the first half of this year. Even if the economy slows down in the second half, we should still end the year with more than 9 percent growth, which means civil servants will get a special bonus.

Our strong economic performance translated into higher wages and better schools, housing, and health care. Everyone has benefited, not just big businessmen, the graduates and professionals, but also small businessmen, workers, stall-owners, and taxi drivers.

Singaporeans living in Housing and Development Board [HDB] flats have seen big improvements in their standard of living. They own more luxury items like hi-fi sets, air conditioners, microwave ovens, and personal computers. Thirty-seven thousand HDB homes have maids, including 4,000 three-roomer households. Each year nearly half the HDB families have some members who go abroad for holidays.

Only with a set of political and social values grounded on sound moral principles can a country develop progressively.

Compare yourself with your counterparts in other countries and see how well you have done. If you are a technician or a teacher, compare yourself with technicians or teachers elsewhere. If you are a taxi driver, compare yourself with taxi drivers in Thailand, Taiwan, London, or anywhere else in the world. How many of them own their homes? How many of them own shares? You are ahead of them.

How far ahead? Singaporeans now have one of the highest per capita incomes in the world. The World Bank ranks us eighteenth among 230 countries. We are ahead of Hong Kong and New Zealand, and just behind Australia.

It will not be easy to repeat the 8.1 percent annual growth of the last five years. But I am optimistic.... The region is booming. We are seeing the greatest transformation in human history since the Industrial Revolution of the eighteenth century.

FAMILY AND MORAL VALUES

◆ ◆ ◆

I am reasonably confident that things will go well for the next five to ten years. At home, sound economic policies are in place. In the region things look calm but of course, one can never predict international relations. For success to continue, correct economic policies alone are not enough. Equally important are the noneconomic factors—a sense of community and nationhood, a disciplined and hard-working people, strong moral values, and family ties. The type of society we are determines how we perform. It is not simply materialism and pursuit of individual rewards which drive Singapore forward. More important, it is the sense of idealism and service, born out of a feeling of social solidarity and national identification. Without these crucial factors, we cannot be a happy or dynamic society.

These noneconomic factors translate into the political values the society has. Some of the political values we have are already ingrained and are good for our development. For example, society's rejection of corrupt practices and demand for a clean government and civil service. This is a basic expectation and it is a good political value. The more we enshrine this value, the more we ensure that crooked people do not assume responsible positions to make decisions affecting our lives. Only with a set of political and social values grounded on sound moral principles can a country develop progressively and win the respect of other nations.

Singaporeans have the right values to progress. Our Asian culture puts group interests above those of the individual. We have strong family and extended family ties. The generation of those over 40 has shared the hardships of the 1950s, 1960s, and 1970s caused by communists and communalists, and the uncertainties after separation from Malaysia when our survival was at stake. These experiences have tempered this older generation.

But societies change. They change with affluence, with technology, with politics. Sometimes changes are for the better, but sometimes changes make a society lose its vitality, its solidarity, make a people soft and [lead to] decline.

Singaporeans today enjoy full employment and high economic growth, and low divorce, illegitimacy, and crime rates. You may think decline is unimaginable. But societies can go wrong quickly. The United States and British societies have changed profoundly in the last 30 years. Up to the early 1960s they were disciplined, conservative, with the family very much the pillar of their societies.

Since then, both the United States and Britain have seen a sharp rise in broken families, teenage mothers, illegitimate children, juvenile delinquency, vandalism, and violent crime. In Britain, one in three children is born to an unmarried mother. The same is true in the United States. A recent BBC program asked viewers to choose from a list of finalists the model British family. They chose a pretty divorcée, her boyfriend, and her five-year-old daughter by a previous marriage. The boyfriend did not even live with the divorcée. He came over only on weekends. This "family" won by an over-whelming majority. *The Times* of London, which reported this story, said that the BBC viewers chose them not just because they looked attractive but because they easily identified themselves with them.

This is a profound change in the British family struc-ture. Many families have no man at the head of the household. The woman raises her children without him. The man is, as the *London Sunday Times* puts it, "a nonessential extra."

Some American and British thinkers are deeply con-cerned with this change in the moral fabric. *U.S. News and World Report* recently carried a series of articles entitled "America's New Crusade" on the loss of values in the United States. Twenty-five years ago the United States was swept by the hippie movement, the "flower power" people who smoked pot, promoted free love, believed in "doing their own thing," and opposed the Vietnam War. Today, one article says:

> Many Americans feel mired in a deep cultural recession and are struggling to escape by restoring old-fashioned values to a central place in their lives. It is Woodstock turned on its head 25 years later, a counter-revolution that esteems prayer over pot, self-discipline over self-indulgence, family love over free love.
> — At the core of this pessimism is an increasingly frantic fear among Americans that the country is suffering a moral and spiritual decline. —

It also quoted President Bill Clinton: "Our problems are beyond government's reach. They are rooted in the loss of values."

Singapore society is also changing. Singaporeans are more preoccupied with materialism and individual rewards. Divorce rates are rising slightly. There are some single parents, and some increases in drug addiction and juvenile delinquency.

Recently the *Straits Times* carried an advertisement showing a boy saying: "Come on, Dad. If you can play golf five times a week. I can have Sustagen once a day." I found the language, the way the boy speaks, most objectionable. Why put an American boy's way of speaking to a father into a Singaporean boy's mouth? Do your children really speak to you like that these days? These advertisements will encourage children to be inso-lent to their parents. Many American children call their fathers by their first names, and treat them with casual familiarity. We must not unthinkingly drift into attitudes and manners which undermine the traditional politeness and deference Asian children have for their parents and elders. It will destroy the way our children have grown up, respectful and polite to their elders.

Lesson 1: Do not indulge yourselves and your fam-ily, especially young children and teenagers.

As Singaporeans become more affluent, parents have increasingly indulged their children's whims and fancies. One small sign of this is the growing number of obese children in schools. Between 1980 and 1993, the obesity rate for primary school students went up three-fold. I see this in kindergarten students in Marine Parade. There are more chubby children today than in the 1970s. Affluent parents who had poor childhoods want to spoil their children.

The schools are tackling the problem, but too many parents are not cooperating. They think chubby children are cute, because in the old days only wealthy people had chubby children. They do not know that doctors have found that fat cells in children make for a lifetime of problems.

In America, indulgent upbringing of children has brought sorry consequences. If you slap your child for unruly behavior, you risk going to jail. At a grocery store in the state of Georgia, a 9-year-old boy picked on his sister and was rude to the mother. The mother slapped him. A police officer saw red marks on the boy's face and asked if he had been slapped before. "I get smacked when I am bad," the boy said. The mother was hand-cuffed and hauled to jail for child abuse. She was released on S$33,000 bail. The charges were later dropped, not because the police felt they were wrong, but because they feared they could not prove to the court that the mother's slapping had caused excessive pain to her son.

British justice also seems to have gone liberal and soft. One teenager committed burglary and other offenses. To reform him, the judge sent him on an 80-day holiday to Africa: Egypt, Kenya, Tanzania, Malawi,

Zambia, and Zimbabwe. I suppose this trip was meant to open his eyes to conditions in poorer countries. The safari cost British taxpayers £7,000 (US$16,000). Within a week of returning from this all-expenses-paid trip, the "Safari Boy," as he was dubbed by the press, went on a burglary spree. He was convicted. The sentence? A six-month stay in a young offenders institution, where the treatment is gentle.

The American and British peoples are fed up with rising crime rates, and want to get tough on crime. This is why Michael Fay's vandalism aroused such interest. Opinion polls showed that the American and British public supported the Singapore government's stand on the caning by large margins. But the liberal establishment, especially in the media, campaigned hysterically against the caning, not least because they felt that the ground in their own countries was shifting against them.

In Confucian society, a child who goes wrong knows he has brought shame upon the whole family.

Compare the attitudes of Michael Fay's parents and the parents of Shiu Chi Ho [a youth arrested along with Fay for vandalism]. Fay's parents were outraged instead of being ashamed. They went on radio, television, [and] talk shows, blaming everyone but themselves. Shiu's parents showed pain, avoided publicity, and considered leaving Singapore because of a sense of shame. On the other hand, Michael Fay, back in America, got drunk, and when his father protested, he tackled the father and wrestled him to the ground. I cannot imagine a Chinese son, or any other Asian son, physically tackling his father. But that may happen when sons call their fathers by their first names and treat them as equals. Familiarity can breed contempt.

In Confucian society, a child who goes wrong knows he has brought shame upon the whole family. In America, he may win instant stardom, like Tonya Harding, the ice skater who tried to fix her rival. The difference is stark between what traditional Asians demand of their children and what many Americans now allow theirs to become.

William Bennet, who was President [Ronald] Reagan's secretary of education, wrote an article in the *Asian Wall Street Journal* [March 16, 1993] titled "Quantifying America's Decline." From 1960 to 1990, the United States GDP grew by nearly 300 percent, wel-

fare spending by 600 percent, and the education budget by 225 percent. During the same period, violent crime increased by 560 percent, illegitimate births and divorces by 400 percent. The only thing which went down was student performance: the [average] Scholastic Aptitude Test score dropped by 80 points.

What went wrong? People demand their rights, without balancing them with responsibilities and a sense of social obligation. As Mr. Bennet puts it: "American society now places less value than before on what it owes to others as a matter of moral obligation; less value on sacrifice as a moral good; less value on social conformity and respectability; and less value on correctness and restraint in matters of physical pleasure and sexuality." This is the result of a me-first-and-society-last attitude to life.

Because we uphold tried and tested traditional values and inculcate them in our young, we are a different society. For instance, the *Straits Times* recently printed a letter from Naresh K. Sinha, a visiting professor at Nanyang Technological University from McMaster University in Ontario, Canada. It was an unsolicited compliment to standards of morality in Singapore. Two days before Mr. Sinha was due to leave Singapore, he went to a CPF [Central Provident Fund, a combination of Social Security, Medicare, and Individual Retirement Account for workers in Singapore] branch office to withdraw his Medisave contributions. To his horror, he discovered he had lost his passport. He panicked and made several phone calls. Meanwhile someone had found his passport and handed it to the police. The police called his office to ask him to go down to the police station and claim it. Mr. Sinha wrote:

> There are two amazing facts about this incident. The first is that someone took it immediately to the police station. The second is the efficiency with which the police were able to locate where I worked and inform me that they had my passport.... This could be possible only because of the tough law enforcement in Singapore, coupled with the fact that the political leaders here have promulgated a strict code of ethics and morality.

Mr. Sinha lamented that during the last 33 years of his stay in North America, he had seen a steady decline in moral standards, followed by increasing crime and falling standards in education in both Canada and the United States.

I know Mr. Sinha's experience is just one example and there are others who lose their things and never get them back. But I cited Mr. Sinha's letter not to make us proud of ourselves or, worse still, smug. It is to highlight and hold up as examples the good deeds when they are done. In the same vein, I am pleased to see our newspapers, television, and police give prominence to Singaporeans who do honest deeds. Society must hold up these examples so that we can all emulate them and retain our strict code of ethics and morality.

Lesson 2: Compassion can be misguided.

We deal severely with criminals and antisocial elements. We have a reason: we have seen that in such cases, to be kind to the individual offender is to be cruel to the whole society and to him.

When Michael Fay was caned for vandalism, the United States media accused us of being barbaric. We know from experience that strict punishment deters criminals. In particular, it deters those who have been punished from repeating the offense. One United States television crew who was here covering the Michael Fay case interviewed a man who had been caned for participating in a gang rape. He told them that the caning was so painful that he would never commit the crime again. In other words, the punishment worked...

Welfare is the other area where misguided government compassion has led to disastrous results. The biggest welfare program in America is Aid to Families with Dependent Children [AFDC]. Under this program, women who are poor, unmarried, and have children receive welfare checks so long as they remain single and jobless. Result? The women don't get married and they don't get a job. For if they do, they will lose the benefits. So they produce more illegitimate babies.

Before 1960, one in twenty Americans was born out of wedlock. Now it is one in three. Among black Americans, two out of three births are illegitimate. Having babies without getting married is becoming the way of life for many Americans.

The AFDC program costs the United States taxpayers US$34 billion a year, enough to support our armed forces for 11 years!

Our compassion must never remove that spur that makes people work and pay for themselves. Nor should we undermine self-control, discipline, and responsibility.

Singapore is still a conservative society. Few children are born out of wedlock—one in a hundred.... I was dismayed that Sumiko Tan, a *Straits Times* journalist whom I know to be a serious-minded young lady, could publicly reveal that she had once entertained the thought of having a child out of wedlock. Japan, despite its wealth, is still conservative, with only one child in a

hundred born out of wedlock. Japanese women feel ashamed to have illegitimate children, and quite rightly so.

Lesson 3: Defend and strengthen family values.

One of our shared values is the family as the basic building block of society. Through the family we transmit values, nurture our young, build self-esteem, and provide mutual support. Schools can teach ethics, Confucian studies, or religious knowledge, but school teachers cannot replace parents or grandparents as the principal models for their children.

Many three-generation Singapore families live together. But this is giving way to single nuclear families. Even so, Singaporeans try to buy HDB flats near their parents so grandparents [can] help out with the grandchildren. Married children still have regular dinners or lunches with their parents.

But we have educated all our women and given them a difficult double role as homemaker and co-breadwinner. If the grandparents look after the children, the kids are not at risk. But they will be at risk if left entirely to the maids, or worse, grow up by themselves in front of televisions.

Furthermore, as we go regional, more families will have fathers who are frequently away, and mothers will have to bear the full burden of caring for the children and aged parents. We must help families to stay together, and encourage wives and young children to follow the fathers abroad, to China, Vietnam, India, or Indonesia.

Women's groups have pressed the government to change the Civil Service rule on medical benefits for family members of female officers. The cabinet has discussed this several times and is reluctant to do so. Changing the rule will alter the balance of responsibility between man and woman in the family. Asian society has always held the man responsible for the child he has fathered. He is the primary provider, not his wife. If a woman has a husband, the husband must be responsible for supporting his children, including meeting their medical costs. If she is an unmarried mother, her children will not be entitled to civil service medical benefits. But if she is widowed or her husband is incapacitated and she is the sole breadwinner, an exception is made and the government extends medical benefits to eligible children. If the boyfriend's child, or the woman's husband, can depend on the woman for medical benefits, [the] Singapore man will become a nonessential extra as in Britain.

I am not saying that woman is inferior to man and must play a subservient role. I believe women should have equal opportunities and men should help out at home, looking after babies, cleaning the house, and washing dishes. But we must hold the man responsible for the child he has fathered, otherwise we will change for the worse a very basic sanction of Asian society. We do not accept unmarried single-parent families.

See what has happened in the United States, the UK, and New Zealand in the last 20 years after their governments took the responsibility of looking after unmarried or divorced mothers and their fatherless children. The number of single-mother families skyrocketed out of control.

America, Britain, and several West European governments have taken over the economic and social functions of the family, and so make [the] family unnecessary and superfluous. Marriage to raise a family is now an extra, an optional extra, like optional extras when buying a car. As the pope observed, two lesbians, a dog, and a cat now form a family.

America's and Britain's social troubles, a growing underclass which is violence prone, uneducated, drug-taking, sexually promiscuous, is the direct result of their family units becoming redundant or nonfunctional. Some 20 to 25 percent of American and British children go to school not to study but to fight and make mischief. Teachers cannot control them. In America, many students carry guns to school and have shoot-outs.

The basic error was for governments to believe that they could stand in place of father and even mother. So they have an underclass which grows up unnurtured by mother or father, no family love and support, no role models, no moral instructions. It started with the best of intentions—compassion for the less fortunate. It ended in the dismantling of their family and the creation of troublesome, uncontrollable youngsters who in turn will become parents without forming proper families.

That is why our Small Families Improvement Scheme insists on the family staying intact. When the family breaks up, the payment stops. I know this is harsh, but it is right. We must never end up with our own version of Aid to Families with Dependent Children....

GOVERNMENT'S ROLE TO SUPPORT THE FAMILY

◆ ◆ ◆

We intend to reinforce the strength of the family. The government will channel rights, and benefits and privi-

leges, through the head of the family so that he can enforce the obligations and responsibilities of family members. We will frame legislation and administrative rules towards this objective. We already give tax rebates for support of parents and children. Children are allowed to top up their parents' CPF. Medisave can be used for parents, siblings, and the extended family. We encourage and will give support to such cross-generational transfers in the family and the extended family.

The government supports Walter Woon's Bill on the Maintenance of Parents. Parents who brought up their children should in turn be cared for by them. They should have legal recourse to seek financial support from their children as a last resort.

Edusave accounts are now in the name of students. We will amend the Edusave Act so that the accounts are jointly held by the students and parents, either the father or mother. The children are too young to have their apron strings cut. Joint accounts will underline and reinforce the family bond.

The government will introduce a new CPF housing grant scheme to help children buy HDB flats near their parents. We will remit a grant of $30,000 into the CPF account of households who purchase, as their first HDB flat, a resale flat in the New Town where their parents live. The $30,000 grant is to be used strictly as a capital payment to reduce the loan principal. The same conditions will apply as for first-time buyers of HDB flats—income eligibility, a five-year minimum period of occupation before resale or reapplication for another flat, and a premium or levy to be paid when they next buy a flat from HDB.

HDB currently allows unmarried mothers to buy HDB flats direct as well as on the resale market. One thousand unmarried mothers have done so. This rule implicitly accepts unmarried motherhood as a respectable part of our society. This is wrong. By removing the stigma, we may encourage more women to have children without getting married. After discovering this slip-up in our rules, we have decided no longer to allow unmarried mothers to buy HDB flats direct from the HDB. They have to buy them from the resale market.

LESSONS FROM TAIWAN

◆ ◆ ◆

Now, let me turn to a related subject. The Western media prescribe Western-style democracy and press freedom for all countries, regardless of their different histories, culture, traditions, and social evolution. They praise countries which follow their prescriptions: a free-wheeling democracy designed to produce alternating parties in government, and a press that treats the government party as an overlord to be gunned down and the opposition party as the underdog to root for. So the Western media praise Taiwan and South Korea but criticize Singapore because we do not heed their advice. We are the "authoritarian," "dictatorial" "PAP [People's Action Party] regime," "strait-laced" and "repressive."

The Economist in a recent report on Taiwan said: "The interests of Taiwan are more likely to be served.... by the evolution of a system of pluralism which enables bad governments to be voted out and good governments to be voted in.... Taiwan will then look just like any other independent democratic country, and have the same moral claims on the rest of the free world."

The Economist argued that Taiwan should become more "pluralistic" and "democratic," even though it acknowledged that Taiwan was "a society where votes are bought and free elections have proved to be very expensive." The *Asian Wall Street Journal* reported that the Taiwanese government is cracking down on election vote-buying, and in March indicted "436 politicians, including 341 of 858 councillors voted into office early in the year." In the Taoyuan county assembly, out of 60 councillors, 30 have been convicted of corruption and are appealing, 24 more are on trial, and 2 have been acquitted. That means only 4 out of 60 had no charges against them.

In the same issue of the *Asian Wall Street Journal*, an American academic, James Robinson, noted that in the forthcoming elections for mayor of Taipei, the Kuomintang candidate has "a budget of some US$20 million—in the league of a United States presidential campaign." Yet Robinson goes on to say: "The Taiwanese themselves marvel at how far their country has come in ten years, reforming itself and making its democratic processes durable. This polity has room to become more democratic, especially in privatization of television and radio and reform of campaign financing, but the democratic core is firm."

Now, let me quote the Taiwanese themselves. They have a serious magazine called *Commonwealth*. Ten years ago, [*Commonwealth*] sent a team here to produce a special edition on Singapore. Five years ago, it sent another team, and this year, a third team. Its editors and journalists have studied us closely over a period of 10 years.

The publisher and chief editor, Diane Ying, in her article "What Makes a Beautiful Dream Come True," says:

> In ten years, Singapore has faced the reality coolly and soberly, sparing no effort in addressing its problems....
>
> [On the other hand,] in ten years, loss of social discipline, confusion of values, rampant gangsterism and drug addiction, a crisis of national identity, poor leadership, and weakening of government power and public trust in Taiwan have left Taiwan further and further behind Singapore.
>
> Taiwan has lost its goal and efficiency after lifting martial law: environmental pollution, backwardness of public construction, and worsening social order....
>
> Most Taiwanese share the dream of having a clean environment, gracious living, a safe and stable society, and a clean and efficient government. What they want is social equality and rule of law, *not greater freedom and democracy*.

These are the words from Taiwan's leading intellectual magazine.

The Taiwanese have good reasons for going democratic, American style. Taiwan's leaders know too well that this is a very complex and delicate operation. But to survive they need the support of the United States media and Congress. Moreover, if Taiwan is democratic and China is totalitarian, then the West may support Taiwan if China uses force for reunification.

Western liberals, foreign media, and human rights groups also want Singapore to be like their societies, and some Singaporeans mindlessly dance to their tune. See what happened to President [Mikhail] Gorbachev because he was beguiled by their praise. Deng Xiaoping received their condemnation. But look at China today, and see what has happened to the Soviet Union. It's gone. Imploded! We must think for ourselves and decide what is good for Singapore, what will make Singapore stable and successful. Above all else, stay away from policies which have brought a plague of social and economic problems to the United States and Britain.

Let me end by quoting from a *U.S. News and World Report* editorial, "Where Have Our Values Gone?" which eloquently describes what it calls America's "moral and spiritual decline":

> Social dysfunction haunts the land: crime and drug abuse, the breakup of the family, the slump in acad-

emic performance, the disfigurement of public places by druggies, thugs and exhibitionists.

We certainly seem to have lost the balance between societal rights and individual freedoms. There are daily confrontations with almost everyone in authority:... children against parents, mothers against matrimony, fathers against child support....

Gone are the habits America once admired: industriousness, thrift, self-discipline, commitment.

The combined effect of these sicknesses, rooted in phony doctrines of liberalism, has been to tax the nation's optimism and sap its confidence in the future.

America was not like this in 1966 when I was there as a student. In one generation, it has changed. Is it for the better or for the worse? That's for Americans to decide. But for me, a Singaporean, it is a change I would not want for my children and my grandchildren. Will Singapore, another generation from now, be like the United States today? This is not an idle question.

Popular culture, television, rock music, the buy-now-pay-later advertisements, conspicuous consumption, the desire for more material goods, all combine to erode the traditional virtues of hard work, thrift, personal responsibility, and family togetherness.

Our institutions and basic policies are in place to sustain high economic growth. But if we lose our traditional values, our family strength and our social cohesion, we will lose our vibrancy and decline. This is the intangible factor in the success of East Asian economies, especially the NIEs [Newly Industrialized Economies] and Japan.

We have a built-in set of traditional values that have made our families strong. These values are tried and tested, have held us together, and propelled us forward. We must keep them as the bedrock values of our society for the next century. With no physical resources but with proper values, we have made the grade. To continue to succeed, we have to uphold these values which bond the family and unite our nation.

Terms & Concepts

authoritarianism
Edusave Act
Housing and Development Board
Maintenance of Parents Bill

People's Action Party
pluralism
pragmatic state capitalism
proactive economy

Small Families Improvement Scheme
traditional social values

Questions

1. Singapore is a country of amazing paradoxes. What appear to be the main ones?

2. What price is paid, in democratic terms, by Singapore's citizens? What aspects of Singaporean government control might Westerners accept? What impression do you get of the role played by women?

3. With what Western political ideology do you think the Singaporean political system is most consistent?

4. Would Singapore's neo-authoritarian model work anywhere else? What are the preconditions for its successful implementation?

5. Does this speech make highly selective use of examples to try and prove that North America's "moral and spiritual decline" is tied to liberalism?

Living in an Antimodern Society: How Russians Cope

Richard Rose

Editors' Note

There are few left who believe that by creating the institutional framework for democracy and by privatizing the economy Russia will become a modern democracy like those in Western Europe. Yet that was precisely the hope of many, including officials at the International Monetary Fund (IMF), who have sunk billions into the Russian economy, which seems to have an infinite capacity to absorb the IMF's dollars.

One reason for our naiveté was that the road to modernization of the successor states of the Soviet Union had been uncharted. Most states developed and modernized more or less gradually. Others planned the process by consciously preparing for accelerated change. But in the former Soviet Union, modernization was forced along an entirely new, and ultimately unsuccessful, route. A capitalist economy was not allowed to develop by

Communist leaders, and political development did not include either the rule of law or genuine, participatory democracy. Rose calls the system antimodern because it rejected important aspects of modernization. Now that the command economy has collapsed and the state has lost its coercive power, societies (looking at many of the successor states of the Soviet Union) are left with a few characteristics of modernity—fairly developed technology; well trained, urban, and modern workforces; and huge state bureaucracies—without many of the social, economic, or political underpinnings of modern developed states.

To use Lenin's famous words, "What is to be done?" There are not many prescriptions for successful Russian political and economic transition. Rose suggests, for example, that the state should cut back its obligations to a level it can actually support, relying on the

remarkable resilience of the Russian people and their ability to adjust to dysfunctional political and economic systems.

Russia's troubles cause us to reflect on the nature of economic and political development. Theorists going back to Marx have argued that economic and political modernization proceeds through inexorable historical stages. Early industrial capitalism emerges from feudalism, goes the theory; late-industrial and postindustrial capitalism develop on the heels of early capitalist forms. Stages cannot be skipped. But the examples of Japan and Singapore, among others, suggest that countries can skip stages—or, more accurately, that the stage theory is simply not universally applicable. The question is whether Russia can be a Japan or whether it must endure generations of slower, more painful transition.

◆ ◆ ◆

Modernization can refer to numerous forms of social change; for example, the replacement of religious faith with secular ways of thinking; replacing arbitrary rule with the rule of law; creating a money or an industrial economy; or bringing in democracy. The idea came to the fore in Central and West European societies because modernization occurred there first, long before it began in Russia. Before the Second World War, Europe could be divided along a north–south line between countries that were

From *East European Constitutional Review* 8 (Winter/Spring 1999), pp. 68–75. Reprinted with permission.

modern or modernizing in the social and economic sense, such as Britain, Sweden, Germany, and the Czech lands, and southern European countries, such as Portugal, Greece, and Bulgaria, countries that were pre-modern. The east–west divide was less important, for the Baltic states were more modern than the Iberian peninsula, and France had as many peasants as Hungary. Now we can see that the division between west and east is a successor to the north–south split, a distinction, roughly speaking, between modern and antimodern.

The culturalist approach to Russia argues for continuity between the Russia of today and the premodern folkways of unreformed czarist rule. Communist rule is seen as modifying patterns of behavior from the past century, adapting (and, in part, being transformed by) what was already there. From a cultural perspective, events of the past half-dozen decades, and even more so, of the past half-dozen years, are assumed to make little difference to the relationship that Russians have to life, nature, work, and vodka. While the truth of this culturalist perspective may be exaggerated, its relevance to us is clear: that the distinctly unmodern past of Russia still exists as an unacknowledged legacy, one with which the country must still come to grips.

The Russian Revolution resulted in communist efforts to modernize a society that was premodern by any standard and thus produced a regime radically different from the communist regimes imposed in Central Europe after 1945. A lot was needed to introduce the attributes of a modern society into Russia. The communist goal, in attempting to transform society, was to create a New Soviet Man. The methods used to accomplish this, such as the mobilization of resources by the organizational weapon of the Communist Party, were radically different from the ways in which modernization had occurred in Western Europe. In Russia, the legacy of the modernization process is different, too.

Political parties were created as readily as a budding entrepreneur might print designer T-shirts.

When the Soviet Union collapsed, many fixed on a new goal: the transformation of Russia into a modern society with a market economy and democratic political institutions. The idea of "plugging in" the market assumed that, if only one followed the appropriate macroeconomic policy and enacted the correct institutional structures for enterprise ownership, behavior would automatically be transformed. "Market bolshe-viks" sought to introduce capitalism into a country that had none of the prerequisites of a capitalist economy, as had England, for example, centuries earlier. In Russia, there was privatization without a private sector. Political parties were created as readily as a budding entrepreneur might print designer T-shirts—and with as little concern about what the logo on the T-shirt represented, as long as it caught the consumer's fancy. The voyage on which the Russian Federation was launched may now be seen for what it was, an attempt to "rebuild the ship at sea." And after the financial collapse of August 17, 1998, one might describe what is happening now as an attempt to "relaunch a holed ship that has run aground"—without repairing the hull.

In the excitement of past and present upheavals, there was much talk about Russia being in transition. Unfortunately, less attention has been given to its starting point before "transition" began. In parts of the former Soviet Union that have been going nowhere or altering only very slowly, the past remains important today, even though the Russian government is committed rhetorically to change. The governors of the Russian Federation cannot "go home" to the Soviet Union, anymore than they (or their successors) can turn the clock back to the era of Stalinist purges or Russia before the introduction of electricity. But the actions of the new government show that "the idea of Europe" is, once more, a minority taste in Russian politics, as it has been in turbulent times past.[1] Since Europe symbolizes a "modern" form of governance and economy, we ought to consider, then, to what extent Russians continue to live in an antimodern society.

RECOGNIZING AN ANTIMODERN SOCIETY
◆ ◆ ◆

The creation of the Soviet bloc split Europe between those countries that were modern in the Weberian sense and those that were modern in the Marxist-Leninist sense. The orthodox communist position was that late-capitalist industrial societies were not modern but decadent, and the more apparently developed they were, the sooner they were doomed to collapse. Marxism-Leninism was trumpeted as the truly modern doctrine, and the Soviet Union as its prime exponent. Even though the communist system had mass education, big cities, and jet airplanes, it was different because it created a nonmarket economy without private property and a party-state that administered affairs without regard for the principles of the *Rechtsstaat*.

A modern society is a knowledge-based society, rich in information. A modern society is transparent; everyone can observe relations of cause and effect and make rational calculations about how to vote or spend money. A democratic government creates, as it were, a cybernetic system with continuing feedback between governors and governed. For all the prattle about cybernetics in the Soviet era, the communist system was opaque. Rulers ignored or repressed feedback. Ideology provided an a priori framework for predicting, prescribing, and interpreting events. To point to evidence contradicting Marxist-Leninist assumptions was to risk being branded an enemy of the state. Neither votes nor prices were used to determine what people wanted. Instead, party leaders and party committees decided what the people were supposed to want, and elections offering no choice meant the party-state did not have to worry about the expression of popular dissatisfaction at the ballot box. A 99.9 percent vote for the party was intended to remind the electorate that they could enjoy only what Václav Havel has called "the power of the powerless."

Communist societies shared two attributes with modern Western societies: they were complex and, up to a point, effective. A communist society was complex, because of the conflicting interests and ambitions within and between communist institutions, and because of the desire of the party-state to centralize control over the political, economic, and social institutions and their respective values. A communist system could also be effective, as was demonstrated by the capacity of the Soviet Union to put a man into space, to maintain an elaborate system of internal surveillance for the repression of political dissidents, or to manage ruthless border controls over thousands of kilometers.

To the casual observer of material phenomena, the subjects of communist systems appeared to be living in modern, if not yet "postmodern," societies. There were increasing numbers of cars on the streets, television sets in rural cottages as well as in high-rise flats, and more people could jet to the seaside for holidays—albeit in enterprise-controlled resorts within the Soviet bloc. Official statistics appeared to confirm modernization, for there was—in theory—a high level of investment, continuing economic growth, full employment, and little or no inflation. But the presence of some elements of a modern society—whether refrigerators or space satellites—does not mean that all materially prosperous societies are the same, much less that they are modern.

In Weberian terms, Russia was not just different, in some small ways, from conventional modern societies; it was antimodern (Table 24.1). The rule of law had limited practical utility; in a system of socialist legality the demands of the party were of overriding importance. And given the absence of the rule of law, subjects could not rely on bureaucrats to deliver services to which they were, from another perspective, legally entitled. Without any sort of predictability, people who wanted things from the state either had to accept, fatalistically, what officials did or had to turn to an "economy of favors" involving *blat*.[2] Money was neither necessary nor sufficient to secure valued goods, since bureaucratic commands allocated resources to enterprises and administered wages in what Janos Kornai characterized as a command economy. In extreme cases, factories subtracted value instead of adding it, as their output could be worth less than the resources used to produce the goods. The unrealistic targets of five-year plans encouraged factory managers routinely to engage in deceit and exaggeration to give the appearance that everything was working all right—on paper.

In a developing country that is modernizing, by definition, a significant portion of the population lives outside the modern economy. Some lead the marginal existence of a first-generation urban underclass or follow a traditional lifestyle in rural areas. The movement of rural offspring to join the urban underclass is a

Table 24.1   Comparing Modern and Antimodern Societies

	Modern	*Antimodern*
Operation	Complex	Complex
Signals	Prices and laws	Rules, politics, bribes, and personal contacts
Openness	Transparent	Translucent, opaque
Lawful	Yes	Rigidity modified by waivers
Cause and Effect	Calculable	Uncertain
Output	Efficient	Inefficient
Effective	Yes	Irregular

collective step leading to a modern society. This is so because a developing country also has a modern sector. Modernization is a process of shifting people between sectors, increasing the proportion living in the modern sector while reducing the number of those living in the traditional rural areas virtually to nil.

The Soviet system was antimodern because the institutions it created to build its new civilization were intended as an alternative rather than as a prelude to "bourgeois" norms and lifestyles. To get things done required much more time and energy than in Weber's paradigm of a modern bureaucracy working with the predictability of a vending machine. The communist system was a perverse example of Weber's dictum that "power is in the administration of everyday things." The power of the communist party-state was evident in the stress created by the maladministration of everyday things.[3]

The power of the communist party-state was evident in the stress created by the maladministration of everyday things.

The legacy of the Soviet era is that of social failure—and the consequences remain palpably evident. The institutions of a market economy have not yet been created by a few "big bang" actions, such as the overnight creation of a stock market. Ironically, the supposedly smart institutions of Western societies, such as commercial banks and the IMF, have paid the biggest dollar price to learn this obvious lesson—of Russia's social failure—from the financial collapse of last August. Ordinary Russians did not need to lose dollars to learn this lesson, nor were they well enough off to have savings in foreign currencies. As John Earle of the Stockholm Institute of Transition Economies has pointed out, long before the Russian Federation defaulted on Western bankers it defaulted on its own citizens, failing to pay the wages and social benefits to which they were entitled.

GETTING THINGS DONE IN AN ANTIMODERN SOCIETY

◆ ◆ ◆

Even in an antimodern society there is no escape from organizations. The modern element of such a society is

represented by the fact that most households depend on large organizations for education, health care, housing, and employment. The "anti" element arises because these organizations do not work as they are supposed to. What do Russians do?

To determine the degree to which formal changes in society have made a difference in the way Russians get things done—and thus, the extent to which Russia is or is not an antimodern society—the seventh New Russia Barometer survey of the Centre for the Study of Public Policy, in 1998, collected data about how Russians deal with organizations that would be crucial to both large, complex, modern *and* antimodern societies. Unlike political-culture surveys, the Barometer study focused on behavior rather than attitudes and opinions. The behavior it emphasized is that required to get the goods and services individuals want, rather than voting behavior, which can produce a Duma or president that few people want. The survey was part of the World Bank's "Global Initiative on Defining, Monitoring, and Measuring Social Capital," supported by overseas-development funding from the government of Denmark. (The author is solely responsible for the survey and for interpretation.[4])

Since institutions differ in how they work—doctors are much more personal than bureaucratic municipal landlords—the questionnaire covered various situations affecting a majority of households. The questionnaire thus treated relations between Russians and organizations as variable, rather than assuming that everything works in Russia as in a modern society or, the opposite error, that nobody knows how to get anything done. Second, the questionnaire dealt with situations in which various formal organizations are the major sources of welfare and income, such as hospital treatment, education, and employment. To focus on the delivery of goods and services that concern ordinary people yields more concrete evidence than questions about trust in distant national institutions, for which the television and press are the primary media of information.[5] Third, individuals were asked what they had done or would advise friends to do to obtain from organizations such things as admission to a university or a job.

The timing of the survey was particularly propitious: the Russian Centre for Public Opinion Research (VCIOM) undertook the actual fieldwork—asking the questions—between March 6 and April 13, 1998. The date was far enough distant from the old regime for evidence of change to have become evident. A total of 1,904 adult Russians were interviewed face-to-face in a multistage, randomly stratified sample covering the whole of the Russian Federation, urban and rural, with 191 widely dispersed primary sampling units. A big, nationwide sample avoids the trap of assuming that "everyone's doing it," however "it" is defined. This is a big limitation of generalizations made by Westerners living in Moscow or anthropologists in rural villages.

ALTERNATIVE TACTICS FOR GETTING THINGS DONE

◆ ◆ ◆

In a modern society, people do not require a repertoire of tactics for dealing with formal organizations. Bureaucratic organizations predictably deliver goods and services to individuals as citizens and customers. In a modern society, a person claims a good or service, to which he or she is entitled by law or payment, and it is delivered, fairly and efficiently, by employees of a large, impersonal organization. In such a society no one thinks it unusual that electricity is supplied without interruption, and bills for payment are regularly received; an airline ticket booked by phone is ready to be picked up at the airport; and wages and pensions are routinely paid each month. If people use informal networks, it is to supplement or complement what is provided routinely by organizations; it is not a vote of no-confidence in the institutions of the state and market.

But what if modern organizations do not work in this way? Given the central importance of money, in a modern society, the inability of organizations to pay wages or pensions is a good indicator of the extent of organizational failure. The New Russia Barometer found that, in the early spring of 1998, three out of five Russians did not routinely receive the wages or pensions to which they were entitled; the proportion had undoubtedly increased since the financial collapse. Moreover, the state itself is more likely to pay wages late to employees of state enterprises, such as those in the military, teachers, and health workers, than the private sector is likely to pay its employees late. Pensions, a state responsibility that is easy to routinize in a modern society, are even more likely to be paid late than wages.

Confronted with organizational failure, individuals have a choice about how to respond. Informal networks can substitute for the failure of modern bureaucratic organizations. Or, for instance, if a landlord will not repair a broken window, you can fix it yourself—or freeze in the winter. In many developing countries, people who have grown up in a traditionally clientelistic culture can try the "premodern" approach of personalizing relations with impersonal bureaucrats. (Similarly, a generation ago, in rural Ireland old people thought they needed a member of parliament to "speak for them" in order to receive a pension to which they were entitled by law.)

Another alternative is the antimodern perversion of the rule of law, using connections or bribery to get bureaucrats to violate rules. In anticipation of frustration, people fatalistically assume that nothing can be done to make an unpredictable organization deliver as it should.

In each module of the questionnaire, respondents were asked what they had done or would advise a friend to do to get something done. For each situation, a multiplicity of tactics was offered in response. A majority of Russians assume that the organizations on which they depend for goods and services do not work with mechanistic predictability (Table 24.2). For example, only 35 percent think the social-security office will pay claimants the money to which they are entitled, and less than half think the police will protect their house from burglary. The percentage ready to rely on other types of organizations is lower still.

Whereas in a modern society, the market offers those with sufficient income an alternative to the failure of government organizations, in Russia choosing what you want from competing shops is a novelty. The great majority have sufficient money to pick and choose their food in the marketplace, and stores now regularly have stocks of food to sell. The 1998 New Russia Barometer survey also found that 86 percent of the households studied had a color-television set and 37 percent a video-cassette recorder, both goods that can only be bought with "hard" currencies. However, when more costly items are involved, the proportion able to turn to the market declines. Fewer than one in three ever expect to have sufficient financial resources to consider buying a house, and only one in six reckons they could borrow a week's wages from a bank (Table 24.2 [1]).

Individuals can end their reliance on organizations by substituting a nonmonetized production organized into a traditional informal network (Table 24.2 [2]). Past experience with food shortages and a desire to save money results in four-fifths of Russian households, including a large majority of city dwellers, continuing to grow some food for themselves. Informal networks are the most practical form of social security, too. While only one out of four Russians has any savings, and a big majority of the unemployed do not receive any state unemployment benefit, most can turn to family and friends for money if in need. Two-thirds report they could borrow a week's wage or pension payment from a friend or relative. In a developing society, such informal networks can be described as premodern, but in the Russian context they are evidence of "de-modernization"—reflecting the failure of large bureaucratic organizations to provide the social protection to which people are entitled.

When a formal organization does not deliver and the market or an informal network cannot be substituted, an individual can try to "de-bureaucratize," that is, find a way to make an organization produce goods and services. The relationship can be personalized (Table 24.2 [3]) by begging or cajoling officials to provide what is wanted or pestering officials until success is achieved. This is a stressful attempt to compensate for the inefficiencies of bureaucratic organizations by taking a step backward into a clientelistic relationship.

Organizations in Soviet times encouraged Russians to adopt antimodern tactics.

Organizations in Soviet times encouraged Russians to adopt antimodern tactics (Table 24.2 [4]); 68 percent of those interviewed said that to get anything done by a public agency, in those days, you had to know party members, and it was even more widely assumed that you had to have connections through friends, friends of friends, or even friends of friends of friends. The Russian concept of *blat* often refers to using connections to misallocate benefits by "bending" or breaking rules on behalf of people in a "circle" *(svoim)*. Connections continue to be seen as significant; for example, close to one-quarter of the respondents endorse connections as the way to get a government-subsidized flat.

Table 24.2   Alternative Tactics for Getting Things Done

	Percent of respondents invoking tactic
Getting modern organizations to work (1)	
Public sector allocates services by law:	
Requesting police to help protect house from burglary	43%
Asking social-security office to pay entitlement when claimed	35%
Using market to allocate services to paying customers:	
Buy a flat if it is needed	30%
Can borrow a week's wage from a bank	16%
Informal alternatives (2)	
Nonmonetized production:	
Growing food	81%
Can borrow a week's wage from a friend	66%
Personalize (3)	
Beg or cajole officials controlling allocation:	
Keep demanding action at a social-security office to get paid	32%
Beg officials to admit person to hospital	22%
Antimodern (4)	
Reallocate in contravention of the rules:	
Use connections to obtain a subsidized flat	24%
Pay cash to doctor on the side	23%
Passive, socially excluded (5)	
Nothing I can do to:	
Get into hospital quickly	16%
Get pension paid on time (pensioners only)	24%

Source: New Russia Barometer Survey VII (1998). Fieldwork by VCIOM; number of respondents: 1,904

The introduction of the market has increased opportunities for overt corruption, that is, paying cash to get officials to break the rules for personal benefit. Whereas one's party connections were most important in Soviet days, the average Russian thinks that dollars or deutsche marks now speak more loudly than a party card.

Taxation illustrates the way in which different defects of the Russian system combine to deprive the state of revenue that would be collected if Russia were modern. There are estimates that more than half the anticipated state revenue is not collected—and some of what is collected is "levied" rather than paid by modern means. Among employed persons, only 41 percent say that taxes are deducted when their employer pays wages; 5 percent that no taxes are deducted; and a little over half (54 percent) do not know whether taxes are deducted. These replies leave open the question of what proportion of taxes deducted by employers are actually paid into the public purse, which institution controls the money, and what is done with it.

A majority of Russians say that there is no need to pay taxes if you do not want to do so, for the government will never find out, and three-quarters believe that a cash payment to a tax official will enable a person to evade payment of the taxes claimed. Altogether, five-sixths think taxes can be evaded; they differ only in whether the best tactic is not to pay at all or that a "tip" to a tax official is needed to avoid legal problems.

The resources that individuals need to get things done are not equally distributed throughout a society. Networks are exclusive as well as inclusive; social exclusion (Table 24.2 [5]) describes the position of individuals lacking networks to secure everyday goods and services. In an antimodern society, vulnerability is greatest when the only network that an individual has is represented by public-sector organizations. When these fail, the vulnerable are effectively excluded from social services by an antimodern state.

To measure exclusion, for each situation the New Russia Barometer survey offered the statement: "nothing can be done." A great majority of Russians are not socially excluded, that is, unable to draw on some form of social capital when problems arise in everyday situations (Fig. 24.1). Depending on the situation, those able to rely on a network to get things done range from 60 percent to more than 90 percent. Similarly, when Russians are asked how much control they have over their lives, on a scale with 1 representing "no control" and 10 "a great deal" the mean reply is almost exactly in the middle, 5.2. Only 7 percent place themselves at the bottom, feeling that they are without any control over their own lives.

Figure 24.1   Measures of Social Exclusion If Organization Fails

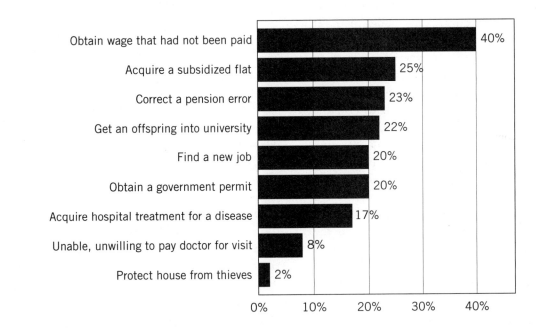

Source: New Russia Barometer Survey VII (1998). Fieldword by VCIOM; number of respondents: 1,904.

Although only a minority are prepared to rely on the police, hardly any Russian thinks nothing can be done to protect his or her home from crime. People invoke alternatives, such as making sure there is always someone in the house, keeping a dog, or even getting a gun. The situation most likely to produce a sense of helplessness is the nonpayment of wages, because enterprises are so short of money that cajoling or bribing is of no avail.

While it is common to talk about categories of people as socially excluded (pensioners, unemployed persons, or women with children), social exclusion tends to be specific to a particular situation. Most Russians have a variety of networks on which they can rely. While very few have the social as well as economic resources to cope with all contingencies, relatively few are consistently without any network at all to fall back on. Across ten different situations, only 18 percent said that "nothing can be done" in a majority of situations, and only 4 percent feel excluded in eight situations out of ten.

IMPLICATIONS

◆ ◆ ◆

For Russians, organizational failure is not a sign that nothing works—but only that organizations do not work as in a modern society. When a formal organization fails to operate routinely, individuals have recourse to a variety of social-capital networks to get things done—informal do-it-yourself cooperation, personal cajoling of bureaucrats, the antimodern bending or breaking of rules, the market, or even—under the right circumstances—the state delivering goods and services.

How common is the Russian experience? Tianjian Shi's ironically titled *Political Participation in Beijing* (Harvard University Press, 1997) describes phenomena familiar to observers of Russia. Shi documents how the Chinese use cronyism, resistance, boycotts, adversarial activities, and personal appeals as standard operating procedures to spur officials to act. Chinese behavior is not a reflection of "Asian" values, for empirical studies in the Republic of Korea show that, even though Korea has its share of elite corruption, there is much less corruption at the grass roots of Korean society, and the market is an effective modern alternative to state failure. In the Czech Republic, where the rule of law existed prior to the arrival of Soviet troops, and there was strong resistance to communist rule, the public today is much less inclined to turn to antimodern techniques to get things done.[6]

Organizational failure in Russia reflects the combination of too many regulations and too little adherence to bureaucratic norms. A surfeit of rules imposes delays and unresponsiveness, as different public agencies must be consulted. Individuals are forced to invest an unreasonable amount of time in pleading with and pushing bureaucrats to compensate for organizational inefficiencies. If bureaucrats offer to waive obstructive regulations in return for a side payment, this delivers a service—but in an antimodern way. The result is popular ambivalence about the rule of law. Among Russians, 71 percent hold that the national government is a long way from the idea of a law-governed state (*pravovoye gosudarstvo*). But not everyone would welcome Russia's becoming such a state, since 62 percent believe the laws are often very hard on ordinary people. In such circumstances, law enforcement may not be desirable.[7] Among Russians, 73 percent endorse the belief that harsh Russian laws are softened by their nonenforcement.

The classic electoral solution for the failure of government to deliver as it should is for the voters to throw the rascals out, giving the opposition an opportunity to show what it can do. But what is to be done if a sequence of elections simply results in the "circulation of rascals," as one unpopular president or Duma representative is replaced by another who appears to be no better? At this point, a society has reached the limit of what elections can achieve.

Among Russians, 73 percent endorse the belief that harsh Russian laws are softened by their nonenforcement.

Where antimodern practices are rampant—and that is the case in most of the successor states of the former Soviet Union—the result is a crisis of governability, such that the state is too weak both to collect taxes and to control its own expenditures. It delivers too much money to the few, who are inside an elite *svoim*, and too little to the great majority. Recognizing this, there are those who argue for strengthening the capacity of the state to promote both welfare rights and classical liberal rights and are optimistic that this can be done. But one does not have to be Riga-born, as was Isaiah Berlin, to know that the paths that may be followed can involve great sacrifices (or a choice between sacrifices) in whichever direction one goes.

Russians, by contrast to the average Western adviser, understand how to survive by working with the system as it actually is. While people might desire better social services from the state, there is a high degree of skepticism about the capacity of the state to deliver the services available in a modern European society. For the time being, at least, the position appears to be a relatively stable, low-level equilibrium trap in which people cope with a system that is inefficient and corrupt. While one can argue that there is a better way, many Russians have also known worse.

Given a state in which bureaucrats, at best, break laws to help people and, at worst, break laws to popular disadvantage, what is to be done? Insofar as the selective enforcement in laws is a major problem in an antimodern society, a logical prescription would be to deregulate, repealing laws that create opportunities for extracting bribes and profiting from connections. A second policy would be to repeal taxes that otherwise can be evaded easily and to concentrate on those that can be collected, for example, on oil exports or on electricity supply. To the extent that public budgets would then have to be reduced, because of less expected revenue (though actual revenue could remain constant, given the current level of tax evasion), cuts in spending should be targeted at nondelivered services and unpaid public employees. While this will reduce the services that individuals and households may rely on, the government could give vouchers so that those affected could make their own choices.

In the abstract, the above prescriptions would reduce the theoretical capacity of the government to behave like a modern Scandinavian or German social-welfare state. In reality, such measures would move in the direction of matching the commitments of the Russian state to its actual capacity. Cutting back national public services, an acknowledgement of government failure, might even stimulate the demand from ordinary Russians for government by the rule of law rather than forcing people to bend or break laws that have ceased to be relevant. This demand by the people is a precondition for the state's having the capacity to deliver, fairly and effectively, the benefits of a modern nation, whether it is a nightwatchman Hayekian state, which concentrates on the law of liberty and the market, or a social-democratic state, delivering a large number of welfare benefits—a goal that is conceivable but remote from the Russia of today.

Notes

1. Iver B. Neumann, *Russia and the Idea of Europe: A Study in Identity and International Relations* (London, 1996).
2. See Alena V. Ledeneva, *Russia's Economy of Favours: Blat, Networking and Informal Exchange* (Cambridge, 1998).
3. Max Weber, *Wirtschaft und Gesellschaft,* 5th ed. (Tübingen, 1972), p. 126.
4. For full details of the survey sample, questionnaire, and answers, see Richard Rose, *Getting Things Done with Social Capital: New Russia Barometer VII,* University of Strathclyde Studies in Public Policy, No. 303 (Glasgow, 1998). On the Internet, see <http://www.cspp.strath.ac.uk>.
5. For details about how Russians evaluate the institutions of society, such as political parties, the police, and private enterprise, see William Mishler and Richard Rose, *Trust in Untrustworthy Institutions,* University of Strathclyde Studies in Public Policy, No. 310 (Glasgow, 1998).
6. See Richard Rose and Doh Chull Shin, *Democratization Backwards: The Problem of Third Wave Democracies,* University of Strathclyde Studies in Public Policy, No. 314 (Glasgow, 1999).
7. Andras Sajo, "Corruption, Clientelism, and the Future of the Constitutional State in Eastern Europe," *East European Constitutional Review,* 7, no. 2 (spring 1998), pp. 37–46.

Terms & Concepts

antimodern states

blat

clientelism

cronyism

de-bureaucratization

de-modernization

Duma

Hayekian state

market bolsheviks

modern states

premodern states

Rechtsstaat

svoim

Questions

1. Why have the Czech Republic, Poland, and Hungary adjusted so much more smoothly to postcommunism than Russia?

2. What makes Russia antimodern?

3. China took a different course than the Soviet Union by concentrating on economic modernization while retaining the coercive state. Would this model have worked better in Russia?

4. Following the previous question, why do you think the Chinese model was not used in Russia?

5. Can a democracy function in as unstable an environment as Russia's?

Reference Re: Secession of Quebec

August 20, 1998

Present: Lamer C.J. and L'Heureux-Dubé, Gonthier, Cory, McLachlin, Iacobucci, Major, Bastarache and Binnie JJ.

Editors' Note

Provincial and federal governments in Canada are able to submit general, hypothetical questions, called references, to high courts and have those courts respond with advisory opinions that are technically non-binding but carry substantial political and legal weight. Courts can refuse to answer reference questions if they think they contain political content that may compromise the judicial function. Judicial sensitivity to the political nature of references is well founded. Politicians have found the reference procedure a convenient way to escape direct accountability for making a tough political decision. In addition, they can use the reference to add legal and constitutional weight to a political position they already hold. References always contain the potential to abuse the functions of high courts.

If governments can force the hand of the judiciary, it is also true that citizens can force the hand of governments. After the election of the Parti Québécois in 1994, led by Jacques Parizeau, the battle lines over Quebec secession were drawn. Parizeau committed the province to secede unilaterally from Canada should a Quebec referendum on the question result in a majority "Yes" vote. The federal government was hesitant to question the legality of such a move and did not press the point in its public reactions to the separatists. Instead, it followed a "Plan A" approach, stressing the benefits of Confederation to Quebec.

A private citizen and former Quebec separatist, Guy Bertrand, forced the issue by initiating a legal action in a Quebec court in August 1995 to stop the Quebec government from holding a referendum that could lead to a unilateral declaration of independence and breach the protection many Quebeckers find in the Canadian Constitution. The court was put into an untenable political and legal position. It agreed with Bertrand in principle, but it made no order to halt the referendum.

The Quebec government lost the October 1995 referendum by a slim margin. Bertrand initiated a new court action in early 1996 to foreclose future referenda, this time with the assistance of the federal government. Quebec political scientist and avowed federalist Stéphane Dion was appointed Minister of Intergovernmental Affairs in January 1996 and steered the federal government in a more "tough love" direction, stressing the costs to Quebeckers should they vote to leave Canada. This was the "Plan B" approach. During the second court proceeding the federal government announced that it would submit a set of questions to the Supreme Court of Canada. The following excerpt is the Court's answer to one of those questions. (In answering the other main question, the Court suggested that Quebec does not have a right to unilateral independence under international law.)

The following is the judgment delivered by THE COURT:

INTRODUCTION

♦ ♦ ♦

This Reference requires us to consider momentous questions that go to the heart of our system of constitutional government....

The [question] posed by the Governor in Council ... reads as follows:

Under the Constitution of Canada, can the National Assembly, legislature or government of Quebec effect the secession of Quebec from Canada unilaterally?

...

THE QUESTION

In order to endure over time, a constitution must contain a comprehensive set of rules and principles which are capable of providing an exhaustive legal framework for our system of government. Such principles and rules emerge from an understanding of the constitutional text itself, the historical context, and previous judicial interpretations of constitutional meaning. In our view, there are four fundamental and organizing principles of the Constitution which are relevant to addressing the question before us (although this enumeration is by no means exhaustive): federalism; democracy; constitutionalism and the rule of law; and respect for minorities.

...

ANALYSIS OF CONSTITUTIONAL PRINCIPLES

... Our Constitution is primarily a written one, the product of 131 years of evolution. Behind the written word is an historical lineage stretching back through the ages, which aids in the consideration of the underlying constitutional principles. These principles inform and sustain the constitutional text: they are the vital unstated assumptions upon which the text is based. The following discussion addresses the four foundational constitutional principles that are most germane for resolution of this Reference: federalism, democracy, constitutionalism and the rule of law, and respect for minority rights. These defining principles function in symbiosis. No single principle can be defined in isolation from the others, nor does any one principle trump or exclude the operation of any other.

... The individual elements of the Constitution are linked to the others, and must be interpreted by reference to the structure of the Constitution as a whole. As we recently emphasized in the *Provincial Judges Reference* [1997], certain underlying principles infuse our Constitution and breathe life into it. Speaking of the rule of law principle in the *Manitoba Language Rights Reference* [1985] ... we held that "the principle is clearly implicit in the very nature of a Constitution." The same may be said of the other three constitutional principles we underscore today.

Although these underlying principles are not explicitly made part of the Constitution by any written provision, other than in some respects by the oblique reference in the preamble to the Constitution Act, 1867, it would be impossible to conceive of our constitutional structure without them. The principles dictate major elements of the architecture of the Constitution itself and are as such its lifeblood.

The principles assist in the interpretation of the text and the delineation of spheres of jurisdiction, the scope of rights and obligations, and the role of our political institutions. Equally important, observance of and respect for these principles is essential to the ongoing process of constitutional development and evolution of our Constitution as a "living tree".... Canadians have long recognized the existence and importance of unwritten constitutional principles in our system of government.

... [T]here are compelling reasons to insist upon the primacy of our written constitution. A written constitution promotes legal certainty and predictability, and it provides the foundation and a touchstone for the exercise of constitutional judicial review. However ... the effect of the preamble to the Constitution Act, 1867, was to incorporate certain constitutional principles by reference.....

Underlying constitutional principles may in certain circumstances give rise to substantive legal obligations ... which constitute substantive limitations upon government action. These principles may give rise to very abstract and general obligations, or they may be more specific and precise in nature. The principles are not merely descriptive, but are also invested with a powerful normative force, and are binding upon both courts and governments.... It is to a discussion of those underlying constitutional principles that we now turn.

1. Federalism

... In a federal system of government such as ours, political power is shared by two orders of government: the federal government on the one hand, and the provinces on the other. Each is assigned respective spheres of jurisdiction by the Constitution Act, 1867.... In interpreting our Constitution, the courts have always been concerned with the federalism principle, inherent in the structure of our constitutional arrangements, which has from the beginning been the lodestar by which the courts have been guided....

The principle of federalism recognizes the diversity of the component parts of Confederation, and the autonomy of provincial governments to develop their societies within their respective spheres of jurisdiction. The federal structure of our country also facilitates democratic participation by distributing power to the government thought to be most suited to achieving the particular societal objective having regard to this diversity. The scheme of the Constitution Act, 1867, it was said in *Re The Initiative and Referendum Act* [1919]... was

> not to weld the Provinces into one, nor to subordinate Provincial Governments to a central authority, but to establish a central government in which these Provinces should be represented, entrusted with exclusive authority only in affairs in which they had a common interest. Subject to this each Province was to retain its independence and autonomy and to be directly under the Crown as its head.

...

The principle of federalism facilitates the pursuit of collective goals by cultural and linguistic minorities which form the majority within a particular province. This is the case in Quebec, where the majority of the population is French-speaking, and which possesses a distinct culture. This is not merely the result of chance. The social and demographic reality of Quebec explains the existence of the province of Quebec as a political unit and indeed, was one of the essential reasons for establishing a federal structure for the Canadian union in 1867. The experience of both Canada East and Canada West under the Union Act, 1840, had not been satisfactory. The federal structure adopted at Confederation enabled French-speaking Canadians to form a numerical majority in the province of Quebec, and so exercise the considerable provincial powers conferred by the Constitution Act, 1867 in such a way as to promote their language and culture. It also made provision for certain guaranteed representation within the federal Parliament itself.

Federalism was also welcomed by Nova Scotia and New Brunswick, both of which also affirmed their will to protect their individual cultures and their autonomy over local matters. All new provinces joining the federation sought to achieve similar objectives, which are no less vigorously pursued by the provinces and territories as we approach the new millennium.

2. Democracy

Democracy is a fundamental value in our constitutional law and political culture. While it has both an institutional and an individual aspect, the democratic principle was also argued before us in the sense of the supremacy of the sovereign will of a people, in this case potentially to be expressed by Quebecers in support of unilateral secession. It is useful to explore in a summary way these different aspects of the democratic principle.

... [T]he democracy principle can best be understood as a sort of baseline against which the framers of our Constitution, and subsequently, our elected representatives under it, have always operated. It is perhaps for this reason that the principle was not explicitly identified in the text of the Constitution Act, 1867 itself. To have done so might have appeared redundant, even silly, to the framers. As [we] explained in the *Provincial Judges Reference* [1997] ... it is evident that our Constitution contemplates that Canada shall be a constitutional democracy. Yet this merely demonstrates the importance of underlying constitutional principles that are nowhere explicitly described in our constitutional texts. The representative and democratic nature of our political institutions was simply assumed.

...

Democracy is not simply concerned with the process of government. On the contrary, as suggested in *Switzman v. Elbling* [1957] ... democracy is fundamentally connected to substantive goals, most importantly, the promotion of self-government. Democracy accommodates cultural and group identities.... Put another way, a sovereign people exercises its right to self-government through the democratic process. In considering the scope and purpose of the Charter, the Court in *R. v. Oakes* [1986] articulated some of the values inherent in the notion of democracy...:

> The Court must be guided by the values and principles essential to a free and democratic society which I believe to embody, to name but a few, respect for the inherent dignity of the human person, commitment to social justice and equality, accommodation of a wide variety of beliefs, respect for cultural and group identity, and faith in social and political insti-

tutions which enhance the participation of individuals and groups in society.

...

It is, of course, true that democracy expresses the sovereign will of the people. Yet this expression, too, must be taken in the context of the other institutional values we have identified as pertinent to this Reference. The relationship between democracy and federalism means, for example, that in Canada there may be different and equally legitimate majorities in different provinces and territories and at the federal level. No one majority is more or less "legitimate" than the others as an expression of democratic opinion, although, of course, the consequences will vary with the subject matter. A federal system of government enables different provinces to pursue policies responsive to the particular concerns and interests of people in that province. At the same time, Canada as a whole is also a democratic community in which citizens construct and achieve goals on a national scale through a federal government acting within the limits of its jurisdiction. The function of federalism is to enable citizens to participate concurrently in different collectivities and to pursue goals at both a provincial and a federal level.

The consent of the governed is a value that is basic to our understanding of a free and democratic society. Yet democracy in any real sense of the word cannot exist without the rule of law. It is the law that creates the framework within which the "sovereign will" is to be ascertained and implemented. To be accorded legitimacy, democratic institutions must rest, ultimately, on a legal foundation. That is, they must allow for the participation of, and accountability to, the people, through public institutions created under the Constitution. Equally, however, a system of government cannot survive through adherence to the law alone. A political system must also possess legitimacy, and in our political culture, that requires an interaction between the rule of law and the democratic principle. The system must be capable of reflecting the aspirations of the people. But there is more. Our law's claim to legitimacy also rests on an appeal to moral values, many of which are imbedded in our constitutional structure. It would be a grave mistake to equate legitimacy with the "sovereign will" or majority rule alone, to the exclusion of other constitutional values.

Finally, we highlight that a functioning democracy requires a continuous process of discussion. The Constitution mandates government by democratic legislatures, and an executive accountable to them, "resting ultimately on public opinion reached by discussion and the interplay of ideas" (*Saumur v. City of Quebec* [1953].... At both the federal and provincial level, by its very nature, the need to build majorities necessitates compromise, negotiation, and deliberation. No one has a monopoly on truth, and our system is predicated on the faith that in the marketplace of ideas, the best solutions to public problems will rise to the top. Inevitably, there will be dissenting voices. A democratic system of government is committed to considering those dissenting voices, and seeking to acknowledge and address those voices in the laws by which all in the community must live.

A functioning democracy requires a continuous process of discussion.

The Constitution Act, 1982 gives expression to this principle, by conferring a right to initiate constitutional change on each participant in Confederation. In our view, the existence of this right imposes a corresponding duty on the participants in Confederation to engage in constitutional discussions in order to acknowledge and address democratic expressions of a desire for change in other provinces. This duty is inherent in the democratic principle which is a fundamental predicate of our system of governance.

3. Constitutionalism and the Rule of Law

... At its most basic level, the rule of law vouchsafes to the citizens and residents of the country a stable, predictable and ordered society in which to conduct their affairs. It provides a shield for individuals from arbitrary state action.

...

The constitutionalism principle bears considerable similarity to the rule of law, although they are not identical. The essence of constitutionalism in Canada is embodied in s. 52(1) of the Constitution Act, 1982, which provides that "[t]he Constitution of Canada is the supreme law of Canada, and any law that is inconsistent with the provisions of the Constitution is, to the extent of the inconsistency, of no force or effect." Simply put, the constitutionalism principle requires that all government action comply with the Constitution. The rule of law principle requires that all government action must comply with the law, including the Constitution....

An understanding of the scope and importance of the principles of the rule of law and constitutionalism is aided by acknowledging explicitly why a constitution is entrenched beyond the reach of simple majority rule. There are three overlapping reasons.

First, a constitution may provide an added safeguard for fundamental human rights and individual freedoms which might otherwise be susceptible to government interference. Although democratic government is generally solicitous of those rights, there are occasions when the majority will be tempted to ignore fundamental rights in order to accomplish collective goals more easily or effectively. Constitutional entrenchment ensures that those rights will be given due regard and protection. Second, a constitution may seek to ensure that vulnerable minority groups are endowed with the institutions and rights necessary to maintain and promote their identities against the assimilative pressures of the majority. And third, a constitution may provide for a division of political power that allocates political power amongst different levels of government. That purpose would be defeated if one of those democratically elected levels of government could usurp the powers of the other simply by exercising its legislative power to allocate additional political power to itself unilaterally.

The argument that the Constitution may be legitimately circumvented by resort to a majority vote in a province-wide referendum is superficially persuasive, in large measure because it seems to appeal to some of the same principles that underlie the legitimacy of the Constitution itself, namely, democracy and self-government.... However, closer analysis reveals that this argument is unsound, because it misunderstands the meaning of popular sovereignty and the essence of constitutional democracy.

Canadians have never accepted that ours is a system of simple majority rule. Our principle of democracy, taken in conjunction with the other constitutional principles discussed here, is richer. Constitutional government is necessarily predicated on the idea that the political representatives of the people of a province have the capacity and the power to commit the province to be bound into the future by the constitutional rules being adopted. These rules are "binding" not in the sense of frustrating the will of a majority of a province, but as defining the majority which must be consulted in order to alter the fundamental balances of political power (including the spheres of autonomy guaranteed by the principle of federalism), individual rights, and minority rights in our society. Of course, those constitutional rules are themselves amenable to amendment, but only through a process of negotiation which ensures that there is an opportunity for the constitutionally defined rights of all the parties to be respected and reconciled.

Canadians have never accepted that ours is a system of simple majority rule.

In this way, our belief in democracy may be harmonized with our belief in constitutionalism. Constitutional amendment often requires some form of substantial consensus precisely because the content of the underlying principles of our Constitution demand it. By requiring broad support in the form of an "enhanced majority" to achieve constitutional change, the Constitution ensures that minority interests must be addressed before proposed changes which would affect them may be enacted.

It might be objected, then, that constitutionalism is therefore incompatible with democratic government. This would be an erroneous view. Constitutionalism facilitates—indeed, makes possible—a democratic political system by creating an orderly framework within which people may make political decisions. Viewed correctly, constitutionalism and the rule of law are not in conflict with democracy; rather, they are essential to it. Without that relationship, the political will upon which democratic decisions are taken would itself be undermined.

4. Protection of Minorities

The fourth underlying constitutional principle we address here concerns the protection of minorities. There are a number of specific constitutional provisions protecting minority language, religion and education rights....

The concern of our courts and governments to protect minorities has been prominent in recent years, particularly following the enactment of the Charter. Undoubtedly, one of the key considerations motivating the enactment of the Charter, and the process of constitutional judicial review that it entails, is the protection of minorities. However, it should not be forgotten that the protection of minority rights had a long history before the enactment of the Charter. Indeed, the protection of minority rights was clearly an essential consideration in the design of our constitutional structure even at the time of Confederation....

Consistent with this long tradition of respect for minorities, which is at least as old as Canada itself, the framers of the Constitution Act, 1982 included in s. 35 explicit protection for existing aboriginal and treaty rights, and in s. 25, a non-derogation clause in favour of the rights of aboriginal peoples. The "promise" of s. 35, as it was termed in *R. v. Sparrow*, [1990] ... recognized not only the ancient occupation of land by aboriginal peoples, but their contribution to the building of Canada, and the special commitments made to them by successive governments. The protection of these rights, so recently and arduously achieved, whether looked at in their own right or as part of the larger concern with minorities, reflects an important underlying constitutional value.

THE OPERATION OF THE CONSTITUTIONAL PRINCIPLES IN THE SECESSION CONTEXT

◆ ◆ ◆

Secession is the effort of a group or section of a state to withdraw itself from the political and constitutional authority of that state, with a view to achieving statehood for a new territorial unit on the international plane. In a federal state, secession typically takes the form of a territorial unit seeking to withdraw from the federation. Secession is a legal act as much as a political one. By the terms of [the question] of this Reference, we are asked to rule on the legality of unilateral secession "[u]nder the Constitution of Canada." This is an appropriate question, as the legality of unilateral secession must be evaluated, at least in the first instance, from the perspective of the domestic legal order of the state from which the unit seeks to withdraw....

The secession of a province from Canada must be considered, in legal terms, to require an amendment to the Constitution, which perforce requires negotiation. The amendments necessary to achieve a secession could be radical and extensive. Some commentators have suggested that secession could be a change of such a magnitude that it could not be considered to be merely an amendment to the Constitution. We are not persuaded by this contention. It is of course true that the Constitution is silent as to the ability of a province to secede from Confederation but, although the Constitution neither expressly authorizes nor prohibits secession, an act of secession would purport to alter the governance of Canadian territory in a manner which undoubtedly is inconsistent with our current constitutional arrangements. The fact that those changes would be profound, or that they would purport to have a significance with respect to international law, does not negate their nature as amendments to the Constitution of Canada.

...

The secession of a province from Canada must be considered, in legal terms, to require an amendment to the Constitution....

The "unilateral" nature of [Quebec secession] is of cardinal importance and we must be clear as to what is understood by this term. In one sense, any step towards a constitutional amendment initiated by a single actor on the constitutional stage is "unilateral." We do not believe that this is the meaning contemplated by [the Reference question], nor is this the sense in which the term has been used in argument before us. Rather, what is claimed by a right to secede "unilaterally" is the right to effectuate secession without prior negotiations with the other provinces and the federal government. At issue is not the legality of the first step but the legality of the final act of purported unilateral secession. The supposed juridical basis for such an act is said to be a clear expression of democratic will in a referendum in the province of Quebec. This claim requires us to examine the possible juridical impact, if any, of such a referendum on the functioning of our Constitution, and on the claimed legality of a unilateral act of secession.

What is claimed by a right to secede "unilaterally" is the right effectuate secession without prior negotiations with the other provinces and the federal government.

Although the Constitution does not itself address the use of a referendum procedure, and the results of a referendum have no direct role or legal effect in our constitutional scheme, a referendum undoubtedly may provide a democratic method of ascertaining the views of the electorate on important political questions on a particular occasion. The democratic principle identified above would demand that considerable weight be given to a clear expression by the people of Quebec of their will to secede from Canada, even though a referendum, in itself and without more, has no direct legal effect, and could not in itself bring about unilateral secession. Our political institutions are premised on the democratic principle, and so an expression of the democratic will of the people of a province carries weight, in that it would confer legitimacy on the efforts of the government of Quebec to initiate the Constitution's amendment process in order to secede by constitutional means. In this context, we refer to a "clear" majority as a qualitative evaluation. The referendum result, if it is to be taken as an expression of the democratic will, must be free of ambiguity both in terms of the question asked and in terms of the support it achieves.

The federalism principle, in conjunction with the democratic principle, dictates that the clear repudiation of the existing constitutional order and the clear expression of the desire to pursue secession by the population of a province would give rise to a reciprocal obligation on all parties to Confederation to negotiate constitutional changes to respond to that desire. The amendment of the Constitution begins with a political process undertaken pursuant to the Constitution itself. In Canada, the initiative for constitutional amendment is the responsibility of democratically elected representatives of the participants in Confederation. Those representatives may, of course, take their cue from a referendum, but in legal terms, constitution-making in Canada, as in many countries, is undertaken by the democratically elected representatives of the people. The corollary of a legitimate attempt by one participant in Confederation to seek an amendment to the Constitution is an obligation on all parties to come to the negotiating table. The clear repudiation by the people of Quebec of the existing constitutional order would confer legitimacy on demands for secession, and place an obligation on the other provinces and the federal government to acknowledge and respect that expression of democratic will by entering into negotiations and conducting them in accordance with the underlying constitutional principles already discussed.

What is the content of this obligation to negotiate?

...

The conduct of the parties in such negotiations would be governed by the same constitutional principles which give rise to the duty to negotiate: federalism, democracy, constitutionalism and the rule of law, and the protection of minorities. Those principles lead us to reject two absolutist propositions. One of those proposi-

tions is that there would be a legal obligation on the other provinces and federal government to accede to the secession of a province, subject only to negotiation of the logistical details of secession. This proposition is attributed either to the supposed implications of the democratic principle of the Constitution, or to the international law principle of self-determination of peoples.

For both theoretical and practical reasons, we cannot accept this view. We hold that Quebec could not purport to invoke a right of self-determination such as to dictate the terms of a proposed secession to the other parties: that would not be a negotiation at all. As well, it would be naive to expect that the substantive goal of secession could readily be distinguished from the practical details of secession. The devil would be in the details. The democracy principle, as we have emphasized, cannot be invoked to trump the principles of federalism and rule of law, the rights of individuals and minorities, or the operation of democracy in the other provinces or in Canada as a whole. No negotiations could be effective if their ultimate outcome, secession, is cast as an absolute legal entitlement based upon an obligation to give effect to that act of secession in the Constitution. Such a foregone conclusion would actually undermine the obligation to negotiate and render it hollow.

The continued existence and operation of the Canadian constitutional order cannot remain indifferent to the clear expression of a clear majority of Quebecers that they no longer wish to remain in Canada.

However, we are equally unable to accept the reverse proposition, that a clear expression of self-determination by the people of Quebec would impose no obligations upon the other provinces or the federal government. The continued existence and operation of the Canadian constitutional order cannot remain indifferent to the clear expression of a clear majority of Quebecers that they no longer wish to remain in Canada. This would amount to the assertion that other constitutionally recognized principles necessarily trump the clearly expressed democratic will of the people of Quebec. Such a proposition fails to give sufficient weight to the underlying constitutional principles that must inform the amendment process, including the principles of democracy and federalism. The rights of other provinces and the federal government cannot deny the right of the government of Quebec to pursue secession, should a clear majority of the people of Quebec choose that goal, so long as in doing so, Quebec respects the rights of others. Negotiations would be necessary to address the interests of the federal government, of Quebec and the other provinces, and other participants, as well as the rights of all Canadians both within and outside Quebec.

Is the rejection of both of these propositions reconcilable? Yes, once it is realized that none of the rights or principles under discussion is absolute to the exclusion of the others. This observation suggests that other parties cannot exercise their rights in such a way as to amount to an absolute denial of Quebec's rights, and similarly, that so long as Quebec exercises its rights while respecting the rights of others, it may propose secession and seek to achieve it through negotiation. The negotiation process precipitated by a decision of a clear majority of the population of Quebec on a clear question to pursue secession would require the reconciliation of various rights and obligations by the representatives of two legitimate majorities, namely, the clear majority of the population of Quebec, and the clear majority of Canada as a whole, whatever that may be. There can be no suggestion that either of these majorities "trumps" the other. A political majority that does not act in accordance with the underlying constitutional principles we have identified puts at risk the legitimacy of the exercise of its rights.

In such circumstances, the conduct of the parties assumes primary constitutional significance. The negotiation process must be conducted with an eye to the constitutional principles we have outlined, which must inform the actions of all the participants in the negotiation process.

Refusal of a party to conduct negotiations in a manner consistent with constitutional principles and values would seriously put at risk the legitimacy of that party's assertion of its rights, and perhaps the negotiation process as a whole. Those who quite legitimately insist upon the importance of upholding the rule of law cannot at the same time be oblivious to the need to act in conformity with constitutional principles and values, and so do their part to contribute to the maintenance and promotion of an environment in which the rule of law may flourish.

No one can predict the course that such negotiations might take. The possibility that they might not lead to an agreement amongst the parties must be recognized. Negotiations following a referendum vote in favour of seeking secession would inevitably address a wide range of issues, many of great import. After 131 years of Confederation, there exists, inevitably, a high level of integration in economic, political and social institutions across Canada. The vision of those who brought about Confederation was to create a unified country, not a loose alliance of autonomous provinces. Accordingly, while there are regional economic interests, which sometimes coincide with provincial boundaries, there are also national interests and enterprises (both public and private) that would face potential dismemberment. There is a national economy and a national debt. Arguments were raised before us regarding boundary issues. There are linguistic and cultural minorities, including aboriginal peoples, unevenly distributed across the country who look to the Constitution of Canada for the protection of their rights. Of course, secession would give rise to many issues of great complexity and difficulty. These would have to be resolved within the overall framework of the rule of law, thereby assuring Canadians resident in Quebec and elsewhere a measure of stability in what would likely be a period of considerable upheaval and uncertainty. Nobody seriously suggests that our national existence, seamless in so many aspects, could be effortlessly separated along what are now the provincial boundaries of Quebec. As the Attorney General of Saskatchewan put it in his oral submission:

> A nation is built when the communities that comprise it make commitments to it, when they forego choices and opportunities on behalf of a nation,... when the communities that comprise it make compromises, when they offer each other guarantees, when they make transfers and perhaps most pointedly, when they receive from others the benefits of national solidarity. The threads of a thousand acts of accommodation are the fabric of a nation....

In the circumstances, negotiations following such a referendum would undoubtedly be difficult. While the negotiators would have to contemplate the possibility of secession, there would be no absolute legal entitlement to it and no assumption that an agreement reconciling all relevant rights and obligations would actually be reached. It is foreseeable that even negotiations carried out in conformity with the underlying constitutional principles could reach an impasse. We need not speculate here as to what would then transpire. Under the Constitution, secession requires that an amendment be negotiated.

The respective roles of the courts and political actors in discharging the constitutional obligations we have identified follows ineluctably from the foregoing observations....

The role of the Court in this Reference is limited to the identification of the relevant aspects of the Constitution in their broadest sense. We have interpreted the questions as relating to the constitutional framework within which political decisions may ultimately be made. Within that framework, the workings of the political process are complex and can only be resolved by means of political judgments and evaluations. The Court has no supervisory role over the political aspects of constitutional negotiations. Equally, the initial impetus for negotiation, namely a clear majority on a clear question in favour of secession, is subject only to political evaluation, and properly so. A right and a corresponding duty to negotiate secession cannot be built on an alleged expression of democratic will if the expression of democratic will is itself fraught with ambiguities. Only the political actors would have the information and expertise to make the appropriate judgment as to the point at which, and the circumstances in which, those ambiguities are resolved one way or the other.

If the circumstances giving rise to the duty to negotiate were to arise, the distinction between the strong defence of legitimate interests and the taking of positions which, in fact, ignore the legitimate interests of others is one that also defies legal analysis. The Court would not have access to all of the information available to the political actors, and the methods appropriate for the search for truth in a court of law are ill-suited to getting to the bottom of constitutional negotiations. To the extent that the questions are political in nature, it is not the role of the judiciary to interpose its own views on the different negotiating positions of the parties, even were it invited to do so. Rather, it is the obligation of the elected representatives to give concrete form to the discharge of their constitutional obligations which only they and their electors can ultimately assess. The reconciliation of the various legitimate constitutional interests outlined above is necessarily committed to the political rather than the judicial realm, precisely because that reconciliation can only be achieved through the give and take of the negotiation process. Having established the legal framework, it would be for the democratically elected leadership of the various participants to resolve their differences.

The non-justiciability of political issues that lack a legal component does not deprive the surrounding constitutional framework of its binding status, nor does this mean that constitutional obligations could be breached without incurring serious legal repercussions. Where there are legal rights there are remedies, but ... the appropriate recourse in some circumstances lies through the workings of the political process rather than the courts.

To the extent that a breach of the constitutional duty to negotiate in accordance with the principles described above undermines the legitimacy of a party's actions, it may have important ramifications at the international level. Thus, a failure of the duty to undertake negotiations and pursue them according to constitutional principles may undermine that government's claim to legitimacy which is generally a precondition for recognition by the international community. Conversely, violations of those principles by the federal or other provincial governments responding to the request for secession may undermine their legitimacy. Thus, a Quebec that had negotiated in conformity with constitutional principles and values in the face of unreasonable intransigence on the part of other participants at the federal or provincial level would be more likely to be recognized than a Quebec which did not itself act according to constitutional principles in the negotiation process. Both the legality of the acts of the parties to the negotiation process under Canadian law, and the perceived legitimacy of such action, would be important considerations in the recognition process. In this way, the adherence of the parties to the obligation to negotiate would be evaluated in an indirect manner on the international plane.

Accordingly, the secession of Quebec from Canada cannot be accomplished by the National Assembly, the legislature or government of Quebec unilaterally, that is to say, without principled negotiations, and be considered a lawful act. Any attempt to effect the secession of a province from Canada must be undertaken pursuant to the Constitution of Canada, or else violate the Canadian legal order. However, the continued existence and operation of the Canadian constitutional order cannot remain unaffected by the unambiguous expression of a clear majority of Quebecers that they no longer wish to remain in Canada. The primary means by which that expression is given effect is the constitutional duty to negotiate in accordance with the constitutional principles that we have described herein. In the event secession negotiations are initiated, our Constitution, no less than our history, would call on the participants to work to reconcile the rights, obligations and legitimate aspirations of all Canadians within a framework that emphasizes constitutional responsibilities as much as it does constitutional rights.

...

SUMMARY OF CONCLUSIONS

◆ ◆ ◆

...

Although there is no right, under the Constitution or at international law, to unilateral secession ... this does not rule out the possibility of an unconstitutional declaration of secession leading to a de facto secession. The ultimate success of such a secession would be dependent on recognition by the international community, which is likely to consider the legality and legitimacy of secession having regard to, amongst other facts, the conduct of Quebec and Canada, in determining whether to grant or withhold recognition. Such recognition, even if granted, would not, however, provide any retroactive justification for the act of secession, either under the Constitution of Canada or at international law.

Terms & Concepts

clear majority
clear question
constitutionalism
constitutional principles

democracy
federalism
minority rights
reference

rule of law
unilateral secession

Questions

1. What are the four main constitutional principles forming the structure of the Canadian Constitution? Which of the four principles do you think had the greatest influence on the outcome of this reference? Which had the least effect?

2. This reference can be understood as a contest between the Quebec and federal governments. Which side does the opinion most favour?

3. Does this opinion effectively settle the secession issue? Why or why not? Is there evidence that the Supreme Court has pushed the matter back into the lap of the politicians?

4. The opinion refers to respect for minorities as a constitutional principle. Which minority groups are involved in the secession debate?

Is There Room for Forgiveness in International Politics?

Jean Bethke Elshtain

Editors' Note

In the summer of 1999, Albanians returning to Kosovo were getting even with the Serb minority. Twenty thousand NATO troops struggled to contain the burning, looting, beatings, and killings. There was little forgiveness in this cauldron of hatred. And yet, forgiveness is the only civilized way out of these collective blood feuds.

Forgiveness is not new. A lot of forgiveness had to be practised before Europe could become the European Union. Most would agree that breaking the cycles of violence between states was well worth it. Professor Bethke Elshtain writes that it takes "knowing forgetting" to pull it off—in other words, recognizing that atrocities and violations occurred but not transferring the guilt to a people, especially not to their descendants. It also requires an acknowledgment that revenge will never bring justice, only more injustice.

Forgiveness, then, is not the same as justice. There is no justice for a people. What could have been done to exact justice for the Holocaust? Nothing could compensate for what was done—not retribution, restitution, restraint, or rehabilitation. Individuals can be and were brought to trial and punished, but it is not clear how this served their victims. Leaders do sometimes face justice, although the mechanisms in international law are limited. But it is doubtful whether the conviction of those accused of war crimes in Kosovo would have prevented Kosovar-Albanians from getting even.

This article focuses on international forgiveness, but similar principles operate in countries that have undergone or are undergoing regime changes, particularly when they change from oppressive to democratic regimes. Here, people have to forgive their fellow citizens. The Truth and Reconciliation Commission in South Africa seems to have been very much about "knowing forgetting": people who publicly admitted what they did to their fellow citizens during the apartheid regime would be given amnesty for their deeds. Other countries took different courses. Germany put on trial former East German leaders and soldiers who were responsible for deaths. STASI files were opened to everyone, so that people could identify the people who spied in their midst. While they were not prosecuted, identification often meant ostracism by friends and family. Chile chose to forget the crimes of the military—or at least to abide by self-serving constitutional guarantees passed by the military as a condition of returning to their barracks. Will burying the past without acknowledging it work? We will have to wait and see. There seem to be enough expatriate Chileans lining up to see General Pinochet prosecuted outside Chile.

Clearly, the world will be a much better place if forgiveness can be practised within and across borders. Not only is it magnanimous, it may be the most practical course.

Sometimes it pays to take a bit longer than one should to revise lectures for publication. As I was putting the finishing touches on [an article], the *New York Times* reported a follow-up to the story about the Sudetenland, detailing the ways in which Germany will apologize for its invasion of the former Czechoslovakia and the Czechs, in turn, "will express regrets for the postwar expulsion of millions of Sudeten Germans...."[1] The Germans apologize for Nazi "policies of violence." The Czechs express regret that their expulsions "caused suffering and injustice to innocent people." But, of course, things are not made right in the eyes of those who suffered most. The story indicates that an organization of Sudeten Germans, a "powerful political lobby in Bavaria," takes strong exception to the agreement that has been hammered out because "it provides them with neither a claim to compensation nor a right to return to expropriated properties." As well, the *Times* tells us, the agreement "seems likely to incense many Czechs because it apologizes for events that many view as an appropriate reaction to Nazi occupation."

No doubt true. Hardliners are already standing in queue waiting for an opportunity to erupt. But still, these small steps, each of which acknowledges violation of "elementary, humanitarian principles" should not be sneezed at altogether. ... Reparation and compensation and return are not in the cards. But acknowledgment and recognition of injustice is forthcoming. Maybe there is a political version of forgiveness that must, not all of the time but most of the time, step back from full reconciliation and certainly from absolution. There are no sacraments, no blessings, no benedictions in politics. Thinking politically, one might ask what sorts of deeds warrant the solemn drama of forgiveness of a sort related to, yet different from, the different acts that constitute a personal redemption narrative.

When Hannah Arendt called forgiveness the greatest political contribution of Jesus of Nazareth to politics, she didn't have in mind a single political figure saying, "Can you forgive me?" Rather, she was gesturing toward a way to break repetitive cycles of vengeance, to forestall the often deadly playing out of horrible deeds done and equally horrible retribution sought. Forgiveness, an unexpected act, disrupts automatic processes and opens a space for something new to begin: for the possibility that bloody deeds will not haunt generation upon generation in perpetuity. Although individual acts of forgiveness—one human being to another—most often take place outside the full glare of publicity, there are others that are noteworthy for the public message they bear. I think here of Pope John Paul II, who barely survived an assassin's bullets, uttering his first public words from his hospital bed to his "brother, whom I have sincerely forgiven," words that preceded his extraordinary visit to his brother and would-be killer in jail once he was up and about. The Pope was practicing what some have called the "craft" of forgiveness and, in so doing, displaying to the world the ways in which forgiveness is not primarily about a singular moment but about an enactment within a particular way of life.

Forgiveness, an unexpected act, disrupts automatic processes and opens a space for something new to begin.

But it would be odd to call John Paul's act of forgiveness a political intervention per se, although it was an undeniably powerful moment, one seared into the memory and locked in the hearts of all who witnessed it, even from afar and through the medium of television news. To be sure, there might have been political consequences: the Pope's words and actions might have quieted the turbulent hearts of many believers who sought revenge for his near-murder. But I doubt this is quite what Arendt had in mind. She was more concerned with interrupting the flow of events that seem to be on automatic pilot when mass murder, acts of retribution, then more killing become the "way we do things here," so to speak. Within the frame of such broad-based events driven by desperate political purpose, *individuals* who are shaped by the practice of forgiveness should practice what they believe or preach. But an individual cannot from himself or herself stem the rushing tide of violence—or, such moments will be quite rare. Can there, then, be authentic acts of political forgiveness? Who forgives whom and for what? Remember: forgiveness isn't a one-way street. It implies a relationship, or requires a transitive dimension, because it is not primarily about self-exculpation but about the creation of a new relationship or the restoration of one that has been broken and torn by violence.

Here one confronts head-on the sheer weight of history—its denseness and thickness. People are often fond of citing Santayana's claim that those who don't know their history are doomed to repeat it. The reverse seems more true, namely, that those who know their history perhaps too well are doomed to repetition. Perhaps a certain amount of "knowing forgetting" is necessary in order to get out of the rut of repetition. By "knowing forgetting" I have in mind a way to release present-day actors from the full burden of the past in order that they not be weighed down by it utterly. Forgetting, in this instance, doesn't mean falling into radical present-mindedness and the delusion that the past counts for nothing; rather, one assesses and judges just what the past counts for in the present, how much it should frame, shape, even determine present events.

Too often when forgiveness is mentioned, it is translated into a bland evocation of nonjudgmentalness of the sort that means I can't say anything at all about anybody else's behavior and words. But if this is the tack one takes, forgiveness is altogether unnecessary. There can never be anything to forgive if no real wrong has been suffered, no real sin committed, no evil deed perpetrated.

Forgiveness is a strenuous discipline, for it aims at the restoration of a relationship when a relationship has been broken; it requires acknowledgment of wrongs perpetrated or wrongly suffered. Forgiveness in public or political life must also involve the painful recognition of the limits to forgiveness itself, if what one seeks is expiation or a full accounting. There are wrongs suffered that can never be put right; indeed, this latter recognition is itself a central feature of an overall structure of political forgiveness, or so I want to suggest. There are many examples one might point to. How does a culture expiate for the Holocaust? For slavery? Wrongs that cannot be righted must, nonetheless, be acknowledged.

Forgiveness ... requires acknowledgement of wrongs perpetrated or wrongly suffered.

Part of that acknowledgment will consist in a knowing and explicit articulation of the terrible fact that full expiation is impossible. This is *not* forgetting as a kind of collective amnesia; rather, it is an explicit recognition of the full scope of a given horror and the inability of a subsequent generation to put things right. The events stand. Acknowledgment of these events is required by those most directly implicated, and even by those not so directly implicated who, perhaps, stood by and did nothing. But, unless one undertakes a course of retribution, the repetition of violence perpetrated must stop even as the remembrance of past violence must go forward in all its fullness, all its detail. In fact, the sheer recitation of

events counts as an ongoing indictment tethered to a tragic recognition that some wrongs cannot be righted.

This must have been what Arendt had in mind, at least in part. In her controversial book, *Eichmann in Jerusalem*, she justifies the hanging of Adolph Eichmann because he had perpetrated terrible crimes against humanity "on the body of the Jewish people," but she did so in full recognition that no scale of justice had thereby been put right and that hanging every known Nazi war criminal would not do that.[2] She also knew that young Germans could not be held accountable for what occurred. But they were obliged to remember in order that they could be free to act in other ways. This is "knowing forgetting," then: recollection of the past, yes, but not being so wholly defined by it that one's options are either to be victim or executioner, in Albert Camus's memorable phrase. Here is one concrete and no doubt modest example of the dynamic I have in mind, although it does take place in the most difficult of all arenas for the dynamic of forgiveness and "knowing forgetting" to play out—the realm of relations between peoples and states. But if forgiveness is to have real political sturdiness, it must be tested in many arenas. My example is drawn from Northern Ireland and its centuries-old troubled relationship with Great Britain. Irish Catholics in Northern Ireland have long been a tormented people, relegated to second-class citizenship in what they perceive to be part of their land. But Irish Catholics, relatively powerless in the overall balance of forces, have also been tormentors, as the history of IRA terrorism and death-dealing attests.

It is, therefore, significant, that on January 22, 1995, Cardinal Cahal Daly of Armagh, Northern Ireland, publicly asked forgiveness from the people of Britain in a speech at Canterbury Cathedral, England, the home (as readers surely know) of the primate of the Church of England, the Archbishop of Canterbury. Cardinal Daly's words on that occasion are worth pondering:

We Irish are sometimes said to be obsessively concerned with memories of the past. It is salutary, however, to recall that the faults we attribute to others can be a projection of faults within ourselves which we have not had the courage to confront.... What is certainly true is that we all need a healing of memories.... Healing of memories demands recognition of our own need for forgiveness; it requires repentance. The original biblical term for repentance, *metanoia,* is a strong word indicating the need for radical conversion, change of attitude, change of outlook, change of stance; and all this is costing and can be painful. The old word *contrition* expresses it well.... This healing, this conversion, this reciprocal giving and accepting of forgiveness are essential elements in the healing of relationships between our two islands and between our divided communities in Northern Ireland.... On this occasion ... I wish to ask forgiveness from the people of this land for the wrongs and hurts inflicted by Irish people upon the people of this country on many occasions during that shared history, and particularly in the past 25 years. I believe that this reciprocal recognition of the need to forgive and to be forgiven is a necessary condition for proper Christian, and human, and indeed *political relationships* between our two islands in the future [emphasis mine].[3]

The Cardinal continued with words about starting "something new" and how frightful it would be to "slide back into violence." What he was saying and doing was avowedly political in the sense of drawing from the Gospel "conclusions which are relevant to our daily living as individuals and as a society...." Reciprocal forgiveness and reconciliation were also offered by the Anglican primate of Ireland as well as the Archbishop of Canterbury himself. A question, then: is this form of forgiveness, to the extent that it is accessible and enactable, available only to communicants of a faith? The Cardinal suggests not when he addresses "human" and "political" relationships more generally. For many, certainly for international relations scholars, this is a hopelessly idealistic stance out of touch with tough realities. But the riposte might be that tough realities invite precisely this stance; indeed, they suggest it as a necessary part of a process of negotiation, reconciliation, starting something new. Of course, there is not yet peace in Northern Ireland. But I am convinced that words and deeds of tough-minded reconciliation and forgiveness are a part of that process. They provide a moral deposit on which future generations can draw in an effort not to slide back into recriminatory cycles.

Nothing I have said should be taken as an injunction to fiddle while Rome burns or pray as the Vandals storm the city. There are times when action is necessary in order to prevent a wrong from being committed. In daily life with those we love, the process of forgiveness is an enactment that is part of the very dailyness of existence: it makes the quotidian livable. But in the affairs of what used to be called men and states, these enactments are not and cannot be so ordinary and so direct. But that does not preclude "knowing forgetting" and an interplay of justice and forgiveness altogether.[4] Over the past several years, the Japanese government has apologized to all those women still alive who were forced into prostitution as "comfort ladies" under Japanese dominion in World War II. This official act was preceded by public acknowledgment and recognition of the wrongs perpetrated upon the bodies of violated women by the thousands. Official recognition; some form of reparation; state-level apology. The scales are somewhat righted. It is such difficult and fragile achievements that politics and forgiveness, or the politics *of* forgiveness, is all about.

Notes

1. Alan Crowell, "Germans and Czechs Agree to Pact on Wartime Abuses," *The New York Times,* December 12, 1996, p. A12.
2. Hannah Arendt, *Eichmann in Jerusalem* (New York: Penguin Books, 1977).
3. The text of this address in full can be found under the title, "Breakdown of the Cease-Fire," *Origins* 25, no. 35 (February 22, 1996), pp. 585–588.
4. This epilogue was written before I made a trip to South Africa, in August 1997. Were I writing the epilogue today, material from this encounter would be incorporated. As it is, that must wait for another day, for yet another essay or book.

Terms & Concepts

contrition	knowing forgetting	reciprocal forgiveness
forgiveness	*metanoia*	

Questions

1. We are frequently called upon to forgive and forget. What is the difference between "knowing forgetting" and just forgetting?

2. Is forgiving more or less difficult within a state than across borders?

3. We are not usually called upon to forgive those who have done us criminal harm as individuals. The justice system does not seem to take forgiving much into consideration. Why, then, is forgiving more important among groups of people or even nations?

4. How does one initiate forgiving between groups with a history of mutual hatred and conflict?

Unit Six   Discussion Questions

1. Is Canada's federal "regime" undergoing major changes? If so, why? If not, why not?

2. Which of the major ideas discussed elsewhere in this reader seem of particular relevance when discussing the problem of regime change?

3. How is the complex relationship between democracy and capitalism linked to the current debate about regime change?

4. In what ways do these selections reveal the importance of political leadership and the need for an honest, efficient, meritocratic state bureaucracy?

Annotated Bibliography

Ash, Timothy Garton. *In Europe's Name: Germany and the Divided Continent.* New York: Random House, 1993. Even when a former Communist state is fully and voluntarily absorbed by the strongest economy in Europe, adjustment to the changes is problematic.

Crick, Bernard. *In Defense of Politics,* 4th ed. London: Weidenfeld and Nicolson, 1992. There are few better at defending the inherent importance of politics and political activity than Bernard Crick. In his inimitable style, he attacks the "enemies" of politics and writes of the attitudes—and the courage—we need if we are to create and maintain a viable and healthy polity.

Chaliand, Gerard, and Jean-Pierre Rageau. *The Penguin Atlas of Diasporas.* New York: Viking Press, 1995. If you want to know who moved where and when, this is the study to consult.

Cohen, Lenard J. *Broken Bonds: Yugoslavia's Disintegration and Balkan Politics in Transition,* 2nd ed. Boulder, Colo.: Westview Press, 1995. Provides essential, detailed information on the crisis leading up to the war.

East European Constitutional Review. This is a quarterly journal jointly published by the New York University School of Law and Budapest's Central European University, and it contains updates and scholarly articles on constitutional politics of the emerging European democracies.

Gibbins, Roger, and Guy LaForest, eds. *Beyond the Impasse: Toward Reconciliation.* Montreal: Institute for Research on Public Policy, 1998. A collection of essays that argue for and explore the nature and implications of a new constitutional, economic, and political relationship between Quebec and the rest of Canada.

Glenny, Misha. "Yugoslavia: The Great Fall," *New York Review of Books* (March 23, 1995). An expert's review and commentary on recent books about the Yugoslavian nightmare.

Goldman, F.M. *Russia, the Eurasian Republics and Central/Eastern Europe.* Guilford, Conn: Dushkin, 1994. An annual edition of news and analysis from the region.

Knop, Karen, Sylvia Ostry, Richard Simeon, and Katherine Swinton, eds. *Rethinking Federalism: Citizens, Markets, and Governments in a Changing World.* Vancouver: UBC Press, 1995. A collection of comparative essays on the cultural and structural forces shaping federal forms of government.

Lee, Kuan-Yeu. *The Singapore Story.* Englewood Cliffs, N.J.: Prentice-Hall, 1999. This is the first volume of memoirs of Singapore's most influential political figure.

Malia, Martin E. *Russia Under Western Eyes: From the Bronze Horseman to the Lenin Mausoleum.* Cambridge, Mass.: Belknap Press, 1999. A penetrating analysis of Western views of changes in Russia.

McGarry, John, and Brendan O'Leary. *The Politics of Ethnic Conflict Regulation: Case Studies of Protracted Ethnic Conflicts.* New York: Routledge, 1993. Note in particular S.J.R. Noel's study "Canadian Responses to Ethnic Conflict." It may not be what you expect.

Schneiderman, David. *The Quebec Question: Perspectives in the Supreme Court Ruling on Secession.* Toronto: Lorimer, 1999. Contains the full text of the Supreme Court's 1998 Secession Reference opinion and a series of critical commentaries.

Sesser, Stan. *The Lands of Charm and Cruelty.* New York: Alfred A. Knopf, 1993. A readable discussion of developments in East Asia, especially the New Authoritarians. Chapter One discusses Singapore and how it has dealt with change.

Smith, Hendrick. *The New Russians.* New York: Avon, 1991. An acclaimed perspective on post-Communist Russia by a Western media correspondent.

Tay, Simon S.C. "Human Rights Culture, and the Singapore Example," *McGill Law Journal* 41 (1996), 743–80. Referring to the Singaporean case, the author rejects the simple view that cultural diversity makes appeals to universal human rights illegitimate.

Conclusion

The first edition of *Braving the New World* appeared four years ago. When changes for a second edition were being contemplated, we considered the concerns and suggestions of our reviewers, the reactions of students, our own sense of what worked and what did not, the extent to which events necessitated reappraisal and comment, and the appearance of new studies to which we wished to direct the reader.

In most respects, the forces in play four years ago, the concepts needed to analyze them, and the political challenges of our era have not changed, at least not markedly. There are differences of degree, and some things that looked important at the time may not look as "foundational" now. But, in the main, the conclusions and comments provided in the first edition still stand. At the same time, we have selected or commissioned new essays to reflect current events, to provide more Canadian content (although still in a comparative context), and to achieve a better balance between sections. One major unanticipated event that will affect Canada, the United States, Europe, Russia, and all NATO members well into the future is the Kosovo situation. It reflects in itself a number of the key themes that surface throughout this edition: ethnicity, institutional arrangements, global connectedness, and civil society, to mention but a few.

The bundle of concepts that are at the heart of introductory political science courses—concepts such as federalism, sovereignty, power, nationalism, democracy, and so forth—must now be seen and set against a 20th-century background of enormous change. It may seem trite to mention such things, but we do forget at times that since 1900 the world's population has more than trebled; the life span in the industrialized world has risen from 45 years to 75 years; old empires have been dismantled (Austro-Hungarian, British, French, Dutch and now Soviet); and new supranational entities have been created, in particular the United Nations and the European Community. Such changes, quite apart from staggering scientific, educational, and social alterations to our ways of life, challenge our understanding of political concepts and political institutions. And, of course, we have witnessed two world wars and countless other conflicts and horrors.

The essays in *Braving the New World* are thus intended to convey a sense of why and how "classical" concepts have mutated and to foster a better understanding of the central role in our lives that such concepts continue to play. Classical concepts still have real political, social, and economic consequences.

In many ways, states still look like states, nowhere more so than when they march off to war supported by bellicose media and appeals to national pride. Yet even this example has to be rethought in light of the Yugoslavia and Kosovo tragedies and NATO's dilemma and response. Yugoslavia casts a pall over Europe as the century ends. A great deal of what we read can lead to pessimism. Canadian political philosopher Charles Taylor has argued that we are experiencing a sense of impending breakdown, to which the name *hypertrophy* is sometimes given. He defines hypertrophy as the fear that we are "becoming too much what we have been— the fear that the very things that define our break with earlier 'traditional' societies, our affirmation of freedom, equality, radical new beginnings, control of nature, democratic self-rule, will somehow be carried beyond feasible limits and will undo us."[1]

Citizens of the wealthy industrial states will continue to face agonizing dilemmas. Who is to be taken aboard the "lifeboat"? What kind of aid—and how much—will be given to the Third World? To what horrors and injustices will the citizens of the "developed" world have to (or choose to) close their eyes? Legally, the democracies of Europe and North America can pride themselves on having abolished slavery and having emancipated women. But in many parts of the world, men, women, and children often toil in appalling conditions to produce the very products we consume so conspicuously, or are even bought and sold as sexual chattels. To some degree, we close our eyes because we do not know what to do; we accept the vagaries of chance and assume that the existence of the unfortunate is unavoidable or even necessary. In these respects, are we not far closer to the Greeks and their attitudes to slavery as a social and economic necessity than we realize? This is an argument developed by Bernard Williams. He concludes that "in important ways, we are, in our ethical situation, more like human beings in antiquity than any Western people have been in the meantime."[2]

Paradoxically, as global economic forces play an increasing role in national economies, Canadians may retreat into ever more parochial identities, stressing local autonomy and control. Why should Albertans care any more about Newfoundlanders than about starving orphans in Bosnia? Why should we allow a remote national government to spend our tax dollars? Thus, under the stress of deficit and debt cutting, some very angry and intolerant sentiments may emerge. How are we to cope with our new world? Is it turning into a cross between a Hieronymus Bosch painting of the apocalypse and a dystopian vision of our future, in which consumerism and entertainment dominate all? To answer, we are drawn back to politics, for such questions raise the not inconsequential matter of what kind of polity we want to create and thus return us to our current dilemmas.

On the Right, there are divisions between staunch free marketers wanting the state out of most if not all forms of regulation, others who are deeply concerned about the erosion of "traditional" values and see the market as responsible for an unacceptable level of corrosive social change, and still others who celebrate, contradictorily, both the dynamism of the market and the need for stable, traditional principles of family and community. On the Left is disarray. The old intellectual left, rooted in the alliance with labour, committed to protectionism and to the preservation of an industrial assembly-line economy (sometimes referred to as "Fordism"), has a difficult time meshing with the new Left of feminists, environmentalists, and other rights-bearing groups. Communitarians of various kinds plead for a renewal of community, but what in practice this really means is unclear. The whole Left/Right debate crumbles on a number of fronts, from the ideological to the pragmatic.[3]

As we approach the end of the 20th century, the international system looks, in some respects, more like the 19th century, at least in the sense that it is a multi-polar world. But the situation is different in that the great powers are not all European, weapons and warfare have changed radically, and there is now only one military superpower. Rivalries in the 19th century were played out over territory in remote parts of the globe. The British and French Empires confronted each other at the forlorn outpost of Fashoda in the Sudan. Nowadays, mere territorial control is not as important to major powers, even though, on the ground, the struggles over who controls a hill or a village are just as important as they always were. Nonstate actors are

extremely powerful. Civilizations may be redefining their boundaries, and cultures are challenging each other in ways not experienced since the Industrial Revolution. Islam confronts the secular world of the Enlightenment. John le Carré estimates that, in Europe alone, there are 35 ethnic or national entities demanding autonomy or sovereignty. He takes issue with "our careless modern assumption that as trade borders fall and systems of communication change, the countries of the world will be brought closer together. Nothing could be further from the truth."[4] We also still face enormous problems of post–Cold War cleanup, with costs expected to be in the hundreds of billions as we realize the legacy of 40 years of nuclear weapons production and environmental pollution, particularly in the former Soviet bloc.

There are numerous reasons for despair and pessimism, and many of the articles in this reader raise excruciatingly difficult questions. What can we do about the extinction of renewable resources and the attendant political consequences? Are we facing the prospect of a quarter-century or more of ongoing moral and spiritual crises that are sapping our political will? How will the forces of liberalism and fundamentalism collide and evolve? What will happen to democracy in the process? Can we invent a kinder, gentler economic marketplace? How is the public domain to coexist with and tame the new world of transnational capitalism and privatization? Are political institutions impotent? Is our civic culture disintegrating? What can be done to tackle the problems of representation, and can we reestablish meaningful forms of public trust, discourse, and conversation? To answer this question, the changes in information and computer technology may enable citizens to participate more actively and in a more informed way; this was certainly the case during the conflict in Kosovo many people in Belgrade were still in touch via e-mail and the Net with friends and colleagues in the West.[5]

We are, according to some, already at the point where consumerism, combined with market and corporate forces, can swamp and co-opt all forms of protest. The predictions of Herbert Marcuse (who wrote a seminal book entitled *One Dimensional Man* several decades ago) may be more realistic now than ever before, as a new generation loses its sense of involvement with political community, or even with political causes.

The possibility that there is now a hollowness at the very heart of civic culture is something that should trouble us, particularly as we can take so many political freedoms for granted and when political cynicism runs so high. For it is only through political activities that certain topics can get onto our collective agendas, and it is only through political institutions—both formal and informal—that a democracy can actually be made to work, however imperfectly. But the price to be paid for involvement in political activity if you are, for example, a Saudi woman, an Algerian journalist, a Burmese democrat, an Italian magistrate, or even a British author, can be very high indeed. You may pay with your life, as well as with the lives of family and friends. Even where political participation is allowed, we seem to have run out of answers, or perhaps we cannot even pose the right questions. Some would argue that our problems are due to too much participation and to excessive demands on the state. At a time when problems appear to be intractable and many citizens are retreating into a privatized world of entertainment, we expect our leaders to have the remedies for what ails us, and we still make facile assumptions about our abilities to identify and solve all our problems.

In the first edition, we wrote a lengthy essay on populism and outlined the paradoxes that accompany the view that all we have to do is to listen to "the common sense of the common people." At the time, populist agendas were once again surfacing, and there was an angry demand for action to cure what ails us, be it crime, deficits, control over those we elect, or moral issues such as abortion and the death penalty. We argued then that such populist political action was as simplistic as it was understandable and was likely to disappoint its proponents, as well as frustrate its opponents.

Populist sentiments have not vanished and never will, but the institutional "establishment" has fought back, at least in terms of posing major challenges to those who have tried to change the institutional status quo.[6] The Reform Party now adopts a "United Alternative" approach designed to win power and wants to do so via a centre–right coalition that will have to drop its populist garb if it is to win over enough voters, especially those in Ontario. Progressive Conservatives are at least as likely to vote Liberal as they are to vote Reform. In the United States there are no more Ross Perots in sight. So even Reform could settle into a familiar pattern of being intent on winning, bereft of any real optimism about significant change, and willing to live with existing institutions. Old institutional habits do die hard.

The only real wild card that might be played is Quebec, for a declaration of Quebec's independence would change a great deal. A favourable constellation of factors could quickly form to create Lucien Bouchard's "winning conditions" for a sovereignty referendum. This issue reveals how difficult it now is for even federal systems to cope with diversity, nationalism, and rights. A multinational Canada needs to deal, as Alan C. Cairns has noted, with three nationalisms: Quebec, Aboriginal, and English-speaking Canadian (as well as multiculturalism). Will Kymlicka argues that multiculturalism is a success story that we do not recognize against a background of globalizing pressures and forces and at a time when the federal system, with its multiple levels of governance, is under review.[7] How do we make governments accountable? How should citizens participate? How are we to have meaningful dialogues about public policies?

The contributions to this volume provide us with the guarded hope that we will be able to cope, or at least muddle through. They urge us to examine history anew and with greater care; they reveal how we must be wary of easy generalizations and undue pessimism; they attempt to see things in context; they do not underestimate the resiliency of democracy or liberalism, or their capacity for reinvention. Democracies may be facing what is, at bottom, a moral crisis, and it is important to see this crisis in historical and comparative perspective. We have experienced many of these problems before, and we have usually proffered similar cures. The trick is to sort out what is different, for history does not simply repeat itself, and the "lessons" to be learned must be related with the greatest of care. What historians are able to do is prevent the overt misuse of historical examples, but the profession itself has become hazardous, and even as eminent an historian as Eric Hobsbawm now admits, "I used to think that the profession of history, unlike that of, say, nuclear physics could do no harm. Now I know that it can."[8]

As we assembled the list of key terms for each piece, it became obvious that certain ideas and concerns are now widespread. What is globalization, how does it affect us, and what can or should be done to ensure appropriate institutional and state responses? There is the stress upon the importance of civil society. There is frequent mention of forms of federalism, or confederalism, as possible avenues of institutional renewal. There is an attempt to defend the very activity of politics and political institutions against the assumed efficiencies of the marketplace. It is not that the pervasiveness of such ideas is novel or unexpected; what stands out are the ways in which the themes pop up in so many different contexts. What is also noteworthy is the repeated stress on the importance of a reasoned and thoughtful historical perspective.

Finally, it is important to remember that actions do not always speak louder; we are not dealing in mere words. Words have great power. They can bring about agreement and compromise and increased tolerance; they can give us hope and confidence. Politics and politicians—though they may be disparaged, reviled, and vilified—remain essential to our collective efforts to cope with change.

We hope that both teachers and students will find that the articles in this volume go beyond what is usually provided in an introductory text. The intent is to provide greater depth, more opportunity for debate, and a challenge to the unthinking acceptance of authoritative definitions, which texts, by their very nature, usually provide. Our political concepts are more nuanced, especially these days, than students are sometimes led to believe. But not so nuanced that we cannot examine and unravel them carefully and see their importance for us as citizens struggling to brave our protean, turbulent, new world.

Notes

1. Charles Taylor, "Alternative Futures: Legitimacy, Identity and Alienation in Late-Twentieth-Century Canada," in *Reconciling the Solitudes* (Montreal: McGill-Queen's University Press, 1993), 60.

2. See Bernard Williams, *Shame and Necessity* (Berkeley: University of California Press, 1993).

3. See Philip Resnick, *The Masks of Proteus: Canadian Reflections on the State* (Montreal: McGill-Queen's University Press, 1990), and Reg Whitaker, "The Changing Canadian State" in Harvey Lazar and Tom McIntosh, eds., *Canada; The State of the Federation, 1998/99: How Canadians Connect* (Montreal: McGill Queen's University Press, 1999), 37–60.

4. John le Carré, "After the Cold War: The Shame of the West," *Globe and Mail* (December 15, 1994), A27.

5. See Cynthia J. Alexander and Leslie A. Pal, eds. *Digital Democracy: Policy and Politics in a Wired World* (Toronto: Oxford University Press, 1998).

6. See David C. Docherty, *Mr. Smith Goes to Ottawa: Life in the House of Commons* (Vancouver: UBC Press, 1997).

7. See the review by Alan C. Cairns of Will Kymlicka's book *Finding Our Way: Rethinking Ethnocultural Relations in Canada* (Toronto: Oxford University Press, 1998) in the *Canadian Journal of Political Science*, 32 (1999), 369–71.

8. Eric Hobsbawm, "The New Threat to History," *The New York Review of Books* (December 16, 1993), 62–64.

Copyright Acknowledgments

Chapter 6: Welfare State Convergence: Paul Bowles and Barnet Wagman, "Globalization and the Welfare State: Four Hypotheses and Some Empirical Evidence"

Tables 2, 3, 4, and A1
For Period 1 and 2 data: OECD, *Social Expenditure 1960–1990: Problems of Growth and Control*. Copyright OECD, 1985. Reproduced with permission.
For Period 3 data: IMF, *Government Financial Statistics Yearbook* (International Monetary Fund, 1995). Reproduced with permission.

Chapter 20: Public Policy and Market Forces: Michael Broadway, "Global Goes Local: The North American Meat-Packing Industry"

Table 1: Distribution of Cattle Slaughtering Activity 1991–1997
Reproduced from Agriculture & Agri-Food Canada publication "Livestock Market Review 1997." Reproduced with the permission of the Minister of Public Works and Government Services Canada 1999.

Table 2: Cattle on Feed in Canada (in thousands), 1985, 1998
Source: Canfax, Canadian Cattlemen's Association. Reproduced with permission.

Table 3: Cattle Slaughtered in Federally Inspected Establishments, by Province: 1985, 1998
Reproduced from Agriculture & Agri-Food Canada publication "Livestock Market Review 1997." Reproduced with the permission of the Minister of Public Works and Government Services Canada 1999.

To the owner of this book

We hope that you have enjoyed *Braving the New World,* by Bateman, Mertin, and Thomas (ISBN 0-17-616745-5), and we would like to know as much about your experiences with this text as you would care to offer. Only through your comments and those of others can we learn how to make this a better text for future readers.

School _____ Your instructor's name _____

Course _____ Was the text required? _____ Recommended? _____

1. What did you like the most about *Braving the New World?*

_____

_____

_____

2. How useful was this text for your course?

_____

_____

_____

3. Do you have any recommendations for ways to improve the next edition of this text?

_____

_____

_____

4. In the space below or in a separate letter, please write any other comments you have about the book. (For example, please feel free to comment on reading level, writing style, terminology, design features, and learning aids.)

_____

_____

_____

_____

Optional

Your name _____ Date _____

May Nelson, Thomson Learning quote you, either in promotion for *Braving the New World,* or in future publishing ventures?

Yes _____ No _____

Thanks!

You can also send your comments to us via e-mail at
college@nelson.com

PLEASE TAPE SHUT. DO NOT STAPLE.

TAPE SHUT

TAPE SHUT

FOLD HERE

Nelson
Thomson Learning™

0066102399-M1K5G4-BR01

NELSON, THOMSON LEARNING
HIGHER EDUCATION
PO BOX 60225 STN BRM B
TORONTO ON M7Y 2H1

TAPE SHUT

TAPE SHUT